PORSCHE
911
PERFORMANCE
HANDBOOK

Bruce Anderson

Motorbooks International
Publishers & Wholesalers Inc
Osceola, Wisconsin 54020, USA ®

P9-ECZ-576

First published in 1987 by Motorbooks International Publishers & Wholesalers Inc, PO Box 2, 729 Prospect Avenue, Osceola, WI 54020 USA

© Bruce Anderson, 1987

All rights reserved. With the exception of quoting brief passages for the purposes of review no part of this publication may be reproduced without prior written permission from the publisher

Motorbooks International is a certified trademark, registered with the United States Patent Office

Printed and bound in the United States of America

The information in this book is true and complete to the best of our knowledge. All recommendations are made without any guarantee on the part of the author or publisher, who also disclaim any liability incurred in connection with the use of this data or specific details

The front cover photograph was taken by Bill Martin at Garretson Enterprises facility in Mountain View, California. In the foreground is a 1976 930 Turbo being worked on by one of Garretson's mechanics; up in the air is Bob Akin's "The Last 935"; below, an IROC RSR built for the first IROC race in 1973; and then a 1978 930 Turbo. The back cover features a RUF Turbo convertible shot in Newport Beach, California, by Tim Parker.

Motorbooks International books are also available at discounts in bulk quantity for industrial or sales-promotional use. For details write to Special Sales Manager at the Publisher's address

Library of Congress Cataloging-in-Publication Data
Anderson, Bruce.
   Porsche 911 performance handbook.

   Includes index.
   1. Porsche 911 automobile—Performance—Handbooks—manuals, etc.   I. Title.
TL215.P75A63   1987   629.2'222   87-18592
ISBN 0-87938-269-4 (pbk.)

Contents

Acknowledgments

I owe a great deal of thanks to all of the people who have helped with my Porsche education. My Porsche education started with my first Porsche, a 356 super, which I bought new in 1961. I first became acquainted with 911s during the winter of 1966-67 when some friends and I bought a half a dozen engines that were badly damaged, but not lost, in a shipwreck in the Azores. These engines had started out in cars, but when the ship that they were being transported in was rammed by another ship, the 911s broke loose in the flooded hold.

Please note that I said engine, my first 911 experience was just with the engines. I didn't actually work on one of the cars until about a year later when we installed one of our refurbished engines into a 912 making it into a 911. By the time we had resurrected all of our engines we had all learned quite a bit about the 911 engines and cars.

My Porsche education continued with rebuilding and hot-rodding 911 engines, and working on a race team that won the prestigious Porsche Cup, Porsche Team Cup, IMSA GTU, GT and GTO championships and the World Endurance Drivers Championship. My education continues today as I help others learn about these great cars with my technical articles and books; by offering instruction in training courses on the Porsches and by giving technical presentation lectures on the 911 engines.

Recommendations in this book for procedures or parts are either based on my own personal experience or friends' experiences. When I make recommendations please realize that someone else may offer a similar service and/or parts, but the ones that I am recommending are the ones that I am familiar with, and you may get just as good or better service and/or parts from someone else.

Many thanks to all of the people who have helped with my Porsche education over the years and contributed to this book either by directly providing information for the book or sharing in the experiences that have been the basis for much of the book. I would like to give everyone who helped credit, but I'm sure to miss someone. My apologies to anyone I may have missed or whose request for anonymity will not allow me to mention them.

Akin, Bob
Anderson, Clark
Bantele, Manfred
Barth, Jurgen
Beach, Cecil and Carol
Behrens, Hartmut
Bingham, Paul
Blakely, Glen
Blendstrup, Gerhard, Dr.
Blitz, Howard
Bohrman, Gary
Bornscheuer, Alexander
Bott, Helmuth, Prof.
Car and Driver
Carlson, Bob
Cohen, Stephania
Collier, Miles
Cousimano, Bob
Daniels, John
de Lespinay, Philippe
Doudy, Steve
Fleck, Dan
Fuess, Lillian
Gaa, Chuck
Garretson, Bob
Garretson, Fred
Gemballa Automobilinterieur Gmbh
Gorissen, Wolfhelm
Gosch, Begonia
Green, Chas R.
Hall, Harry
Hammill, John
Hampton, Fred
Hanna, Tom
Hensler, Paul
Home-Anderson, Stephanie
Jopp, Ursula
Klym, Dave
Krag, Scott
Kremer Brothers Porsche Racing
Krull, Donald R.
Lateer, Jeff
Lemke, Eugene
Martin, Bill F.
Mezger, Hans
Miller, Dale
Newton, James
Padermderm, Joe
Parker, Rick
Parr, Richard
Porsche Aktiengesellschaft
Porsche Cars of North America
Porsche MotorSport North America
Rapp, Leo F.
Raven, Greg
Reichert, Klaus
Riley, Lori and Richard
Robinson, Ted
Ruf, Alois
RUF Automobile W. Germany
Schenk, Paul
Schutz, Peter
Speer, Doug
Spence, Scott
Sprenger, Rolf
Springer, Alwin
Strange, Robert
Strosek Auto Design
Stroth, Achim
Struffert, Hans
Union Oil Company
Urbaniak, Tom
Walton, Gary
Weber, Greg
Weber, Jim
Woods, Jerry
Zimmermann, Ekehard

Foreword

It has been my privilege to serve as "Vostandsvorsitzender" of Porsche AG since January 1981. In this capacity, one comes into close contact with a variety of unique and exciting things, including a number of automotive engineering classics from the original 356 to the latest 959. Historical racing cars such as the 917 of the 1970s, through the 935 and 936 of the late-seventies and 1980-81, to today's 956 and 962. Include the McLaren-TAG Formula One successes and the coming Indianapolis-Cart program, and they constitute a breathtaking array of engineering achievements.

The technical centerpiece of all this has been the Porsche 911 sports car. This unique engineering achievement departs from virtually all conventional practice in that it is air-cooled and rear-engined. It "breaks all the rules," and yet continues to dominate its particular corner of the Automotive scene. The unique basic 911 six-cylinder engine has won every long-distance race in the world, many repeatedly, including Paris-Dakar, and is now about to make its debut as an aircraft and helicopter powerplant.

But beyond all the hardware, commercial and competitive successes, the most outstanding dimension of my personal Porsche experience has consisted of the people that I have met in my tenure as chief executive of this unusual company. World renowned entertainers, athletes and artists; business people and politicans; all leaders in their chosen field comprise a star-studded array of achievers that share a Porsche Fascination.

Just as the Porsche 911 is unique and fascinating among the world's sports cars, there are a few people who stand out in the distinguished crowd of Porsche people it has been my privilege to know. One such person is Bruce Anderson.

Bruce is one of those rare persons who never does anything halfway. His knowledge of Mexican food and jazz music is exceeded only by his love and knowledge of Porsche, and particularly the 911 in all its variations. (There is little truth to the rumor that he learned all that he knows about everything else including food, Mexican or otherwise, from his best friend, conscience, advisor, critic and wife, Stephanie.) It is thus in the true Bruce Anderson style that he has decided to share his love and knowledge of the Porsche 911 with the rest of us, in this book; beyond all else, Bruce is a sharing person.

I hope that you will enjoy the book as much as I know Bruce has enjoyed the many years that it took to put it together. *Peter W. Schutz, 1987*

Porsche 911 performance history

Like the 356 before it, the 911 has always been a performance car. We heard rumors before the 911 was introduced that the replacement for our beloved 356 would not be a performance car or sports car at all, but instead it would be a larger, four-passenger grand touring car. Fortunately that turned out not to be true and the new car was, in fact, a more efficient, comfortable and sporting two-plus-two.

In the early years of postwar sports cars, the British had tried to convince the world in general and the United States in particular that sports cars had to have sidecurtains, a top that didn't work, and ride like an ox cart to actually be considered a sports car. By the time the 911 came along, we were already spoiled by the 356 and knew that a sports car didn't *have* to be a hard-riding, uncomfortable roadster.

Porsche built the Speedster for its customers who needed to be reassured that they had indeed bought a sports car. But the Porsche Speedster didn't even do *that* right. The top actually worked pretty well and the ride was great. Of course the sidecurtains leaked, but did you ever hear of a car that used sidecurtains that didn't leak?

I first heard about the coming of the 911 from a friend and fellow 356 owner in the early 1960s. He had just returned from a business trip to Europe on behalf of the company that we both worked for, and a business associate had booked him on a tour of the Porsche factory. On his tour he saw Porsche's new car, which turned out to be the not-yet-introduced 911. He came back concerned that Porsche was ruining "our" car and was going to make it too expensive for any of us to afford. At the time, he and I had some plain-Jane pushrod 356 Porsches that sold then for about $4,000 to $5,500. The high-performance and high-priced Porsche of the time was a 2.0 Carrera, available for about $7,500 in the United States.

The 901, as it was then called, was introduced at the September 1963 Frankfurt International Auto Show.

The front of preproduction 901 prototype; the 356s in the background are a 1963 B model and two 1964 C models. The differences between the preproduction 901 and the production 911s were the shape of the gas filler lid in the fender and the absence of the trim strip under the door. Werkfoto, Porsche AG

US introduction of 1966 model in San Francisco by Porsche Car Pacific, July 23, 1965. Porsche Car Pacific

Porsche built 125 of the original 901 prototypes from 1963 through the end of 1964. A friend, Leo Rapp, tells me that he was in Germany to visit friends in 1962 and got a ride in a 356 Carrera 2 with Edgar Barth. Leo said that he was trying to buy a Carrera 2 at the time and mentioned this to Barth who told him to wait; something better was coming. That something was the 911, or as it was called then, the 901.

Porsche helped to finance the development of the 901 by asking its 100 best dealers to put up what, in effect, was a deposit on one of these cars. The deposit was 8,000 DM, which back in 1962 was some $2,000. My friend Leo had a friend, Jochen Piper, with one of the larger German dealerships, Max Moritz. Piper arranged for Leo to put up the deposit for Max Moritz in exchange for its 901. Leo actually did get the 901 and shipped it to the United States in November 1964.

The 901 was introduced at the Frankfurt show of September 1963, and actual production of the 1965 model started in September 1964. It was now called the 911. The new 911 two-liter cost 22,900 DM ($5,800) in Germany and $6,500 in the United States.

The reason the car was renamed, or renumbered from 901 to 911, was that French auto maker Peugeot had registered the use of three-digit numbers where the center digit was a zero. Porsche was ready for production at the time of this decision, which explains why so many of its part numbers and designations for the 911 use the 901 prefix.

Competition with the new 911 started as early as January 1965 when Porsche prepared a 911 for competition in the famed Monte Carlo Rally. It placed seventh in that first attempt. The 911 went on to win most of the major European rallies, including three victories at the Monte Carlo Rally and a win in the Tour de Corse. The special race preparation of these very early cars was limited to minor suspension modifications, more powerful versions of the 901 six-cylinder engine, and a wide selection of different gear ratios.

As the 901 model matured, several special versions of the 911 were built for touring car races and grand touring (GT) racing and rallying. These 911 derivatives at one time or another have won most of the major races and rallies of the world: The 959 has already contributed to this record by winning the Paris-Dakar. Competition is an integral part of Porsche 911 performance.

It was no surprise that with the 1967 model introduction, Porsche had also added as a new model the higher-performance 911S model with 160 DIN horsepower. When the 911 was introduced it was available only in coupe form and with only one engine configuration, the 130 DIN horsepower engine. The coupe body had been designed by Ferdinand "Butzi" Porsche who had also designed the body for the 904 and went on to establish his own company, Porsche Design. It was inevitable that sooner or later there would be a hot-rod version of the 911—it has always been a Porsche tradition. The price for the new 911S was $6,990, while the price of the standard 911 was lowered $500 dollars to $6,000.

In addition to the increased power, the 911S also introduced the Fuchs forged-aluminum wheels which have added character to the car's appearance for twenty years now. The originals were 4.5x15 in. and had all-silver spokes. The Fuchs forged-alloy wheels were standard on the 911S and a $375 option for the 911 and 912. When these wheels were introduced they were not considered attractive. In fact, a friend of mine said they looked as if they belonged on a circus bandwagon. The wheels were lighter, stronger and provided better brake

Dashboard of the original 911. Notice wood dashboard insert and wood-rimmed steering wheel.

The 1967 911S introduced more power, better handling and styling changes too. The 1967 911S with its "mag" wheels was one of the first production cars in the world with alloy wheels. Actually they were 4½ in. wide Fuchs forged aluminum-alloy wheels.

The rubber trim strips on the sides and bumpers were made much larger and had a square profile. The front bumper guards were left off altogether on the European version of the 911S. Werkfoto, Porsche AG

cooling than the steel disc wheels, but they were also expensive.

The 1967 model also marked the addition of the rear antisway bar which improved the 911's already superb handling. In addition to the wheels, different side trim and bumper trim with a larger, squared-off rubber insert marked the visual differences between the 911S and the standard 911 and 912. The 911S also had an all-leatherette dashboard, with leatherette replacing the wooden inserts of the earlier standard 911. For 1967 an aluminum dash insert was used for the standard 911 and the 912. The 911S also had a new leather-covered steering wheel for 1967.

At the 1965 Frankfurt show, Porsche introduced its new, unconventional solution for the open car—a cabriolet-like car that it called the Targa to honor Porsche's many successes at the Sicilian Targa Florio race. This cabriolet was unique with its six-inch-wide stainless-steel-covered roll bar. It couldn't help but be noticed. Porsche was the first to put a roll bar on a production car, an idea that several other manufacturers followed. It was over a year before the Targa was finally added to the Porsche line-up in the 1967 model year.

Some people called it the Porsche with a handle, and others called it the safety cabriolet. Porsche said the Targa was its car with four personalities: first, the Targa Spyder, a fully open car with the roof off and the rear window folded flat; second, the Targa Bel Air, like a sunroof, with the top off and the rear window in place for draft-free sunshine; third, the Targa Voyage, with the soft cabriolet top in place and the rear window folded flat; and fourth, the Targa Hardtop, with the roof attached and the rear window zipped in place.

At the end of 1967, Porsche built a small series of twenty-three 911 units for racing and designated them as 911R (R for rennsport, or racing). The 911Rs were extensively modified 911s with fiberglass bodywork, plexiglass windows and a 210 hp Carrera Six type engine.

These Spartan 911Rs weighed only 1,830 lb. And although not much racing was done with the 911Rs, they paved the way for future 911 racing cars. One 911R was fitted with the Type 916 engine for the Targa Florio in 1969. The Type 916 four-camshaft version of the 901 engine produced 230 hp, twenty more than the Carrera Six engine. The only notable accomplishments for the 911R were in establishing a series of fourteen

international and five world records at the Monza track in 1967, and winning the 1969 eighty-four-hour Marathon de la Route.

For 1968, Porsche added a less expensive version of the 911, the 911T which was only sold to the European market in 1968. For the European, or the Rest of the World (R.o.W.) market there were three different 911 models— the 911T, 911L and 911S—and the four-cylinder 912. The 911L was the successor to the standard 911 for the R.o.W.

While Porsche was expanding its R.o.W. product line, it was actually

reducing the models available to the US market. The United States was reduced to the 911 and the 912 for that year. Admittedly, there were two 911 models. In addition to the standard 911 there was a 911L, the L designating luxury. The 911L had most of the features of the 911S except one, the important one; the 911L had the same engine as the plain-Jane 911. The reason for this was stricter US emission laws.

New for the 1968 models was the dual circuit brake system for the world market, with a warning light added for the US market. The 1968 models had 5½-inch-wide wheels replacing the orig-

1967 also introduced the 911S dashboard— note leatherette dash insert in place of the wood in the earlier car, and the leather-covered steering wheel in place of the earlier wood-rimmed wheel. Werkfoto, Porsche AG

Porsche first showed its 911 Targa at the 1965 Frankfurt Auto Show. Porsche said the Targa was its car with four personalities. The first personality, Targa Spyder, was a fully open car with the roof off and the rear window folded flat. The second personality, Targa Bel Air, was like a sunroof, with the top off and rear window in place for draft-free sunshine. The third personality, Targa Voyage, had the soft cabriolet top in place and the rear window folded flat. The fourth personality, Targa Hardtop, had the roof attached and the rear window zipped in place. Porsche was the first to put a roll bar on a production car, an idea that several other manufacturers were to follow. It was over a year before the Targa was finally added to the Porsche line-up in the 1967 model year. Werkfoto, Porsche AG

inal 4½-inch wheels for all models T, E and S. In addition, the wiper blades now parked on the left side instead of the right side to get them out of the driver's line of sight.

An interesting addition for the 1968 model year was the semi-automatic Sportomatic transmission. Porsche felt that none of its customers would really want to give up complete control of their transmission, so instead of a *total* automatic Porsche engineers combined a torque converter, an automatic clutch and a four-speed transmission. Porsche took its excellent four-speed transmission and added a torque converter and a vacuum-servo-controlled clutch.

The Sportomatic's torque converter was what could be considered a loose one, with a stall speed of 2600 rpm. The clutch was disengaged by the vacuum servo when it received a signal from the microswitch on the shift linkage, so that when you grabbed the shift lever the clutch would release and you could shift. When you let go of the shift lever, the clutch would engage again. With the high stall speed of the torque converter you could be a lazy driver with one of these transmissions, starting out in second gear and shifting directly to fourth when the car came up to speed. Or if you wanted, the car could be driven quite aggressively using all four gears and it would give very little away to the 911s, with their more conventional four- or five-speed manual transmissions.

The 911s with these Sportomatic transmissions were a good solution for people who still wanted a sporty Porsche, but who spent quite a bit of driving time stuck in commuter traffic, because the semi-automatic greatly reduced the amount of shifting necessary. Unfortunately for the Porsche customers who liked their Porsche driving *sans* clutch, this transmission was not an idea that really caught on in the United States, and ten years after its introduction Porsche ceased production of the Sportomatic.

There are still some people who swear by these transmissions, saying that they offered the best of both worlds. It would be very difficult to pin down exactly when Porsche quit building the Sportomatic cars. The newest Sportomatic that I know of in the United States is a 1978 911SC that belongs to a friend in the Porsche club. The 1980 was the last model year the Sportomatic transmission was listed as an option, even in Europe. I did notice at Le Mans in 1985, however, that the car Wolfgang Porsche was driving had a four-speed Sportomatic installed. The car was a Carrera turbo-look cabriolet, so it had to be either a 1984 or 1985 model. But then this was a special case, wasn't it?

The most notable changes for 1969 were the increased wheelbase length and

At the end of 1967 Porsche built a small series of very special 911s—the 911R. The 911Rs were extensively modified 911s, with fiberglass bodywork, plexiglass windows and a 210 hp Carrera Six type engine.

These very Spartan 911Rs weighed only 1,830 lb. They were fitted with six-inch front wheels and seven-inch rear wheels. Werkfoto, Porsche AG

911R had oil tank mounted in front of the right rear wheel to better balance the car's weight. The windshield was made of a thin glass and the rest of the windows were plexiglass.

911R Interior. Sheel bucket seats were used. The 911R's trunk space was filled with a plastic 100-liter (22 gal) fuel tank.

the fender flares. The 911S received the Bosch twin-row mechanical-injection pump. The 911L also received a mechanical-injection system and was renamed the 911E, the E standing for *Einspritzung*, the German word for injection. There was also more differentiation between the various models, with the 911S being the performance model, the 911T the economy model and the 911E the luxury model with a softer ride. This softer ride was provided by what Porsche called its "comfort group," which consisted of the Boge hydro-pneumatic struts in front instead of torsion bars.

These Boge hydro-pneumatic struts were self-leveling and did ride much softer than the conventional suspension. The comfort-group cars also came without a front sway bar, and with 14x5½ in. wheels with the high-profile 185/78x14 tires. This comfort group was standard equipment on the 911E with Sportomatic and optional on the 911T, 911E and 911S. The standard-equipment wheels on the 911T were 15x5½ in., and for the 911E and 911S they were 15x6 in.

All three of the 911 models were available to the world market for 1969. Due to the mechanical injection, the 911E and 911S complied with US emission specification. The new-to-the-United States 911T used a decel valve on its carburetors and a vacuum unit on its distributor to meet the emission test.

For the 1970 model year a new production Porsche was introduced, the VW-Porsche 914. This model was a joint venture between Porsche and Volkswagen, and was marketed everywhere except in the United States as a VW-Porsche. In the United States the 914/6 was sold as a Porsche by the newly formed Porsche-Audi distribution organization. The 914/6 was offered from 1970 to 1972, during which time 3,360 914/6s were built and 1,788 were sold in the United States. The 914/6 used 2.0 911 engines built to specifications similar to the 1968-69 911T.

A 914/6 GT version was produced to International Group 4 (GT class) rules for racing and rallying. It is impossible to speculate on the true number of 914/6 GTs that were produced because Porsche attempted to homologate the car into the Sports Car Club of America's B-production class. In an effort to comply with SCCA's requirement of 500 production cars, Porsche made some real 914/6 GTs, some look-alike GTs and a lot of kits to convert production 914/6 models to the GT configuration. Porsche's efforts did not meet with SCCA's approval, and in July 1971 the

The 911R's doors, hood, engine lid and front and rear bumpers were made of fiberglass by Karl Baur of Stuttgart. The doors used on the later 935s were very similar to these.

1969 911T and 911S with fender flares and a change to the longer wheelbase. Note the Fuchs alloy wheels introduced in 1968, with new paint scheme and wider 5½ in. width. Most people felt that painting the background for the spokes flat-black improved the appearance of the alloy wheels. Werkfoto, Porsche AG

914/6 GT was thrown out of B-Production and placed instead in B-Sports Racing where it just was not competitive.

The 914/6 was not as successful in sales or competition as Porsche had intended. Even so, in 1970 a Porsche 914/6 GT won the GT class at Le Mans and placed sixth overall. Peter Greg and Hurley Haywood won the IMSA GT championship in 1971 driving a 914/6 GT. In 1976 and 1977 Walt Maas successfully ran his 1971 914/6 GT in the IMSA GTU series, winning twelve races and the 1977 GTU championship.

The 916 was to have been the civilized street version of the 914/6 GT, but the project was killed by the accounting department at Porsche. Thirteen prototypes were built in 1972-74; they had a version of the 2.4 liter 911S engine, larger seven-inch wheels, a steel welded-on roof and deluxe appointments. Porsche kept half of them for family members and sold the rest to Porsche company friends.

Another very interesting car in the 914 family was the 914/8. Only two of these cars were built, and those only for the use of Porsche family members; one for Ferdinand Piech, then Porsche's engineering manager, and the other a present for Professor Ferry Porsche's sixtieth birthday in September 1969. Both of these 914/8s used the 908 racing engine. The engine in the Professor's 914 was modified to a more subdued state of tune, while the only concession Ferdinand Piech's car made for its use as a street car was the addition of mufflers.

For 1970 and 1971 the 911 engines were increased to 2.2 liters, actually 2195 cc, but the cars looked pretty much the same as they had in 1969, aside from some interior changes. The 1972 911s had yet another displacement increase to 2.4 liters (2341 cc).

The 1972 models also had the oil tank moved up in front of the right rear wheel, like the tanks on the 911Rs. The oil tank returned to its previous location in 1973, however. Some said it was because it had become an attractive nuisance, and that some gas station attendants had put gas in the oil tanks, and children had put rocks and sticks into the tank. Whatever Porsche's reason for moving the tank back to the rear of the fender, someday it will probably move back to the position in front of the rear wheel. That was actually a good, out-of-the-way location. It left the rear corners of the car available for more important things, such as intercoolers for turbocharged cars.

The 911s remained pretty much the same for model year 1973 as they had

The 914/6 roadster was powered by the 2.0 liter engine with specifications that were nearly identical to the 1969 911T engine. The 914/6 was offered by Porsche from 1970 to 1972 during which time 3,360 were built and sold, 1,788 of these were US versions. Jeff Lateer

1963-68 911 with short wheelbase. Note distance from the edge of the fender to the torsion-bar cover in the fender.

The 914's mid-engine layout was tailor-made for racing; here is Walt Maas' 914/6, the IMSA GTU champion in 1977. Note the over-emphasized wheel arches, front air dam and rear-deck spoiler mounted on the trunk lid of the car.

1969 911 with long wheelbase. Again note distance from the edge of the fender to the torsion-bar cover in the fender.

been for 1972. The fuel injection was changed from mechanical to CIS on the US 911T for January 1973. The new ATS "cookie cutter" wheels were introduced and made standard equipment on the 911E. The ATS wheels were originally available only in the 15x6 in. size.

In 1970 and 1971 several 911s were specially built for racing and rallying, based on the 2.2 liter 911. These cars used some of the development work from the 911R such as lightweight bodywork and deletion of any sound-deadening material. They remained slightly modified street 911s in most other respects, however. They included modified suspensions and an extensive selection of alternate gear ratios. There were different engines available for different applications, with the rally version usually being nearly stock 911S. For racing there were special 2.2 and 2.3 liter versions, and a prototype version with the soon-to-follow increased stroke.

Some of the racing 911s that Porsche built during this period were very specialized. One example was a car that was prepared for the 1970 Tour de France. Porsche reduced the weight of this car even further than that of the 911R to 1,720 lb. The powerplant for the Tour

de France car was a 2.4 liter engine producing 245 hp. These extensive modifications were permitted because the car was raced as a prototype rather than as a GT car.

Another example of specialized 911 developments was the cars created by Porsche for the East African Safari. The

Safari cars were lighter in weight than the production cars, but the biggest difference was in the special preparation for the rigors of off-road racing which included extra reinforcement, raised suspension settings and skid shields. Though the cars were successful in the East African Safari, they never won this

The 1970 911S-style dashboard.

Opening the oil-filler hatch on the 1972 911. To check the oil level in any of the 911s it is necessary to run the engine to get it up to operating temperature of 80 deg C (176 deg F). The car should be level and running at idle speed, and the oil level should be about halfway between the two marks on the dipstick. (The dipstick should always be believed before the gauge.) Perhaps the oil filler was too accessible when the filler was in the right rear fender. Anyway, the filler lasted there only one model year and in 1973 was returned to the engine compartment, and the tank was returned to the rear of the right rear wheel.

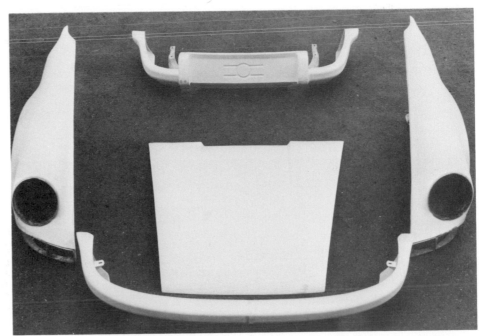

In 1970, Porsche produced a complete kit for converting a normal-production 911S into a Group 4 race car. The kit not only included all of the engine parts, but also several of the body panels in fiberglass

which were considerably lighter than the production steel components. The body kit consisted of front and rear bumpers, front hood and front fenders. Werkfoto, Porsche AG

event—one of the few in the world that a 911 or 911-based car has not been able to win.

For 1972, Porsche used its new 2.4 liter as the basis for a 2.5 liter racing engine that it developed for GT racing. At the Paris show of 1972, Porsche introduced the 2.7 liter Carrera RS and planned to build 500 to homologate them as a series into Group 4 for GT racing.

The production RS actually came in three different versions: first, the M471 RS Sport, the version that has become known as the "lightweight"; second, the M472 RS Touring, the most common version with more standard-comfort options similar to the 911S; and, third, the M491 RS Rennsport, the 2.8 RSR racing version of the Carrera. The Carrera RS was a much larger commercial success than Porsche expected and by April 1973, 1,000 had been produced and the Carrera qualified for the Group 3 category of GT racing. By the end of 1973, more than 1,590 of the touring and lightweight 2.7 Carrera RS models had been built, including the first ten prototypes.

When Porsche built these cars, it incorporated a larger engine, several aerodynamic aids, larger wheels and fenders, and a lower bodyweight. This new Carrera RS was also the first production Porsche with larger wheels on the rear than the front. The Carrera RS 2.7 became the basis for a very successful racing version, the 2.8 Carrera RSR. Forty-nine 2.7 Carrera RS cars were rebuilt as the option 491 2.8 RSR models.

Except for the 911R, this was the first *real* series of racing cars based on the 911. The success of the RSR started even before it was homologated as a Group 4 car, with its win at the Daytona 24-Hour race in 1973. By Sebring, the next race for the RSR, it had been homologated for Group 4 and won GT class and overall.

For the 1974 model year the displacement expanded to 2.7 liters for the base models.

The 1974 models had a new simplified front sway bar which went under the front of the body and was mounted in rubber bushings to each of the front A-arms. The size was 16 mm on the 911 and 911S, and 20 mm on the Carrera, which also had an 18 mm rear sway bar. The rear trailing arms were now aluminum castings which were stronger, lighter and cheaper to make. In 1974 Porsche introduced the US Carrera with its larger wheels, fender flares and ducktail.

The year 1974 brought what was probably the most significant visual change to the 911 in its existence—the US-legal bumpers. When these were introduced, I can remember that everyone objected to their appearance. But after a year had passed, everyone thought the earlier cars looked old-fashioned.

The 1974 was the last model year that steel wheels were standard equipment on the 911. Having the steel wheels as standard equipment created a misleading base price for the cars, since no one bought their 911 with steel wheels.

For 1974 the Carrera RS was upsized

Carrera RS lightweight under hood area. The car had an 85-liter (22.5 gal) gas tank. Spare wheel was 6Jx15 in. forged light-metal wheel with collapsible spare tire.

Only one battery was used, instead of the normal two used in the other production 911s. James D. Newton

The Carrera RS lightweight had its interior visibly stripped down to save weight. The sound-deadening material was left out and the carpeting was replaced with rubber floor mats. The emergency rear seats, clock, passenger's visor and glove compartment lid were also left off. Seats were simple lightweight Recaro bucket seats with a thumbscrew adjustment for the backrest angle. The interior came in black. The windshield and side glass were made of a special thinner, lighter Glaverbel safety glass, and the rear quarter windows were fixed. The Carrera RS was also the first production car with larger rear fender flares to accommodate larger seven-inch rear wheels. James D. Newton

to 3.0 liters, and 109 were built for homologation purposes. As an evolution version of the original Group 3 1973 2.7 Carrera RS, only 100 cars were required for the 1974 homologation. Of the 109, forty-four were the extremely desirable street version, while the remainder were prepared as race cars with fifteen for the IROC series and the remaining fifty for factory and customer race cars. The resulting competition car was the familiar 3.0 RSR which was so successful in GT racing over the next several years. The 3.0 RSR was the first 911-based car built from scratch as a race car, and some sixty-five were produced.

In 1974, Porsche raced four extensively modified Carrera RSRs with turbocharged 911 engines in the prototype class. This was done as preparation for the upcoming Silhouette formula for Group 5 cars, which was supposed to begin in 1975 but was delayed until 1976. These highly modified GT cars were run in the prototype class, and as such had to meet the 3.0 liter class limit which, with the 1.4 multiplier imposed on turbocharged cars, limited their displacement to 2142 cc. The 2142 cc engine Porsche developed for this car produced 480 hp at 8000 rpm.

Several things were done in these cars that showed up in later 911-based racing cars. A raised rear-roof section with a raised rear window was used to improve the aerodynamics at the rear of the car. Coil-over springs were also used as the spring media, front and rear, and front and rear suspensions were lightweight fabrications.

Porsche introduced the Type 930 Turbo as a 1975 model at the Paris Auto Show in October 1974. In September 1973 at the Frankfurt Auto Show, Porsche had shown a prototype turbocharged 911 show car to test the market potential of such a car. The Type 930 was originally placed on the market in 1975 to gain homologation for the Group 4 and Group 5 cars that Porsche intended to race in 1976. The original plan was to build the necessary 400 required for homologation, but the car became such a success that it is still in production after thirteen model years. More than 14,750 were built between 1974 when production started and the end of Porsche's 1986 fiscal year.

It took Porsche quite a long time to realize that it was actually going to continue to build these wide-fendered cars indefinitely. When the factory started to produce the 930, it actually welded the fender flares onto the fender stampings as it built the cars. Finally in 1986, the fenders for the Turbo were made as a one-piece part without the welded flares.

2.7 Carrera RS (lightweight option M471) and 2.8 Carrera RSR (option M491). The Carrera RS was the basis for the 2.8 RSR. The RSR was the car that Porsche wanted to build, so it determined what was required as a basis for homologation and reverse-engineered the required homologation car as the 2.7 Carrera RS. When Porsche built these cars, it incorporated a larger engine, several aerodynamic aids, larger wheels and fenders and a lower weight. This new Carrera RS was also the first production Porsche with larger wheels on the rear than the front. Conversion to RSR (option M491) specifications were performed after production. Werkfoto, Porsche AG

The 1974 US Carrera brought what was probably the most significant visual change to the 911 over its whole life, the US-legal bumpers. For 1975, the ducktail was replaced with the whaletail which only lasted one year as well. Dale Miller

The racing rule changes finally came in 1976, and Porsche produced two new 911 race cars for the new classes, the 934 and 935. The 934 was homologated as a Group 4 car and sold to racing customers for GT racing. The 935 was a Group 5 car which the Porsche factory raced itself and won with in the 1976 World Championship of Makes.

The basis for the homologation of the 934 was the 930 Turbo Carrera and the requirement was for 400 to be produced in two model years. Because of the 1.4 multiplier for turbocharged cars, the 934 Turbo RSR could not be considered a lightweight model like its predecessor the 3.0 RSR had been. The multiplier placed the 934 in the 4001 to 4500 cc class requiring the cars' weight to be 2,469 lb. The 934s had power windows,

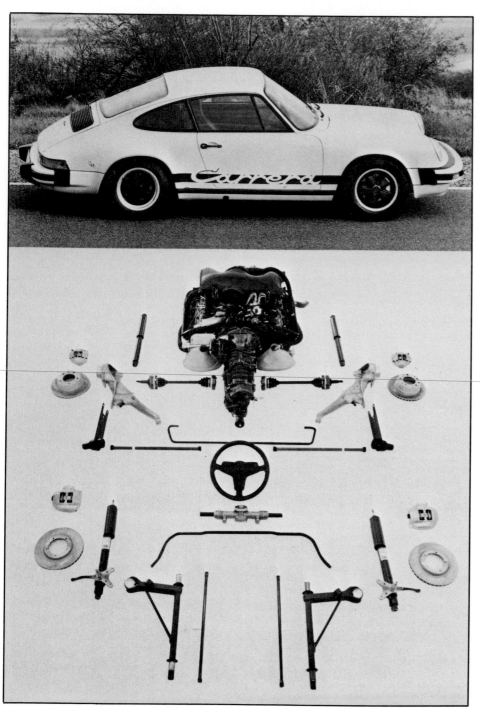

The 1974 2.7 Carrera was the successor to the very popular limited-production series of the 2.7 Carrera RS. The 2.7 Carrera still featured its mechanical fuel-injection engine with 210 hp, but otherwise fit right into the standard R.o.W. 911 program with the 2.7 CIS 911 and 911S. The Carrera rear wing was an option. Werkfoto, Porsche AG

and still required eighty-eight pounds of lead in the front trunk to bring them up to weight. Thirty-one of these Group 4 934s were produced for Porsche's racing customers. Most of these cars remained in Europe and competed in the Group 4 category; Toine Hezemans won the 1976 European GT Championship in a 934.

In the United States, IMSA had said no to the Porsche Turbos, preferring to encourage Porsche to continue to build and support the normally aspirated RSRs. SCCA welcomed the Group 4 934s with open arms, however. Vasek Polak bought five and Al Holbert bought one to race in the popular SCCA Trans-Am series. Several different drivers drove the Polak cars during the year, but George Follmer drove for Vasek most of the season and was rewarded for his efforts with a Trans-Am championship. Al Holbert spent most of his time with his Chevrolet Monza winning the IMSA championship, and had little time to race his 934 in the Trans-Am series.

For 1977, Porsche produced a special series of ten IMSA-legal 934s that took full advantage of the more liberal IMSA rules and used many of the mechanicals from the 935. The IMSA cars were able to run with a lighter weight, wider fifteen-inch wheels, larger Group 5 rear wing and the Bosch plunger-type mechanical injection instead of the CIS system. This change made the cars more pleasant to drive, more reliable and able to produce nearer the 600 hp of the 935 instead of the 500 hp of the Group 4 version.

In Europe over the 1976 season, a number of Porsche's racing customers had been converting their Group 4 934 racers to Group 5 specifications, so for 1977, Porsche also produced a small series of thirteen cars for its customers to race in Group 5. The cars were a customer version which were, in effect, replicas of the two 1976 factory single-turbo 935s.

Porsche built three additional 935s for the factory team's use for the 1977 season, taking advantage of the liberalized Group 5 rules. Porsche entered its factory team in eight of the nine races counting toward the 1977 World Championship of Makes. The factory team won three of the races it entered and the private teams won the rest, giving Porsche another championship.

The Group 5 rules had been revised in an effort to help some of the other makes be competitive. The new rules let the competitors raise the floor up to the doorsills, let them move the bulkhead (firewall) between the engine and the cockpit 20 cm (7.9 in.) into the cockpit, and defined the body structure as the part between the front and rear bulkheads.

The true effect of these rule changes did not completely take effect until 1978 and later. Nevertheless, the new factory cars had improved aerodynamic bodywork, made of fiberglass, which had a greatly revised rear section with a false plexiglass rear window over the existing stock window. The rules said the cars had to retain the original rear window, but they didn't say that a car couldn't have two.

The air inlets for the twin-turbo engine were at the rear edges of the rear vent windows and used a portion of the false roof. The front bodywork was changed to include a pair of front mirrors flared into each of the front fenders, and the cars had running boards under the doors and between the fenders on each side.

The engines were changed quite a bit on these 1977 factory cars, including twin turbochargers and an improved intercooler system. The twin turbochargers were added not so much to increase the engine's horsepower as they were to improve the engine's throttle response. This was done by using the twin-turbo system to create a pair of smaller systems which had half of the inertia to start moving and get up to speed, and then to slow down and stop every time the engine was accelerated or decelerated.

The new intercooler installation took advantage of the rule change that allowed the firewall between the engine and cockpit to extend the 20 cm (7.9 in.) into the cockpit. The intercooler was moved around to the flywheel-end of the engine, and the plumbing from the turbochargers was routed forward, utilizing the increased space from moving the firewall forward into the passenger compartment.

The 3.0 liter Carrera was introduced for 1976 in Europe as Porsche's top-line street car; this version of the Carrera was the forerunner of the 911SC. The 3.0 liter Carrera had an engine that was based on the new, stronger aluminum engine that had been developed for the 930 Turbo, and retained the larger fender flares from the earlier Carreras. In 1978 the 911 became the 3.0 liter 911SC for the entire world market. The 911SCs were built for six model years, from 1978 until 1983.

In 1976, the US version of the Carrera had been discontinued. Nevertheless, in addition to the 911 and the 911S, the 911 Turbo was available for the US market.

Porsche started to experiment with advanced rustproofing techniques as early as 1967 for the 911s with three cars with polished, unpainted stainless steel bodywork. One of these cars was shown at the Frankfurt Auto Show in 1967. Three of these cars were built; two were damaged in accidents and the third retired to the Deutsche Museum in Munich in 1975 after seven years of extensive testing and 95,000 miles. These

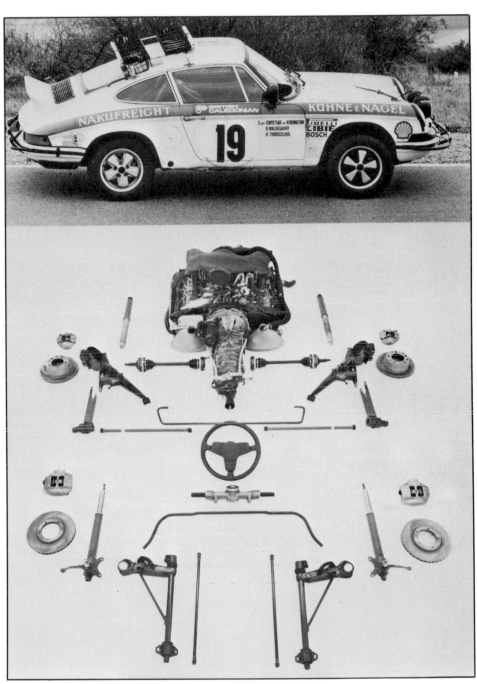

The 1974 2.7 liter Safari was a very slightly modified 1973 Carrera RS, with only some minor reinforcement done to the chassis. The ride height was raised to provide more clearance. Reinforced front-suspension A-arms were used as well as reinforced fabricated rear-suspension arms, with the mounting of the stub axle mounted lower on the arms to increase the ride height. The Safari retained the 210 hp mechanically injected 2.7 Carrera RS engine. Underbody skid plates were used to protect the front suspension and the engine and transmission. The transmission utilized an oil pump, and had an external loop cooler mounted in the left front fender. Werkfoto, Porsche AG

tests were done in collaboration with the German stainless steel industry. The stainless was great and showed no signs of corrosion, but the process was far too expensive for a production car, even a Porsche.

The second choice was to galvanize the exposed portions of the cars' underbody sheet metal, which Porsche started to do to the 911s in the summer of 1970 for the 1971 2.2 liter models. In 1973 the theme of the Frankfurt Auto Show was the "longlife" car which would last twenty years and provide 180,000 miles of use. Porsche built a longlife car for this show, and one of the topics of discussion was extending the body life to twenty years by using special metals, coatings or other materials to prevent corrosion.

In 1975, Porsche introduced its fully rustproofed body to go with the galvanized chassis at the Frankfurt Auto Show. This new combination rustproof body and chassis would enable Porsche to offer a six-year longlife warranty for the 911. All of the body metal had a hot-galvanized coating on both the inside and outside of the sheet metal panels.

From mid-1976 on, all of the 911 Porsches have been made of galvanized sheet metal. For the first few months after the introduction the roof section was not galvanized, but by the end of the production year the roof was galvanized as well. This process has proven so successful for reducing rust that the longlife warranty was increased first to seven years in 1981 for the world market and then to ten years in 1986 for the US market.

In addition to the galvanized body sheet metal, Porsche increased the use of corrosion-resistant aluminum components over the years so that by 1976 they included the bumpers, the rear trailing arms, the front suspension cross-member and the engine crankcase. The stainless steel exhaust system and Targa roll bar were also corrosion-resistant. The exhaust system heater boxes were aluminized, as was the dry-sump oil tank to extend their useful lives.

The 1977 911 was changed very little from the 1976 model except that the US version had only one type of engine for all fifty states, with thermal reactors, EGR and air injection to comply with US emission standards. The specifications for these engines were the same as those for California engines in 1976.

The 1977 911s and 911 Turbos had power-assisted brakes for the first time. The 3.0 liter Carrera was continued for 1977 for the R.o.W. For the US only the 911S and 911 Turbo (930) were available. The 1977 Turbo was the first model to have a boost gauge built into the tachometer. The rear suspension spring plates were made of two pieces and had eccentric adjustment to permit the two pieces to be adjusted with relationship to each other. This was done to permit fine-tuning of the suspension. The Turbo received the new simpler front sway bar that had been used on the 911s since 1974, with a 20 mm front bar and an 18 mm rear bar. The 911 also had its front bar increased in size from 16 to 20 mm and a rear 18 mm was added. This was the same combination as the Carrera had used since 1974.

For a little additional excitement in 1977, Porsche took on BMW in the two-liter class of the German Group 5 series with the 935 Baby. Because Porsche was

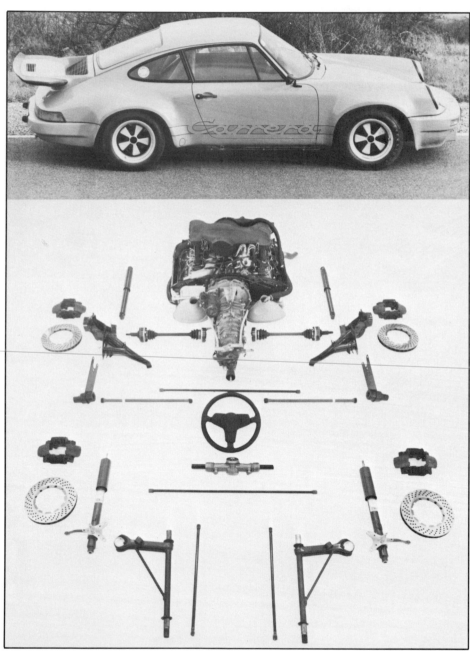

The 1974 3.0 Carrera RS was an even more exciting model than its predecessor the 2.7 Carrera RS had been. The 3.0 Carrera RS was still a mechanically injected car, which was still just an extension of the 911S philosophy with 230 hp. Because Porsche was sure that most of these cars would be converted to race cars, all were delivered with 917 brakes and an oil pump with an external loop cooler for the transmission. They also had special shortened rear trailing arms with revised rear pickup points, eight-inch-wide front wheels and nine-inch-wide rear wheels. Werkfoto, Porsche AG

running unopposed in its own class, it decided to go after the competition in the under-two-liter class. The Baby was turbocharged, so the displacement had to be less than 1425 cc with the 1.4 multiplier. For the Baby, Porsche built a special 370 hp engine with a 60 mm stroke and 71 mm bore. Porsche used air-to-air intercooling for this little engine because it was able to fit the smaller intercoolers under the engine lid.

The Baby was raced only twice; unsuccessfully the first time, but winning by more than half a lap in its second—and last—race. This was the first 935 to use aluminum tube subframes, a technique later applied to the 935/78.

In the mid-seventies all of the new car models were having difficulties meeting US emissions and safety standards, and because the 911 was so different in concept from other cars it was hit particularly hard by all of the drastic new law changes. The majority of the cars in the world are front-engined cars with water-cooling so the new emissions and safety legislation was written for these cars. With the 2.7 liter models the 911 did not seem to be gracefully adapting to this new legislation and as a result, many anticipated its demise, expecting each new year to be the last year for the 911. The new-generation transaxle Porsches were introduced in the mid-seventies, first the 924 in 1976 and then the 928 in 1977. Surely this spelled the end for the 911.

With the introduction of the Turbo model in 1975, Porsche had the means to build a much stronger normally aspirated 911 engine by simply using the same basic components as those used for the Turbo engine. If Americans had been paying close attention they would have noticed that Porsche had done just that when in 1976 it produced the Carrera 3.0 liter for the European market.

In 1978 the 3.0 liter 911SC replaced the Carrera 3.0 in Europe and 2.7 liter 911 models in both Europe and the United States to become the 911 for a world market. The 911SC engine, besides being larger at 3.0 liters and more powerful at 180 horsepower than the 2.7 liter engine, was essentially an all-new engine, and at the time was the best 911 engine produced. By adapting the 911 Turbo technology to the normally aspirated engines, Porsche had solved most of the problems caused by the engine's

rapid growth in the 1970s. By developing more graceful emission control devices for these 1978 911SC engines Porsche was able to make great progress toward meeting the world's ecological needs without making either the driver or the engine suffer for it. Even further progress was made in 1980 with the inclusion of the oxygen sensor system and three-way catalytic converter.

The body for the 911SC model was a fairly logical progression from the Carrera and continued to use larger rear

fender flares with larger wheels in the rear than in the front. The standard wheel and tire combination was 6x15 with 185/70VR-15 tires in the front and 7x15 with 215/60VR-15 tires in the rear. The 1978 was also the first model year that the sixteen-inch wheels and tires were offered as an option with 6x16 with 205/55VR-16 tires in the front and 7x16 with 225/50VR-16 tires in the rear. The rear torsion bars were increased in diameter from 23 to 24.1 mm in 1980.

The black window trim was also made

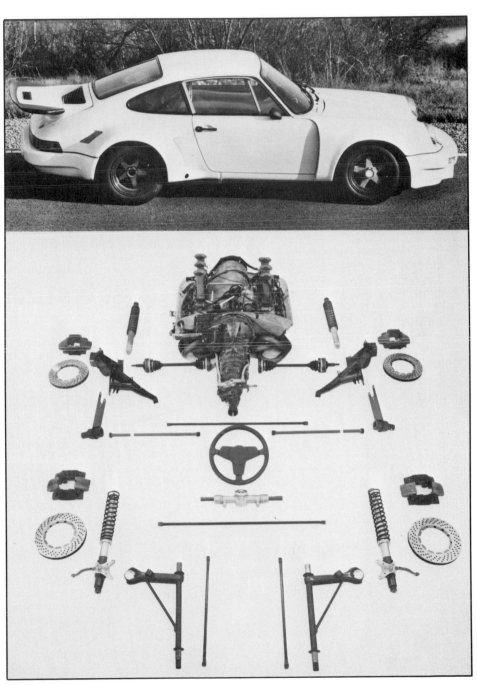

The 1974 3.0 Carrera RSR was basically the 3.0 Carrera RS modified for racing, with wider fenders for the 10½ in. front wheels and the 14 in. rear wheels. The engine was modified to produce 330 hp. Werkfoto, Porsche AG

standard in 1981. In 1981 the additional turn-signal lights were added to the front fenders on the European model 911SC. The 911SC continued to be available in both coupe and Targa model, with the cabriolet becoming available as a 1983 model.

For 1978, Porsche built a series of fifteen customer 935s and let customers defend the World Championship of Makes. The cars looked similar to the first series of customer cars, but they had some refinements and they did have a twin-turbo version of the 935 engine, a big improvement. The bodywork was a little different for these cars in that the rear fenders were removable for the first time on the 935s. This made the cars much easier to work on and, of course, easier to repair. The rear wing was changed to a two-stage wing to provide improved rear downforce, and the cars had running boards to improve aerodynamics.

In 1978, Porsche drastically revised the concept of the Group 5 cars by taking advantage of the rule change that had been made in 1977. The 935/78 Moby Dick Porsche was created just to race at Le Mans where the emphasis is more on straightaway speeds rather than cornering speeds as with most other courses. The results had a great influence on the future of Group 5 racing.

In addition to the rules that Porsche exploited in building the 1977 factory 935s, the Moby Dick also took advantage of the bulkhead or firewall rule which stated that the chassis ends at the front and rear bulkheads. The Moby Dick was built with an aluminum roll cage-tube frame, and the center section of the car was lowered and the floor section raised up to regain the ground clearance. All new bodywork was developed to take advantage of the car's lower profile for improved aerodynamics.

Moby Dick was nine seconds per lap faster at Le Mans than the 935/77 had been, and the speed on the straight was increased from 205.7 to 222.0 mph. Moby Dick was raced only four times, winning only at Silverstone, but the concept led the way for many more innovative Group 5 cars. Moby Dick had a newly developed 3.2 liter version of the venerable 901 engine with four valves, dual overhead cams and water-cooled heads for increased power and reliability.

Again in 1979, Porsche produced an updated version of the 935 for its customers to defend the World Championship of Makes title. The 935/79 incorporated some of the innovations from the 935/78 Moby Dick, and was the basis with which private teams were able to develop their own more-competitive versions of the 935, winning the World Championship of Makes in 1979.

In 1979, Porsche again left the defense of the World Championship of Makes to its customers. For both the 1978 and 1979 seasons, Porsche customers did bring home the World Manufacturers' Championship for the name Porsche. In 1980 and 1981, Lancia threw Porsche a curve by running its cars in the under-two-liter Group 5 class unopposed. The under-two- and over-two-liter Group 5 classes competed equally for the championship, so all Lancia had to do to achieve a perfect score was to finish all the races. The Porsche private teams had good seasons both years but did not achieve perfect scores, so Lancia was able to defeat Porsche by the smallest margin both years.

The 1974 Carrera RSR Turbo 2.1 was a development tool for the future. Porsche developed and raced these cars in preparation for the upcoming Silhouette formula for Group 5 cars. The brakes and titanium axles from the 917 were used. Werkfoto, Porsche AG

The outstanding example of privately developed 935 racers were the Kremer brothers' all-conquering K3 and K4 versions which won the Porsche Cup in 1979, 1980 and 1981. Other significant and successful 935 developments were the Joest Moby Dick copies, Akin's two cars, ANDIAL's Moby Dick copy and John Paul's 935s. There was also a small series of three or four customer 935s made by Porsche for some of its special customers in 1980. By 1980 the Kremer K3 was the "in" customer car and the private teams that did not buy a K3 made their own 935s. One was even rumored to have been made from an old 912 chassis from a wrecking yard.

The K1 and K2 had been versions of the 935 that the Kremers had developed for their racing use in the World Endurance Championship and the German National Championship. The K1 was their original 935, which was based on a 934, with a flat front end and very short rear fenders built in 1976. The K2 was their 1977 car, but with the different rear fenders that had fins on the top to hold more air on top of the fenders, and a different rear spoiler. Both of these changes were in an effort to increase the downforce and improve the handling. The Kremers had developed their K3 935 for their own use during the 1979 season. In 1979, they won eleven of the twelve races in the German National Championship. They also won the prestigious Le Mans race with one of their K3s, the only 935 to ever win Le Mans.

The K3 had bodywork designed in collaboration with Ekehard Zimmermann of Design Plastics. The bodywork was both effective and attractive. All of the bodywork was done in Kevlar instead of fiberglass, which is much stronger and lighter than fiberglass, but more expensive as well. The K3 had wings, or "fences," on both the front and rear fenders to keep the air from spilling off and improving the downforce. The K3 also had a raised false rear-roof section to clean up the airflow over the car, and a unique engine lid and rear wing. Both the front and rear of the chassis were reinforced with aluminum tubes. The rear reinforcements replaced some of the original unit-body construction and made it much easier to remove and install the engine.

The car's main advantage over its predecessors and competition, however, was its air-to-air intercooler. This had been the Kremers' unfair advantage in 1979 and one of the main reasons the car

The 1974 Carrera RSR Turbo 2.1 engine lid and rear wing. Notice the air inlet to the turbo on the left side from the scoop on the passenger side of the car. The big NACA duct in the center pulled the air into the intercooler, and the rectangular opening in the rear exited the air. The air inlet on the right was for cooling air for the engine.

The 1974 Carrera RSR Turbo 2.1 fuel cell. Some versions of the Carrera RSR Turbo 2.1 had their fuel cell mounted inside the passenger compartment, to shift more of the weight toward the rear.

The 1974 Carrera RSR Turbo 2.1. Notice that the outlet of the turbo went directly to the inlet of the intercooler, and the outlet of the intercooler went directly to the intake plenum. Also notice the flat engine-cooling fan.

had been so successful. With the air-to-air intercooler they were able to run with higher boost pressure for longer periods of time without overheating the engine's charge air.

In 1980 the Kremers built replicas of their winning K3 and sold them as customer cars to anyone who wanted to win for 350,000 to 375,000 DM, depending upon the equipment supplied and parts prices. In all, the Kremers built thirteen from Porsche spare-parts race chassis. Additionally they converted three 935s to K3 specifications; two of them were their own 1978 cars and the other was shipped from Japan by a customer. In addition to the Kremer K3s, they also sold several conversion kits so the 935 owners could convert their own 935s to K3 specifications. The K3 was so popular that there were a lot of copies or K3 look-alikes made in addition to the cars and conversion kits from the Kremers. The customer cars were almost as successful as the original had been, and John Fitzpatrick won the IMSA championship and the Porsche Cup in K3 customer cars.

In 1981, Porsche gave two of the German private teams copies of its plans for the Moby Dick so they could build their own copies. Joest built its first Moby Dick replica for its own use in the German championship and World Endurance Championship (WEC), and raced its replica three times in Germany with Jochen Mass as driver. Mass won the Hockenheim race and then Joest sold the car to Gianpiero Moretti, who brought the car and Mass to the Riverside race in April. Mass and Moretti were in contention until they dropped back with a rocker-arm problem and ended up fourteenth.

Dr. Moretti successfully raced the Moby Dick replica in the IMSA series for a couple of years. In 1982 John Fitzpatrick had Joest build him an additional copy of Moby Dick for David Hobbs and himself to drive at Le Mans, where they placed fourth behind the three factory 956s. The 935s were no longer eligible for the World Endurance Championship after 1982, where they had been allowed a one-year grace period after the change to Group C. After racing his Joest Moby Dick car at the Le Mans, Fitzpatrick brought it to the United States and raced it in the IMSA series.

The Kremer brothers also built a 935 that they called the K4 using the information they gained from having access to the factory's Moby Dick plans. Moby Dick had been built as a compromise for Le Mans; Porsche had given up some downforce and resulting cornering power in exchange for some extra speed down the long Mulsanne straightaway. When the Kremers built their tube-frame Moby Dick-type car, they changed the bodywork to get more downforce since most of the tracks the car would race on would place more demands on handling than sustained high speed. They also revised the suspension design, but their revision wasn't quite as successful as their body design. Even with its problem, however, the K4 was successful enough for the Kremers' driver, Bob Wollek, to win the Porsche Cup in 1981. The Kremers also built a second K4 for Interscope Racing and Ted Field and Danny Ongais.

Interscope did not like its K4 and never raced the car. Thus, the Interscope K4 is now part of Vasek Polak's collection.

John Fitzpatrick bought the Kremers' original K4 from them for use in the US

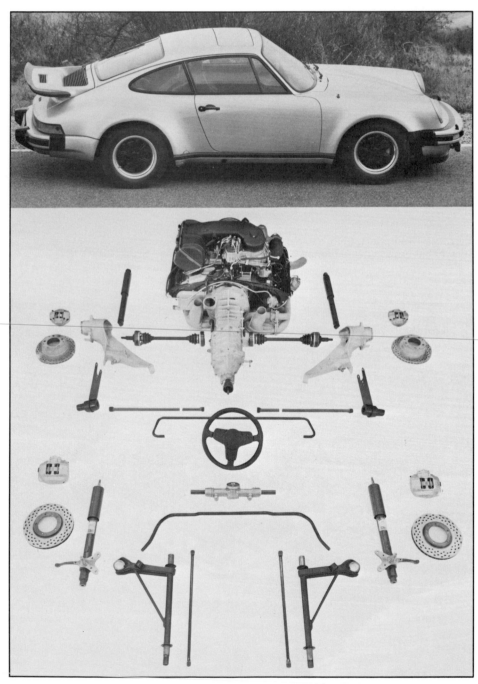

Porsche introduced the Type 930 Turbo at the Paris Auto Show in October 1974. Werkfoto, Porsche AG

IMSA series. Fitzpatrick and his people extensively modified the body and the suspension, and won four IMSA races with it during the 1982 season. "Fitz" still raced the K4 at the beginning of the 1983 IMSA season and then moved his operation to England to race a 956 team in the World Endurance Championship. The K4 was sold to a Porsche club member in Southern California, who uses it for club events.

In 1982, Glen Blakely and ANDIAL built another Moby Dick copy for Howard Meister. They raced the car at Riverside and sold it to Preston Henn. In 1983, Bob Wollek put the ANDIAL Moby Dick on the pole and then he, Henn, Claude Ballot-Lena and A. J. Foyt drove it to its first victory. Foyt and Hurley Haywood won again at Daytona in July. Foyt, Wollek and Derek Bell drove this copy to second place at Daytona in 1984 and the same trio placed third at Sebring. Foyt and Wollek also placed fourth at Miami. By 1984, however, these wonderful old beasts were no longer competitive in IMSA against the always-improving GTP cars, and the 935s won just a single race for the season—Sebring.

John Paul and John Paul, Jr., had a series of cars that they either modified or had built for them. The first two, JLP1 and JLP2, were modified 935s with some tube-frame modifications. The JLP3 was the first car that was really all of their own construction, and was made for them by Graham "Rabbit" Bartills at Chuck Gaa's GAACO in Norcross, Georgia. The only Porsche body or chassis points used in its construction were the door frames, cowl, window frame and roof section which were from a 1972 or 1973 911 rusted-out wreck from an Atlanta wrecking yard.

The JLP3 was new at Sebring in 1981, where it had some engine-oil-supply problems. In the end, the race itself became just a testing exercise for the Pauls and their JLP3. The JLP3 was built along conventional lines and still utilized all of the standard Porsche 935 suspension pickup points and suspension components.

The Pauls' next "Porsche 935" was the much more adventuresome JLP4, which was designed by Lee Dykstra and built by Dave Klym's FABCAR in Tucker, Georgia. This car was built from scratch and had a combination monocoque and tube-frame chassis. The center section of the car was a monocoque, and the front and rear were tube frame to support the suspension components, engine and transmission. The front of the car was also a tube frame which was only sixteen inches wide where the front suspension attached. This was an extremely sophisticated car, with fully independent suspension based on inboard-mounted coil-over shock absorbers. The JLP4 was a ground-effects car

A 1976 Group 4 934, based on the 1976 930 which was produced for homologation purposes. Werkfoto, Porsche AG

The fuel tank was replaced with a 120-liter (32 gal) fuel cell. This same fuel cell was also used in the 935s.

The early 1976 935s had very conventional-looking bodywork, with normal front fenders with headlights. And even though the rear fenders had scoops and air inlets, they were still fairly conventional in appearance. The original 935 had an air-to-air intercooler mounted up in the rear wing. The rules, and Porsche's cars, were scrutinized after the first couple of races, and it was determined that Porsche's intercooler installation did not comply with the rules. The rules said that in all circumstances, the bonnets and bootlids must be interchangeable with the original homologated ones, and in this case the stock engine lid (bonnet or bootlid) did not fit over the intercooler. Porsche was forced to change to a water-cooled intercooler system much like the one used with the 934. It used the leading edge of the fenders for the air inlet to the intercooler water radiators. The rear 930 intercooler and resulting rear engine lid from 1978-on were similar to the original location of the air-to-air intercooler on the 935. In fact, I wouldn't be surprised if you could make a stock engine lid fit onto one of those original 935s over the air-to-air intercooler. Werkfoto, Porsche AG

and it, like its predecessor the JLP3, spent a great deal of time in the Lockheed wind tunnel in Murietta, Georgia.

The JLP4 was a very complex car; it took 2,004 hours to build originally. Because it was complex, it was more difficult to maintain than the more conventional 935s, and as a result the JLP3 stayed in service in the Pauls' team. During the 1981 and 1982 seasons, John Paul, Jr., won six poles and a total of nine races with these two cars, and actually won five races in a row with the JLP3. In 1982 John Paul, Jr., won nine of the eighteen-race IMSA series and the IMSA championship using these two Porsches and a Lola T-600. The JLP4 was sold at auction to an attorney who plans to convert the car for street use.

Bob Akin had two 935s built in Georgia as well. Chuck Gaa of GAACO made Akin's first Georgia 935 a monocoque chassis 935. The car looked like a cross between a Lola T-600 and a 935.

Although this car was incredibly fast in a straight line, its handling could best be described as diabolical. The car went out after only two hours at Le Mans in 1982, and Akin was quoted as saying, "Good," he wasn't looking forward to driving it for twenty-four hours. The car was crashed at the end of the 1982 season and was never repaired. Akin went back to racing his reliable Kremer K3 for the 1983 season.

In the summer of 1983, Akin had Dave Klym of FABCAR make "The Last 935" for him. There was nothing really new about The Last 935; in fact, it was fairly conventional. The chassis was a steel tube frame and it used all Porsche 935 suspension components. When Klym built the car, he concentrated on building a strong, reliable car, optimizing the suspension pickup points and getting the car down to the IMSA weight limit of 2,060 lb. The body used an adaptation of the Kremers' K4 nose, and the rest was pretty much Klym and Akin's own. The original bodywork was all done in aluminum, and then, when Klym and Akin were happy with it, a fiberglass mold was taken off of it.

The Last 935 was completed and tested in Atlanta at the end of October, where it proved to be four seconds faster than Akin's K3. They tested it again at Daytona, and had The Last 935 ready in time for its first race at the Daytona three-hour Finale where Akin and John O'Steen placed second to IMSA champion Al Holbert in his Porsche March 83G. It's too bad The Last 935 was built so late—it was a marvelous 935. The handwriting was on the wall in 1983, when Holbert won the IMSA championship with a Porsche March, and 1984 would be the year of the GTP cars in IMSA.

In 1982 the FIA rules were changed, replacing Groups 4, 5 and 6 with the current Groups A, B and C. Two hundred cars had to be built to qualify for Group B. Once the 200 were built, an "evolution" was permitted and only twenty cars were required for this additional evolution homologation. When the rules changed in 1982, Porsche homologated evolution models of both its 911SC and 911 Turbo to help its customers with their racing efforts. In 1982 Porsche included performance updates such as the through-the-body front sway bar; reinforced suspension front and rear; improved brakes front and rear and dual master cylinder with balance beam; and central-locking wheel nuts and reinforced axles.

Interior of 935/77. This one was modified to gain access to the engine from inside the passenger compartment, and the water tank for the intercooler was moved inside the passenger compartment. The original Group 5 rules didn't allow any of the engine components to extend into the passenger compartment.

935/77 after a blown tire had ripped up the rear fender. Having the rear fenders as a permanent part of the car had two disadvantages—this was one of them. The other disadvantage was that the fenders were in the way when the mechanics needed to work on the car.

The 911SC RS (Type 954) was an example of the evolution homologation procedure. The homologation was based on the standard 1983 3.0 liter 911SC. Twenty evolution cars were built and homologated January 1, 1984. These cars embodied all of the high-performance features necessary to win the European Rally Championship. The 911SC RS had an engine that was modified to produce 250 hp. Other changes to the 911SC RS included turbo brakes, aluminum hood and doors, and the use of fiberglass for the bumpers and rear engine lid.

In 1983, when Porsche added its Cabriolet to the model line, it again had six distinct body styles for the first time since 1961. The new Cabriolet was a welcome addition to the 911 line—Porsche's first *true* open car since the 356C Cabriolet was discontinued in 1965. The body and interior changes have continued through the years, with the most significant appearance changes being the introduction of the Targa model in 1967 and the bumper change in 1974. The Cabriolet was introduced as a 1983 model at the tribute to Porsche at Laguna Seca in August 1982.

At the Frankfurt International Auto Show for 1983, Porsche introduced its new 959 Group B car as an evolution of the 911 concept. The Type 959 Group B car was a technical exercise that was put into limited production; it incorporated technical advancements that should keep the 911 concepts current until the year 2000.

Even though the 959 showed a strong relationship to the 911, it was an exciting, all-new car with totally new developments in engine, drivetrain, body and chassis. Most of the visible parts of the new aerodynamic body were made of Kevlar mounted on a load-bearing steel-chassis structure. The front hood and doors were made of aluminum, and the rear engine lid with integrated rear wing was also made of Kevlar.

The 450 hp 2.85 liter engine was based on the 911 engine, using the concept of four-cam, four-valve, water-cooled cylinder-head design developed for racing for the 935, 936 and 956 engines. Although the concept was the same, the cylinder heads for the 959 engine were single castings for each bank of three cylinders instead of individual cylinders and cylinder-head assemblies.

The engine was twin-turbocharged for flexibility, and also utilized the electronic performance optimization designs based upon Porsche's experience with the 956. Power was put to the ground through Porsche's then-new electronic program-controlled all-wheel-drive transaxle design with six-speed transmission. The suspension was fully independent, using dual transverse arms front and rear with dual shock absorbers at each corner.

For the 1977 season, the factory team had a new 1977 version of the 935 for its own use. The factory 935/77 had new bodywork which included running boards and a new front end that had faired-in mirrors at the edge of the fender, which also served as a fence to keep the air from spilling off the front end, improving the downforce. It also had a raised false-roof section to clean up the airflow over the back of the car, making the rear wing more effective. The running boards were used to improve the air management, and were the beginning of efforts to provide some ground effects for the 935. The rules said that the car had to retain its original rear window in its original location, but they did not say there couldn't be a second rear window over the original—so that's what Porsche did. This new false roof faired into a new rear wing. The edges of this false rear-roof section were used as air inlets for the engine. Werkfoto, Porsche AG

The ride height and shock absorber stiffness were adjustable from the driver's seat while the car was under way.

The 959 was not only an exercise in high technology, it also was a very attractive new car that looks somewhat like a cross between a 911, a 928 and a 356. Two hundred of these cars were built so

The 935 Baby. For a little additional excitement in 1977, Porsche took on BMW in the two-liter class of the German Group 5 series with this 935 Baby. Werkfoto, Porsche AG

1977 Kremer K2 at Daytona 24-Hour race, February 1978. The Kremer K2 incorporated some aerodynamic improvements as well as some styling changes. The rear fenders were the Kremers' own design, with a smoother leading edge for the rear fender and fences to prevent air from spilling off the fenders. Notice that the lower lip on the front spoiler is adjustable. Manfred and Erwin Kremer are at the rear of the car. The K2's rear fenders were removable and held on with Dzus fasteners at a time when the factory cars still had the fenders bonded on.

The 911SC was introduced for the 1978 model year and remained in production through 1983. Porsche-Audi Division of VWoA

The 930 Turbo received a major revision in 1978. Its engine was increased in displacement to 3.3 liters and an intercooler was added to the engine for improved efficiency. The addition of the intercooler could be detected by the change in the rear wing. The 1978-and-later Turbos had the much larger and more efficient 917-type brakes. Porsche-Audi Division of VWoA

that they would comply with the Group B homologation requirements that were in effect when the car was conceived. Porsche had planned to build the two hundred required for homologation, selling 959-derived cars for street, sport and racing.

The Group B rules replaced the old Group 4 rules that were in effect for cars like the 934. Production of the 959 started in the late spring of 1987, and customer deliveries began in May 1987. Unfortunately, by the time the two hundred required for homologation had been built, FISA had changed the rules and cars like the 959 were no longer eligible as race cars.

Jacky Ickx competed in the 1983 Paris-Dakar rally and wanted Porsche to be the first sports car to compete in the event. Porsche took advantage of the opportunity to do some development work on its all-wheel-drive system that would be used in the 959. Porsche ran three all-wheel-drive 953s in 1984, winning the event on its first try.

In 1985, Porsche again entered the Paris-Dakar rally with three prototypes of the 959. This time they were not so lucky, and some teething troubles ended up delaying the cars with suspension problems. Eventually all of the cars failed due to different weaknesses, some driver-induced. The cars that Porsche ran in 1985 had the chassis and all-wheel-drive of the 959, but used a 3.2 liter Carrera engine. For 1986, Porsche entered three rally versions of the 961 and won again. All three finished, the first two placing first and second.

In 1984, Porsche again applied the Carrera name to its 911 product line. The new 911 Carrera is the best 911 to date, with its new, larger 3.2 liter engine and DME-controlled (Digital Motor Electronics) fuel and ignition system. The Carrera is the fastest road-going 911 ever offered in the United States. For 1984, Porsche also offered the turbo-look body, which it called the 911 Carrera with 930 Performance Body/Chassis option. The turbo-look body included the turbo bodywork, brakes and larger turbo wheels and tires. The front wheels and tires were 7x16 in. with 205/55VR-16, while the rear were 8x16 in. with 226/50VR-16.

Beginning with the 1985 models, the turbo-look was also made available for both the Targa and Cabriolet, in addition to the coupe. The turbo-look was also made available without front and rear spoilers.

Porsche also introduced its short-shifter in 1985. The reason for shortening the shift travel was to avoid having the shift lever scrape the seat going into second gear, when the car had sport seats. Porsche shortened the shift travel by about ten percent by moving the pivot point up by 4 mm. Starting with the 1985 model, Porsche also used Boge GZ double-tube gas-pressure shock absorbers as an option to the Bilstein single-tube gas-pressure shocks.

For 1986, the 930 or 911 Turbo was reintroduced to the United States. For its reintroduction, Porsche used a catalytic-converter system with oxygen-sensor fuel control to comply with the US emission laws. A number of changes were made to the 911 Turbo since it was last available in the United States in 1979, and they have all been incorporated in the new US version.

The 1986 911 Carreras had Boge double-tube low-pressure gas shock absorbers as standard equipment. The front sway-bar diameter was increased from 20 mm to 22 mm. The rear torsion bars were increased in diameter from 24.1 to 25 mm. The rear sway bar was also increased in size from 18.8 to 21 mm.

The 911 Turbo and turbo-look models had different size tires and rims on the rear wheels. The rim size was changed from 8Jx16 in. with a 10.3 mm rim offset with 225/50VR-16 tires, to 9Jx16 in. with a 15 mm rim offset with 245/45VR-16 tires. The 1986 model year also included the introduction of the US additional third stop light. For the Cabriolet, this third stop light was mounted on the engine lid.

For 1986, the Cabriolet also had an electrically actuated cabriolet top available as an option. This was also the first year that the Turbo fenders, with their fender flares, were made as one piece for the front and rear instead of welded-on flares as they had been previously.

In 1987, Porsche made both the Targa and a Cabriolet available as a Turbo model as well as the traditional coupe. In addition to the standard production cars, Porsche has been doing custom work for its customers in Europe at its customer service department in Werk I for several years. A few years ago it started a program called the *Sonderwunsche-Programm* (Special Wishes Program), where Porsche offered its customers a catalog of conversions, modifications and customizing work. Starting with the slant-nose body option, Porsche Car of North America is starting to offer a version of this program to its US customers as the Porsche Exclusive Program.

The 1987 Carrera had a completely new five-speed transmission, Type G-50. The clutch was increased from 225 to 240 mm in diameter. The new larger clutch was also activated by a hydraulic master-and-slave cylinder. The rear torsion-bar tube had a bent center section to provide additional clearance for the transmission; the additional clearance was required for the new clutch disc with larger rubber-damper center section.

The 1987 911 Carrera and 911 Turbo had new headlights that were optically

The rear of a 935/78 customer 935, with its removable rear fenders. Pip pins retained the fenders, and after removing a few of these fasteners the whole fender could be removed, which made it much easier to work on the cars. The 935/78 used twin turbochargers to improve the power and throttle response. The intercooler installation took advantage of the 1977 rule change that permitted engine components to protrude into the passenger compartment 20 cm (7.9 in.).

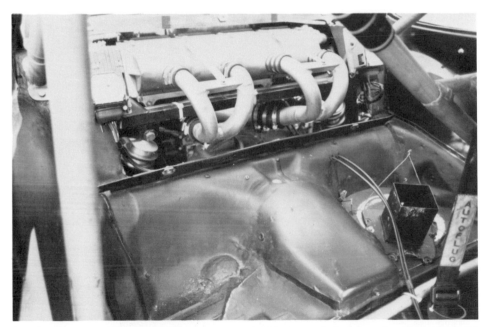

935/78 customer 935 passenger compartment with intercooler installation, which took advantage of the 1977 rule change. A new mount for the rear shock absorbers had to be made to take advantage of this 20 cm rule. There was an aluminum cover that went over this and hid it from the outside.

standard for R.o.W. and US models. The 911 Carreras and 911 Turbos equipped with catalytic converters had an additional electric blower mounted on the oil cooler in the right-front wheelhousing to prevent excessive oil temperatures. The fan was controlled by a temperature switch mounted in the top of the oil cooler. This switch turned on the fan when the oil temperature reached 118 deg C (244 deg F).

Originally, Porsche had planned to produce an evolution version of the 959 in the form of the 961, but by the time Porsche completed its run of 200 cars, the rules had been changed and FISA no longer accepted cars like the 959 into Group B. In addition to the rally versions of the 961 run in the Paris-Dakar event in 1981, Porsche also built a racing version of the 961 which was raced three times as an IMSA GTX car, placing seventh at the 1986 Le Mans 24-Hour, and later raced at the Finale at Daytona. The best finish for the 961 was seventh at the 1986 Le Mans race. Unfortunately it crashed at the 1987 Le Mans and was badly damaged by the resulting fire.

IMSA has agreed to accept the 961 into its GTO class after the 200 have been built for homologation. Porsche has talked about building twenty-five of these cars for its American customers at 430,000 DM FOB Stuttgart, but at the present time there is not much interest in these cars at over a quarter of a million dollars a copy, so no customer version of the 961 is planned.

In April of 1987, Porsche offer a new car which will be a replica of the 953s that the Porsche factory entered in the Paris-Dakar rally in 1984. Porsche will be building a limited series of these cars for its customers who would like to run either the Paris-Dakar rally or the Paris-Peking rally. The new car will be the Type 953. The 953 will have an engine derived from the production 3.2 liter Carrera engine, with 9.5:1 compression, 228 hp at 5900 rpm and a peak torque of 195 pounds-feet. The engine will retain the Motronic management system and require a minimum of 95 RON (Research Octane Number) octane fuel.

The 953 will have permanent four-wheel drive using the technology derived from the 959 and components from the future 911 four-wheel-drive called the 964. The transmission is five-speed Type 964 with laminated-clutch differential locking. An additional laminated clutch is used for the center differential to the front wheels as well. The front suspension is double control arm with two shock absorbers per wheel. Front torsion bars are 24.1 mm and the front sway bar is 22 mm. The rear suspension is semi-trailing arm with torsion bar and coil spring. Rear torsion bars are 24.1 mm and the rear sway bar is 20 mm. Front wheels are 6x15 in. and the rears are 7x15 in.

The chassis is a reinforced Carrera coupe chassis. The doors, fenders and front hood are made out of aluminum as are the front and rear bumpers. The windows are made out of thin glass. The car has racing seats and full-harness safety belt, and weighs 2,756 lb.

The 911 may be phased out of production someday, when it fails to sell enough to justify production. But for now it seems safe with eighty cars produced per day and 16,454 cars per year. The end of 1987 will mark the 911's twenty-fifth anniversary, with nearly a quarter of a million 911s having been built. Let us hope that when and if it is ever replaced, its replacement retains the spirit and character of the 911 we have all grown to love.

Peter Greg's 1979 IMSA version of the 935/79. For the 1979 season, IMSA tried to handicap the Porsches and increased the multiplier for turbocharged cars, with an even higher multiplier for the twin-turbocharged cars. Porsche made a special IMSA version of the 935 for 1979, which had a special engine with a larger single turbo, in an effort to give the Porsche private teams the biggest advantage, or least handicap, possible. Only Greg was able to win races with this single-turbo engine, and all of the other teams went back to the easier-to-drive twin-turbo 935s with an added weight penalty. Bill Martin

The factory team raced only one 935 in 1978—Moby Dick. The Moby Dick was built with an aluminum roll cage-tube frame. The center section of the car was lowered and the floor section was raised up to regain the ground clearance. All new bodywork was developed to take advantage of the car's lower profile for improved aerodynamics. Werkfoto, Porsche AG

The 935/77 customer cars were essentially identical to the late 1976 935/76 factory race cars. The body was revised and the results were the beginning of the slope-nose front ends and squared-off and raised rear fenders. W. H. Murenbeeld

The 1977 Kremer K2 at Daytona 24-Hour Race, February 1978. Notice the shape of the rear fenders and the fact that they were removable. By adding the bumper guards, the Kremers extended the rear of the car and thus how far the rear wing could extend.

The 1978 Moby Dick 935 was created with the intention of doing well in just one race, Le Mans, where the emphasis is more on straightaway speeds rather than cornering speeds. Hence, the car's aerodynamics were compromised toward high speed versus downforce. The concepts Moby Dick established had a great influence on the future of Group 5 racing cars. Werkfoto, Porsche AG

Kremer K3, one of their customer cars that they sold to Dick Barbour. John Fitzpatrick won the IMSA championship and the Porsche Cup with this car. Bill Martin

The Last 935 at the Daytona 24-Hour 1985. This car did race twice again in 1985 placing seventh at the Daytona 24-Hour and finally breaking at the Sebring 12-Hour. Bill Martin

One of Georg Loos' 935/79 customer cars. Fuel cell and oil tank filled the whole trunk area in these cars. Jerry Woods

The new 935/79 customer version had a great number of changes over its predecessors, using a lot of the technology gained from Moby Dick. The 935/79 had the Moby Dick's upside-down transmis-sion and the new "big" brakes. The upside-down transmission allowed these cars to run revised-suspension geometry, and with a lower center of gravity without severe axle angles. The 19 in. diameter rear wheels with their larger tires had caused the axles to operate at some fairly extreme angles as the 935s were lowered. Notice that more and more of the rear of the car was being cut away to accommodate these changes.

Gianpiero Moretti raced this 1981 Joest
Moby Dick replica in the IMSA series for a
couple of years. Bill Martin

Dashboard of the Kremer K3. Bill Martin

The Cabriolet introduced as a new model
for 1983 was one of the most significant
changes in the 911's history. Porsche Audi
Div. VWoA

The Kremer brothers also built a 935 that they called the K4, using the information they gained from having access to the factory's Moby Dick plans. The Moby Dick cars were based on an aluminum-tube frame but retained enough of the original homologated body parts to comply with the rules. They were required to have the roof section, the door frames and the windshield frame. The rulemakers said that the floor could be raised up to the bottom of the doorsill, and by requiring that the cars have a complete door frame they could establish the overall height of the cars. This is an early construction of the Kremers' first K4 with their driver "Smiling" Bob Wollek at the wheel. H. Peter Boss, Porsche-Kremer Racing

ANDIAL Moby Dick 935 winning 1983 Daytona 24-Hour endurance race with A.J. Foyt, Bob Wollek and Claude Ballot-Lena as drivers. Bill Martin

John Fitzpatrick bought the Kremers' original K4 from them for use in the US IMSA series. Fitzpatrick and his people extensively modified the body and the suspension, and won four IMSA races with it during the 1982 season. Fitz still raced the K4 at the beginning of the 1983 IMSA season, and then midseason moved his operation to England to race 956s in the World Endurance Championship. (Note that the original Moby Dick, Joest replicas and Kremer K4s were right-hand-drive cars.) Bill Martin

959 prototype shown at the 1983 Frankfurt Auto Show. Werkfoto, Porsche AG

John Paul, Jr., won the Daytona 24-Hour endurance race 1982 with his dad and Rolf Stommelen in their JLP3. JLP3 was a very reliable fast car, and John Paul, Jr., did very well with it. Bill Martin

JLP4 was the Pauls' next "Porsche 935." It was a much more adventuresome car. This car was built from scratch and had a combination monocoque and tube-frame chassis. Bill Martin

Bob Akin had Chuck Gaa of GAACO make a monocoque chassis 935 for him. The car looked like a cross between a Lola T-600 and a 935. Although this car was incredibly fast in a straight line, its handling could best be described as diabolical. The car was crashed at the end of the 1982 season and was never repaired. Akin went back to racing his reliable Kremer K3 for the 1983 season. Hal Crocker

Porsche ran three all-wheel-drive 953s in the 1984 Paris-Dakar race winning the event on its first try. Cutaway drawing of 953 Paris-Dakar car. Werkfoto, Porsche AG

The 911SC RS (Type 954) was an example of the evolution homologation procedure. Werkfoto, Porsche AG

1984-87 3.4 liter Carrera Cabriolet. Note the "telephone dial" cast wheels which became standard equipment in 1984 when the Carrera was introduced. Werkfoto, Porsche AG

A number of changes had been made to the 911 Turbo since it was last available in 1979 as a 1980 model, and were all incorporated in the new US version. Werkfoto, Porsche AG

Rear photo of cutaway 959. Werkfoto, Porsche AG

Rear view of 959 engine compartment.
Werkfoto, Porsche AG

The 959, rally version, street version and racing 961 version. Werkfoto, Porsche AG

The 961 race car based on the 959, placed seventh at Le Mans in 1986, and also raced at the IMSA Finale at Daytona that year.

The only 961 built was destroyed by fire at Le Mans 1987. Werkfoto, Porsche AG

959 interior. Werkfoto, Porsche AG

Paris-Dakar 959. Werkfoto, Porsche AG

Construction of both Paris-Dakar 959 and 961 race cars at Weissach. Werkfoto, Porsche AG

The 961 engine.

In 1987, Porsche made the Turbo available
as a Targa and a Cabriolet as well as the
traditional coupe. Werkfoto, Porsche AG

Porsche also produced the slope-nose as a limited series, and for the first time made the factory slope-nose, or slant-nose, available to the United States through Porsche Car of North America's "Exclusive Program." PCNA

953. Replica of cars that ran and won the Paris-Dakar rally in 1984. The 953, customer's version of Paris-Dakar rally car. Werkfoto, Porsche AG

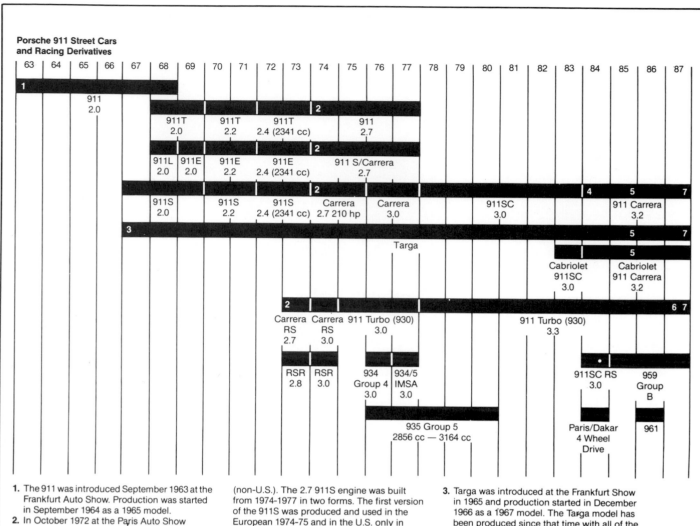

Porsche 911 Street Cars and Racing Derivatives

| 63 | 64 | 65 | 66 | 67 | 68 | 69 | 70 | 71 | 72 | 73 | 74 | 75 | 76 | 77 | 78 | 79 | 80 | 81 | 82 | 83 | 84 | 85 | 86 | 87 |

1

911
2.0

2

911T 2.0 — 911T 2.2 — 911T 2.4 (2341 cc) — 911 2.7

2

911L 2.0 | 911E 2.0 — 911E 2.2 — 911E 2.4 (2341 cc) — 911 S/Carrera 2.7

2 ... **4** **5** **7**

911S 2.0 — 911S 2.2 — 911S 2.4 (2341 cc) — Carrera 2.7 210 hp — Carrera 3.0 — 911SC 3.0 — 911 Carrera 3.2

3 **5** **7**

Targa

5

Cabriolet 911SC 3.0 — Cabriolet 911 Carrera 3.2

2 **6 7**

Carrera RS 2.7 | Carrera RS 3.0 | 911 Turbo (930) 3.0 — 911 Turbo (930) 3.3

RSR 2.8 | RSR 3.0 | 934 Group 4 3.0 | 934/5 IMSA 3.0 — 911SC RS 3.0 | 959 Group B

935 Group 5 2856 cc — 3164 cc — Paris/Dakar 4 Wheel Drive | 961

1. The 911 was introduced September 1963 at the Frankfurt Auto Show. Production was started in September 1964 as a 1965 model.
2. In October 1972 at the Paris Auto Show Porsche introduced the 2.7 Carrera RS for 1973 production. The introduction of the 2.7 engine and the Carrera name set the stage for a series of engine and designation juggling which would last through 1977. The 2.7 liter 210 horsepower Carrera engine was built 1973-75 and used only in European cars (non-U.S.). The 2.7 911S engine was built from 1974-1977 in two forms. The first version of the 911S was produced and used in the European 1974-75 and in the U.S. only in 1974 for both the 911S and the U.S. version of the Carrera. The second of the 911S engine was the U.S. version 1975-77 which produced 157 horsepower. The straight 911 engine produced 150 horsepower and was used in Europe 1974-77 and in the U.S. only in 1974.

3. Targa was introduced at the Frankfurt Show in 1965 and production started in December 1966 as a 1967 model. The Targa model has been produced since that time with all of the normal street 911 engines.
4. Turbo Look Coupe body for 911 in 1984.
5. Turbo Look Targa and Turbo look Cabriolet added to product line in 1985.
6. 911 Turbo Targa and Cabriolet.
7. 911 Turbo Slope Nose Coupe, Targa and Cabriolet were made available for the U.S. market as a production option.

911 family tree.

Flat-six engine development

In the January 1985 issue, *Car and Driver* magazine selected the Porsche 911 engine as one of the ten best engines of all time. When this issue came out, the first thing I did was turn to the article to see if the 911 had made the list. I would have been disappointed if it had not.

The 911 engine has become an extremely reliable high-performance engine. Even though, there have been some times during its life that its longevity and potential future may have been seriously in doubt. And, perhaps in spite of the fact that some people still consider the Porsche 911 models to be merely hopped-up Volkswagens, the 911 engine has indeed become one of the great engines of all time.

Over the years, Porsche has put a great deal of effort into its yearly effort to win the Le Mans 24-Hour race. And indeed it did win Le Mans with the fabulous 917 in 1970, after twenty years of trying. Another 917 won again in 1971. And 911-based engines have gone on to win that prestigious victory for Porsche ten additional times since then, including the past seven consecutive races. Le Mans is one of the most important races in the world, and Porsche has made Le Mans its own.

In its article about the ten best engines, *Car and Driver* said, "In automotive history there have been many noteworthy cars whose distinction and fame have rested largely on their great engines. Conversely, there have been cars of great potential that have slipped into obscurity for lack of a decent powerplant." The article goes on to say that the engines selected for the ten best list had to be both innovative and successful in the marketplace to be chosen. The other nine engines that made this list were: the 1901 35 hp Mercedes; the 1909 Ford Model T; the 1928 Alfa Romeo 6C 1500; the 1932 Ford Flathead V-8; the 1945 Volkswagen Flat-four; the 1947 Ferrari-Colombo V-12; the 1949 Cadillac High-Compression V-8; the 1949 Jaguar XK Six; and the 1955 Chevrolet Small-Block V-8.

Type 821 prototype engine was one of the early prototype engine designs for the 901. The Type 821 was actually very similar to the first production engine, except that it was still a wet-sump engine. Werkfoto, Porsche AG

Type 901 prototype engine with more conventional triple-throat Solex downdraft carburetors. This prototype engine also had an exhaust system that was very similar to those used on the four-cylinder Carrera engines. This was the version of the engine that was in the 901 shown at the Frankfurt show in 1963. Werkfoto, Porsche AG

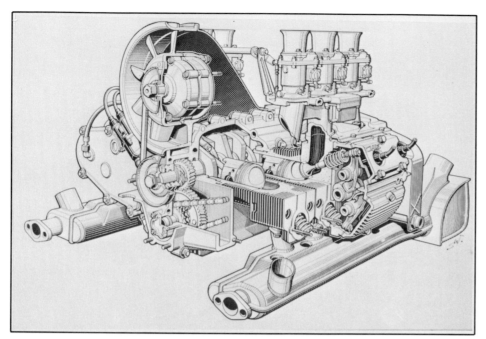

Cutaway drawing of early Type 901 engine. Notice early-style heat-exchanger system. The exhaust manifolding was a simple welded-up arrangement that looked very much like headers for a flat-head Ford V-8. Werkfoto, Porsche AG

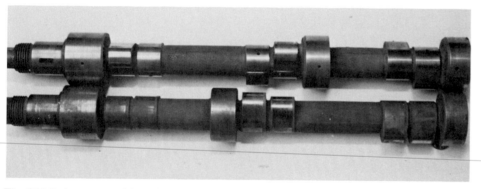

The 901 Solex cams with and without center lube. Note oil holes in the bearing journals and at the base circle of each lobe.

When the 911 engine was developed in the early 1960s, a series of six-cylinder prototype engines led up to what became the 911 engine, or the 901 engine as it was known in the beginning. The Type 745 was a flat-opposed six-cylinder engine with two camshafts located down at the center of the engine, with one above and the other below the crankshaft driving the valves through pushrods.

Probably even more significant was the Type 821 engine which was the first of the prototypes that shared much of its technology with the final design. In fact, this engine actually used the same Solex overflow-type carburetor design that the first 901 engines had when the car went into production in late 1964. The most significant differences between the Type 821 engine and the next prototype engine, Type 901, was that the Type 821 was still a wet-sump engine like the 356 pushrod engines. The near-hemispherical head design and the cam drives used to this day were originally used on this prototype engine.

The next prototype engine in this series was the prototype Type 901 engine which used the more conventional triple-throat Solex downdraft carburetors. This engine also had an exhaust system that was very similar to those used on the four-cylinder Carrera engines. The exhaust gases first went forward to a pair of heat exchanger and expansion chamber premufflers, then to the rear of the car to one large rear muffler with twin tailpipes.

This was the version of the engine that was in the 901 shown in the Frankfurt show in 1963. This prototype engine had the spark plugs angled upward at a

Left-hand chain-housing cover (cyl 1-3) for Type 901/01, showing mount for mechanical pumps for fuel recirculation, and fitting for oil line for center-lubed camshaft.

Inside of left-hand chain-housing cover for Type 901/01, showing axial sealing ring for supplying oil to center-lubed camshaft.

steep angle so that they were more nearly parallel to the intake ports. Because of the steep angle, the intake-valve covers had a unique appearance. They were smaller and only had a pair of small notches in them to provide clearance for the spark plugs.

The 901/911 engine and car went into production in the fall of 1964 as a 1965 model 911. The engine was designed as a 2.0 liter (1991 cc) with an 80 mm bore and 66 mm stroke, with room for expansion up to 2.5 liters. Professor Ferry Porsche has been quoted as saying that if he had known the engine had as much room for expansion—3.3 liters in production engines and as much as 3.5 liters in some experimental racing and street engines—he would have requested that the engineers redesign the engine as a smaller, lighter unit.

The basic layout of the 911 engine was a flat-opposed boxer six-cylinder engine with eight main bearings. The crankcase was split vertically along the crankshaft axis. The crankshaft was of forged steel with its six rod throws spaced out at 120-degree intervals so that one of the cylinders fires for every 120 degrees of crankshaft rotation, making this a very smooth-running engine design.

The crankshaft was nitrated using the German Tenifer process. This process is a surface treating that is performed on the crankshaft by submerging it in a molten cyanide salt bath at elevated temperatures for extended periods of time. This process, similar to the United States' Tufftriding process, increases the fatigue strength and improves the surface wear of the crankshaft journals. Although the two processes are very similar, they are performed at different temperatures and for different periods of time, thus the results are not exactly the same.

Under the forged crankshaft was the layshaft, or counter-rotating shaft which was driven by a gear on the crankshaft. This layshaft used a hunting system to reduce gear wear and noise by reducing the frequency so that the same two gear teeth on the mating gears came together. This was done by using not the expected 1:2 gear ratio but twenty-eight teeth on the crankshaft and forty-eight teeth on the driven layshaft gear, thus requiring nine crankshaft revolutions before the same two teeth meshed.

The layshaft had two drive sprockets for the camshaft chains. This is where the odd ratio of the layshaft was compensated for, by using a twenty-four-tooth drive sprocket and a twenty-eight tooth driven sprocket on the camshafts to achieve the required ratio of half the crankshaft at the camshafts. The layshaft also drove the dry-sump oil system's tandem scavenge and pressure pumps through an internally splined interconnecting shaft between the layshaft and the oil pumps. The distributor also was driven at half crankshaft speed by another drive gear on the crankshaft.

The engine had six individual piston-and-cylinder sets on which six identical cylinder heads were mounted. The 911 pistons were cast and used Biral cylin-

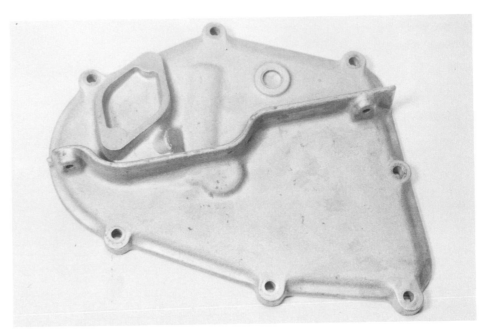

Left-hand housing cover for Type 901/05. Notice that casting still had provisions for both fuel pump and center-lubed cam, and neither were used.

Left-hand chain-housing cover for Type 901/14, with seal for camshaft-driven smog pump. This was only used for 1968 US models.

ders. The Biral cylinder was a cast-iron cylinder with aluminum fins cast in place to improve the cooling. The heads had a near-hemispherical combustion chamber, with one intake and one exhaust valve at an included angle of fifty-nine degrees from vertical.

With the final version of the Type 901 engine, Porsche changed the spark-plug angle to one that put the spark plug right in the center of the intake-valve cover. This change was made because of the simultaneous development of the Carrera Six (906) engine which had twin-plug cylinder heads. To work out a symmetrical arrangement with the plugs centered in the combustion chamber for twin plugs, Porsche changed the angle from the one used on the earlier Type 901 prototype engine. With this change, the normal spark plugs came out spaced down the center of the intake-valve covers. For racing engines, the second plug for the twin ignition came out spaced down the center of the exhaust-valve cover.

The engine was a single overhead cam engine, with the cams running directly in the aluminum cam housings mounted on each set of three cylinder heads. The cams were driven by a pair of duplex chains which were each guided by three guide ramps. Each chain was tensioned by a spring-loaded hydraulic tensioner. The cams operated the valves via rocker arms, which also mounted in the cam housing in a unique manner. Each individual rocker arm was retained by an expansion shaft which also acted as an oil seal in the cam housing.

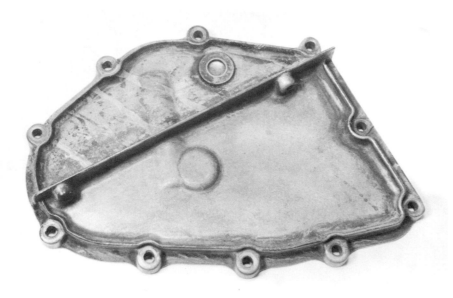

Left-hand diecast magnesium chain-housing cover as used on most engines from 1968 until late 1977, when they were changed to aluminum diecastings.

Lubrication in the engine was also unusual in that the main bearings were fed oil from the main oil gallery, using the crankcase through-bolt holes as oil passages. The eleven crankcase through bolts were used to hold the two crankcase halves together around the main-bearing saddles, and shared their passageways through the case with the pressurized oil for the engine main bearings. Oil pressure was then fed through radial drillings in the bearings at the front and rear of the crankshaft (main bearing numbers one and eight), and then through the drilled passage the entire length of the crankshaft to lubricate the connecting-rod bearings.

In early production engines (up to engine number 903069), and in 911-derived racing engines, the lubrication was supplied to the camshafts from the end of the main oil circuit and fed to the end of the center-drilled camshafts by a special axial sealing ring. There were drillings to each of the cam's three journal bearings and the cam lobes to lubricate the cam running surfaces. Oil splashed from these points lubricated the rocker arms, rocker-arm shafts and the valve stems.

The first production engines, Type 901/01, utilized permanent-mold aluminum sand-castings for all major engine assemblies: crankcase, heads, cam housings, chain housings and covers, and valve covers. These early engines had a pair of simple three-into-one exhaust systems which were enclosed in heat exchangers.

Another oddity of these early engines was that they retained the 109-tooth 6-volt starter-ring gear pattern that had been used on the 356 engines and all

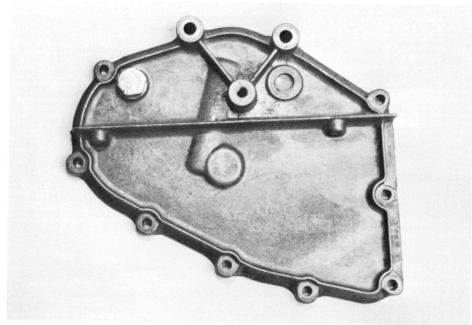

Left-hand diecast aluminum chain-housing cover as used from late in the production year 1977 until 1984, when they were replaced by covers with fittings for the pressurized chain tensioners.

Volkswagens since the beginning of time, rather than the later 12-volt 130-tooth pattern.

The engine-cooling fan used on the 911 engine was a 245 mm-diameter, eleven-blade axial-flow fan which was driven at a 1.3:1 ratio from a pulley on the front of the crankshaft. The alternator for the 911 was mounted coaxially inside the eleven-blade fan. The fan produced approximately 1,390 liters per second at 6100 engine rpm.

After the first 3,069 engines had been built, Porsche replaced the center-lubed camshaft lubrication with a squirter-bar-type lubrication. Starting with engine number 903070, an aluminum tube was installed in each of the cam housings to lubricate the valve-actuating mechanism. Three 3 mm holes provided lubrication to the cam journal bearings, and six additional 1 mm holes sprayed lubricant for the cam lobes, rocker arms and shafts, and the valve stems. This change was made because the rocker arms and the valve stems were not getting adequate lubrication during low-rpm use. Oil for this new spray-bar system was still derived from the end of the main oil circuit.

All Type 901/01 engines had six individual Solex PI 40 mm overflow-type carburetors mounted on a pair of manifolds which contained overflow chambers (float bowls). A Bendix electric fuel pump supplied fuel to the overflow chambers where a pair of mechanical pumps "siamesed" together took over the task of recirculating the fuel past the overflow carburetors. Each of the six carburetors had a fuel well with an overflow dam. The mechanical pumps supplied more fuel than was needed to these fuel wells; the excess ran over the dam, down the spillway and back to the overflow chambers.

The mechanical pumps were driven by the left-hand camshaft (cylinders one to three) via a strange-looking wobble cam nut. These were pesky carburetors. Their biggest problem was a severe flat spot in the 2500 to 3000 rpm range, which was not satisfactorily solved until after use of the carburetors had been discontinued.

The Solex overflow-type carburetor had been successful in a side-draft version of the German-made Glass S1004 of 1962. Because of this, and Porsche's close relationship with Solex, Porsche tried to make these carburetors work.

The flat-spot problem was more acute in the United States, probably both because of differences in the density of US fuels and because of different driving styles and conditions. In the end, the problem was fairly simple to correct by changing the emulsion tubes and rejetting the carburetors.

In February 1966, with the introduction of the Type 901/05 engine, the Solex carburetors were replaced with Weber 40 IDA-3C carburetors. The Weber carburetors were an existing model, having been designed for use on the Lancia V-6. Because the Webers were smaller, the two end tubes on each mani-

Left-hand sand-cast magnesium chain-housing cover as used on most 911-derived racing engines that retained center-lubed camshafts.

Left-hand diecast aluminum chain-housing cover as used from the introduction of the 1984 Carrera, which provided a hole and sealing boss for the oil-pressure-fed chain tensioners.

47

Permanent mold-aluminum sand-cast crankcase used for engines from Type 901/01 until crankcase was replaced in 1968.

Inside sand-cast aluminum crankcase, lay-shaft ran in aluminum crankcase without insert bearings. This particular layshaft was used only in these early sand-cast aluminum crankcases.

First in a series of high-pressure cast-magnesium crankcases first introduced in spring of 1968 and used with changes and updates through the 1977 2.7 911 production.

fold were slightly inclined. An inexpensive update kit to change over to Weber carburetors was initially offered to all Solex-carbureted 911 owners.

The first racing version of the 901 engine was actually developed in conjunction with the production engine, which benefited both projects. The 901 engine was first raced in 1965 in a 904. The engine was actually the Carrera Six or 906 engine Type 901/20, which introduced many concepts that are still used in Porsche racing engines today.

The Carrera Six engine differed from the production engine in that the majority of the engine castings were unique castings made of magnesium instead of aluminum. The connecting rods were made of titanium, as were the rod bolts. Forged high-compression (10.3:1) pistons were used along with special Chromal cylinders. The Chromal cylinders were made of aluminum, and the wear surface for the piston was hard-chromed. The surface was lined with small indentations to help retain the oil film on the cylinder under the stress of racing.

The engines used one-piece forged rocker arms and the valve clearance was set by valve-lash-adjusting caps. The heads had larger valves, larger ports and dual spark plugs which were fired by the Marelli twin-plug distributor. The carburetors used on the Carrera Six engine were the 46 IDA-3C Webers. The Carrera Six also used a smaller-diameter (226 mm) cooling fan driven at the same 1.3:1 ratio as the fan used on the production cars. Because the racing engine would be run at consistently higher rpm, Porsche determined that the standard fan used on the production engine would produce more cooling air than was necessary if the fan was not changed. As a result, it reduced the diameter from the street cars' 245 to 226 mm.

With the experience gained from the Carrera Six engine, Porsche developed the 911S model for street use. Introduced in late 1966 as a 1967 model, the 911S used the Type 901/02 engine. The engine differed from the 911 Normal engine in that it had higher compression, larger valves and ports, and the cam timing was modified. Forged pistons were used rather than the cast units used in the 911 Normal, and the Biral cylinders were retained.

The exhaust system had been greatly improved, with two equal-length three-into-one header systems enclosed within a heat exchanger. The Weber carburetors for these first 911S engines were modified cast-aluminum 40 IDA-3Cs with S stamped on the side after the 40 IDA-3C and 3C1 designations. From engine serial number 960502 on, the 911S used Webers with a 40 IDS-3C (right) and 40 IDS-3C1 (left) designation.

The 911S also used an aluminum pressure plate for lower inertia and better cooling. That contact surface of the pressure plate and the contact surface of the flywheel were coated with a thin layer of bronze to improve cooling and to provide a wearing surface for the aluminum pressure plate.

The header-heater system developed for the 911S was then used on the 911 Normal engine. The change in the exhaust system increased the horsepower, however, from 130 to 140 DIN hp. Porsche felt that the difference between the S and the Normal would not be enough and took steps to reduce the Normal engine's power to the original 130 DIN hp. To solve the problem initially, a restrictor ring was installed at the end of the header system where it joined to the muffler. In November of 1966 (for the 1967 models) new, milder camshafts were introduced to provide a broader and more elastic power curve and to restrict the power to its former value for advertising purposes. The restrictor ring was removed from the exhaust system. The type number of this new engine was 901/06.

During the 1967 model year, the forged-steel rocker arms were replaced with cast-iron rocker arms, which were less expensive to produce and had the side benefit of acting like a shear pin if there was a failure in the valvetrain. In the earlier engines that had used the forged rocker arms, if the camshaft lost its timing for *any* reason, the valves would be forced into the pistons, usually bending the valves and breaking the pistons, and sometimes bending the connecting rods. The cast-iron rocker arms in the same situation usually break, resulting in much less damage.

These first cast rocker arms had no bronze bushings. Usually, when two similar materials like steel and cast-iron are run together, some form of bushing or bearing is used to prevent the mating surfaces from galling. Porsche tried a surface-treating process on the rocker-arm shafts in an attempt to cure this potential problem. Unfortunately, after a few thousand miles, this surface treating wore through and the rocker arms started to gall both the rocker arm and

the rocker-arm shaft, resulting in premature failure.

These rocker arms with bushings were finally replaced in 1970 with a third version of the rocker arm, which was still made of cast-iron, but now with the bronze bushing again, eliminating the galling problem altogether.

Another change made in the 1967 model year was the addition of three

more holes in each cam spray bar for a total of nine in each spray bar. The added holes sprayed up toward the intake-valve covers, and were added to insure proper lubrication for the intake rocker arm.

In 1968, the 911T (T for Touring) was introduced for the European market with the Type 901/03 engine. This new engine was the economy model and as a result many of the changes were made to

Inside the early magnesium crankcase, there was no provision for rear layshaft bearing; the rear-bearing journal of the layshaft ran in the magnesium as it had in *the aluminum crankcase. The magnesium did not prove to be durable enough in this application, however, and a shell-insert bearing was installed in 1970.*

By 1970, provisions had been made for a bearing insert for the rear layshaft-bearing journal.

reduce the cost. It differed from its predecessors in that it had a cast non-counterbalanced crankshaft, cast-iron cylinders, lower compression and single valve springs. The heads utilized valves the same size as the 911S, but with smaller ports and milder cam timing for very tractable performance. A new version of the Weber carburetor, the 40 IDT-3C, was developed for the 911T.

Several other changes were introduced in the 1968 model year to improve the growing 911 engine family. One change was to the one-piece rubber (soft plastic) chain-guide ramps, which were later found not to have been an improvement at all. These new ramps replaced the aluminum-backed plastic ramps that had been used in 1965-67. New sealed chain tensioners were used on all models,

replacing the original open-reservoir type previously used.

From engine number 4080733 on, the 40 IDS-3C Weber carburetors used on the 911S had an added high-speed enrichment circuit for improved engine safety. The circuit provided an overly rich mixture at higher rpm to minimize the possibility of destructive detonation, but offered no increase in performance.

Another change was to use permanent mold-magnesium high-pressure castings in place of the sand-cast aluminum parts for all the major engine castings. This started after the beginning of the 1968 model year by replacing the castings of the chain housings, their covers, the engine breather and the valve covers with magnesium castings. Along with the change to magnesium for the valve covers, the number of studs retaining the lower valve covers was increased from six to eleven in an attempt to solve the leaking problem. It didn't work—but it was a nice try.

In the spring of 1968, the crankcase itself was changed to a high-pressure cast-magnesium casting. At the time, there were several advantages to this change: the pressure-cast magnesium crankcase was a more precise piece requiring less machining; magnesium machines move easily saved additional machining time; and the finished crankcase weighed twenty-two pounds less than the aluminum crankcase it replaced. In 1969, Mahle won a design award from the Magnesium Association for the Porsche crankcase which, at that time, was the largest magnesium pressure die-casting ever made.

A new series of engines was introduced to be compatible with the Sportomatic transmission. These engines were the Type 901/13 for the 911T, 901/07 for the 911 Normal, and 901/08 for the 911S. The engines differed from the standard engines in that they had all of the fittings, vacuum lines and external oil pump to operate the Sportomatic transmissions.

For the United States, there were just two versions of the 911 Normal engine available in 1968, the Type 911/14 for the standard transmission and the Type 901/17 for the Sportomatic transmission. These engines differed from those sold in the rest of the world in that they had air-injection pumps, distributor with a vacuum unit, and a throttle position valve to meet US emission regulations.

In 1969, Porsche introduced mechanical fuel injection to street models with

In 1971, case squirters were installed in the main-bearing webbing to provide additional cooling for the pistons. Note:

Cylinder-head studs have been removed and Time Serts installed.

The strongest of the magnesium crankcases were the ones with casting number 901.101.101.7R. Note the extra reinforcement webs for the main-bearing saddles. This version of the layshaft has been used in all of the production engines since the magnesium crankcase was introduced for the 1968 model year. The aluminum gear and the steel chain sprockets are replaceable.

both the 911E and the 911S. In 1966, the 906E was produced with a fuel-injected version of the Carrera Six engine, Type 901/21. The Bosch mechanical-injection system increased the power from 210 to 220 DIN hp. This same technology was applied to the street cars in 1969, increasing their performance and allowing them to meet the 1969 US emission standards by more precise fuel metering.

The basic concept of the fuel-injection system was similar to that used on the 906E engine but with a much-improved injection pump with an engine-speed-controlled space cam. With the space cam, the quantity of fuel was controlled by both the throttle position and the engine rpm, providing much better fuel economy and low-rpm throttle response.

The 911E engine, which replaced the midrange 911 Normal, had the same size intake and exhaust valves as the 1968 911S and 911T engines. The cam timing for the 911E was the same as with the 911 Normal and 911L engines. The cams used for the 911E were the same as those used for the engine Type 901/06—at least the right one was. Porsche had to make a new one for the left side with the mechanical-fuel-injection belt drive.

The larger valve size and the Bosch twin-row plunger fuel-injection pump increased the power from 130 (911 Normal) to 140 DIN hp (911E), and dramatically improved throttle response and low-rpm power. One basic engine was produced for the world market as the Type 901/09 for the standard transmission and Type 901/11 for the Sportomatic version.

For the fuel-injected 1969 911S engine, Porsche again increased its valve size, making them the same size as the valves in the 906 engine, Type 901/20. The larger valves in conjunction with the Bosch twin-row plunger fuel-injection pump increased the power from 160 to 170 DIN hp. Porsche changed the facing on the aluminum pressure plate to an iron coating because the bronze that had been used on the contact surface for the 911S pressure plate and flywheel proved to be too fragile to provide adequate service life in a street-car application. The bronze surface was also deleted from the flywheel at the same time. Only one 911S engine was available for the world market, the Type 901/10.

The 911T engine was introduced to the US market as the Type 901/16 for the standard transmission and 901/19 for the Sportomatic. The specifications were the same as those for the 1968 European 911T engine, Type 901/03, except for compliance with the US emission standards.

Competition layshaft. The shaft and driven gear were a one-piece forging for high strength, while all of the chain sprockets, including the idler sprocket and the cam drive sprockets were made of aluminum.

An additional area in need of reinforcement was back in the flywheel area on the left-hand side (cyl 1-3) of the engine. Note that the early style had little reinforcement.

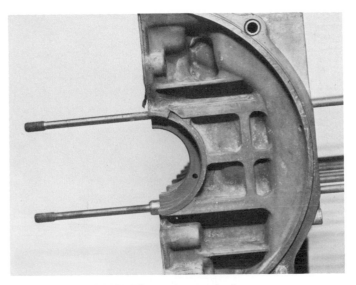

The later 901.101.101.7R crankcases had additional reinforcement webs back in the area where the flywheel mounted.

Other changes for 1969 included changing the valve springs on the 911T to the same double valve springs as used on all other 911s instead of the single springs used in 1968 on the European 911T engines.

Both the 911E and the 911S engines had the more efficient Bosch capacitor discharge ignition system. The CD system proved to be such a big improvement in the running of the 911E and 911S engines that Porsche later offered a capacitor discharge update kit for 911T owners. The system virtually eliminated the plug-fouling problem that had plagued the 911 engines from the beginning. Because of the additional heat created by the added horsepower in the 911S, an external oil cooler was added in the right-front fender. The external oil cooler was thermostatically controlled to open at 83 deg C (182 deg F). Through the various subsequent models, the thermostat operating temperature has varied from 83 to 87 deg C (182 to 189 deg F).

The 1970 model year was another of big changes for the 911 engine. The displacement was increased to 2.2 liters (2195 cc) by increasing the bore from 80 to 84 mm. The cylinder heads were standardized with 46 mm intake valves and 40 mm exhaust valves, with only the port sizes changing between the T, E and S models. The contour of the near-hemispherical combustion chamber was changed to a more shallow, larger-diameter, smaller-volume combustion chamber to accommodate the larger valves and larger bore. This change of the combustion chamber had the added benefit of eliminating all of the detonation problems that had existed with the earlier combustion-chamber shape.

During the 1975 model year, the main bearings were changed so that the locating tab moved from one side of the bearing saddle to the other. Because of this change there were some crankcases with notches on both sides of the bearing saddle.

Split-shell bearing inserts were added to the crankshaft halves at the inner end of the layshaft because the magnesium had not provided as durable a bearing surface as the original aluminum crankcase had. The other end of the layshaft was already supported by split-shell bearing inserts because Porsche had changed it to a thrust bearing to establish the layshaft position and end play when it went to the magnesium crankcase.

Previously, the layshaft end play had been established by measuring the end play and setting it with shims. The spark plugs threaded directly into the aluminum rather than using Helicoil inserts. They were changed because Porsche felt the inserts caused inconsistent effective spark plug heat ranges.

At the same time, the clutch was changed from 215 to 225 mm diameter, and changed to the stronger pull-type clutch. The pull-type clutch also permitted the use of a larger-diameter clutch without increasing the overall diameter of the flywheel and bell housing.

Another change implemented in 1970 was the use of CE-type head gaskets. The CE-ring-type head gasket is a thin metal C-shaped ring that encloses a tubular spring. This gasket fits in a groove in the upper cylinder flange. From 1970 on, the CE-ring head gasket was used on all 911 street engines and most racing engines up to three liters in displace-

These later 901.101.101.7R crankcases came with both the original 92 mm cylinder spigots and the later, larger 97 mm spigots for the 2.7 engines. The thick cylinder-base surface for cylinders indicates that this was one of the 901.101.101.7R crankcases with 92 mm spigots. These are the best of the magnesium crankcases for building any 911 engine from 2.0 to 2.4 liters. The "7R mag cases" were the strongest of the magnesium crankcases.

ment. First in 1978, the 911 Turbo did away with any head gasket at all, and then in 1984 when the 3.2 liter Carrera was introduced, it also was *sans* head gasket.

In 1970 the power was increased for all three versions of the 911 engine—the T, E and S. The 911T had a new carburetor, the Zenith 40 TIN. The 911T also received as standard equipment the capacitor discharge ignition as used on both the 911E and 911S in 1969. All models received new reinforced connecting rods with a much more substantial bottom end and longer rod bolts. Engine type numbers were changed from 901 to 911, the European 911T being the Type 911/03 for standard transmission, and 911/06 for Sportomatic.

The US emission 911T engines were 911/07 for standard transmission and 911/08 for Sportomatic. The emission control on these engines consisted of a lean-idle circuit and a deceleration-idle fuel shutoff valve. The 911E and 911S engines were still suitable for a world market, the 911E being Type 911/01 for standard transmission, 911/04 for the Sportomatic, and the 911S being Type 911/02.

The 914/6 was introduced as a 1970 model with an engine that was identical in specifications to the 1969 911T engine. The 914/6 was the 901/36 for the European standard transmission and Type 901/37 for Sportomatic. The US 914/6 engine was the Type 901/38 and Type 901/39 for the Sportomatic. This engine remained unchanged throughout its production life, except for the addition of crankcase oil squirters to cool the pistons with the 1971 model change. But more about that later. There was a 2.4 liter version of the 911T engine developed for use in the 914/6, Type 911/58, but it was never used in production.

The year 1970 was also the beginning of larger racing engines for the racing 911s. Up until 1970 there had been but two versions of the 2.0 liter 911 engines used in racing 911s; the small-valve Type 901/30 rally engine with 46 IDA Webers and 911S cams, which produced 150 DIN hp, and the Type 901/22, called the 911R engine, which was similar to the Carrera Six and produced 210 DIN hp at 8000 rpm. The Type 916 engine was also used in the 911R racing cars.

The Type 916 engine was a 911-based engine that had chain-driven dual overhead cams (for a total of four) and which produced 230 DIN hp at 9000 rpm, but proved to be too peaky in use to be prac-

tical. There were also two versions of the 2.0 liter racing engines for the 914/6. Type 901/25 was a continuation of the Carrera Six type engine, with 46 IDA Webers which produced 210 DIN hp at 7800 rpm and a maximum torque of 152 lb-ft at 6200 rpm. The other engine was for rallying and produced 180 DIN hp at 6800 rpm. Maximum torque was 132 lb-ft at 5200 rpm. This engine utilized 911S cams and 40 IDS Webers.

930 crankcase of aluminum-silicon alloy (Al-Si) was introduced for the Turbo. A version of this same crankcase is used for the current Turbo and Carrera engines.

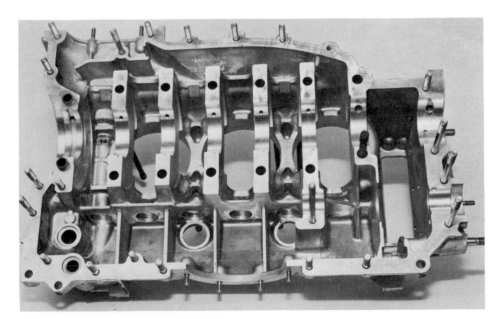

In addition to being made out of the stronger aluminum alloy, the construction of this crankcase was also greatly reinforced.

In 1970, the move to 2195 cc for the production cars put the 911 in the 2.0 to 2.5 liter class for racing. Cars competing in this class were allowed to increase their displacement up to the class limit, provided it was done with a bore increase only. Thus began a series of larger-displacement 911 racing engines.

The first was a small increase to 2347 cc by increasing the bore 1 mm to 85 mm. These engines used Carrera Six

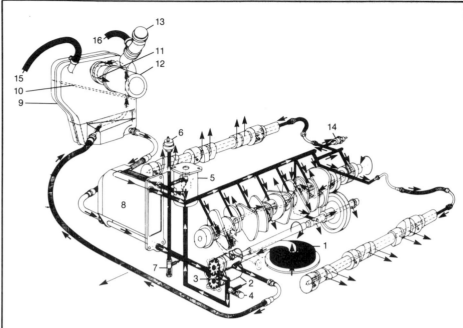

1. Oil pick-up mesh
2. Scavenge pump
3. Pressure pump
4. Safety valve (opening pressure 113.7 psi)
5. Thermostat (opens to pass oil through cooler at approx. 80° C)
6. Oil pressure gauge
7. Pressure release valve (opening presure 76.8 psi)
8. Oil cooler
9. Oil tank
10. Perforated plate (to prevent foaming)
11. Bypass valve
12. Full-flow oil filter
13. Oil filler pipe
14. Oil temperature gauge
15. Crankcase breather into oil tank
16. Oil tank breather to intake air filter

911 engine-oiling diagram for early 911 engines with center-lubed camshafts. The center-lubed cam oiling was always used for Porsche's racing engines because it provided better camshaft lubrication.

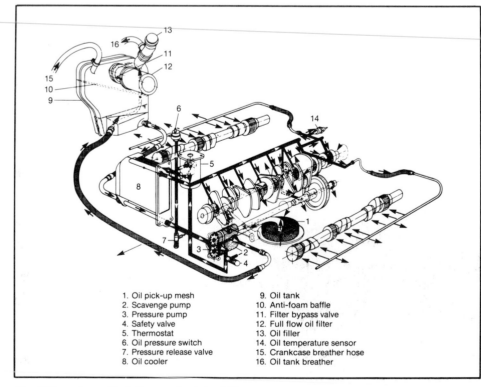

1. Oil pick-up mesh
2. Scavenge pump
3. Pressure pump
4. Safety valve
5. Thermostat
6. Oil pressure switch
7. Pressure release valve
8. Oil cooler
9. Oil tank
10. Anti-foam baffle
11. Filter bypass valve
12. Full flow oil filter
13. Oil filler
14. Oil temperature sensor
15. Crankcase breather hose
16. Oil tank breather

The 911 engine-oiling diagram for later 911 engines with spray-bar-lubricated camshaft.

cams and retained the stock valve diameter. There were two versions of these engines. One was the Type 911/20 with mechanical injection and the Type 911/22 with 46 IDA Weber carburetors. The power claimed for both versions of the engine was 230 DIN hp. The next version was the Type 911/21 with an 87 mm bore for a displacement of 2380 cc with 250 DIN hp at 8000 rpm. Other than the increased bore, this engine was unchanged from the Type 911/20. The final version of this series of engines was actually developed after the longer-stroke engines came out and were used in racing. It was the Type 911/73 with an 89 mm bore and 66 mm stroke, for a displacement of 2466 cc. These Type 911/73 engines produced 275 DIN hp at 8000 rpm.

This large bore was achieved by utilizing the newly developed thin-wall aluminum cylinders of Nicasil construction. These Nicasil cylinders were centrifugally-cast, finned aluminum with their bores electroplated with a very thin layer of nickel-silicon carbide. These cylinders provided several advantages over all the other types of cylinders Porsche had previously used: the thin plating allowed larger bores within the same head-stud spacing; they wore very well; and because of reduced friction and a better surface for the rings to seal with, they actually produced a small increase in horsepower. The Nicasil cylinders were originally developed in 1971 for the 917 racing engines.

In 1971, production 911 engines remained unchanged with the exception of the addition of oil squirters for additional piston cooling. These were installed in the crankshaft main-bearing webbing and were fed from the main oil gallery to spray oil onto the bottom of each piston crown. The supply to the squirters was controlled by a check valve in each squirter, which opened under pressure at 45 to 55 psi oil pressure. The squirters reduced the operating temperatures at the crown of the pistons by 50 deg C (90 deg F).

The next big change was in 1972 with the increase to 2.4 liters, with 2341 cc actual displacement. This displacement increase was achieved by lengthening the stroke from 66 to 70.4 mm. Porsche increased the length of the stroke by decreasing the crankshaft rod-journal diameter off center and increasing the journal width to retain bearing capacity. The rod journal was decreased from 57 to 52 mm, and the rod journal width was increased from 22 to 24 mm. The connecting rods were changed because of the smaller crank journal. They were also shorter by half of the increase in stroke, 2.2 mm, allowing the wrist pin to remain at the same height in the piston. The cylinders were the same as those used on the 2.2 liter 911 engines, while the pistons had material removed from the dome to reduce the compression, both to counter the effect of the longer stroke and to lower the overall compression and the required fuel octane.

The noncounterweighted cast crankshaft was discontinued for the 911T, and all engines shared a common forged crankshaft. The valve diameters of 46 mm for the intake valves and 40 mm for the exhaust valves were continued from the 2.2 liter engines. The change to 2.4 liters was also when Porsche finally changed the clutch shaft spline from 13/16x24 splines that had been used since the early VW days, to ⅞x20, which was used through the 1986 3.2 911 Carrera. At the same time, the 901 transmission was replaced with the more substantial 915 transmission, which also lasted through the 1986 3.2 911 Carrera.

There were still T, E and S versions of the 2.4 liter engines. In Europe, the 911T engine retained the Zenith 40 TIN carburetors as Type 911/57 for standard transmission and Type 911/61 for the Sportomatic. The US version 911T had mechanical fuel injection to comply with the emission standards as Type 911/51 for the standard transmission and Type 911/61 for the Sportomatic. The carbureted European version of this engine produced 130 DIN hp, while the mechanically injected US version produced 140. The cams remained the same in the 911T engines; they were timed a bit differently however.

Both the 2.4 liter 911E and 911S engines retained their mechanical injection. The 911E engine had its cams timed differently as well, and produced 165 DIN hp with Type 911/52 for the manual transmission and Type 911/62 for the Sportomatic. The 911S engine produced 190 DIN hp with the Type 911/53 for the standard transmission and Type 911/63 for the Sportomatic.

In 1972, Porsche moved the oil tank from its more normal location behind the right rear wheel to in front of the right rear wheel, between the wheel and the doorjamb. This location offered the advantages of better weight distribution, and also freed up space that could be better used for other purposes, in

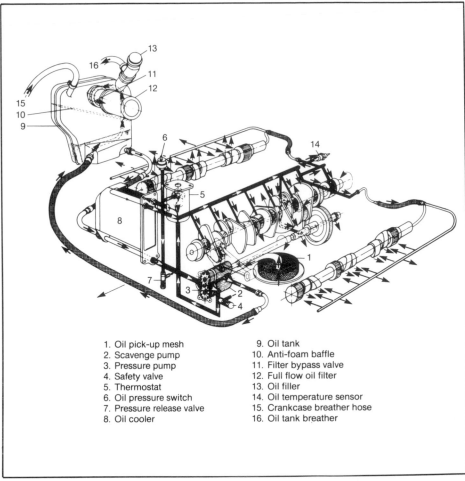

1. Oil pick-up mesh
2. Scavenge pump
3. Pressure pump
4. Safety valve
5. Thermostat
6. Oil pressure switch
7. Pressure release valve
8. Oil cooler
9. Oil tank
10. Anti-foam baffle
11. Filter bypass valve
12. Full flow oil filter
13. Oil filler
14. Oil temperature sensor
15. Crankcase breather hose
16. Oil tank breather

The 911 engine-oiling diagram for the turbocharged race cars, such as the 935. These engines used a combination of the center-lubed and the spray-bar cam lubrication. They used the center-lubed oiling system because of its superior cam lubrication, and the spray-bar lubrication for enhanced cooling.

The 935 engines used both the center-lubed and the spray-bar cam lubrication, so the oil lines were modified to provide oil to both connections.

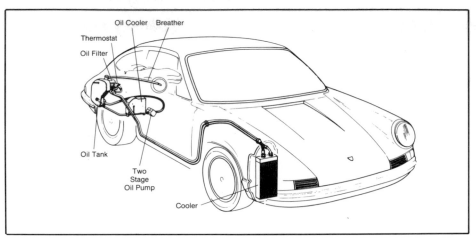

In 1969, because of the additional heat created by the added horsepower in the 911S, an external radiator-type oil cooler was added in the right front fender. Oil flow to this external cooler was controlled by a thermostat unit mounted in the engine compartment. The thermostat was in series with the scavenge return line to the oil tank. When the oil temperature reached 87 deg C (189 deg F) the oil was routed forward to this additional cooler before being returned to the oil tank. This version of the front-mounted or external oil-cooler system was used from 1969 through 1971.

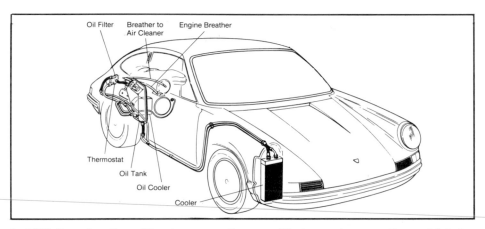

In 1972, the relocation of the dry-sump oil tank necessitated a new system for the front-mounted external oil cooler. Porsche designed a new oil-filter housing which in addition to providing the filter mount had both the thermostat and an oil by-pass valve built into it. This unit had fittings that permitted remote mounting, which has made it popular for use by people building their own oil systems in racing and time-trial cars. The oil filler for these tanks was in the right rear fender, just behind the door, and the filter mount was in the engine compartment.

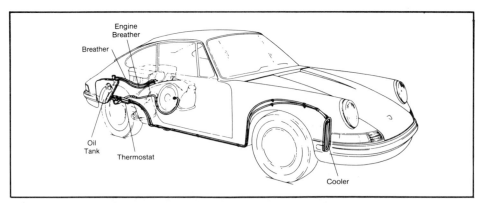

In 1973 the oil tank returned to its original position at the rear of the rear fender, and again Porsche designed a new front-mounted oil-cooler system. This system mounted on the oil tank under the car. 1973 was also the first year of the serpentine or loop oil cooler. These oil coolers were now optional unless the cars were ordered with an air-conditioner, but were standard equipment on the new Carrera RS.

exchange for a space that was inconvenient to use.

This installation used a new oil-filter housing which, in addition to providing the filter mount, had both the thermostat and an oil by-pass valve built in. This unit had fittings that permitted remote mounting, which has made it popular for use by people building their own oil systems in racing and time-trial cars. The oil filler for these tanks was in the right rear fender, just behind the door.

A special version of the 911S engine was produced for the limited series of 916s that were built. The specifications were the same as those of the 2.4 liter 911S engine, but the exhaust and fittings were different for the mid-chassis installation in the 916. The type number for these engines was 911/56. The execution of the unique parts that were required for this installation indicated that Porsche intended to produce far more than the thirteen 916s that were actually built.

There was a racing version of the 2.4 liter-based engine with a larger 86.7 mm bore for a displacement of 2492 cc, Type 911/70. This engine produced 270 DIN hp at 8000 rpm and a peak torque of 191.6 lb-ft at 5300 rpm. It was the first 911 racing engine to reach the limit for the 2.5 liter GT racing class.

For 1973, the 911E and 911S engine specifications remained unchanged for the world market. The 911T engine remained the same in Europe, but went through some changes for the US market. For the beginning of the 1973 production year, the 911T was still sold with mechanical injection, offering the same specifications as for the previous year.

Starting with January production, Porsche introduced the Bosch CIS injection on the 911T, called K-Jetronic, or the KA Injection in Germany (K for continuous, A for nonpowered). These engines had the compression increased from 7.5:1 to 8.0:1 and required new, very mild cam timing because the CIS injection was very sensitive to pulsations in the intake system. This system required cams with little or no overlap.

This injection system was introduced on the 911T because Porsche could no longer meet the US emission standards with carburetors, and the mechanical-injection system was too costly for its low-priced car. The new 911T engine with CIS injection was Type 911/91 for the standard transmission and Type 911/96 for the Sportomatic version.

The horsepower for this new CIS-injected 911T engine was claimed to be the same 140 DIN hp as the previous mechanically injected 911T engine.

For 1973, the oil cooler in the right front fender of the 911S was replaced with a serpentine (or loop) cooler. These oil coolers were optional unless the cars were ordered with an air-conditioner, but were standard equipment on the new Carrera RS.

The new loop coolers actually relied on the pipe running to and from it to do most of the cooling; the loop itself was just a way to turn the oil around and start it back to the oil tank. The more effective aluminum radiator-type oil coolers used since 1969 were deemed too fragile for general street use. One problem they had was that the salt used to melt the snow caused corrosion of the cooler. A car could run around all winter without getting warm enough to open the thermostat to the front cooler. When spring came with its warmer temperatures, the thermostat to the front cooler would open. When his happened, the cooler would cause a bad oil leak. This was particularly a problem with the cars built in 1969 through 1971 because they did not have an oil by-pass circuit built into the external cooler circuit.

The oil tank was also returned to its original location behind the right rear

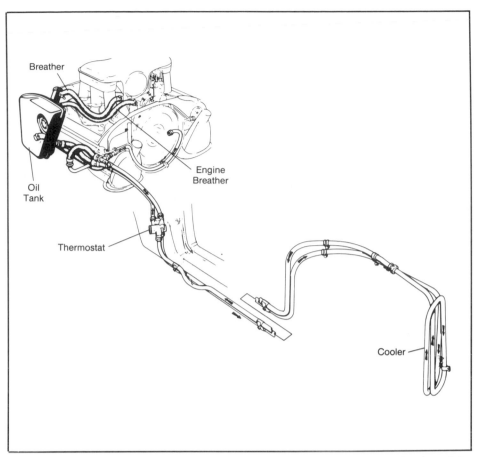

The current version of the front-mounted oil-cooler system was introduced in 1974 and has proven to be a practical and reliable system. The cooler itself has changed several times since the introduction of the current front-mounted oil-cooler system, but the rest of the plumbing has remained the same.

The serpentine or loop-style cooler was introduced in 1973 for use on the 911S and Carrera RS. James D. Newton

911 engine used the through-bolt holes as part of the oiling system, providing oil for the main bearings and the piston squirters. Note pieces of crankcase with through bolt. These pieces were cut from a pair of damaged crankcase halves, up by the main-bearing saddles. Also note main-bearing oil holes in the crankcase main-bearing saddles. The main-bearing journals were lubricated from this right-hand side of the crankcase (cyl 4-6).

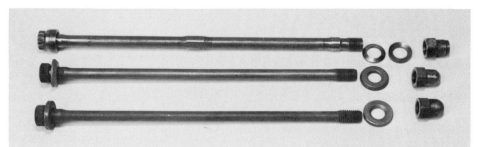

Crankcase through bolts. The one on the bottom of this photo was used in early-style street cars up until 1978 with the introduction of the 911SC. The middle bolt has a finer 1.25 mm thread pitch for more even torquing, and was used on some of the racing 911 engines, such as the RSRs and then on all production engines since the introduction of the 911SC in 1978. The top bolt is a special aircraft-quality bolt used in some of the more recent racing 911 engines. Porsche originally developed these bolts for use on the 917 as a weight-saving measure. The bolts use a pair of specially ground self-aligning spherical washers that fit inside each other at each end which, along with the special nut, will not introduce a bending stress on the bolt. The threaded portion of the stud and the nut were also designed to eliminate the notch effect of the threads. Porsche found that it could reduce the bolt by one unit size so that in some applications these bolts could be used as a weight-saving measure.

Through-bolt washers from production engines. The washer on the left was used on all production engines up until the 2.7 liters of 1973 and 1974. When the change was made to these larger-diameter cylinders for the 90 mm bore, it was found necessary to chamfer these washers to prevent them from interfering with the cylinder fit and from holding up the base of the larger-diameter cylinders and causing them not to seat properly. The washer on the right has this chamfer and has been used on all of the 911 engines from the 2.7 liter.

Various types of cylinder-head studs used on the 911 engines. One of the original steel head studs is at the bottom. The next (second from bottom) was an early Dilavar stud from a racing engine. These studs had fiberglass jackets that were supposed to keep them warm so they would be able to expand at a similar rate to the aluminum cylinders. On later engines the cylinders themselves provided the jacket for these Dilavar studs. The next (third from bottom) was one of the shiny silver ones that was the style of Dilavar stud first used in production 930s in 1975 and later for the bottom row on 1977 911s. The next (fourth from bottom) was the next-style Dilavar stud which had a textured finish and was gold in color. There had been some problems with the studs fracturing because of corrosion. The gold version was made to combat this problem. The next (fifth from bottom) is the current style which has a black epoxy finish, which goes further to help prevent corrosion pits and possible resulting fractures starting from these corrosion pits. The last is a special stud made for use on some of Porsche's racing engines. The difference between this and the other studs is that it is 9 mm in diameter and the others all neck down to 8 mm.

wheel in 1973. As a result, the thermostat and plumbing for the front-mounted oil cooler were changed again. The thermostat for this system was mounted on the oil tank where the oil return line is normally attached to the oil tank. This location made the thermostat and fittings vulnerable to the elements.

The big news for 1973, however, was the reintroduction of a car called the Carrera. The Carrera for that year was the Carrera RS with its 2.7 liter engine. The Carrera RS was not available in the United States. Because only a limited series was planned, no effort was made to make the Carrera RS meet US emission standards.

Its 2687 cc engine introduced the use of Nicasil cylinders on a production-model Porsche. The displacement increase was obtained by increasing the bore to 90 mm and retaining the 70.4 mm stroke. The crankcase was reinforced both internally at the base of the main-bearing webs and at the base of the cylinders, and the diameter of the cylinder spigots was increased from 92 mm, which had been used for 2.0 to 2.4 liter engines, to 97 mm to accommodate the larger cylinders.

There were actually two versions of this, the final version of the magnesium crankcase casting number 901.101.101. 7R for both versions. One version was the one described here for the 2.7 engine, the other version had all of the modifications except for the larger spigot bore. The spigot bore remained 92 mm, making this case suitable for all 2.0 through 2.4 liter engines.

This 2.7 Carrera RS engine, Type 911/83, was identical to the Type 911/53 911S engine except for the 90 mm bore and a different space cam in the mechanical-injection pump. Power output was 210 DIN hp at 6300 rpm.

A racing version of this Carrera RS was built in 1973 called the RSR, with a Type 911/72 engine. The bore was increased 2 mm to 92 mm for a displacement of 2808 cc. The thin-wall Nicasil cylinders were used to achieve the 2.8 liter displacement with a 92 mm bore, which was deemed the safe limit for the magnesium crankcase with its 80 mm cylinder-head-stud spacing and a 70.4 mm stroke.

The RSR engines used production rods that were polished in the areas of high stress, and soft-nitrated to make them more resistant to failure. The 2.0, 2.2 and some of the 2.4 liter 911S connecting rods also utilized this soft-nitrating process for extra strength and added reliability.

To strengthen the 70.4 mm crankshaft for the high-rpm racing application, Porsche used a large, round and smooth radius for the transition between the crankshaft journal and the counterweight or cheek of the crankshaft. These larger-radius fillets on the RSR crankshaft necessitated special connecting-rod bearings with clearance provided for the fillets.

The 2.8 RSR engines had a new cylinder head with a larger-diameter, more open, larger-volume combustion chamber and 49 mm intake and 41.5 mm exhaust valves. With this larger combustion chamber and the new larger valves, the valve angle was reduced to an included angle of 55 deg 45 min., with an exhaust angle 30 deg 15 min. from vertical, and an intake angle 25 deg 30 min. from vertical. The 2.8 liter RSR used what is called high-butterfly injection, with the throttle butterfly high up in the injection stacks. These Type 911/72 engines produced 308 DIN hp at 8000 rpm.

There were some RSR engines built with 95 mm bores for 3.0 liter displacement using the magnesium cases with the old 80 mm cylinder-head-stud spacing. These engines had some reliability problems, which were caused by the fact that the metal separating and surrounding the cylinder spigots had become too thin to hold up under the rigors of racing.

The new 3.0 RSR engine was introduced for the Riverside IROC race September 1973 with engine Type 911/74. A new, more substantial crankcase made of aluminum was introduced for this new 3.0 liter engine. The crankcase had larger 103 mm cylinder spigots as well as a wider 83 mm head-stud spacing to accommodate the larger cylinders. The head-stud spacing in all previous 911 engines had been 80 mm. New cylinder heads, pistons and cylinders were produced to match the new crankcase with its wider head-stud spacing.

The 49 mm intake and 41.5 mm exhaust-valve size and the larger, open combustion chamber were carried over from the 2.8 RSR engine, but with the changed head-stud spacing. The cams retained the same timing as the Carrera Six; however, the lift was increased from 12.1 to 12.2 mm on the intake, and the exhaust from 10.5 to 11.6 mm—these cams were referred to as Sprint cams. The 3.0 RSR also had a new Bosch breakerless capacitor dual ignition as

Early 911 engine tandem oil pump with sand-cast aluminum housing. Pressure pump is at left end and scavenge pump at right with scavenge pickup.

In the late 1960s the pump housing was changed to diecast magnesium; the size of the pumps and the operation remained unchanged.

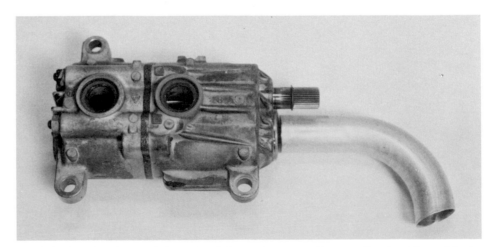

In 1976, Porsche changed the ratio of the oil pumps with the pressure-pump section being made larger. However, the scavenge section was reduced in size, while retaining its original overall dimensions. The oil bypass system was changed to compensate for this ratio change. This was essentially the same oil pump that is still used in the current Carrera model. The only difference is that in 1983 the oil pickup was changed to match the newer-style crankcases without a removable sump cover.

used in the 917. The power for this new engine was 316 DIN hp at 8000 rpm.

Late in the summer of 1973, an update kit was offered to some of the people racing the 2.8 RSRs which would allow them to update their 2.8 RSRs to 3.0 liter displacement. These kits consisted of a new crankcase, a new set of 95 mm pistons and cylinders, the cylinder heads that would fit on the new crankcase and a set of the new high-performance camshafts.

A revised version of the 3.0 liter RSR engine was built in 1974 as Type 911/75, which was identical to its predecessor with the exception of the change to slide-valve fuel injection in place of the high-butterfly type used previously. This new version of the engine produced 330 DIN hp at 8000 rpm, with a peak torque of 231 lb-ft at 6500 rpm.

The United States got the Carrera and the 2.7 liter engines in 1974; however, the US Carrera was not the same as the European version. Only two 911 engines were available to the United States for 1974—the 911 and the 911S. The US Carrera shared engines with the 911S. To add salt to the wound, there was an additional 3.0 Carrera in Europe

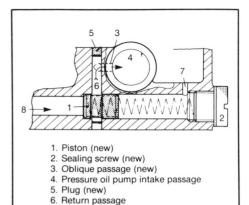

1. Piston (new)
2. Sealing screw (new)
3. Oblique passage (new)
4. Pressure oil pump intake passage
5. Plug (new)
6. Return passage
7. Vent passage
8. Pressure oil passage

In 1976 the 911 engine's oil by-pass system was changed to make up for the different scavenge-to-pressure ratio of the new-style oil pump. The by-passed oil was returned to the pressure-pump inlet rather than being by-passed into the crankcase's sump.

The oil by-pass pistons were changed when the oil pump and oil by-pass circuit were changed in 1976. The piston on the left was necessary with the modified system. The piston on the right was used in the oil system from 1964 until the by-pass circuit was changed. If the old-style pistons are accidentally used with the post-1976 by-pass system, the engine will not produce proper oil pressure.

In 1980 the intake tube of the oil pump was fitted with a suction venturi, which was surrounded by a screen. This venturi pickup was added to eliminate an oil-scavenge problem that some 911SCs had when driven at sustained high rpm. This photo shows this venturi pickup as viewed from the bottom. The oil-pump pickup fit through the hole, and the dent to the left was to provide clearance for the oil-drain plug.

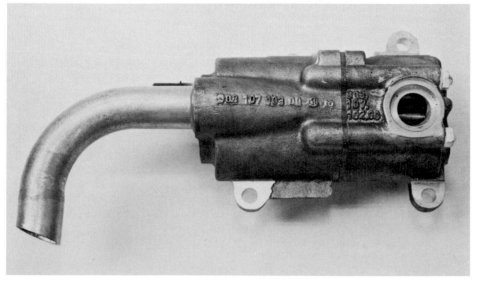

The larger 908 oil pump was used by Porsche in its racing 911 engines until the even larger 3.3 Turbo oil pump was introduced in 1978. The increased need for oil volume was because of Porsche's extended use of oil for cooling in its turbocharged racing engines.

Venturi pickup added in 1980 to eliminate scavenge problem, top view.

with a Type 911/77 engine. These engines were the basis for the 3.0 liter RSR engines that had the new 3.0 liter heads, crankcase, and cylinders with 83 mm head-stud spacing. They had 9.8:1 compression, the 911S cams and mechanical fuel injection.

The European Carrera produced 230 DIN hp at 6200 rpm, with a peak torque of 203 lb-ft at 5000 rpm. To be fair, the 3.0 Carrera RS was an homologation special, and few more than the 100 required were ever produced. The purpose of the car was to make the 3.0 liter engine parts and chassis changes legal for GT racing.

In 1974, the emission-legal US engines for the 911 were 150 DIN hp, Type 911/92 for the standard transmission and Type 911/97 for the Sportomatic. For the 911S and the US Carrera there were the 175 DIN hp 911S engines, Type 911/93 for the standard transmission and Type 911/98 for the Sportomatic. The engines for the United States both had CIS fuel injection and consequently much milder cam timing. They also had cast pistons rather than the forged pistons of the European 2.7 and 3.0 liter Carrera RS engines. Both Nicasil and Alusil cylinders were used on the US engines.

The Alusil cylinders were a special 390 eutectic aluminum-silicon alloy (Al-Si) used with a special cast-iron-plated (ferrocoat) piston. The cylinders were electrically etched to leave a surface of exposed silicon particles protruding from the aluminum. This provided a durable surface for the pistons and rings to wear on, the ferrocoat pistons preventing galling or excessive wear during break-in. This process was originally used for the 1970 Chevrolet Vega, and is currently used on all 928 and 924S/944 engines and on some 911 engines.

There was another oil system for the front-mounted external oil cooler for 1974. (This new thermostat and plumbing has been used ever since 1974, although the coolers themselves have changed several times since.) The thermostat, with its built-in oil over-pressure by-pass circuit, was mounted in front of the right rear wheel where it was protected from physical damage, if not the elements.

Porsche breathed some new life into the old 911 engine in 1974 when it started developing the Carrera RSR Turbo in the sports-prototype racing class. This development program was

done in preparation for the 1976 season and the new Group 5 Silhouette racing formula. There was a multiplier for sports-racing cars which considered any turbocharged engine to be 1.4 times its actual size. To compete as a 3.0 liter prototype, Porsche's engine could be no larger than 2143 cc in displacement.

The engine that Porsche built had an 83 mm bore and 66 mm stroke for a displacement of 2143 cc. The engine was built using the old magnesium crankcase and 2.0 liter crankshaft and heads. The cam timing was changed for these engines and the lift reduced to 10.5 mm for both the intake and exhaust valves.

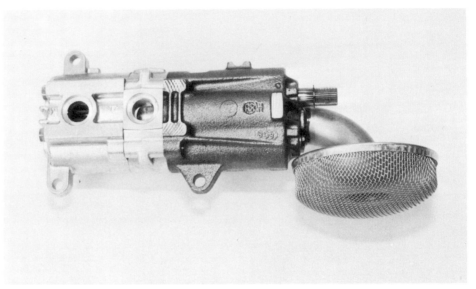

The "big" 930 oil pump introduced with the 3.3 liter Turbo in 1978 had much larger scavenge and pressure pumps. The pressure-pump housing was made of aluminum and the scavenge-pump housing was made of cast-iron to reduce thermal expansion to maintain closer tolerances. The crankcase was changed in model year 1983, and at that time a screen and built-in venturi were installed on the pump's oil pickup. This screen and pickup were to replace the ones that Porsche had installed in 1980 to solve an oil-pickup problem.

Indy oil pump developed in 1979/80 for the 911-based Indy engine that Porsche was working on with Interscope Racing. They found that the centrifugal force threw the oil to the right rear of the crankcase, so Porsche added a second scavenge pump to scavenge for this area. Even though the Indy program was abandoned, some of these oil pumps were used to improve the scavenging in the 935 engines. This new racing pump had dual scavenge pumps to get more of the used oil out of the engine.

There were two versions of these engines: Type 911/76 which was used in the Carrera RSR Turbo, and Type 911/78 which was used later in the 936.

The year 1975 was intended to be one of very little change for the production cars; however, this was the first year of the abominable thermal reactors and EGR (exhaust-gas recirculation) for California cars, Type 911/44 for the standard transmission and Type 911/49 for the Sportomatic.

All US engines were called 911S this year. The forty-nine-state cars (California excluded) had an exhaust like the European engines, with a primary muffler, and all the US engines had air-injection pumps to meet US emission standards. The forty-nine-state engines were Type 911/43 for standard transmission and Type 911/48 for Sportomatic.

The rest of the world had a very nice selection of engines for the 1975 model year. The straight 911 was still available as Type 911/41 with 150 DIN hp at 5700 rpm. The 911S was available as Type 911/42 with 175 DIN hp at 5800 rpm. The 2.7 Carrera was still available as Type 911/83 with mechanical injection and 210 DIN hp at 6300 rpm.

The R.o.W. and the forty-nine-state engines received one new exhaust system, while the California cars received another. The new R.o.W. exhaust system had a pair of new heat exchangers that merged into a single tube going back through a primary muffler to the final muffler. The beautiful three-into-one header-type heat exchangers were gone forever. The noise-pollution laws in Europe and air-pollution laws in the United States had won out.

The California exhaust also had two new heat exchangers, but they were each fed from a thermal reactor. Then, from the heat exchangers the exhaust gases were fed back to a double-inlet muffler like those used before with the three-into-one exhaust systems. There was an interesting midyear change during the 1975 model year; the main bearings were changed so that the locating tab moved from one side of the bearing saddle to the other. Because of this change there were some crankcases with the locating-tab notches on both sides of the bearing saddle.

The 930 Turbo was introduced with the engine Type 930/50. The 930 used another new aluminum-silicon alloy (Al-Si) crankcase with 86 mm cylinder-head-stud spacing and 103 mm cylinder-spigot diameter. These engines had new cylinder heads with the 49 mm intake valves and the 41.5 mm exhaust valves like 3.0 RSR engines, set at the new, more shallow angle. The combustion chamber in these new cylinder heads was even larger and more open than the ones used by the 2.8 and 3.0 RSRs.

The turbocharged engine still used CIS fuel injection, the unit being the one used on the Mercedes V-8, with two outlets plugged. Four-bearing cam housings and camshafts were used for these engines. Bosch breakerless capacitor discharge ignition was also a feature of the 930 engine. To transmit the extra power, the clutch was again increased in size from 225 to 240 mm in diameter, and the splined hub in the center was also increased in size again. To provide

Indy oil pump developed in 1979/80 for 911-based Indy engine that Porsche was working on with Interscope Racing. They found that the centrifugal force threw the oil to the right rear of the crankcase, so Porsche added a second scavenge pump to scavenge for this area. Even though the Indy program was abandoned, some of these oil pumps were used to improve the scavenging in the 935 engines.

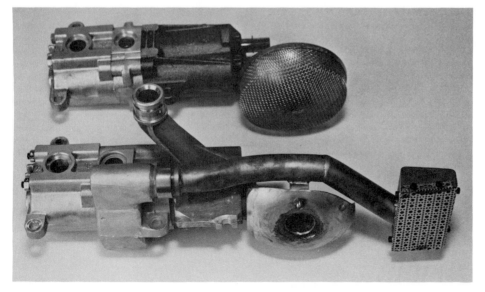

Comparison of the standard 3.3 Turbo oil pump and the 935 racing oil pump introduced for use with the 935s in 1981. This version of the twin-scavenge oil pump placed the second pickup toward the front of the engine where more of the used oil accumulated. There was a newer version of this pump used on the 956/962C engines that actually had three scavenge pumps and three different pickups, with the third pickup even further forward to better scavenge the used oil from the cam drive gears.

additional cooling for this higher performance, Porsche speeded up the fan ratio from 1.3:1 to 1.67:1, increasing the fan air-transfer rate from approximately 1,390 liters per second to approximately 1,500 liters per second. The new turbo fan had a smaller pulley which in conjunction with a larger crankshaft pulley speeded up the fan. The new 930 engine produced 260 DIN hp at 5500 rpm, to be the most powerful road-going Porsche up to that time.

The 1976 was another good model year for the 911. The United States still had two 911s—the US engine and the California engine, with the same power claimed for both at 165 DIN hp at 5800 rpm. The forty-nine-state engine was Type 911/82 for standard transmission, and Type 911/89 for Sportomatic for both forty-nine-state cars and California cars.

The engine-cooling fans were changed from eleven-blade to five-blade fans, and the pulley ratio was speeded up from 1.3:1 to 1.8:1. The purpose of this change was to run the alternator at a higher speed for more efficient charging while reducing the fan noise. The five-blade fans were the same diameter (245 mm) as the eleven-blade fans used on all previous 911 street engines.

There was also the US version of the 930 Turbo with engine Type 930/51. This version had 245 DIN hp at 5500 rpm—a loss of 15 hp from the European version due to thermal reactors, air-injection pumps and different ignition timing used to comply with US emission standards. A new car was introduced in Europe for the 1976 model year, a 3.0 liter Carrera with CIS fuel injection, engine Type 930/02 for standard transmission and Type 930/12 for the Sportomatic. This engine shared its crankcase, head design and valve size with the Turbo, and was forerunner of the 911SC engine. This Carrera engine produced 200 DIN hp at 6000 rpm.

There was also a 911 Normal engine for Europe for 1976, which retained the specifications of the European 1975 911S. The 911 had engine Type 911/81 for standard transmission and Type 911/86 for the Sportomatic. All 911 engines now used the four-bearing camshaft housings, although the engines with the 911 type numbers still used three-bearing camshafts. A new version of the chain tensioner and new, hard-plastic chain-guide ramps were used first on the Turbo engines and then phased into the rest of the 911 engine line. The

oil pumps were changed in all engines for the 1976, as was the oil by-pass system.

Porsche increased the size of the pressure portion of the pump and reduced the size of the scavenge portion, while keeping the overall size the same. Because the scavenge section was reduced, the by-pass was changed to route the by-passed oil directly back to the oil pressure-pump inlet rather than to the crankcase sump. This was done to min-

imize the work that the new, smaller scavenge pump had to do and to avoid filling the crankcase with oil.

The racing engines for 1976 were very interesting, with the 934, 935 and 936 all using the 911 engine as the basis for their power source. All were turbocharged, the 934 and 935 engines based on the 930 while the 936 engine was based on the 911 engine. The 934 was a racing version of the production 930 homologated into Group 4 for GT rac-

The 935 racing pumps required some additional modifications to fit the pump in the crankcase. They siamesed the oil-return tubes so that they could utilize the oil-return-tube drain hole in the crankcase for the second scavenge outlet. A special adaptor and bolt connected the normal scavenge line and the new scavenge line so that the oil could be returned to the tank.

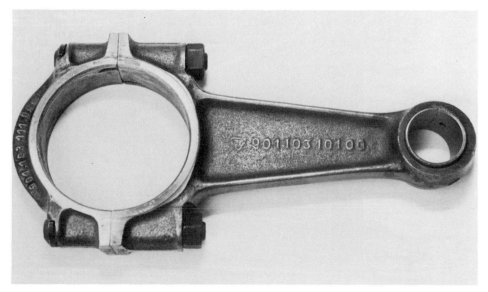

2.0 liter 911 connecting rod used in production cars.

ing. Four hundred 930s had to have been produced over a two-year period to allow a racing version to compete in the GT races as a Group 4 car.

The 1976 934 engine was Type 930/71 which was actually changed very little from the production 930 engine. To improve its performance, Porsche increased the ports to 41 mm, used different cam timing and a modified CIS fuel-injection system that utilized a metering cone rather than the normal sensor-plate arrangement.

Water intercooling was incorporated to cool the turbocharged air before it reached the engine, providing a denser charge and allowing higher boost pressure to be used. The intercooler system reduced the air-charge temperature from 150 deg C to 50 deg C (300 deg F to 120 deg F). The engine also utilized a horizontal cooling fan for more cooling and more even distribution of cooling air over the engine.

The 1976 935 engine was 2857 cc in displacement which, with the 1.4 multiplier applied to turbocharged cars, made it a 3999 cc engine for the 3.5 to 4.0 liter weight group in the Group 5 World Championship of Makes racing. The

2.0 liter 906 titanium connecting rod used in 2.0 liter racing engines Type 906 and 910.

2.8 and 3.0 liter RSR connecting rods, balanced and polished before being soft-nitrated.

2.2 liter 911 connecting rod with reinforced big end and longer rod bolts. Note that the black color indicated this was a nitrated 911S connecting rod.

Porsche nitrated the connecting rods for the 911S engines from the 2.0 liters in 1967, until the 2.4 liter 911S engines.

2.4 liter 911S connecting rod, also nitrated like the RSR rod.

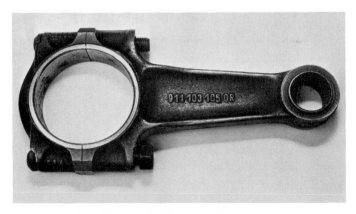

2.4 and 2.7 liter 911 and 911S connecting rod, redesigned for longer-stroke engine.

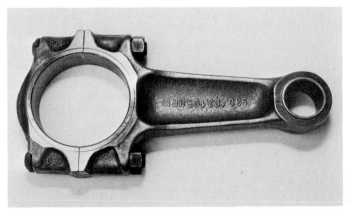

3.0 liter 911SC connecting rod used from 1978 through 1983.

A 3.3 liter Turbo and 3.2 liter connecting rods.

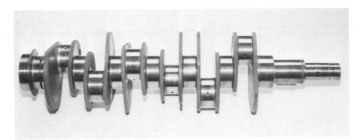

Crankshaft used for 2.4 through 3.0 liter Carrera engines.

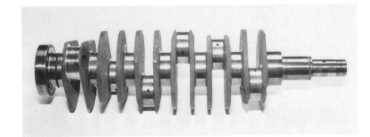

Crankshaft used for 3.3 Turbo and 3.2 Carrera engines.

Titanium 935 connecting rod.

Cup-type flywheel and push-type pressure plate used on 911s from 1965 model through 1969.

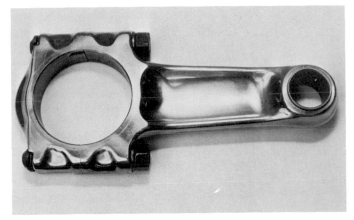

Crankshaft used from 2.0 through 2.2 liter engines.

Crankshaft without counterweights used for 2.0 through 2.2 liter 911T engines only.

Flat-type flywheel and pull-type pressure plate used on all 911s since 1970.

The cylinders used on the original production-model 911s were of Biral construction, which was a cast-iron cylinder with aluminum fins cast around the cylinder.

Pilot bearings; at left is the type used from 1980 on, and at right is the type used in the flat-type flywheels from 1970 through 1979.

Crankshaft and flywheel, showing how the 1980-and-newer pilot bearing mounted.

1976 935 engine, Type 930/72, used a production 930 crankcase, crankshaft and heads, although all were modified and the heads had larger 41 mm ports.

The rest of the engine was typical of Porsche's racing tradition: titanium connecting rods, 908 oil pump, Bosch mechanical plunger-pump fuel injection, and forged rocker arms with valve lash caps for valve adjustment. These forged rocker arms did not use any bushings; instead the rocker-arm shafts used a nitrating process similar to the one used

At the same time Porsche was using the Biral cylinder on its production engines, it was using a cylinder that it called Chromal on its 906 racing engine. These Chromal cylinders consisted of an aluminum cylinder with a chrome-plated working surface. Their chrome surface had what appears to be small serrations all around the cylinder to help retain an oil film on the working surface.

The 911Ts produced from 1968 through 1973 used a cast-iron cylinder to reduce the production expense.

on Porsche's crankshafts and some of its special connecting rods.

This process worked much better than the one used on the production engines with cast-iron rocker arms in the late 1960s, however. The rocker-arm shafts had special retainers to make sure they could not slide out of place and let a rocker arm slip out.

The rocker-arm shafts also used a special seal at each end to prevent oil leaks in this area. The seals fit down into the

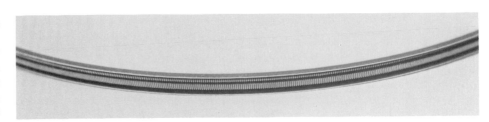

The CE-ring type head gasket was a thin, metal C-shaped ring that enclosed a tubular spring.

In 1973 the Nicasil cylinders were used on the 2.7 Carrera RS. The Nicasil cylinders were originally developed in 1971 for the 917 racing engines, when they increased the displacement from 4900 cc to 5000 cc.

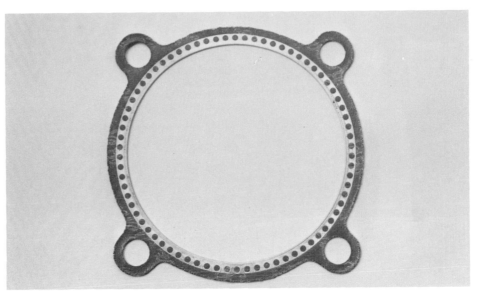

Cylinder-head gasket for 2.0 liter.

In 1974, Alusil cylinders were used as an alternative to the more expensive Nicasil cylinders for some of the production 2.7 911 engines. The Alusil cylinders had some of the advantages of the Nicasil cylinders in that they had the same sort of thin-wall construction. However, it has been my experience that they do not provide as good service as the Nicasil cylinders do.

The 911SC exploding clutch. These rubber-centered clutches were used to dampen out the vibration noises of the transmissions. When the rubber failed, the drivetrain vibrated. Often a piece of rubber jammed between the clutch and the pressure plate and caused the clutch to cease operating. These clutches should be replaced with spring-centered clutches. The new Carreras are again using a rubber-centered clutch, but it is a much larger, more substantial example.

compression grooves at each end of the shaft. When the rocker shaft is installed and the center pinch bolt is tightened, the seals are compressed and forced against the cam-housing rocker-arm-shaft bores forming a good seal.

These engines used both the center-lubed racing cams and the spray-bar lubrication to ensure adequate lubrication but more importantly for additional cooling. Besides the larger ports, the heads were also modified by adding a second spark plug and special guides with additional oiling provided to the finned exhaust guides. The horizontal fan was used both for more cooling and more even cooling of all six cylinders. The airflow from the normal vertical production fan does not like to make the abrupt turn necessary to provide adequate airflow over the front two cylinders (one and four).

Special crankcase through bolts were used on these high-specific-output, turbocharged 935 engines. Porsche originally developed these bolts for use on the 917. The bolts used a pair of special-ground self-aligning spherical washers at each end that fit inside each other, with a special nut that would not put bending stress on the bolt. The threaded portion of the stud and nut were also designed to eliminate the notch effect of the threads. Porsche found that in many applications it could reduce the bolt by one unit size so that in some applications these bolts could be used as a weight-saving measure. When this type of bolt is used for the crankcase through bolts, it is because the through-bolt holes are used as part of the main oil galleries and it is very critical that these bolts not break. The enlarged portion in the center of these bolts is to stop, or at least limit the travel of, any sympathetic harmonic vibrations that may have been set up in the bolts.

Initially, air-to-air intercooling was used on the 935s, but because of a reinterpretation of the rules, Porsche's placement of its intercooler was deemed illegal. The FIA required that an original stock engine lid fit on the car, and with Porsche's air-to-air intercooler it would not. A water intercooler system similar to the one used on the 934 was quickly developed midseason for use on the 935 engines. Fuel consumption for these engines was 4.38 mpg.

The 1976 936 engine was essentially the same engine that had been used in the 1974 Carrera RSR Turbo, and carried the 911/78 type number. The accessories and plumbing were changed to allow mounting in a mid-engined car, but the specifications remained the same as for the Type 911/76, but with the power increased to 540 DIN hp. The 936 was able to continue using the more efficient air-to-air intercooling.

For 1977, the United States had only one type of engine for all fifty states—Type 911/85 for the standard five-speed transmission and Type 911/90 for the Sportomatic. These engines had thermal reactors, EGR and air injection to comply with the US emission standards. The specifications for these engines were the same as for the 1976 California engines, and all of the United States, Canada and Japan shared the exhaust system with thermal reactors that had been used for California since 1975.

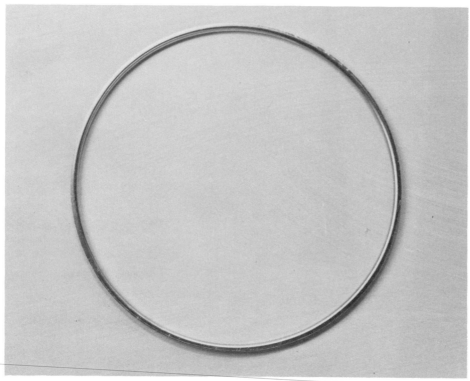

CE-type cylinder-head gasket as used on all 2.2 through 3.0 911SC production engines and some of the racing engines.

1969 911T cylinder head with 42 mm intake valves and 38 mm exhaust valves.

The late 1977 911 engines utilized Dilavar studs for the bottom row of cylinder-head retaining studs. These studs were used to help eliminate the head-stud pulling problem that the 2.7 liter engines had experienced. These Dilavar head studs had been used in racing engines from the early 1970s, and also in the 930 Turbo engines.

Dilavar, a steel alloy that has a thermal expansion rate closer to that of aluminum and magnesium (which are about the same)—used for the crankcase, cylinders and cylinder heads—was about double that of the steel cylinder-head retaining studs. The effect was that the cold, or room-temperature, stress was increased by different thermal expansion rates, resulting in overstress of the steel head studs at higher operating temperatures. In time, many of the head studs pulled and deformed the crankcase where the head stud screwed in.

To explain further, steel has an expansion coefficient of 11.5×10^{-6} per degree Celsius, which is only about half of what the light alloys are at 22×10^{-6} to 24×10^{-6}. Dilavar has a heat-expansion coefficient of about 20×10^{-6}, and a tensile strength of 100-120 kp/mm². Specifications of Dilavar as manufactured by DEW, Krefeld, are as follows:

Carbon	0.065%
Silicon	0.2
Manganese	5.0
Chromium	3.5
Nickel	12
V+FE	78.65

In 1977, we also saw the reverse of the procedure we had seen in 1968; the chain housings, chain-housing covers and valve covers changed back to an aluminum alloy. These new castings were pressure-cast aluminum-silicon alloy (Al-Si).

The 1977 Turbo engine had some minor revisions in the fuel injection and the wastegate. The US version received EGR to comply with the emission standards. The European engine became Type 930/52, while the US version became Type 930/53.

For 1977, there was even a US version of the 934 engine—only this time we came out ahead. This version was built to the then-looser IMSA GT rules. These cars were a blend of the Group 4 934 and Group 5 935, and as such were called 934/5s. The engines were actually more like the 935 engine than the 934, aside from the fact that it retained the single-plug ignition system from the 934. The big change between them and

1965 911 cylinder head with 39 mm intake valves and 35 mm exhaust valves.

906E/910 cylinder head with 45 mm intake valves and 39 mm exhaust valves and twin plugs.

1969 911S cylinder head with 45 mm intake valves and 39 mm exhaust valves.

2.7 911 cylinder head with 46 mm intake valves and 40 mm exhaust valves. All cylinder heads used from 1970 through 1977 were essentially the same, with the same combustion chamber and valve sizes.

Only the ports were changed for the various versions of the engines. The combustion chamber for the 2.2 to 2.7 liter heads were in the range of 68 cc.

the Group 4 934 engines was the Bosch mechanical twin-row plunger-type fuel-injector pump from the Group 5 935 engine. These engines were Type 930/73 and produced 590 DIN hp.

Porsche produced a customer version of the 935 for 1977, with the same engine used in the factory cars in 1976, engine Type 930/72. Most of these customer cars had their engines updated to 3.0 liter configuration by increasing the bore to 95 mm. With the 1.4 multiplier applied, these cars fell into the 4.0 to 4.5 liter weight group for Group 5 racing, which required that the cars carry an additional 122 lb. The 3.0 liter-displacement version of the Type 930/72 engine produced 630 DIN hp at 8000 rpm. Late in the year a second engine became available as Type 930/76. This engine still had the 3.0 liter displacement and used the new twin-turbocharger intercooler system, but retained the single turbo. The power for the Type 930/76 was 630 DIN hp at 7800 rpm.

For 1977 the factory 935s retained their 2857 cc displacement but had twin turbochargers and a new, more efficient intercooler system; this engine was Type 930/77. These changes not only increased the power to 630 DIN hp at 7900 rpm, but also greatly improved the throttle response because there was less inertia in each of the two smaller parallel systems than with one large system.

When Porsche took on BMW in the under-two-liter class of the German Group 5 series in 1977 with the 935 Baby, the engine was turbocharged, of course, so the displacement had to be smaller than 1425 cc with the 1.4 multiplier. The car was called the 935-77-20 and it had engine Type 911/79. Development of an engine this small necessitated a new crankshaft with a 60 mm stroke, and pistons with a 71 mm bore. For this engine, Porsche returned to the air-to-air intercooler system. The cooling effect of the air-to-air intercoolers was improved by using an exhaust-gas-activated system called Jet Cooling.

This Jet Cooling system had originally been developed and tested for Porsche by an American company, Fletcher Aviation, in the early 1950s. Fletcher installed its Jet Cooling system on a then-new 1952 Cabriolet and sent it to Porsche for evaluation in 1953. The Jet Cooling was an interesting scheme that saved the power required to drive a cooling fan. Porsche did a great deal of development work with the cooling system for several years, and even tried it on one of its racing spyders before concluding that the exhaust noise was excessive and abandoned the Jet Cooling program.

It is interesting that Porsche tried this concept again for this project that was so important to the company. This time it was not used for engine cooling, but instead more effective intercooling of the charge air. The power for the Type 911/79 was 370 DIN hp at 8000 rpm.

For 1978 the 3.0 liter 911SC was introduced as the only 911 for the world market. Based on 930 components, the engine was Type 930/04 for the US forty-nine-state car; Type 930/06 for the California car; and Type 930/03 for the R.o.W. The differences between the engines were minor, and the same specifications and performance were claimed for all. All of the engines had air-injection pumps when the 911SC was introduced. The US engine additionally had a catalytic converter, and the California engine also had EGR to meet the various emission standards.

The engine-cooling fans were changed again, this time to the smaller-diameter 226 mm eleven-blade fan, while retaining the higher-speed 1.8:1 drive ratio of the five-blade fan. The air-delivery rate in this configuration was approximately 1,380 liters per second. These smaller-diameter fans had been used on most of the racing engines from the 906 on, but with the slower 1.3:1 pulley ratio. The front-mounted serpentine (loop) oil cooler was made standard equipment on the 911SC.

The 1978 911SC introduced the Porsche clutch disc with a large rubber damper in the center. These rubber-centered clutches were to dampen out the vibration noises of the transmissions. The problem with these clutches, however, was that they were prone to failure because of the rubber damper. Often when these clutches fail, a piece of rubber will jam between the clutch and the pressure plate and cause the clutch to cease operating. Porsche used these clutches from 1978 until 1983, when they were replaced with a spring-centered clutch disc.

The 1978 930 Turbo engine received some major changes, some of which were shared with the new 911SC engine. Both engines received new crankshafts with larger main-bearing journals; bearings one through seven on both were increased from 57 to 60 mm, and number eight on the Turbo was increased from 31 to 40 mm. The crankshaft's rod-

2.8 RSR cylinder head with 49 mm intake valves and 41.5 mm exhaust valves. These heads had 43 mm ports, and larger combustion chamber with 80 mm head-stud spacing. With the 2.8 RSR head's more open combustion chamber, the combustion volume increased to 76 cc.

3.0 RSR cylinder head with 49 mm intake valves and 41.5 mm exhaust valves. These heads had 43 mm ports, and larger combustion chamber with 83 mm head-stud spacing. These heads were very similar to the 2.8 RSR heads, with essentially the same size combustion chamber at 77.2 cc. Only the larger 3 mm cylinder-head-stud spacing made these heads unique to the 3.0 liter RS and RSR engines.

71

3.0 911SC cylinder head with 49 mm intake valves and 41.5 mm exhaust valves. These 930-type cylinder heads had an even larger (90 cc) combustion chamber than the 2.8 and 3.0 liter RSR engines, and the head-stud spacing was increased an additional 3 mm to 86 mm.

A 1980 935 cylinder head with 49 mm intake valves and 41.5 mm exhaust valves and twin spark plugs. Note the groove machined in the cylinder sealing surface, which was for an interlocking ring Ni-Resist head gasket.

bearing journals were also increased in size from 52 to 53 mm for the 911SC and to 55 mm for the Turbo. This change required that the crankcase bores be increased from 62 to 65 mm for the 911SC and the Turbo.

The flywheel mounting-bolt circle was increased from 44 to 70 mm, and nine bolts were used to fasten the flywheel rather than the six used before. The flywheel seal was increased in size to 110 mm and the 928 seal used.

Both engines used the Bosch breakerless capacitor discharge ignition system with distributors that rotated in a counterclockwise direction instead of clockwise, which had always been the 911 tradition. These new-style pointless distributors were originally used on the racing 917s and the RSRs. They had a toothed rotor which caused a magnetic flux change and acted like a pulse generator. There were six little tabs on the rotor so that one turn of the distributor produced six pulses which drove the electronic capacitor discharge unit. The rev limiter was changed to a fuel-pump-cutoff type set for 6850 rpm, plus-or-minus 150 rpm for the 911SC. The chain ramps were changed again in an effort to quiet the chains. One brown plastic ramp was retained while the other five were replaced with the new, taller black ramps.

Several other changes were unique to the Turbo engine, now Type 930/60 for the R.o.W., Type 930/61 for the US forty-nine-state cars, and Type 930/63 for the California cars. The displacement was increased on the Turbo by using both a longer 74.4 mm stroke and a larger 97 mm bore. New connecting rods, in addition to accommodating the larger journal diameter, were 0.7 mm shorter, and the wrist-pin diameter was increased 1 mm to 23 mm.

The cylinders no longer used any type of head gasket at all, for the first time on any 911-type engine. The cylinder-cooling fins were drastically altered in an effort to even the cooling effect of the fan. The fins were completely left off the top of the cylinder (side nearest the fan), and the fins were lengthened on the bottom of the cylinders, particularly at the end nearest the cylinder head.

Both portions of the oil pumps were greatly increased in size to improve oil circulation. The new pumps were larger than the 908 pumps used in the 935 engines. The pressure pump was 51 mm long and the scavenge pump was 80 mm long. To improve the quality of the intake charge air, an air-to-air intercooler was added between the turbocharger and the engine.

All Turbos had air-injection pumps. The US engine had additional thermal reactors and the California engine had a distributor with a double-vacuum unit to retard the timing at full load to meet the various emission standards of the world. The power for the European Turbo was 300 DIN hp at 5500 rpm, while the emission controls reduced the US models to 265 DIN hp at 5500 rpm.

For 1978, the customer's 935 received engine Type 930/78. This engine was similar to Type 930/77 used by the factory cars in 1977, using twin turbochargers and an improved intercooler system. A pair of turbocharger scavenge pumps were driven off the end of the layshaft, scavenging oil from the turbochargers and returning it to the engine's sump. These customer engines continued to be 3.0 liter. Power output was 720 DIN hp at 7800 rpm.

An interesting change in these engines was that Porsche had replaced the CE-ring head gasket with a solid-steel ring which fit in a groove in both the upper cylinder flange and the cylinder head, forming an interlocking seal. The ring was originally made of stainless steel and later made of Ni-Resist, a high-nickel-content alloy steel able to withstand very high temperatures. This is the same material the turbocharger hot housings are made of.

Engines for both the factory 935 and 936 were greatly changed for 1978. They were both still based on 911 components, but had new water-cooled four-valve heads with cog-gear-driven dual overhead cams. These changes were made because of Porsche's desire to produce more reliable power from these engines. The forerunners were not at their mechanical limit, however, they were at their thermal limit. A good example of this thermal limit phenomenon was the 1979 Daytona 24-Hour race where ten of the thirteen 935s that entered, failed. The majority failed by exceeding the thermal limits of the engine, resulting in such problems as melted pistons, burned valves and most commonly a blown head gasket or burned-out cylinder.

To obtain more power it was necessary to go from two valves to four valves which, with air-cooled heads, would have been an additional thermal liability because the valves and their ports would severely reduce the cross section of the

One of the ways the 935 was able to utilize the extra oil for cooling was the use of specially modified cylinder heads. The head on the left was a standard-production 911 cylinder head and its valve guides, and the head on the right was the 935 head and its valve guides. The drilling that you can see on the 935 head provided a constant source of fresh oil to the exhaust guide about halfway down its length. There was another drilling up in the finned area that provided additional oiling in this finned portion of the guide as well. This additional oil in the exhaust guide ensured that there was a path for the heat to be conducted from the exhaust valves to the guides and then out into the airstream. The finned guide also took advantage of the oil-spray mist created by the spray-bar cam lubrication to provide additional cooling.

962 cylinder head with 49 mm intake valves and 41.5 mm exhaust valves, with single plug and special squish area to improve combustion in the absence of the second plug.

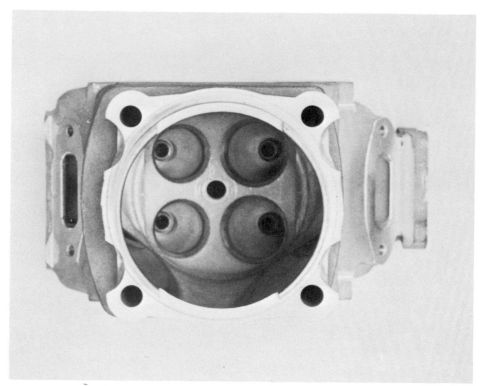

The 956/962C air-cooled cylinder and water-cooled cylinder head assembly with two 35 mm intake valves and two 30.5 mm exhaust valves.

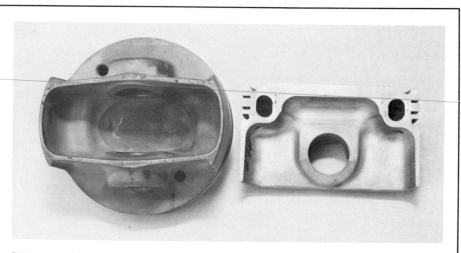

Oil-cooled engines

Porsche has continued to expand the use of oil cooling for its engines over the years. The piston oil squirters were first used in racing engines to provide additional cooling for the pistons, and then incorporated into all of the production 911 engines from 1971 on. The turbocharged racing engines further expanded the use of oil cooling by using an oil mist over the finned valve guides, and using direct-exhaust-guide oiling.

The IMSA 962 engine used a different form of oil cooling for the pistons. Instead of the squirters, they aimed a steady stream of oil at a hole in the bottom of the piston

crown, so that there was a continuous supply of fresh oil to the gallery built into the piston's dome. This additional piston cooling relieved the top compression rings of one of its added-on jobs—cooling the piston crown—and let it get down to its *real* job of sealing the piston to the cylinder for compression.

By so relieving the compression ring, the designers were able to make the ring narrower, 1 mm instead of the normal 1.5 mm, and thus make the rings seal to the cylinder better and increase the engine's performance. These pistons were made of multiple forgings and then were electron-beam-welded together.

head used for cooling. Water cooling was essential if four-valve heads were to be used.

In addition to offering a power increase, the four-valve layout reduced the thermal stress on the valves because of their smaller size. Experience gained from experiments with four-valve heads with water cooling for the 908 engine in 1970 and 1971 was applied to this project.

Cylinders were welded to the heads by an electron-beam-welding machine, eliminating the critical head gasket, an area where the thermal limit was often approached and sometimes exceeded in these turbocharged racing engines. The four-valve head used a very simple pent-roof-design combustion chamber, with one centrally located spark plug. Spark plugs were fired by a high-tension distributor unit driven by the intake cam for cylinders one through three, while the inductive driver for the electronic-ignition unit was driven by the intake cam for cylinders four through six. Camshafts were spur-gear-driven rather than by chains, and the valves were actuated by cup tappets.

Both the 935 and the 936 engines utilized twin turbochargers for improved throttle response. The 935 twin-turbo engine used water intercooling and twin wastegates. The smaller 936 twin-turbo engine retained the air-to-air intercooling and used one wastegate. The Type 935/73 936 engine had to remain under 2146 cc because of the 1.4 multiplier and the 3.0 liter limit for Group 6 cars. The 60 mm stroke crankshaft from the 935 Baby was used in conjunction with an 87 mm bore to achieve 2140 cc displacement. The Type 935/73 936 engine produced 580 DIN hp at 9000 rpm.

The 935 engine was increased to 3211 cc which, with the 1.4 multiplier, brought the equivalent displacement to the 4.5 liter weight-group limit, with 4495 cc. The displacement increase was achieved by using a new 74.4 mm crankshaft derived from the 3.3 liter street Turbo combined with the 95.7 mm pistons. The Type 935/71 engine was for the factory Moby Dick; power output was 750 DIN hp at 8200 rpm.

Both the 911SC and the 930 Turbo engines remained unchanged for the world market in 1979, although in 1979 a special version of the 935 was built for the United States and the IMSA multiplier for turbocharged cars. New rules gave single-turbo cars a 1.5 multiplier, while twin-turbo cars had a 1.8 multiplier. As such, a 3.0 liter twin was required to weigh 88 lb. more than the 3.122 liter single-turbo cars that Porsche made especially to comply with the IMSA rules.

Porsche chose the single-turbo approach with its Type 930/79 engine because it felt that it could make the engine as effective as the 3.0 liter twin-turbo engine by increasing the bore to 97 mm and developing a new, larger and more efficient single turbocharger—using the same type intercooler used on the Type 930/78 engine.

Porsche's solution to the IMSA rules was not entirely effective and only Peter Greg won races with the Type 930/79 engine. Most of the other teams that had these engines converted them back to the 3.0 Type 930/78 specifications because they felt that this configuration had better throttle response. The power output of the Type 930/79 was 715 DIN hp at 7800 rpm.

In 1980 the 911SC engine was revised for all markets. The US version became the Type 930/07 with 9.3:1 compression and retained its 180 DIN hp. The emission-control devices consisted of a three-way catalytic converter with an oxygen-sensor-controlled frequency valve to control the "control pressure" in the fuel distributor. This was the Lambda system, which very precisely controlled the fuel/air-mixture ratio of the engine to provide the correct combustion byproducts to the very critical three-way catalytic converter. The Lambda system was a great advancement in performance and driveability for emission-legal engines.

The US cars also used both vacuum-advance and retard distributors. The R.o.W. cars retained their air-injection pump to comply with the emission laws. The oil pump was fitted with a suction venturi surrounded by a cylindrical filter screen. This venturi pickup was added to eliminate an oil-scavenge problem that some 911SCs had when driven at sustained high rpm. The lower valve covers received extra reinforcement to both help quiet the engine and provide a better oil seal.

These new reinforced "turbo" valve covers actually solved the problem of leaking valve covers that had been with the 911 engine since its introduction. The pilot bearing was mounted onto the end of the crankshaft with three bolts rather than pressed into the flywheel as had been the case with all previous 911 engines. The fan size was increased again

to the 245 mm diameter, the pulley ratio was increased to the 1.67:1 ratio of the Turbo, and the fan air-transfer rate was increased to approximately 1,500 liters per second.

The 911SC engine for the R.o.W., Type 930/09, had 8.6:1 compression and produced 188 DIN hp at 5500 rpm. All of the 1980 911 and 930 engines received revised chain tensioners. The tensioners were still hydraulic and, in

fact, the internals had not changed. The body, however, had been made thinner where it goes onto the support spud in the chain housing. This change was to provide room for the new chain-sprocket carriers (chain idler arms) which were now wider and had two bronze bushings. These changes were made to relieve the binding stress and galling, which Porsche had determined was causing most of the premature chain-tensioner

959 cylinder head with two 35 mm intake valves and two 32 mm exhaust valves, and very similar pent-roof combustion chamber that was used in the racing cars.

Original sand-cast aluminum 911 valve covers. Note that the exhaust cover used only six mounting studs.

failures. This problem was determined to be similar to the one Porsche had with its change to the rocker arms without bushings in 1967.

Another change for the R.o.W. cars was the replacement of the front-fender-mounted loop oil cooler with a brass-tube-type cooler for improved oil cooling. The US cars retained the serpentine (loop) cooler that had been standard equipment since the introduction of the 911SC. There was a limited series of 930

Turbos for the United States in 1980, built to 1979 specifications and delivered before January 1980, after which the Turbo was discontinued for the US and Canadian markets.

The Porsche racing program for 1980 was to have been an Indy program with Interscope Racing. The engine for this car was the Type 935/72, a 2650 cc development of the four-valve engines used in Groups 5 and 6 racing in 1978. Porsche, as it turned out, attempted to

enter US Championship Car racing at the wrong time in history—right in the middle of the USAC versus CART feud, and the rules were changed out from under the company.

Porsche had been told that it would be allowed to run with a boost of 54 in. of mercury, but on April 21, Porsche was told the company would be limited to 48 in. of boost, like the eight-cylinder cars. When the boost was reduced, Porsche withdrew, feeling that the reduction would require a complete redesign and that there was not enough time left before the early May practice.

Porsche was beaten before it started—not on the track but at the conference table. The type 935/72 was designed to run on methyl alcohol. The engine used electronic injection with dual injectors. The compression ratio was 9.0:1 and the power output depended on the boost it was allowed to run: At 60 in. boost (1.03 bar), the engine produced 630 DIN hp at 9000 rpm; at 54 in. boost (0.83 bar), it produced 570 DIN hp at 9000 rpm; at 48 in. boost (0.63 bar) we will never know. Porsche decided not to play.

The customer 935 engine for 1980 was the 930/80, an extension of the all-conquering version of the 935 engine the Kremer brothers had developed for the 1979 season. In 1979, the Kremers won eleven of the twelve races in the German National Championship, and they also won the prestigious Le Mans race, with the only 935 to ever do so.

Magnesium 911 valve covers used from 1968 until changed to diecast aluminum midyear 1977.

The 930/80 had a bore of 95 mm and a stroke of 74.4 mm, for a displacement of 3163 cc. It also had a Bosch-Kugelfischer injection pump with electronic regulation of fuel mixture and air-to-air intercooling.

The Kugelfischer injection, with its electronic regulation, was Porsche's first real effort to reduce the fuel consumption on the racing turbocharged 911 engines. The engine with 7.2:1 compression and 1.7 bar boost produced 800 DIN hp at 8000 rpm. When run at a more conservative 1.4 boost, the Type 930/80 engine produced 740 DIN hp at 7800 rpm, and was an extremely reliable endurance racing engine.

The intercoolers for the Type 930/80 were various forms of air-to-air intercooler systems. Porsche had one system, and several major teams developed their own systems. One thing was sure, air-to-air was the way to go. No more heat build-up in the intercooler system, and with a cooler, denser charge, the engines

Diecast aluminum 911 valve covers introduced with 930 Turbo in 1975 and phased into production on the 911s midyear 1975.

Top cover has remained unchanged since then, but the lower cover was changed again in 1980.

could produce more horsepower for extended periods of time.

In 1981 there were minor revisions in the 911SC engine for the US market. Most of the changes were in the fuel injection system. The fuel distributor was made nonadjustable to comply with US emission laws. A cold-start-mixture distributor was added inside the air box to provide more uniform distribution of the mixture to all cylinders. Previously, cold-start fuel was injected into the air-distributor housing. All fuel lines and injector lines on the engine were changed to steel. An acceleration-enrichment circuit was added to the injection system to improve reliability when the engine and/or the oxygen sensor was cold. The engine type number was changed to Type 930/16 for the United States and Canada. Power remained unchanged at 180 DIN hp.

The year 1981 also saw the return of the 930 Turbo to Canada with the Type 930/60 R.o.W. 300 DIN hp engine. Canadian laws required Porsche to use a US-approved version of the car if there was one, and allowed it to import the R.o.W. version in the absence of a US-approved car. The R.o.W. version of the 911SC engine was revised for 1981 as Type 930/10. The compression ratio was increased to 9.8:1 and the effective combustion chamber changed to improve the thermal efficiency and increase the horsepower to 204 DIN at 5900 rpm.

The 1981 935 engine Type 930/81 had only minor revisions over the Type 930/80. The changes were an improved oil-scavenging system, improved cooling and larger 43 mm intake ports. The main changes to the cooling system were the use of a new drive system and higher drive ratio for the flat fan.

The change to the oil-scavenging system was more significant, however. There was a new 935 racing oil pump with dual scavenge pumps and oil pickups to get more of the used oil out of the engine. There are a couple of advantages in doing a more thorough job of oil scavenging. By getting the oil out of the engine more quickly, you can reduce the windage and prevent frictional horsepower losses from the crankshaft operating in the oil. Without efficient scavenging, as much as a couple of quarts of oil can be in the engine at one time. The crankshaft will whip this excess oil into a fog by introducing air into the oiling system. The added air in the oil makes it much more difficult to effectively cool

Comparison of various chain tensioners, left to right: early open-reservoir-style chain tensioner; early-style sealed-reservoir chain tensioner; late-style sealed-reservoir chain tensioner; and the superior, current Carrera-style pressure-fed chain tensioner.

Diecast aluminum 911 valve covers; 1980 update, which reinforced the Turbo lower valve cover.

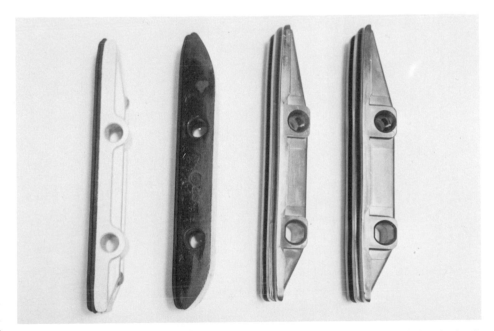

Comparison of chain ramps, left to right: composite aluminum-backed plastic ramps used in early 911 engines; black soft-plastic ramps used 1968 to 1976/77; brown hard-plastic ramps introduced for the Turbo in 1976; and the taller, black hard-plastic ramps, five of which were used in conjunction with one of the earlier brown ramps for quieter operation.

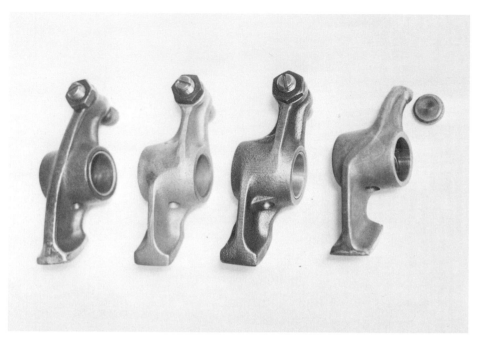

Comparison of various rocker arms, left to right: early-style forged rocker arm with bushing; first-style cast rocker arm without bushing; current-style cast rocker arm with bushing; and the forged racing rocker arm without bushing or adjustment screw, *shown with lash cap used for valve adjustment (these rockers have been used on most single overhead cam racing 911 engines from the 906 to the present IMSA 962 engine).*

the scavenged oil. There was a later version of this pump, with three stages of scavenging and three oil pickups to even further improve the engine's oil scavenging.

These changes were made to allow the engines to run higher boost for longer periods of time, which meant they could produce more power with more reliability. Power for the Type 930/81 engine was increased to 760 DIN hp at 7800 rpm, but in short races the boost was increased to the 1.7-1.8 bar range, with more than 800 DIN hp on tap.

The real excitement for 1981 was the good use that Peter Schutz and Porsche came up with for the Indy engine design. The Indy engine was converted to run on racing gas, using a Bosch-Kugelfischer injection pump with twin turbochargers as Type 935/75, and installed in the venerable 936 chassis to win again at Le Mans for Porsche's sixth win. When converted to gasoline, Porsche claimed a power output of 600 DIN hp at 8200 rpm for the Type 935/75. The reason these larger engines were now eligible in Group 6 was that the year before, FIA had made an emergency change in an effort to give a car a place to compete. For 1981, the class limit had been

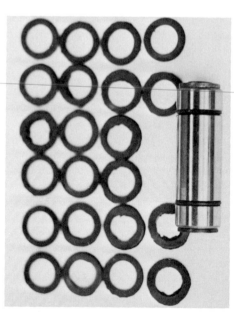

Racing rocker-arm-shaft seals. The rocker-arm shafts also used a special seal at each end to prevent oil leaks in this area. The seals fit down into the compression grooves at each end of the shaft. When the rocker shaft was installed and the center pinch bolt tightened, the seals were compressed and forced against the cam-housing rocker-arm-shaft bores, forming a good seal. Note seals shown in production steel-rocker-arm shaft, in an effort to show contrast between shaft and seal.

Comparison of rocker-arm shafts. On the right, early example with 5 mm pinch bolt, used in 1965 and 1966 models. On the left, an example of the later rocker-arm shafts, with a 6 mm pinch bolt. The pinch bolts were too small in the originals and had to *be overtorqued to retain shaft in the cam housing. The small bolts used in these early shafts often stretched, causing the shafts to loosen up and work their way out of the cam housings.*

increased up to 6.0 liters, so almost anything could compete as a Group 6 car. There were weight penalties for the larger engine sizes, but obviously this didn't prove to be much of a handicap to Porsche.

Only minor changes were made in 1982 in the 911SC and the 930 Turbo engines. The largest change was that the camshaft drive gears were mounted to the cams with a bolt rather than the large nut used previously. The alternators were changed to units that had a built-in voltage regulator rather than those used previously with remote-mounted voltage regulators. The 930 had an oil trap installed in the crankcase vent line to separate the fumes and return the oil to the oil tank. The type numbers remained the same for 1982: Type 930/10 for the R.o.W. 911SC, Type 930/16 for the US 911SC, and Type 930/60 for the R.o.W. Turbo.

245 mm five-bladed fan used for 1976 and 1977 only.

226 mm eleven-bladed fan with large pulley used for racing Types 906 on.

Comparison of various chain-sprocket idler arms, right to left: early 911 arm with bushing; arm without bushing used from the late 1960s until 1980; 1980-and-later sprocket idler arm with a broader stance and two bushings. This later style was introduced after Porsche determined that the binding of these idler arms on the mounting spud was causing the majority of the premature chain-tensioner failures.

Comparison of various rocker-arm shafts, left to right: early-style plain steel rocker shaft; nitrated racing rocker shaft; surface-treated shaft used with non-bushed cast-iron rocker arms; and current-style plain steel rocker shaft. Notice that the surface treatment on the treated shaft has worn through.

245 mm larger-diameter eleven-bladed fan with small pulley as used on Turbo.

Eleven-bladed 245 mm fan with 1.3:1 drive ratio as used in production 911, from 1965 to 1975 model.

In 1982 the Indy engine was again pressed into service in the all-new 956 Group C car. The Group C rules required a 100 liter fuel tank and limited overall fuel consumption to fifty-five liters per 100 km (5.14 mpg). The new fuel-economy requirements were hard to meet with the Type 935/76 version of this engine, with its Bosch-Kugelfischer injection. The Kugelfischer injection was a mechanical-injection system with some limited electronic compensation devices to improve the fuel economy. Porsche did everything it could to improve the fuel economy, and it did get better with each race. The company had its biggest problems at the beginning of the season, and at Silverstone actually had to race at a pace almost ten seconds off its qualifying speed. Even so, Porsche was able to win at Le Mans in 1982 with this car. As a result of the company's conservation effort, the winning car went further for its win than 1981's winning 936 and in doing so consumed less fuel and won the Le Mans Index of Energy Consumption for the car that achieved the best ratio of fuel used for the distance run.

The year 1983 was again one of little change for the 911SC. The engines had a modified acceleration control unit and a new oxygen sensor. Additionally, the California cars had a new oxygen-sensor control unit. These changes were made to improve throttle response while the engine was still cold, and still comply with the various emission laws. The US cars received the tube-type oil cooler.

The Turbo engine received enough changes to justify a new type number, Type 930/66, for the R.o.W. Most of the changes were made to improve running while complying with the world (exclusive of the United States) emission laws. There was a new warm-up regulator to improve cold running performance and throttle response. The fuel distributor was modified by the addition of what Porsche called a "capsule" valve, to improve the fuel enrichment when the throttle was opened suddenly during fast acceleration. The engines also had a new distributor with a double-vacuum unit with a temperature-controlled vacuum advance for emission control. The exhaust system was also changed to by-pass the wastegate exhaust through its own muffler. Porsche made this change to reduce the noise level without restricting the power output which was still 300 DIN hp at 5500 rpm.

In 1983, Porsche produced a series of eleven 956 race cars for its racing customers, with essentially the same Type 935/76 engine used in its own factory-team cars in 1982. Then it began to develop a new, more fuel-efficient version of the Indy engine for Group C, as the Type 935/77. This new version produced 620 DIN hp at 8200 rpm with 1.3 bar boost.

A very sophisticated electronic ignition and engine fuel-management system was used to cope with the changing conditions and provide more precise fuel control and timing. The system was developed by Bosch for Porsche, and had some similarities to the DME (Digital Motor Electronics) used in the production Porsches. The system used six input signals that were fed to the fuel-injection and ignition-control computer: current rpm, engine temperature, bat-

Eleven-bladed 226 mm fan with 1.3:1 drive ratio as used in race cars from 906 through the 956/962C engines with water-cooled cylinder heads. With the exception of Moby Dick, all of the 934s and 935s were cooled with the larger flat fans for additional cooling.

Five-bladed 245 mm fan with 1.8:1 drive ratio as used on 911s for 1976 and 1977.

tery voltage, idling adjustment, inlet air temperature and turbocharger boost pressure. This new car won at Le Mans in 1983.

1984 marked the beginning of the third decade of the 911 and the introduction of the new-and-improved version of the Carrera engine. Its larger displacement produced more power and was more efficient, providing better fuel economy than the previous models. The basic engines for the world market were identical except for their emission control devices and compression ratios. The high specific output was due mainly to the resonance-type intake system and the increased compression ratios.

In addition to the increased power, there were also several significant mechanical changes for the 1984 Carrera engines. The displacement was increased to 3.2 liters by using the 74.4 mm crankshaft and connecting rods from the 3.3 930 Turbo engine, with the same 95 mm bore that had been used on the 911SC engines for a displacement of 3164 cc. The cylinders for the 3.2 liter 911 Carrera engine did not have the groove for the CE-ring-type head gasket that had been used on all other normally aspirated engines from 1970 until this change. Instead, the cylinder sealing surface was cut at a slight angle and no head gasket at all was used.

Porsche also changed the crankcase which no longer had a removable sump plate and sump screen. The benefit of the new crankcase, for our purposes, was that it was stronger and less likely to leak oil along its bottom seam. This change was actually introduced on the 911SC production engines the previous April (1983) because the old molds had worn out.

Another major mechanical change in these engines was the all-new pressure-fed chain tensioner. This tensioner is actually best described as a spring tensioner that is hydraulically dampened. The chain tensioners were pressure fed from the engine's lubrication system through oil lines that "T" off the oil lines which provide lubrication to the cam and valve-gear mechanism. These new tensioners proved to be a simple, reliable, trouble-free solution to an old problem.

The exhaust system remained the same in concept as the 911SC, except for larger-diameter tubes for the larger-displacement engine. There were two identical heat exchangers that crossed over at the rear of the engine (flywheel

end), combined and passed down the left side of the engine. The R.o.W. cars had a new, larger-volume pre-muffler, while the US-Japan version had a three-way catalytic converter in place of the pre-muffler. An oxygen sensor was installed at the input of the catalyst on these cars. This sensor was electrically preheated for faster response time. The exhaust from either the pre-muffler or the catalytic converter then went to the final

Eleven-bladed 226 mm fan with 1.8:1 drive ratio as used on 1978 and 1979 911SCs.

Eleven-bladed 245 mm fan with 1.67:1 drive ratio as used on all Turbos and 1980-and-newer 911s.

muffler at the rear of the car, as before. There was a new final muffler which had a new interior with approximately ten percent greater flow rate.

The big change for the 1984 3.2 liter Carrera was Porsche's use of the Bosch-Motronic-controlled fuel injection and ignition system, which Porsche calls its DME system.

The DME system combined separate ignition, fuel and in the case of the US-

Solex 40 PI overflow carburetors used on the Type 901/01 engines. Note wobble nut used to drive recirculating fuel pumps, tandem fuel pumps and special chain-housing cover with mount for fuel pumps.

Weber 40 IDA carburetor as used on 911 engines from midyear 1966 through 1969.

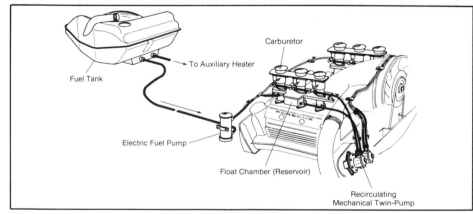

Cam nuts, and at left wobble nut used with Solex carburetors. At center is normal street-car nut, and at right is racing nut. The differences were that the street-car nuts had a 2 mm thread pitch and used a 46 mm wrench, and the racing nut had a 1.5 mm thread pitch and used a 41 mm wrench. The current method is a much simpler bolt.

Weber 40 IDS carburetor. Note high-speed enrichment tube. The high-speed enrichment circuit was added for improved engine safety. The circuit provided an overly rich mixture at higher rpm to minimize the possibility of destructive detonation, and offered no increase in performance.

Drawing of Solex carburetor fuel flow shows electric supply fuel pump which pumped fuel from the tank to a pair of float chambers, one on each bank of three carburetors. A pair of mechanical fuel pumps, driven by the left camshaft, then recirculated the fuel past the jets in the overflow carburetors. The fuel level, normally called the float level, was established by a spillway in each of the six carburetors. The fuel that ran over the spillway was returned to the float chambers to be recirculated again.

Weber 40 IDA with no high-speed enrichment circuit. The carburetor design was essentially the same, it just didn't use the extra circuit.

Japan car, oxygen-sensor systems into a single control system. The control system was a microcomputer with microprocessors. These microcomputers differed among countries because of different emission regulations and fuel grades. Complete performance maps for both the ignition and electronic injection were stored within the DME control unit. Sensors on the engine provided the control system's microcomputer with instantaneous information which then provided the engine with the correct amount of fuel and the optimum ignition timing for all engine operating conditions. The DME system allowed the 911 engine to be optimized for performance, economy and exhaust emissions without causing any problems with the way the car drove.

To achieve its goal of a high specific output, Porsche optimized the compression ratio for the R.o.W. cars at 10.3:1 and for the US cars at 9.5:1. The company also optimized the effective combustion-chamber shape within the normal hemispherical combustion chamber with a squish hump on one side of the piston. Porsche continued to use the same camshafts it had introduced with the 3.0 Carrera in 1976 and then had used with all of the 911SC engines.

When these cams were first used in the 3.0 Carrera engine, they were timed so that they opened the intake at 1 deg BTDC and closed it at 53 deg ABDC, and so that they opened the exhaust valve at 43 deg BBDC and closed it at 3 deg ATDC. In the various versions of the 911SC engines, Porsche first advanced the cams by 6 deg and then retarded them again by the same 6 deg. Sometimes the Euro version of the engine was more advanced than the US version, and at other times it was the other way around.

For the 3.2 liter Carrera engine, the timing was a compromise between the

Belt drive for 906E and 910 injection engine, Type 901/21. Special cams were made just for this application, where there was an extension on the cam billet, which had a key way drive for the Gilmer belt drive for the injection pump.

Bosch mechanical injection for 906E and 910 engines, Type 901/21. Simple inline injection pump with simple speed and throttle-position control.

Zenith 40 TIN carburetors were used on the 1970/71 US 911T engines, and 1970 through 1973 R.o.W. 911T engines.

High-butterfly injection manifolds as used on 2.8 liter RSR and early 3.0 liter RSR.

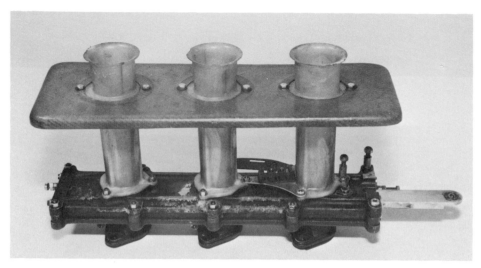

Slide-valve injection manifolds for 906E and 910 engines, Type 901/21.

two extremes and was 3 deg more advanced than the 911SCs it replaced. The Carrera engine used resonance-type tuning for the intake system to optimize the power output. The R.o.W. version had 73 hp per liter, which was a higher power output than any of the other normally aspirated engines since the 1973 Carrera RS engine at 78.2 hp per liter. The R.o.W. engine had 231 hp and the US version had 207.

There was another new 911 engine type for 1984, Type 930/18, which was the engine for the Type 954 911SC RS. This new engine was an evolution of the 3.0 liter 911SC engine for racing or rallying. The engine retained the 95x70.4 mm bore and stroke ratio of the 911SC

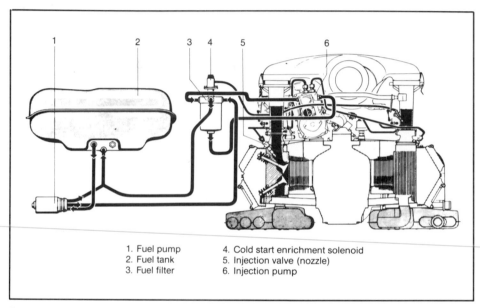

1. Fuel pump
2. Fuel tank
3. Fuel filter
4. Cold start enrichment solenoid
5. Injection valve (nozzle)
6. Injection pump

Drawing of mechanical-injection system used on production-model 911s from 1969 through 1975 with the R.o.W. 2.7 Carrera engine. Fuel was fed to the mechanical-injection pump by an electric fuel pump with a pressure-regulating by-pass circuit.

The mechanical pump then supplied a timed mixture to each of the six cylinders. There was an auxiliary cold-start circuit which squirted fuel into the top of the intake stacks.

Twin-row Bosch injection pump used on 911E and 911S. This was essentially the same technology used on the 906E race car applied to the street cars in 1969, but with a much-improved injection pump with an engine-speed-controlled space cam.

Three-dimensional space cam used in Bosch twin-row mechanical-injection pumps.

Auxiliary cam drive for mechanical-injection pump on racing engines. This auxiliary cam drive was part of the camshaft on production cars with mechanical injection. Camshafts that did not have a pump drive could be modified using this drive piece.

for a displacement of 2944 cc. The standard valve size of 49 mm intake and 41.5 mm exhaust was retained for these engines, and their ports were increased to 43 mm for both the intake and the exhaust.

These engines had a new sport camshaft which opened the intake valve at 82 deg BTDC and closed the intake valve at 82 deg ABDC. The cam opened the exhaust valve at 78 deg BBDC and closed the exhaust valve at 58 deg ATDC. The maximum valve lift for the intake valve was 11.70 mm and for the exhaust valve 10.25 mm. This engine used the Bosch-Kugelfischer mechanical fuel-injection pump and high-butterfly injection system. The power output for the Type 930/18 was 255 DIN hp at 7000 rpm with a peak torque of 184 lb-ft at 6500 rpm.

For 1986, the 911 Turbo was reintroduced to the US market after six years of absence. The new US version with Type 930/68 engine used a catalytic converter and oxygen sensor to meet the US emission laws. The engine was designed for operation on unleaded premium-grade gasoline and met all of the US laws as one version. The power output was 282 hp at 5500 rpm with a peak torque of 287.4 lb-ft at 4000 rpm.

In the three model years since its introduction, in 1984 and 3.2 Carrera engine had remained relatively unchanged. In 1985, Porsche changed the front-mounted oil cooler to a finned radiator-type heat exchanger, or cooler. This new finned cooler was mounted in the right front fender, in place of the former brass-tube-type oil cooler. The change was actually made in July 1984 to both the Turbo and the Carrera. A notch in the lower portion of the front bumper was opened up to let more airflow into the new radiator-style cooler.

This type of cooler works very well at high sustained speed, 100-plus mph, such as you would enjoy on the *autobahns*, but were not necessarily an improvement over the tube-type cooler for US driving where there is not much airflow from that small hole or notch in the front bumper. In 1987, Porsche installed a thermostatically controlled fan on the front-mounted radiator-type cooler on all catalyst cars, which should solve the cooling problems on the US cars. The thermostat turns on the fan when the oil temperature reaches 118 deg C (244 deg F).

Also for 1987, Porsche was able to wring a little more power out of the catalytic-converter version of the engine, increasing it up to 217 hp. The R.o.W. version remained at 231 hp, and there were two new versions of the 3.2 Carrera engine. One was for Australia, which carried the same type number as the US version, but with a modified control unit that reduced the fuel octane require-

ments by four points RON and also dropped the power back to 207 hp.

The second version was Type 930/26 which had the same performance specifications as the R.o.W. version, but with engine encasement to conform with the Swiss 75 dBA noise restrictions for 1987. A noise-reducing panel was

Kugelfischer injection pumps used on 1980- and-newer 935s and the original customer 956 race cars in 1983. The Kugelfischer injection system was also used on the 1984 911SC RS (Type 954).

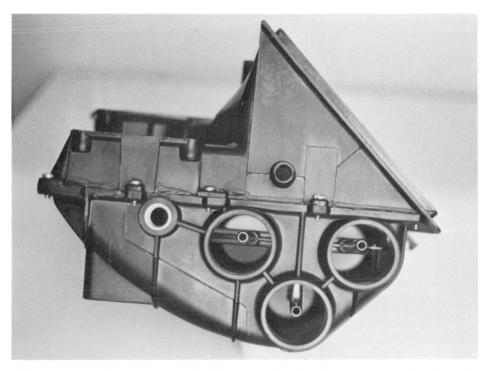

CIS air box. A cold-start-mixture distributor was added inside the air box to give more uniform distribution of the cold-start mixture to all cylinders. Previously, cold-start fuel was injected into the air-distributor housing.

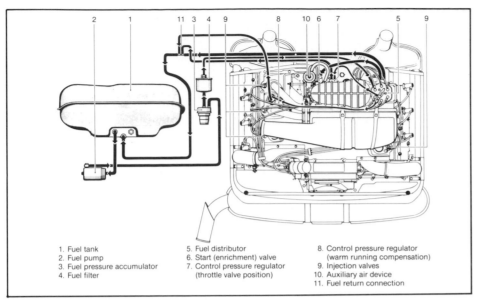

1. Fuel tank
2. Fuel pump
3. Fuel pressure accumulator
4. Fuel filter
5. Fuel distributor
6. Start (enrichment) valve
7. Control pressure regulator (throttle valve position)
8. Control pressure regulator (warm running compensation)
9. Injection valves
10. Auxiliary air device
11. Fuel return connection

Drawing of CIS injection system shows overall layout of the CIS fuel injection which was introduced on the 1973 US 911T.

mounted on the underside of the car and almost completely enclosed the engine compartment on the bottom. This was in addition to the special muffler that had already been installed for 1986.

There was also a new transmission for the Carrera for 1987, the G-50, replacing the 915 transmission that the 911s had used since 1972. A new development was the hydraulically operated, rubber-dampened clutch which was increased in size from the 225 mm that had been used with the 915 transmission to 240 mm. This was a new, larger version of the rubber-damper unit which provided enough dampening action to absorb the torsional oscillation of a slow-running engine without the rattling noise in the transmission. In order to take pressure off of the torsion damper's rubber package in high-torque applications, there were mechanical stops

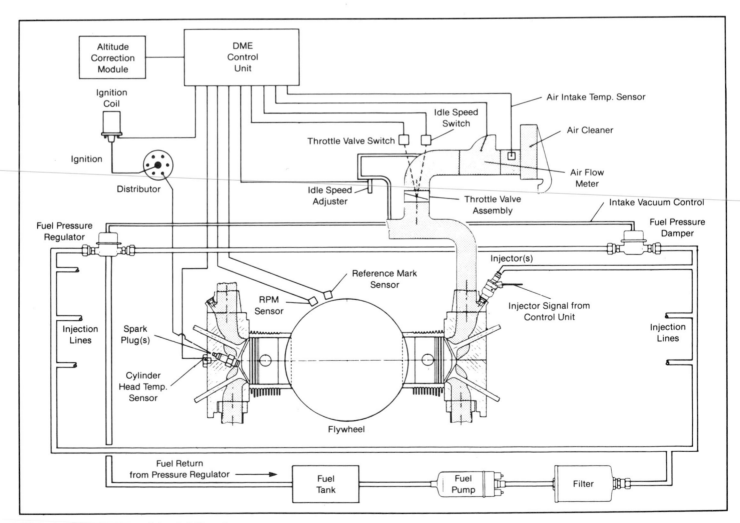

With the introduction of the 3.2 liter Carrera engine in 1984, the Bosch Digital Motor Electronics (DME) was introduced to the 911.

built-in that restricted the torsional angle from 44 to 47 deg.

Porsche continued to develop its racing engines for the 956/962C as well as its engine for the US IMSA version of the 962. The IMSA 962 engine was forced down in displacement from 3.2 to 3.0 liters for the 1987 season. And at the same time, Porsche increased the size of the WEC version up to 3.0 liters and added water cooling for the cylinders as well as the heads, which allowed Porsche to produce more power and increase the engine's reliability at the same time. Porsche ran a preliminary version of this engine in the German Super Cup in 1986. The reason IMSA forced Porsche to reduce the displacement of its IMSA 962 engine from 3.2 to 3.0 liters was to give its competitors a better chance to compete with the Porsches.

Type 901/20 Carrera Six engine right-side view (cyl 4-6). Note tachometer drive at rear of camshaft and oil-filter housing, which mounted where oil cooler was installed on production engines.

Racing oil-filter housing had a full-flow oil filter made up of metal disc in its pressure circuit, whereas the production cars had their full-flow oil filter in the scavenge circuit. This casting also incorporated an adjustable oil-pressure by-pass for setting the operating oil pressure. This same casting was used on all of Porsche's racing 911 engines from the 906 through the 956 and 962 engines.

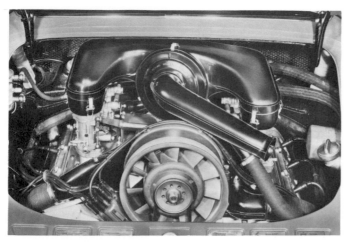

1967 911S 160 hp 2.0 liter engine. Werk-foto, Porsche AG

1967 911R engine. Specifications were the same as for the carbureted 906 engine.

1968 916, 2.0 liter four overhead cam engine installed in 911R. Sloniger, Porsche AG

Oil-filter unit used in racing 911 engines, disassembled for cleaning.

Mechanical tachometer drive and cam drive as used on early 901-derived racing engines before Porsche grew to trust the electronic tachometers.

1973 2.7 liter Carrera RS engine. The RS engine was the first of the 911 engines to use the then-new Nicasil cylinders which allowed a larger bore within the same cylinder-head stud spacing. Aside from the larger 90 mm bore, the 2.7 Carrera RS engines were very much like the 2.4 911S engines from 1972 and 1973, with 8.5:1 compression and mechanical fuel injection. James D. Newton

1974 3.0 IROC RSR engine with high-butterfly injection.

1974 3.0 RSR engine with slide-valve injection. Jeff Lateer

A 1976 934 engine for Group 4. Notice air-flow sensor for CIS injection system, and that this engine also used the flat-fan cooling system from the Carrera RSR Turbo. Werkfoto, Porsche AG

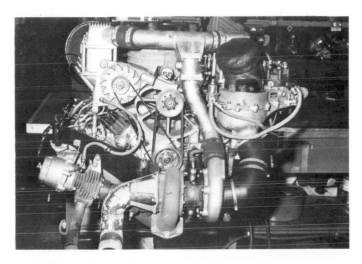

A 1976 factory 935 engine with water intercoolers, Type 930/72. This was the second version of this engine; the original used air-to-air intercooling. Werkfoto, Porsche AG

Early version of 3.0 911 Turbo engine.
Werkfoto, Porsche AG

1974 Carrera RSR Turbo 2.1 engine. This
was an early version of the Type 911/76
RSR Turbo engine that still used the 226
mm vertical cooling fan, which had been
the standard for racing 911 engines up until
this engine. Werkfoto, Porsche AG

1974 Carrera RSR Turbo 2.1 engine. This
version of the 911/76 engine had the horizontal cooling fan that was used on all of
the air-cooled turbocharged racing engines. The flat fan provided more even
cooling to the hotter-running turbocharged
engine. Werkfoto, Porsche AG

A 1976 936 engine Type 911/78. This engine was essentially the same as the 911/76 that had been used in the Carrera RSR Turbo 2.1, but with all of the accesso- ries turned around to facilitate the mid-engined application in the 936. Werkfoto, Porsche AG

Customer engine for 935/77, engine for Type 930/72, with bubble-type water intercooler. Werkfoto, Porsche AG

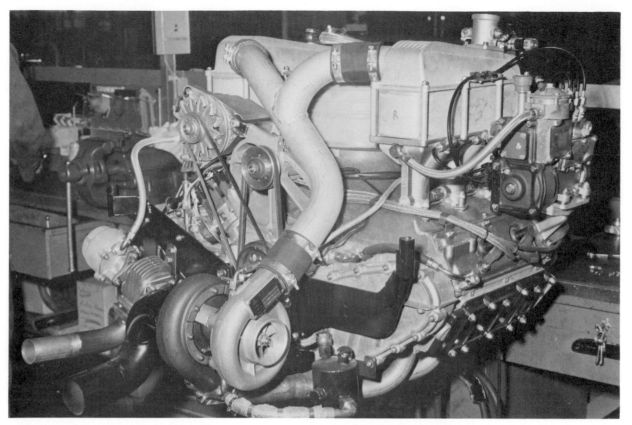

The 1977 IMSA version of the 934 engine Type 930/73. This was an interesting engine in that it retained the 934 intercooler system, but utilized the mechanical injection of the 935 engine. Note that it still used only single ignition. Werkfoto, Porsche AG

1978 Type 930/60 300 hp 3.3 911 Turbo engine for the 930. Werkfoto, Porsche AG

1978 Type 930/78 twin-turbo 935 engine with water intercooler. Werkfoto, Porsche AG

1978 Type 935/71 Moby Dick engine with water-cooled heads and four valves. Werkfoto, Porsche AG

1978 Type 935/71 Moby Dick engine with 226 mm vertical-mounted cooling fan. With the water-cooled heads the cooling job was reduced, and the old-standby fan proved adequate to cool the cylinders. Werkfoto, Porsche AG

1979 Type 930/79 "big" single-turbo 935 side view.

1980 Type 930/80 3.2 twin-turbo 935 engine with air-to-air intercooler.

1981 Type 930/81 3.2 twin-turbo 935 engine with air-to-air intercooler, Kugelfischer injection pump and upside-down transmission.

1981 Type 930/81 3.2 twin-turbo 935 engine with speeded-up fan drive for improved cooling.

Type 935/72 Indy engine in Interscope Indy car for testing in 1979. Werkfoto, Porsche AG

Type 935/76 956 engine. Werkfoto, Porsche
AG

Type 959 engine. Werkfoto, Porsche AG

Indy engine converted to gasoline as Type 935/76 in prototype 956 for Group C racing for the World Endurance Championship (WEC). Werkfoto, Porsche AG

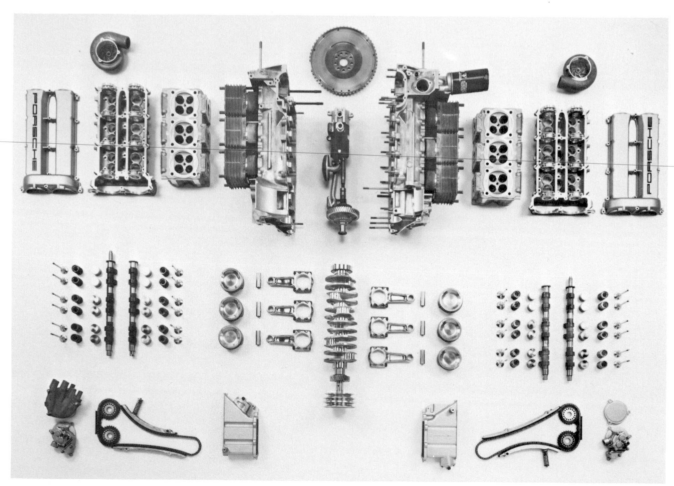

Type 959 engine components laid out. Note three-stage scavenge oil pump with the standard pickup in the center, an additional pickup up front under the chain sprocket and the third pickup back at the rear, near the pressure portion of the pump. Werkfoto, Porsche AG

The Porsche PFM 3200 aircraft engine.
Werkfoto, Porsche AG

Porsche added water jackets over the cylinders to the 962C engine, which already had water-cooled cylinder heads, and made it a water-cooled engine. The best of the private German and Swiss teams now have these all-water-cooled engines.

Engine type number summary

Type #	Year	Characteristics	Displacement (bore x stroke) in mm, cc	Valve size (intake, exhaust) in mm	Port size (intake, exhaust) in mm	Valve timing in degrees	Compression ratio	DIN in hp @ rpm	Peak torque in lb-ft @ rpm
901/01	65	911, Solex carbs	80x66, 1991	39, 35	32, 32	In opens 29 BTDC closes 39 ABDC Ex opens 39 BBDC closes 19 ATDC	9.0:1	130@6100	128@4200
901/02	67/68	911S, Weber carbs	80x66, 1991	42, 38	36, 35	In opens 38 BTDC closes 50 ABDC Ex opens 40 BBDC close 20 ATDC	9.8:1	160@6600	132@5200
901/03	68/69	911T, Euro version, Weber carbs	80x66, 1991	42, 38	32, 32	In opens 15 BTDC closes 29 ABDC Ex opens 41 BBDC closes 5 ATDC	8.6:1	110@5800	116@4200
901/05	66/67	911, Weber carbs	80x66, 1991	39, 35	32, 32	same as 901/01	9.0:1	130@6100	128@4200
901/06	67/68	911, revised cams & heat exchangers	80x66, 1991	39, 35	32, 32	In opens 20 BTDC closes 34 ABDC Ex opens 40 BBDC closes 6 ATDC	9.0:1	130@6100	128@4200
901/07	67/68	911, for Sportomatic same as 901/06							
901/08	67/68	911S, for Sportomatic same as 901/02							
901/09	69	911E, mechanical injection	80x66, 1991	42, 38	32, 32	In opens 20 BTDC closes 34 ABDC Ex opens 40 BBDC closes 6 ATDC	9.1:1	140@6500	129@4500
901/10	69	911S, mechanical injection	80x66, 1991	45, 39	36, 35	same as 901/02	9.9:1	170@6500	134@5500
901/11	69	911E, for Sportomatic same as 901/09							
901/13	68/69	911T, for Sportomatic same as 901/03							
901/14	68	911, US emissions same as 901/06							
901/16	69	911T, US emissions same as 901/03							
901/17	68	911, US emissions for Sportomatic same as 901/06							
901/19	69	911T, US emissions for Sportomatic same as 901/03							
901/20	65	906 racing, Weber 46 IDA carbs	80x66, 1991	45, 39	38, 38	In opens 104 BTDC closes 104 ABDC Ex opens 100 BBDC closes 80 ATDC	10.3:1	210@8000	152@6200
901/21	66/67	906E racing slide-valve, mechanical injection	80x66, 1991	45, 39	38, 38	same as 901/20	10.3:1	220@8000	152@6200
901/22	67/68	911R racing, Weber 46 IDA carbs	80x66, 1991	45, 39	38, 38	same as 901/20	10.3:1	220@8000	
901/23		911 racing, mechanical injection	80x66, 1991					210	
901/24		911 racing, mechanical injection	80x66, 1991					180	
901/25	70	914/6 racing, Weber 46 IDA carbs	80x66, 1991	45, 39	38, 38	same as 901/20	10.3:1	220@8000	152@6200
901/26	70	914/6 rally, Weber 40 IDS carbs	80x66, 1991	42, 38	32, 32	same as 901/02	9.9:1	180@6800	132@5200
901/30	67/68	911 rally, Weber 46 IDA carbs	80x66, 1991	39, 35	32, 32	same as 901/02	9.8:1	150	
901/36	70-72	914/6, Euro version	80x66, 1991	42, 38	32, 32	same as 901/03	8.6:1	110@5800	116@4200
901/37	70-72	914/6, for Sportomatic same as 901/36							
901/38	70-72	914/6, US emissions	80x66, 1991	42, 38	32, 32	same as 901/03	8.6:1	110@5800	116@4200
901/39	70-72	914/6, for Sportomatic same as a 901/38							
911/01	70/71	2.2 911E, mechanical injection	84x66, 2195	46, 40	32, 32	same as 901/09	9.1:1	155@6200	141@4500
911/02	70/71	2.2 911S, mechanical injection	84x66, 2195	46, 40	36, 35	same as 901/02	9.8:1	180@6500	147@5200
911/03	70/71	2.2 911T, Euro version Zenith 40 TIN carbs	84x66, 2195	46, 40	32, 32	same as 901/03	8.6:1	125@5800	130@4200
911/04	70/71	2.2 911E, for Sportomatic same as 911/01							
911/06	70/71	2.2 911T, for Sportomatic same as 911/03							
911/07	70/71	2.2 911T, US emissions same as 911/03							
911/08	70/71	2.2 911T, for US version for Sportomatic same as 911/03							
911/20	70	911 racing, fuel injection	85x66, 2247	46, 40	38, 38	same as 901/20	10.3:1	230@7800	170@6200
911/21	71/72	911 racing, fuel injection	87.5x66, 2380	46, 40	38, 38	same as 901/20	10.3:1	250@7800	188@6200
911/22	71	911 racing, Weber 46 IDA carbs	85x66, 2247	46, 40	38, 38	same as 901/20	10.3:1	230@7800	170@6200

Type #	Year	Characteristics	Displacement (bore x stroke) in mm, cc	Valve size (intake, exhaust) in mm	Port size (intake, exhaust) in mm	Valve timing in degrees	Compression ratio	DIN in hp @ rpm	Peak torque in lb-ft @ rpm
911/41	75	2.7 911, CIS injection	90x70.4, 2687	46, 40	32, 32	In opens 1 ATDC closes 35 ABDC Ex opens 20 BBDC closes 7 BTDC	8.0:1	150@5700	173@3800
911/42	75	2.7 911S, CIS injection	90x70.4, 2687	46, 40	35, 35	In opens 6 ATDC closes 50 ABDC Ex opens 24 BBDC closes 2 BTDC	8.5:1	175@5800	175@4000
911/43	75	2.7 911S, US (49-state emissions) same as 911/42 but with reduced power					8.5:1	165@5800	167@4000
911/44	75	2.7 911S, for California same as 911/42 but with reduced power					8.5:1	160@5800	162@4000
911/46	75	911, for Sportomatic same as 911/41							
911/47	75	911S, for Sportomatic same as 911/42							
911/48	75	2.7 911S, for Sportomatic for US (49-state emissions) same as 911/43							
911/49	75	2.7 911S, for Sportomatic for California specs same as 911/44							
911/51	72/73	2.4 911T, for US mechanical injection	84x70.4, 2341	46, 40	32, 32	In opens 16 BTDC closes 30 ABDC Ex opens 42 BBDC closes 4 BTDC	7.5:1	140@5600	148@4000
911/52	72/73	2.4 911E, mechanical injection	84x70.4, 2341	46, 40	32, 32	In opens 18 BTDC closes 36 ABDC Ex opens 38 BBDC closes 8 ATDC	8.0:1	165@6200	151@4500
911/53	72/73	2.4 911S, mechanical injection	84x70.4, 2341	46, 40	36, 36	same as 901/02	8.5:1	190@6500	158@4000
911/56	72	916, same as 911/53 with different exhaust and fittings for installation in 916							
911/57	72/73	2.4 911T, Euro version, Zenith 40 TIN carbs	84x70.4, 2341	46, 40	32, 32	same as 911/51	7.5:1	130@5600	144@4000
911/58		2.4 914/6, developed but never used	84x70.4, 2341	46, 40	32, 32	same as 911/51	7.5:1	130@5600	144@4000
911/61	72/73	2.4 911T, US, for Sportomatic same as 911/51							
911/62	72/73	2.4 911E, for Sportomatic same as 911/52							
911/63	72/73	2.4 911S, for Sportomatic same as 911/53							
911/67	72/73	2.4 911T, Euro for Sportomatic same as 911/57							
911/70	71	911 racing, mechanical injection	86.7x70.4, 2492	46, 40	41, 41	same as 901/20	10.3:1	270@8000	191.6@5300
911/72	72	911 2.8 RSR racing, mechanical injection	92x70.4, 2808	49, 41.5	43, 43	same as 901/20	10.3:1	308@8000	217@6200
911/73	72	911 racing, mechanical injection	89x66, 2466	46, 40	41, 41	same as 901/20	10.3:1	275@8000	
911/74	73	3.0 RSR racing, mechanical injection	95x70.4, 2994	49, 41.5	43, 43	same timing as 901/20, greater lift	10.3:1	315@8000	231@6500
911/75	74	3.0 RSR racing, slide-valve, mechanical injection	95x70.4, 2994	49, 41.5	43, 43	same as 911/74	10.3:1	330@8000	231@6500
911/76	74	2.1 Carrera RSR Turbo	83x66, 2143	47, 40.5	43, 43	In opens 80 BTDC closes 100 ABDC Ex opens 105 BBDC closes 75 ATDC	6.5:1 (@ 1.4 bar boost, 20 psi)	480@8000	340@5900
911/77	73/74	3.0 Carrera RS, mechanical injection	95x70.4, 2994	49, 41.5		same as 901/02	9.8:1	230@6200	203@5000
911/78	76/77	2.1 turbocharged 936	83x66, 2143	47, 40.5	43, 43	same as 911/76	6.5:1 (@1.4 bar boost, 20 psi)	540@8000	362@6000
911/79	77	935 Baby	71x60, 1425				6.5:1 (@1.4 bar boost, 20 psi)	370@8000	
911/81	76/77	2.7 911, R.o.W.	90x70.4, 2687	46, 40	35, 35	same as 911/42	8.5:1	165@5800	176@4000
911/82	76	2.7 911S, US 49-state, CIS fuel injection	90x70.4, 2687	46, 40	35, 35	same as 911/42	8.5:1	165@5800	176@4000
911/83	73/75	2.7 Carrera RS, mechanical injection	90x70.4, 2687	46, 40	36, 35	same as 901/02		210@6300	188.4@5100
911/84	76	2.7 911S, California	90x70.4, 2687	46, 40	35, 35	same as 911/42	8.5:1	165@5800	176@4000
911/85	77	2.7 911S, US 50-state engine	90x70.4, 2687	46, 40	35, 35	same as 911/42	8.5:1	165@5800	176@4000
911/86	76/77	2.7 911S, R.o.W. Sportomatic specs same as 911/81							
911/89	76	2.7 911S, California for Sportomatic same as 911/84							
911/90	77	2.7 911S, US for Sportomatic same as 911/85							
911/91	73	2.4 911T, US 50-state engine, CIS injection	84x70.4, 2341	46, 40	30, 33	In opens 0 at TDC closes 32 ABDC Ex opens 30 BBDC closes 10 BTDC	8.0:1	140@5700	148.5@4000

Type #	Year	Characteristics	Displacement (bore x stroke) in mm, cc	Valve size (intake, exhaust) in mm	Port size (intake, exhaust) in mm	Valve timing in degrees	Compression ratio	DIN in hp @ rpm	Peak torque in lb-ft @ rpm
911/92	74	2.7 911, US 50-state engine, CIS injection and R.o.W.	90x70.4, 2687	46, 40	32, 32	same as 911/41	8.0:1	150@5700	175@3800
911/93	74	2.7 911S and Carrera, US 50-state engine, CIS fuel injection. Same engine also used as 911S engine for Euro car.	90x70.4, 2687	46, 40	35, 35	same as 911/42	8.5:1	175@5800	187@4000
911/94	77	2.7 911S, Japan	90x70.4, 2687	46, 40	35, 35	same as 911/42	8.5:1	165@5800	176@4000
911/96	73	2.4 911T, US 50-state for Sportomatic same as 911/91							
911/97	74	2.7 911, US 50-state for Sportomatic same as 911/92							
911/98	74	2.7 911S and Carrera, US 50-state for Sportomatic specs same as 911/93							
911/99	77	2.7 911S, Japan for Sportomatic same as 911/94							
916	68	2.0 twin ovehead cam racing, mechanical injection	80x66, 1991	46, 40		In opens 104 BTDC closes 104 ABDC Ex opens 105 BBDC closes 57 ATDC	10.3:1	230@9000	152@6800
930/02	76/77	3.0 Carrera, CIS fuel injection for R.o.W.	95x70.4, 2994	49, 41.5	39, 35	In opens 1 BTDC closes 53 ABDC Ex opens 43 BBDC closes 3 ATDC	8.5:1	200@6000	188@4200
930/03	78/79	3.0 911SC, R.o.W.	95x70.4, 2994	49, 41.5	39, 35	In opens 7 BTDC closes 47 ABDC Ex opens 49 BBDC closes 3 BTDC	8.5:1	180@5500	189@4200
930/04	78/79	3.0 911SC, US 49-state	95x70.4, 2994	49, 41.5	39, 35	same as 930/02	8.5:1	180@5500	175@4200
930/05	78/79	3.0 911SC, Japan	95x70.4, 2994	49, 41.5	39, 35	same as 930/02	8.5:1	180@5500	175@4200
930/06	78/79	3.0 911SC, California	95x70.4, 2994	49, 41.5	39, 35	same as 930/02	8.5:1	180@5500	175@4200
930/07	80	3.0 911SC, US	95x70.4, 2994	49, 41.5	34, 35	same as 930/03	9.3:1	180@5500	175@4200
930/08	80	3.0 911SC, Japan	95x70.4, 2994	49, 41.5	34, 35	same as 930/03	9.3:1	180@5500	175@4200
930/09	80	3.0 911SC, R.o.W.	95x70.4, 2994	49, 41.5	34, 35	same as 930/03	8.6:1	188@5500	189@4200
930/10	81-83	3.0 911SC, R.o.W.	95x70.4, 2994	49, 41.5	34, 35	same as 930/02	9.8:1	204@5900	
930/12	76/77	3.0 Carrera, R.o.W. for Sportomatic same as 930/02							
930/13	78/79	3.0 911SC, R.o.W. for Sportomatic same as 930/03							
930/14	78	3.0 911SC, US for Sportomatic same as 930/04							
930/15	78/79	3.0 911SC, Japan for Sportomatic same as 930/05							
930/16	81-83	3.0 911SC, US	95x70.4, 2994	49, 41.5	34, 35	same as 930/03	9.3:1	180@5500	175@4200
930/17	81-83	3.0 911SC, Japan	95x70.4, 2994	49, 41.5	34, 35	same as 930/03	9.3:1	180@5500	175@4200
930/18	83	3.0 911SC RS, Kugelfischer mechanical injection	95x70.4, 2994	49, 41.5	43, 43	In opens 82 BTDC closes 82 ABDC Ex opens 78 BBDC closes 58 ATDC	10.3:1	255@7000	184@6500
930/19	80	3.0 911SC, R.o.W. for Sportomatic same as 930/09							
930/20	84-87	3.2 911 Carrera, Euro	95x74.4, 3164	49, 41.5	40, 38	In opens 4 BTDC closes 50 ABDC Ex opens 46 BBDC closes 0 TDC	10.3:1	231@5900	209@4800
930/21	84-86	3.2 911 Carrera, US	95x74.4, 3164	49, 41.5	40, 38	same as 930/20	9.5:1	207@5900	192@4800
930/25	87	3.2 911 Carrera, US	95x74.4, 3164	49, 41.5	40, 38	same as 930/20	9.5:1	217@5900	195@4800
930/50	75/76	3.0 Turbo, R.o.W.	95x70.4, 2994	49, 41.5	32, 36	In opens 3 ATDC closes 27 ABDC Ex opens 29 BBDC closes 3 BTDC	6.5:1	260@5900	253@4000
930/51	76	3.0 Turbo, US	95x70.4, 2994	49, 41.5	32, 36	same as 930/50	6.5:1	245@5500	253@4000
930/52	77	3.0 Turbo, R.o.W.	95x70.4, 2994	49, 41.5	32, 36	same as 930/50	6.5:1	260@5500	253@4000
930/53	77	3.0 Turbo, US	95x70.4, 2994	49, 41.5	32, 36	same as 930/50	6.5:1	245@5500	253@4000
930/54	77	3.0 Turbo, Japan	95x70.4, 2994	49, 41.5	32, 36	same as 930/50	6.5:1	245@5500	253@4000
930/60	78-82	3.3 Turbo, R.o.W.	97x74.4, 3299	49, 41.5	32, 34	same as 930/50	7.0:1	300@5500	304@4000
930/61	78/79	3.3 Turbo, US 49-state	97x74.4, 3299	49, 41.5	32, 34	same as 930/50	7.0:1	265@5500	291@4000
930/62	78/79	3.3 Turbo, Japan	97x74.4, 3299	49, 41.5	32, 34	same as 930/50	7.0:1	265@5500	291@4000
930/63	78/79	3.3 Turbo, California	97x74.4, 3299	49, 41.5	32, 34	same as 930/50	7.0:1	265@5500	291@4000
930/64	80	3.3 Turbo, US	97x74.4, 3299	49, 41.5	32, 34	same as 930/50	7.0:1	265@5500	291@4000
930/65	80-82	3.3 Turbo, Japan	97x74.4, 3299	49, 41.5	32, 34	same as 930/50	7.0:1	265@5500	291@4000
930/66	83-87	3.3 Turbo, R.o.W.	97x74.4, 3299	49, 41.5	32, 34	same as 930/50	7.0:1	300@5500	321@4000
930/68	8-87	3.3 Turbo, US	97x74.4, 3299	49, 41.5	32, 34	same as 930/50	7.0:1	282@5500	287@4000
930/71	76	3.0 934 Turbo, CIS fuel injection	95x70.4, 2994	49, 41.5	41, 41	In opens 54 BTDC closes 90 ABDC Ex opens 95 BBDC closes 49 ATDC	6.5:1 @ 1.35 bar boost	530@7000	434@5400
930/72	76/77	2.8 935 Turbo, factory 935 version	92.8x70.4, 2856	49, 41.5	41, 41	same as 911/76	6.5:1 @ 1.45 bar boost	590@7900	438@5400
930/72	77	3.0 935 Turbo, customer 935 verson	95x70.4, 2994	49, 41.5	41, 41	same as 911/76	6.5:1 @ 1.45 bar boost	630@8000	

Type #	Year	Characteristics	Displacement (bore x stroke) in mm, cc	Valve size (intake, exhaust) in mm	Port size (intake, exhaust) in mm	Valve timing in degrees	Compression ratio	DIN in hp @ rpm	Peak torque in lb-ft @ rpm
930/73	77	3.0 934/5 Turbo, mechanical injection	95x70.4, 2994	49, 41.5	41, 41	same as 911/76	6.5:1 @ 1.45 bar boost	590@7500	
930/76	77	3.0 935 Turbo	95x70.4, 2994	49, 41.5	41, 41	same as 911/76	6.5:1 @ 1.45 bar boost	630@7900	
930/77	77	2.8 935 Turbo	92.8x70.4, 2875	49, 41.5	41, 41	same as 911/76	6.5:1 @ 1.4 bar boost	590@7900	
930/78	78/79	3.0 935 Turbo	95x70.4, 2994	49, 41.5	41, 41	same as 911/76	6.5:1 @ 1.4 bar boost	720@7800	
930/79	79	3.12 935 IMSA	97x70.4, 2122	49, 41.5	41, 41	same as 911/76	6.5:1 @ 1.4 bar boost	715@7800	
930/80	80	3.2 935 Turbo	95x74.4, 3164	49, 41.5	41, 41	same as 911/76	7.2:1 @ 1.4 bar boost	740@7800	
930/81	81	3.2 935 Turbo	95x74.4, 3164	49, 41.5	43, 41	same as 911/76	7.2:1 @ 1.4 bar boost	760@7800	
935/71	78	3.2 935/78 Turbo	95.7x74.4, 3211	2x 35, 30.5	43, 41	same as 911/76	7.0:1 @ 1.4 bar boost	750@8200	
935/72	80	Indy Turbo, electronic injection	92.3x66, 2650	2x 35, 30.5	43, 41	same as 911/76	7.0:1 @ 1.03 bar boost	630@9000	
935/73	78/79	2.1 936 Turbo, mechanical injection	87x60, 2140	2x 35, 29	43, 41	same as 911/76	7.0:1 @ 1.4 bar boost	580@9000	
935/75	81	2.7 936 Turbo, mechanical injection	92.3x66, 2650	2x 35, 30.5	43, 41	same as 911/76	7.5:1 @ 1.3 bar boost	600@8200	
935/76	82	2.7 956 Turbo, mechanical injection	92.3x66, 2650	2x 35, 30.5	43, 41	same as 911/76	7.5:1	620@8200	
935/77	83	2.7 956 Turbo, D-Motronic injection	92.3x66, 2650	2x 35, 30.5	43, 41	same as 911/76	7.5:1	620@8200	
959/	86	959 Group B, D-Motronic injection	95x67, 2849	2x 35, 32	43, 41	same as 911/76	8.0:1	450@6500	369@5500
962/70	84	2.8 962	93x70.4, 2869	49, 41.5	43, 41	same as 911/76	7.5:1	650@7800	
962/71	85	3.2 962	95x74.4, 3164	49, 41.5	43, 41	same as 911/76	7.5:1	700@7800	

Engine-rebuild fundamentals

3

When a 911 engine has high mileage, it will require some form of major maintenance. And when it does, the decision will have to be made whether or not to perform a top-end overhaul or a complete overhaul. You may be wondering, just what is the *difference* between the two, and why should you do one instead

Valve failure caused by worn valve guides. The valve guide wore to the point where there was no longer adequate valve cooling, thus the valve failed.

of the other, or why should you do either? Those are good questions, because this is a very complicated decision with any engine. And although the 911 engine isn't just *any* engine, it is certainly no exception.

During the life of the 911 engine, it has gone from the extremely long life of the very reliable 2.0 liter engine to the much shorter life of the not-so-reliable 2.7 liter. Over the past decade, it has again returned to a long life with the extremely reliable 3.0 liter 911SC and 3.2 Carrera engines. Because of this wide range of durability, my advice will have to be quite different for the various versions of the 911 engine.

For the 2.0, 2.2 and 2.4 liter engines, for instance, my advice would be quite different than for the 2.7 911 engines. For the 2.4 and smaller engines, probably the best thing to do would be a top-end overhaul at 60,000 to 70,000 miles, when the exhaust guides wear out. Then after the top-end overhaul, drive the car for another 50,000 miles or so. Between 120,000 to 130,000 miles seems to be a

nice, safe life expectancy for these engines.

With the 2.7 liter engines, however, other complications enter into this decision equation that will make it a little more difficult to decide just what to do. The problem with this engine is that it had gotten just a little too big for its britches, and there are a few things that will not last an acceptable period of time.

Magnesium is a wonderful material in some applications, and in fact served us well for our 911 engine crankcases for a number of years when the engine was smaller in displacement, 2.0 to 2.4 liters. As the engine grew in size and the power was increased, however, the heat produced was also increased. While magnesium has a very good strength-to-weight ratio, strength alone is not one of its main attributes. The Nicasil and Alusil cylinders that were so advantageous to the future of the 911 when they were introduced for the 2.7, were also unfortunately among the things that taxed the strength margins of the magnesium crankcase.

The thermal expansion of the aluminum-alloy cylinders and the aluminum-alloy cylinder heads put a tremendous strain on the steel cylinder-head studs. Porsche solved this problem very quickly by changing the cylinder-head studs to a material called Dilavar, which

Valve failure caused by excessively worn valve guides. Notice the carbon trails up the valve stem of the failed valve, and several others from the set of six exhaust valves. Failure necessitated a complete overhaul of the engine and ruined one cylinder head and one piston and cylinder.

Cylinder-head damage caused by pulled head studs. Some of the magnesium crankcases used for 911 engines from 1968 through 1977 experienced the problem of pulled cylinder-head studs, particularly the 2.7 liter engines made from 1974 through 1977.

is a steel alloy with a thermal expansion rate like that of aluminum and magnesium alloys. Unfortunately, this change did not take place until 1977, when Porsche changed the lower row of head studs to studs made of Dilavar. On the 2.7 liter engines with steel cylinder-head studs, one or more of these cylinder-head studs normally would "pull." When the head studs pulled, they actually pulled the threads out of the magnesium crankcase.

Another problem that had become more acute with 2.7 engines because of their larger size and higher power output was the copper-alloy valve guides that Porsche continued to use until 1977, when they were finally changed to a silicon-bronze alloy. With the larger-displacement 2.7 liter engines, the exhaust-valve guides wore out at 30,000 to 60,000 miles because of the extra heat. The 911 engines with the thermal reactors were, of course, the engines that had worn out guides at 30,000, but it is not at all uncommon to see one of the Normal 2.7 911 engines with these copper-alloy guides worn out by the time the engine had 60,000 miles on it.

What is a top-end overhaul, then? Well, it actually means a lot of different things to a lot of different people. If someone is selling a car, it may mean any work that person may have had performed on the top end of the engine. For instance, it could mean the replacement of one burned exhaust valve to make the engine run on six cylinders again. But then again, it could be a *proper* top-end overhaul. I feel that a proper top-end overhaul is one that reconditions or certifies serviceable the pistons and cylinders, valves and as much of the valve-actuating mechanism as possible.

Some mechanics will recommend against top-end overhauls and instead recommend only a complete overhaul for an engine with top-end problems such as burned valves, low compression, high cylinder leakage, broken piston rings or pulled head studs. I do feel, however, that a top-end overhaul is a legitimate solution for some specific engine problems under most conditions.

I also feel that the bottom end of the 911 engine has a safe life of at least 100,000 to 120,000 miles. Sometimes it is necessary to perform a top-end overhaul to enable a given engine the opportunity to last until it has enough mileage to require a complete overhaul. Any 911 engine with less than 60,000 to 70,000 miles use with top-end problems is a per-fect candidate for a top-end overhaul. For engines exceeding this mileage, top-end overhauls may be of questionable value, since it is desirable to perform a complete overhaul on engines with 100,000 to 120,000 miles. If your engine has only a few miles to go before the complete overhaul, a top-end overhaul would be a waste of money. People planning to sell a car often have a top-end overhaul performed when the engine has this kind of mileage on it, so that it will

Cylinder damaged by pulled head studs.

Overall low compression and excessive oil consumption can be caused by broken compression rings. Re-ringing is the most probable cause for the top piston ring to be broken. Because the 911 is air-cooled, the top ring gets some excessive abuse from the added heat. If a piston is re-ringed when the top-ring groove has excessive clearance, the new ring with its better bite on the cylinder wall will beat up and down in the groove, making it even larger and finally breaking the ring.

Loss of compression can be caused by a burned valve. Burned valves will usually have a pie-shaped notch burned out of them. Generally speaking, the first indication of a burned valve will be rough running at idle and lower speeds that will smooth out as the engine speed is increased. In a 911 engine, a burned valve is most often caused by improper valve adjustment.

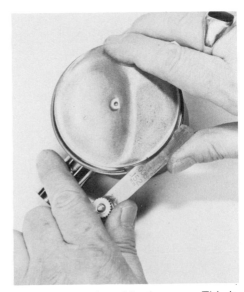

Checking top-ring side clearance. This is probably the most important piston measurement that can be made. Clearance should not exceed 0.004 in. If this top-ring side clearance in the piston is excessive, the rings will break prematurely.

run well at the time of sale. Buyer beware!

The most common problem you are likely to have with the 911 engine that would require a top-end overhaul is worn-out valve guides. This problem became more and more acute in the early to mid-1970s as the engines first became larger in displacement and then had to cope with all of the various emission-control devices.

The basic problem was the soft-copper valve-guide material. When the engines were still 2.0 liters in displacement they did not generate enough heat to cause excessive premature wear of these soft-copper valve guides, so it took quite a while to realize the extent of the problem.

As the engines became larger in displacement, the problem became more obvious. The 2.0 liter engines wore out their exhaust guides also, but usually not until the engines had at least 100,000 miles, so it was acceptable. When the engine size was increased to 2.2 and then 2.4 liters, the guides started to wear out at a lower mileage than was acceptable. And when the displacement was increased to 2.7 liters, it was not at all uncommon for the guides to wear out at 50,000 to 60,000 miles. And finally, when the thermal reactors were used to help these engines meet the emission laws in California in 1975 and 1976, and then for all US cars in 1977, it was not at all uncommon for the guides to be worn out at 30,000 miles.

Worn valve guides can be a larger problem than most people realize, par-

A connecting rod can be removed and the rod bearing inspected for wear and condition. I feel that a thorough inspection of all the top-end components should be performed anytime the top end of a 911 engine is disassembled. These bearings show some wear, but were holding up well.

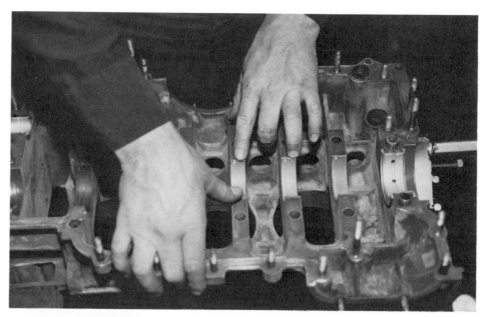

After the crankcase is cleaned and prepared, install the bearing inserts. Put a light coat of motor oil on each of the bearing surfaces.

These bearings show some major wear, and in fact the bearing on the right shows excessive wear and is "showing copper." If the engine was driven much further with bearings in this condition, it would have failed.

Assemble the connecting rods onto the crankshaft and lightly oil bearings with motor oil.

106

ticularly in the air-cooled 911 engines. All of the Porsche 911 engines have used sodium-cooled exhaust valves. Actually the sodium cools the valves only inasmuch as it helps to transfer heat from the valve head, down the valve stem to the valve guide, into the cylinder head, and thus to be carried away in the airstream that flows past the fins on the cylinder head.

For this heat transfer to work properly, the close proximity of the valve stem to the valve guide must be maintained so that the heat can be transferred through the oil film between them as the stem slides up and down in the guide. Wear in the guide creates an air gap that acts like the one in a vacuum bottle, causing the heat to remain in the valve stem just below the head of the valve. When the valves overheat, the metal is weakened and the valve head can and will break off of the valve stem, allowing the head to fall into the combustion chamber.

Unfortunately, there is not enough room in the combustion chamber for a loose valve head when the piston is at top dead center. I have seen several engines completely destroy themselves with this type of failure. I first became aware of how serious this problem was when I saw two engines in one month with exactly this problem. If the valve guides are ignored long enough they can wear as much as 2 mm oversize. I have seen valve guides so badly worn that there were black carbon trails all the way up the valve stem, and the valve spring and retainer were blackened with carbon, with carbon trails from the engine combustion.

Other engine malfunctions that can necessitate a top-end overhaul are low compression, excessive oil consumption, or in the case of some of the magnesium crankcases used for some of the 911 engines (1968-77), pulled cylinder-head studs. Compression loss or high cylinder leakage are usually caused by a burned valve, broken piston rings, damaged pistons or cylinders. High oil consumption is usually caused by worn, broken or sticking piston rings or worn cylinders.

Uneven cooling can cause the premature failure of one or two cylinders on an engine. I know of a 930 Turbo that required a top-end overhaul at an early mileage because rats had built a nest on top of one bank of cylinders causing them to overheat. The overheating cylinders distorted and the rings lost their spring tension causing both a loss of performance and excessive oil consump-

tion. This was a Porsche with very low mileage, and initially the mechanic working on the car had difficulty diagnosing the source of the problem. That was until he found the dead baby rats. The rodents had gained access to the underside of the cooling shroud through the heater exhaust under the car. The way the heater works is that a flapper valve diverts the hot air into the car to warm its passengers, or it exhausts the hot air under the car. So with the heater in the off position, the flapper valves provide

an open door to mice, rats or other rodents into your engine-cooling ducts.

Some mechanics advocate patching only the damage that necessitated the top-end overhaul. For example, if the problem is a burnt valve, they recommend replacing the burnt valve and reassembling the engine without inspecting the rest of the engine for any wear or damage. Once the top end of a 911 is torn down, it is very easy to make a thorough inspection of the condition of all the top-end components. One of the

Torque-rod bolts. Use a mixture of motor oil and moly lube to ensure an even, accurate torquing. Remember, the 911 rod bolts are malleable, which means they stretch, and may only be torqued once. The risk you will be running if you either reuse old bolts or for any reason re-torque your new bolts is the possibility of having them fail.

Install the oil pump and layshaft with chains in the crankcase half.

cylinders of an air-cooled engine can be removed and the condition of both the piston and cylinder evaluated for condition. A connecting rod can be removed and the rod bearing inspected for wear and condition.

I feel that a thorough inspection of all the top-end components should be performed anytime the top end of a 911 engine is disassembled. All of the components must be evaluated, considering the mileage on the engine and its use, by someone with the experience to judge the engine's condition in its proper context. To put this in perspective, remember I said I would expect the bottom end on the 911 engine to last 100,000 to 120,000 miles; however, a high-revving racing 911 engine running in IMSA races would be expected to last less than forty hours before requiring a complete overhaul.

There are other conditions that can cause the top-end life to vary, such as cars that are driven infrequently. When the engine sits idle, the moisture and acids will corrode the engine's internal components. The only way to avoid this corrosion is to drive the car frequently so the engine heat dries out the moisture. Frequent oil changes will also prolong the life of an engine that is not used as often as it should be. Regular operation also helps keep the rings free and will help avoid carbon build-up on the piston and combustion chamber. When an engine sits, the moisture will soften the carbon buildup and pieces of carbon can get caught between the valve and the valve seat, which can cause a burnt valve.

I have also seen an engine in which all of the carbon mysteriously fell off of the piston and combustion chamber into a pile at the bottom of the cylinder and head. The carbon was piled up so thick that the engine would not turn over, and acted as if something mechanical was preventing its turning over. This type of problem would not occur in a normal inline engine, but because the 911 is a flat-opposed engine, it could happen in the 911. The owner had the car towed into a repair shop because he could not get the engine to turn over and start. The mechanic working on the car assumed the engine had a broken valve that was preventing its turning over. The mechanic could turn the engine over backward until it would hit solid in the backward direction as well. He concluded that the problem must be mechanical and removed the cylinder heads only to find that the problem was only the carbon collection.

As with all Porsche maintenance work, the quality of the top-end overhaul work is vital. When you are looking at a used car that has had a top-end overhaul, ask to see the records and then check into the reputation of the Porsche repair shop that performed the maintenance work. Finally, call the repair shop that performed the work and ask to review the records. Complete records of the work performed should be available. When they are, you will feel more comfortable about your prospective purchase.

If you are considering having a top-end overhaul performed, make sure you have the work done by a Porsche repair shop that you feel you can trust. The top-end overhaul of a Porsche engine is not an inexpensive venture, so make sure you choose someone who has the experience and the judgment to do proper,

Install assembled crankshaft in crankcase half.

Use a small paint roller to apply the German Loctite 574 sealant to the other half of the crankcase. If instead you are going to be using the Dow-Corning RTV 730 fluorosilicone sealant, put a small bead all around the crankcase.

thorough and complete maintenance on your Porsche.

Many small Porsche repair shops perform excellent maintenance, but it is up to you to investigate and make sure the shop you select will do the quality of work that you expect and your Porsche 911 deserves. You may even want to do the work yourself. If you decide to, please be sure you take time to learn enough about your 911 engine to ensure that you can do the job properly.

If you determine that your engine actually needs a complete overhaul instead of just a top-end overhaul, you should be at least as careful in your selection of a repair shop as you would for the top-end overhaul. And again if you decide to do the work yourself, make sure you spend the time to learn what you are doing. You should purchase both the factory workshop manual and the Porsche technical specifications booklet for your specific model 911.

The factory workshop manual is far from perfect, but is vastly superior to any other manual you can buy. The manual, like the car, has evolved over the past twenty-three and some odd years and is now in the form of three separate manuals. The first manual (Porsche part number WKD 480 520) covers 1965 through 1971 and consists of two volumes. The second manual (Porsche part number WKD 481 021) consists of an additional four volumes and covers 1972 through 1983. This second manual was written as additional information to the first, and relies on basic information and the tutorial information from the first manual. With the introduction of the Carrera in 1984, Porsche came out with an additional four-volume manual (Porsche part number WKD 482 020) which was written to stand alone, and covers the 1984 and newer 911 Carreras. Some of the aftermarket workshop manuals may seem to be written in an easier-to-use style, however none of them are as complete or as accurate as the factory workshop manual.

Before you start your rebuild project, become thoroughly familiar with the organization and content of the engine section in the factory workshop manual. Read the section from beginning to end, supplements and all. Note any questions you may have as you read through your manuals and resolve them before you proceed with the actual work.

As a do-it-yourself engine builder, your biggest problem will probably be in coordinating everything so that your overhaul will happen in a timely fashion. First, you will need to get everything organized or your overhaul project can take forever. Make a list of all the work you are going to have to do, the work you will be sending out and a list of all parts you are going to need.

Start your engine rebuild by removing and disassembling the engine. The condition of many components can be judged while you are taking the engine apart, so be sure to check the condition of all parts as you take them off. It will save you time later. Check for broken or damaged fasteners and studs, and check the rocker-arm-shaft bores in the cam housing as you remove each shaft. Completely remove the bolts and taper cups from both ends of the rocker-arm shafts before attempting to remove rocker shafts. Applying pressure to the shafts

Using the factory straps to hold up the chain and a couple of the connecting rods, assemble the other half of the crankcase.

Install the crankcase through bolts. Remember, many of these through-bolt holes are main oil galleries for lubricating the engine's crankshaft, so it is important to seal up both ends.

with the taper cups in place will expand the ends of the rocker shafts, making them very difficult to remove and damaging the cam housing.

Also, you should only attempt to remove the rocker arms and shafts when the rocker is on the back, or heel, of the cam. Continue to rotate the engine as you are removing the rockers so that each one you remove is on the heel. If the cam-housing rocker-arm-shaft bores are damaged, your engine will leak oil when you put it back together. Nonetheless, if you do encounter an engine with damaged rocker-arm-shaft bores in the cam housing, all is not lost. Some special seals were made for the 911 racing engines that can be used and may solve the oil-leaking problem where the shafts are supposed to seal to the cam housing—if the housings aren't too badly damaged. (The part number of the seal is 911.009.103.52.)

Next, thoroughly clean all the engine components, and at this time, check and measure the components for wear and condition. Compare your measurements with those in the Porsche spec book. The cylinder heads and crankcase are best cleaned in an aluminum-only-type hot tank which will clean the grit, grime and varnish deposits of age from your crankcase and heads more effectively than almost any other method. You must be careful when using a hot tank, however, since there are special hot tanks made for use with magnesium and aluminum alloys. Normal hot tanks for use with cast-iron engine blocks will melt Porsche crankcases, so be careful.

The hot tanks will soften, but not remove the carbon from the cylinder heads. The best way to finish cleaning the heads is with a walnut-shell or glass-bead blaster. These blasters are great for cleaning the carbon from cylinder heads, but should not be used on the crankcase because they can contaminate the oil passages in the crankcase. I prefer using the walnut-shell blaster because it cleans the aluminum surface without altering its finish, whereas the glass-bead blasters will actually alter the metal's finish much like a sandblaster would.

Now that you have cleaned and measured your parts, you can make a list of work that needs to be performed and parts that need to be ordered. The following is a work-estimate sheet for a Porsche repair business that rebuilds Porsche engines on a regular basis. This worksheet should help you with a couple of things. First, if you want to, you can plug in your current local shop rates and crank out your own estimate. The labor rate used for the estimate is $50.00 per hour, and the sublets were priced at the going market rate at the time. Second, this worksheet will help you to organize all of the operations necessary for rebuilding a 911 engine, and will give you a list to work with of parts needed for a rebuild.

With a torque wrench, tighten the crankcase through bolts to the correct torque specifications.

All magnesium crankcases should have Time Serts installed the first time they are apart and Dilavar studs installed upon reassembly. To install the head studs properly, measure up from the crankcase cylinder-base surface 135 mm (5 5/16 in.) to the top of the studs. These studs should be installed with high-strength number 172 red Loctite.

Work needed	Estimated time required	Estimated cost
R&R and rebuild engine	40.0 hrs	$2,000.00

110

Magnaflux and polish crankshaft (sublet)		$48.00
Magnaflux and recondition rods (sublet)		$133.00
Regrind camshafts (sublet)		$250-350
Resurface and recondition rocker arms (sublet)		$230.00
Polish or replace rocker shafts	1.0 hrs	$50.00
Strip and powder paint sheet metal (sublet)		$300.00
Repair head studs	6.0 hrs	$300.00
Remove and replace head studs	2.25 hrs	$112.50
Install piston squirters on updates	5.8 hrs	$290.00
Modify oil by-pass on oil-pump updates	1.5 hrs	$75.00
Modify crankcase for layshaft bearings	2.6 hrs	$130.00
Install valve guides	2.5 hrs	$125.00
Grind valves	5.0 hrs	$250.00
Resurface cylinder heads	2.4 hrs	$120.00
Resurface flywheel	1.0 hrs	$50.00
Rebuild carburetors	6.0 hrs	$300.00
Remanufacture carburetor throttle bodies (sublet)		$350.00

To remove and install these cylinder-head studs, either use one of these special collet-type-style removing tools or one of the threaded collet-type Snap-On-style stud removers. These special stud-removal tools will prevent damaging the studs during removal of installation.

Install pistons onto connecting rods. Original pistons had a light press on the pin fit and pistons had to be heated slightly to facilitate installation. The modern-version pistons have a slight clearance so that the pins may be pressed in with a finger. It is a good idea to lay out all of the pistons, cylinders, wrist pins and pin clips before you start assembly to make sure they are all there and that there are no extras. I have had the occasion to get all of the pistons assembled only to find that there was an extra wrist-pin clip, which meant that I had to remove all of the cylinders just to make sure I hadn't left out a pin clip.

Lightly oil the piston rings and put a drop of oil on the piston skirt. Use your finger to spread that drop of oil around so that the same drop of oil is used to lubricate both the top and bottom piston skirts. I recommend aligning the rings so that the oil-ring gap is pointed straight up, and spacing the two compression rings so they are 120 deg apart. Use a quality ring compressor to ready piston for installation of cylinder.

Tap cylinder over compressed rings, being sure to keep the cylinder square to piston.

Rebuild injection pump (sublet)	$500.00
Remanufacture FI throttle bodies (sublet)	$350.00
Clean crankcase and oil passages	
R&R and clean cam squirters	
Pressure-test oil cooler	
Check oil thermostat	

Parts needed

motor oil
gas
paint
sealant
miscellaneous hardware
complete gasket set
  or
gasket set, upper
  and
gasket set, lower
miscellaneous gaskets
main bearings
#8 main bearing
rod bearings
layshaft bearings
layshaft thrust bearings
valve guides
intake valves
exhaust valves
valve springs
valve-spring retainers
valve-spring keepers
valve-spring shims
rocker arms
rocker-arm shafts
elephant's-feet valve adjusters
upper valve covers
lower valve covers
cam drive chains
black chain ramps (5)
brown chain ramps (1)
chain tensioners (early one not recommended)
chain tensioners (1980 style)
  or
left chain tensioner (1984 style)
  and
right chain tensioner (1984 style)

chain guards
left idler arm (1980 and later)
right idler arm (1980 and later)
left cam-housing oil line
right cam-housing oil line
scavenge oil line
supply oil line
left camshaft (cylinders 1-3)
right camshaft (cylinders 4-5)
layshaft, complete
layshaft sprockets, steel
layshaft gear, aluminum
pistons and cylinders
cylinder heads
Dilavar head studs
rod bolts
rod nuts
flywheel bolts

oil pump
oil cooler
oil thermostat
oil-pressure switch
oil-gauge sender
oil-pump/layshaft lock tabs
oil-return tubes
oil-relief piston
oil-pressure safety-valve piston
fan belt
air-conditioner belt
smog-pump belt
carburetors
carburetor rebuild kits
FI-pump belt
injection-pump pulley, upper
injection-pump pulley, lower
injection pre-heat hose, rubber

injection pre-heat hose, paper out
injection pre-heat hose, paper in
injector nozzles
alternator
alternator brushes
spark plugs
distributor
distributor cap
distributor rotor
points
condensor
ignition coil
spark-plug wires
spark-plug connectors
air filter
oil filter
smog-pump filter
fuel filter
CV gaskets
pressure plate
driven disc
throw-out bearing
pilot bearing
heater hoses, fresh-air
heater hoses, orange
any other forgotten parts

Cylinders installed on engine. Notice the cylinder holder screwed onto one stud for each cylinder. These are very handy to have since part of the process of installing all six pistons necessitates continually turning the engine over, which would cause the cylinders to go in and out with the pistons were it not for these cylinder holders.

Installing CE-style cylinder-head gaskets before installing cylinder heads.

Once you have made your list, you should plan to deal with the long-lead items first, so that everything will be ready when you are ready to reassemble your engine. Send the crankshaft and connecting rods out to someone you are sure you can trust to be magnaflux-inspected for cracks. If the crankshaft and connecting rods pass the crack test, you should have the crankshaft micropolished and the connecting rods reconditioned.

I am not fond of regrinding Porsche crankshafts. If your crankshaft is damaged and must be reground, I recommend that you either replace it, or do as the workshop manual recommends and send any crankshafts that require grinding back to the Porsche factory to have them reground and Tenifer-hardened properly. This process increases the fatigue strength of the crankshaft and improves the surface wear of the crankshaft journals.

If your crankshaft did pass the magnaflux test and you had the journal surfaces micropolished, you must now thoroughly clean the crankshaft to remove any trapped dirt and grit. I don't recommend removing the plugs in the crankshaft to do this cleaning. I have seen more damage done by the improper replacement of these crankshaft oil-passage plugs than I have seen caused by dirty crankshafts. I have, however, seen engines ruined within the first few hundred miles because they were put back together with dirt or polishing grit still in the crankshaft.

The best method of cleaning the oil passages is to use an aerosol can of carburetor cleaner with a long plastic nozzle. Thoroughly spray in each passage and then blow out with compressed air.

Remember that the drillings in the crankshaft start from each end (number one and number eight main journal) and work their way toward the center, providing oil drilling for each connecting-rod throw.

Reconditioning of the connecting rods consists of resizing the big-end

Preparing oil-return tubes by lubricating O-rings with either grease or silicone paste. Dow-Corning 111 compound works well here.

A proper valve job is a necessary part of any top-end or complete engine overhaul. The valves and guides should be measured and replaced as necessary, and then a three-angle valve job performed. The seat is ground at 45 deg, and 75 deg and 30 deg are used as the topping and throating angles to narrow the seats.

bores, installing new wrist-pin bushings, boring the wrist-pin bushing to re-establish the end-to-end length and honing the pin bushing to size. All of the dimensions are critical, so this operation must be performed by a competent automotive machine shop. Specifications are given in the workshop manual and spec books.

If any of the connecting rods require replacement, be sure to replace the damaged connecting rod with one from the correct weight group. Porsche recommends no deviation greater than nine grams among the rod weights in an engine.

For the 911, you can usually match the rods up fairly well into three pairs weightwise, and install the heaviest pair on cylinders three and six, across from each other at the rear of the engine. The next pair would go on cylinders two and five, and the final pair on cylinders one and four. If the whole set of rods was originally balanced within factory specs, this sub-balancing will give the engine a nearly perfect balance.

You will also have to send your cylinders heads out to have the valves reground. Be prepared to have new valve guides installed, particularly the exhaust guides, because the exhaust valves are sodium-cooled and conduct more heat into their guides so that the guides wear more. On high-mileage engines, the intake guides will also be worn and require replacement, but they will never be as worn as the exhaust guides. Be sure that the machine shop you have chosen knows how to install guides in 911 heads. The sizing is critical to a successful job. If the guides are improperly sized, they can fall out if too loose or crack the cylinder heads if too large.

Make sure the machine shop doing your heads measures the valve stems for minimum size and taper. I recommend not letting the taper exceed .0013 mm (.00005 in.) over the valve-stem length. The intake valves have softer stems and will often show more wear than the exhaust valves. If your valves are worn, replace them. Reusing them is like putting the engine back together with worn-out valve guides. You should also probably have your cylinder heads resurfaced so that they will seal to the cylinder properly.

You're not done with the heads and valve mechanism yet. If your camshafts show any signs of wear or pitting, you should either have them reground or replace them with new or serviceable used camshafts. Check your rocker arms. The bushings are usually worn out of tolerance in a high-mileage engine. If they are, you can have them reconditioned or replaced with new rocker arms. You should check the elephant's-feet adjusters for excessive wear and replace them also, if necessary. The valve-spring condition should also be checked with a spring tester to ensure that they are still within specifications. Again, replace if necessary.

Check all the chain sprockets and idler arms for wear. If excessive, replace the offending sprockets. Check the condition of the intermediate (lay) shaft aluminum gear. These gears as well as the chain sprockets are available as separate replacement parts for the later-version layshaft used since 1968. There are, however, no replacement aluminum gears for the early-style layshaft used in the original aluminum crankcase. Check the backlash of the aluminum gear on the intermediate shaft before you remove the crankshaft and intermediate shaft from the crankcase half while you are disassembling the engine. The chains should be replaced as a matter of course while the engine is apart.

Resurfacing of 911 cylinder heads creates special challenge because of the counterbore in the cylinder head to accept the mating cylinders. For this reason, the 911 cylinder heads cannot be machined by conventional means. It is essential that they be machined square to the cam- housing mounting surface, and that all six cylinder heads be machined the same amount so they will not put the camshaft in a bind. The best way to machine a set of these 911 cylinder heads is with a lathe, which requires a special mounting fixture.

Install cam housing onto cylinder heads.

Checking all of the valve springs before installing them. First, check the spring pressure at 30.5-31.0 mm (1.201-1.220 in.) which will simulate the spring in the valve-open condition. The pressure should be 80 kp (176.4 lb). Next, check the spring pressure at 42.0-42.5 mm (1.6535-1.6731 in.) which will simulate the seat pressure; the pressure should be 20 kp (44.09 lb). The 911 valve springs are very high quality and will usually last the life of the car. With the exception of some special applications, none of the aftermarket valve springs are nearly as good as the original equipment, so do not replace them unless absolutely necessary. There was apparently a bad batch of springs from late 1977 to mid-1978, because I have seen several cars built during that time with broken intake-valve springs. The way to check for this is when you are adjusting the valves, press on the intake rocker arms. If you can move the rocker arms by hand, you must have a broken valve spring. The springs can be replaced with the engine in the car by pressurizing the cylinder with compressed air and using the 906 valve, adjusting to compress the valve springs.

Next are the chain tensioners. No matter which tensioners your engine has, you should replace them. Either use the 1980 and later type with the updated idler arms or the new pressurized type used on the 1984 911 Carrera. The pressure-fed chain tensioner should last forever and be a maintenance-free component. The sealed-type chain tensioner (1968-1983) probably should be replaced every 40,000 miles as preventive maintenance, however.

If you are rebuilding a 911 engine with a magnesium crankcase (1968-77), you should remove the cylinder-head studs and install timed, threaded inserts. If you will be using either Nicasil or Alusil cylinders, you should also replace the steel cylinder-head studs with the later-style Dilavar head studs. This is particularly true for the 2.7 liter engines that

All of the cam-housing nuts are installed and tightened to their proper torque. There are 18 nuts retaining the cam housing to the three cylinder heads, six per head.

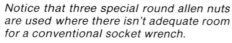

Notice that three special round allen nuts are used where there isn't adequate room for a conventional socket wrench.

When you clean the chain housing, it will usually disturb the epoxy used to seal the pins used to mount the chain ramp and tensioner in the chain housing. It is a good idea to clean them off and reapply a new coat of epoxy.

To time the cams it is necessary to measure the valve travel relative to the crankshaft's rotation. To keep track of the crankshaft rotation, we will use the crankshaft pulley with its markings at TDC and each 120 deg of rotation. Illustration shows the crankshaft pulley with the Z top dead center (TDC) mark lined up with the seam in the crankcase. The crankshaft has its throws at 120 deg intervals and the firing order is 1 - 6 - 2 - 4 - 3 - 5. In our example, the crank pulley is marked with 1 and 4 at Z1, and then at 120 deg 3 and 6, and again after another 120 deg 2 and 5. At TDC and each of these 120 deg marks, two of the engine's pistons will be at top dead center. Before the camshafts are installed and timed, it does not matter which TDC is number 1 and which is number 4, it is actually the cam timing that makes this determination.

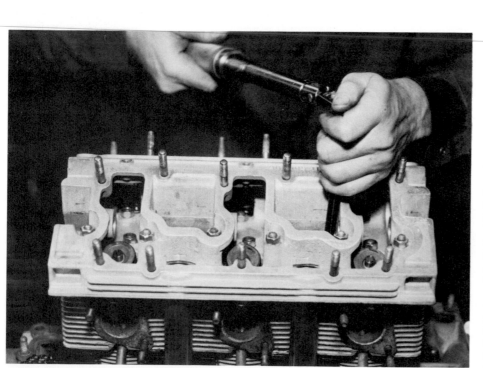

Install heads on cylinders and torque the 12 head nuts to their proper torque. The steel studs should be torqued to 25 lb-ft, and the Dilavar head studs to 29 lb-ft.

had their crankcases a little overstressed. The reason for doing this while the engine is apart, even though everything may look all right, is that once the studs have been disturbed by the process of rebuilding the engine, they will very likely pull soon after the rebuild. While on the subject of repairing potential problems, the 8x1.25 mm stud that holds the case halves together at the inner-layshaft bearing also has been known to pull and should have a timed insert installed while the case is apart. I know of no way to repair this stud if it has pulled *after* the engine is assembled, other than disassembling the crankcase again.

The main-bearing bores should be measured while you have the engine disassembled for the rebuild. If the crankcase bores are too tight, they should be reamed or honed to size. If the crankcase bores are too large, they should be reamed or line bored for the first oversize bearings. If the crankcase shows any other signs of damage, possibly the crankcase should be replaced. Nothing lasts forever. Check the crankcase mating surfaces for any nicks or damage. If any nicks are found, carefully dress them down with a file.

Clean all oil passages in the crankcase with solvent and compressed air. While you are blowing compressed air through the passages, make sure that the air passes freely through each and every passage. Note that the through-bolt holes are used as part of the main oil system, with the main bearings receiving their oil through drillings from these through-bolt holes. Be sure to remove both the oil-pressure relief valve and the oil-

pressure safety valve from the crankcase prior to cleaning the crankcase.

Examine both the pistons and their bores for any damage. If the pistons are damaged, replace them. Make sure the replacements are the same type as those you removed. If you mix up the types of by-pass pistons, you will create oil-pressure mysteries for yourself. Damaged bores can usually be repaired by polishing any score marks with fine crocus cloth. Inspect the oil pump. It should be replaced if any wear or damage is found. Before reassembly of the engine, check for worn or damaged parts—washers, spring washers, nuts, studs and so on—and replace if necessary. All elastic lock-type nuts, aluminum crush washers, and seals should be replaced. These aluminum crush washers are actually a silicon-magnesium alloy and not dead soft aluminum.

As with many of the parts you will purchase for your rebuild, you will have to make sure you get the real thing. There are a number of aftermarket parts available for you to use when you are doing your rebuild, and some of those parts are just not up to the job. This is one area where you can actually test the part yourself. Take a nut and a bolt and a couple of these crush washers and assemble them. Then take your torque wrench and torque the nut to 15 lb-ft.

Installing camshafts in their respective cam housings. It is important that you make sure you get the correct camshaft in the correct housing. The housings are identical, so either cam will fit in either housing.

Camshaft identification drawing. When you look at the cams from the nose, or nut end, the left cam has the first two lobes that you see spread out like a L, and the L stands for "left," so this is the left cam. The right camshaft when viewed from the front will have its lobes closer together so that it looks like a rabbit with its ears up in the air, and the first letter in "rabbit" is R and R stands for right, so this is the right cam.

Measuring the fixed offset to the front chain sprocket on the layshaft. Use Porsche's method for checking sprocket alignment by first measuring the position of the front chain sprocket, and then measuring from a straight edge the right-hand camshaft (cyl 4-6) drive sprocket. The cam drive sprocket should have the same reading as the chain sprocket on the layshaft. The maximum permissible difference is 0.25 mm. The shims for adjusting sprocket position are 0.20 mm thick.

The washers should hold their shape. If they don't and they squish out, you clearly did not get the right stuff.

In purchasing *all* your rebuild parts, you will have to be careful to get the real thing. Almost everyone will try to sell you aftermarket parts wherever they can because they make more money on them. Unfortunately, I don't have a nice simple test like the one for the crush washers for all parts. You will just have to use your own judgment. Be careful; most aftermarket parts are not as good as the real thing.

When reassembling your engine, be sure to use either the graphite-coated or the new green-style gaskets, and either Loctite 573 (European product) or Dow-Corning RTV 730 (US product) sealants. The sealant is only used on the crankcase halves and where the heads are sealed to the cam housing. All other joints are sealed by using the graphited or green-coated gaskets on a clean, dry surface with no sealant. The sealant can cause these treated gaskets to slip, causing leaks. There are some very good

aftermarket suppliers of these treated gaskets. This is one area where you *can* get the real thing in the aftermarket.

There are several O-ring-type seals used on the 911 engine in various applications. To help seal the O-rings used on the return tubes, the camshaft O-ring seals, the thermostat O-ring and the number eight main-bearing O-ring, lubricate the O-rings with a silicone paste or grease-type lubricant. Dow-Corning 111 compound works well here.

The advantage of the silicone paste or grease over petroleum grease here is that they will withstand very high temperatures and will not run off. The reason for lubricating these O-rings is so that they will reseal themselves anytime they have been disturbed by the thermal expansion of the engine. Do *not* use silicone sealer or any other sealant in this application, however. These O-rings, by design, must be free to move to do their job correctly.

For assembling the engine, an assembly lubricant should be made by mixing engine oil and molybdenum disulfide compound (not moly grease). Molybde-

num disulfide (moly) is a sulfide of molybdenum MoS_2. Pure molybdenum disulfide is a soft black solid with many interesting uses. The only use we are really interested in here is its ability to act as an effective lubricant under severe operating conditions. When used as a lubricant, moly can withstand extremely high temperatures and extremely high pressures. This is important because the camshaft and rocker arms will see their most severe wear when the engine is first started.

Proper lubrication during this first start-up procedure will go a long way toward extending the life of any engine. The assembly lube should be used on the camshafts and cam thrust plates. Use engine oil for the connecting-rod bearings, main bearings, pistons and cylinders. Lightly oil the rings and pistons with engine oil. If you make them too slippery, your rings will not seat.

Your mixture of assembly lube should also be used on the rod bolts and any other bolts or studs where the torque is critical. Exceptions would be the studs where elastic-stop-type lock nuts are used (which are best assembled dry or with a light coat of engine oil) and the flywheel bolts, where I would recommend using red Loctite.

When people are assembling 911 engines, they always worry about the cam timing. It's a shame they don't have the same concern for some of the other more subtle pitfalls of building 911 engines; there are several other things that must be done correctly as well. These are carefully explained in the workshop manual, but are often not correctly performed.

The cam timing is a fairly simple, straightforward procedure which is well described in the workshop manual. For most engines, you will need to refer to your Porsche spec books to determine the intake-valve lift at overlap TDC for your engine.

It is *doubly* important, however, to install the rocker arms and rocker-arm shafts properly because, in addition to carrying the rocker arms, the rocker shafts also seal-in the camshaft housing to prevent oil leakage. The rocker-arm shafts must be centered in the rocker arms to avoid damage to the rocker-arm bushings and camshaft housings, and to ensure proper sealing in the camshaft housing.

The rocker shafts are made so that they expand at the ends when the allen head bolt is tightened. One end has a

Measuring sprocket alignment for the chain sprocket on the left-hand side (cyl 1-3) is a little more difficult because you can't actually measure the position of the layshaft drive sprocket for that bank, and have to calculate its position using the offset provided in the spec book. After the offset has been checked and adjusted, rotate both cams until the punch mark's point stamped in the faces points straight up, which will provide an initial rough setting and establish which is the number 1 cylinder and which is the number 4 cylinder at TDC. Note some camshafts may not have the punch mark to indicate this rough setting. You can use the key way for the woodruff

key as an indication of which direction to point the camshafts; the key way should point up. Next find the hole in the camshaft sprocket that is in alignment with the hole in the camshaft sprocket mounting flange, and install the dowel pin through the aligned holes. Be sure that when you install the dowel pin, you face the threaded portion outward so that it can be removed again. There is a special tool available for pulling this pin out, but the threaded end of a spark plug will work just as well. Install the washers and nuts on each of the cams and tighten to the specified torque.

tapered, threaded cap and the other a tapered cap that the bolt fits through. When the allen head bolt is tightened, these tapered ends expand the ends of the rocker-arm shaft, sealing and retaining the rocker-arm shaft in the housing.

If the rocker shafts are off center, this wedging action will occur in the rocker-arm bushing and both loosen the rocker shafts and ruin the rocker-arm bushing. The rocker shafts should also be installed so that they can be removed at a later date in case it is necessary for maintenance. All of this is carefully explained in the workshop manual, but somehow is often overlooked.

It is also important to be able to tell the left cam from the right. Proper cam identification can be made by looking at the camshafts from the nose or drive end and examining the relationship of the first two lobes on each cam. There is a little gimmick for remembering which is which. The left cam has the front two lobes spread out and looks like an L, whereas the right cam has the lobes close together and looks like a pair of rabbit ears, and the first letter in "rabbit" is R, as is the first letter in "right."

Rocker-arm shaft. When installing the rocker-arm shafts, be sure they are centered in the rocker arms. There is a procedure in the workshop manual for installing these rocker shafts, but it may be easier, and just as accurate, to visualize where the shaft will be when it is installed relative to one end or the other of its bore in the cam housing. When torquing the shafts in the housing, it is essential that you make sure they are tight in the housing; otherwise they can work their way out. To make sure they are tight, use a torque wrench in the 5 mm bolt end and hold the 6 mm nut end just enough so it starts to tighten in the housing. Then torque the 5 mm bolt end up to the 15 lb-ft torque specified. If they tighten up in the housing without requiring the 6 mm end to be held before the 15 lb-ft torque is reached, they will probably be all right. However, if they turn in the housing, you may have a problem with the shafts working their way out of the housing.

This picture shows the mechanic setting the camshaft timing for cylinders 4 through 6. The cam nuts must be tightened up to their torque setting and the chain and chain-tensioner idler arms installed. You may want to use something other than the tensioners to hold the chains tight during the cam-timing process. The tensioner on the left side will get in your way while you are trying to tighten the cam nut. I recommend a mechanical tensioner for the right side and a C-clamp for the left side. The C-clamp is used to reach over the top of the chain housing so that the idler arm can be pulled tight against the chain. The mechanical tensioner can be used on the right side to tighten the chain. For the timing procedure you will want the chains a little tighter

than normal so that the resulting timing is accurate. Install the rocker arm for the number 1 intake valve and adjust the valve lash for 0.10 mm (0.004 in.). A dial indicator with feeler pin 40 mm long is needed to measure the valve travel in relationship to the rotation of the crankshaft. Using a wrench, rotate the engine 360 deg until you align Z1 with the seam in the crankcase again; this is TDC overlap. The dial indicator should indicate the inlet-valve lift specified for the camshaft you are timing. If the reading is not correct, readjust the cam and try again. After you have successfully adjusted the camshaft for the number 1 intake valve, you can install the rocker arm for the number 4 intake valve and repeat the procedure for that camshaft.

Completed long block with pressure-fed chain tensioners.

The reason it is so important to make sure you do install them correctly is that if you don't, you may not catch it as you go through the remainder of the cam timing and valve-adjustment procedure. But then when you get done, the engine will try to run backward.

Another common error is to install the cam chain sprockets incorrectly. This error would be caught if the whole procedure for setting up the chain sprockets were followed.

The camshaft sprockets are identical and are thus interchangeable. They are offset, and the left-hand sprocket is installed with the offset *toward* you. The right-hand sprocket is installed with the offset *away* from you. Then there is a procedure that measures the alignment of both sprockets, so that any misalignment can be adjusted out. If this procedure is followed, it is impossible to end up with the sprockets installed incorrectly.

While on the subject of chain sprockets, there is one other thing I have seen done that is equally inexcusable. I have seen an engine assembled with only one row of the duplex chain on the layshaft sprocket; the other half was flapping in the breeze.

The importance of the O-rings on the crankcase through-bolts is also often overlooked. Because the through-bolt holes in the crankcase are used as part of the main oil system, feeding oil from the main oil gallery to the main bearings, it is very important that the through-bolts are properly sealed. When you install the crankcase through-bolts, you must be sure that the O-rings and chamfer washer are installed on each end of the through-

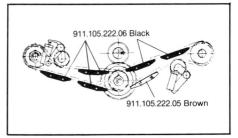

Chain-ramp identification and installation diagram. The 911 engines used five black (911.105.222.06) chain ramps and one brown (911.105.222.05) chain ramp. The brown ramp went in the lower right-hand side of the engine. Also notice that the long end of each of the ramps pointed toward the nearest sprocket. The four ramps that were actually mounted in the crankcase halves pointed toward the sprockets on the layshaft, while the remaining two ramps pointed toward the cam drive sprockets.

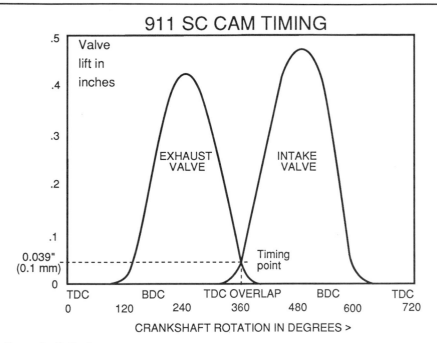

Camshaft timing

The 911 engine is a four-stroke engine. The timing of this cycle is described in degrees of crankshaft rotation. Each stroke takes 180 deg of crankshaft rotation, and a total of 720 deg for the four cycles to be completed. The camshafts are directly timed to the crankshaft in a 1:2 ratio so that the camshaft rotates at one-half the crankshaft speed.

The process of timing the camshafts is performed to synchronize the camshafts with the rotation of the crankshaft. This illustration shows both the exhaust-valve travel and the intake-valve travel for number 1 cylinder through two complete rotations of the crankshaft. Since the camshaft runs at half the crankshaft speed, it takes two complete revolutions to complete one full cycle. The exhaust-cam profile is shown just to give the complete picture of what happens with both of the valves opening and closing, but for the cam timing we are actually interested only in the intake profile. However, showing both the intake and exhaust profile does clearly illustrate why this point is called TDC overlap. It is where the exhaust valve is still open and the intake valve has already started to open. When the crankshaft is rotated 360 deg from 0 deg TDC to TDC overlap, you reach a point where the camshaft is just starting to lift the intake valve. I have called this point the "Timing point." At this Timing point the valve lift should be what is specified as the "Intake-valve lift at Overlap TDC with 0.1 mm (0.004 in.) valve clearance" for the camshafts being used. If you are using any of the factory camshafts, this checking value will be given in the technical specification booklets. And if you are using a special camshaft grind, the manufacturer of the

cam should be able to provide the lift specifications.

If the reading is too high, the camshaft is advanced, and if it is too low, the camshaft is retarded. If you advance the cams you will improve the bottom-end performance, and if you retard the cams you will improve the top-end performance. There is usually a range given for this check. For example, for the 911SC engine in this illustration, the range is 0.9 to 1.1 mm (0.035 to 0.043 in.). This timing specification is only one of three timings that have been used for these camshafts since they were first introduced as the 3.0 Carrera cams in 1976.

Originally these cams were set for 0.9 to 1.1 mm (0.035 to 0.043 in.) for the 1976 and 1977 3.0 liter Carrera. When the 911SC was introduced in 1978, Porsche advanced the camshaft timing six degrees for the R.O.W. version. Checking clearance increased to 1.4 to 1.7 mm (0.055 to 0.067 in.). The camshaft timing for the 1978 US version of the 911SC remained the same as it had been for the 1976/77 R.o.W. 3.0 Carrera. The cam timing, however, for the 1980 US version of the 911SC was advanced to the same timing that had been used for the R.o.W. version since 1978. In 1981 the R.o.W. 911SC had its timing retarded to what had been the original cam timing for the 1976/77 3.0 Carrera. The cam timing was changed again when the 3.2 Carrera engine was introduced in 1984, when Porsche split the difference and set the timing halfway in between the two settings that it had used before; three degrees more advanced than the original 1976/77 3.0 Carrera, with a checking height of 1.1 to 1.4 mm (0.046 to 0.055 in.).

bolts to ensure sealing. The later-model 911s with their larger cylinders also have an external chamfer on these washers to provide clearance for the larger cylinders. The O-rings should be lubricated with assembly lube or silicone compound to ensure that they seat properly and seal each end of the through-bolts.

The rod bolts are another often-overlooked potential problem. The rod bolts used in the 911 engines are malleable and must be replaced whenever the engine is disassembled. What malleable means, in this instance, is that the stretch bolts take a stretch when they are torqued, and if they are reused, they will not torque properly. Be sure that when you send your rods out for reconditioning, you send them out with the old bolts. In the course of reconditioning the rods, the machine shop will torque your rod bolts, which would ruin your new rod bolts.

When you are installing the connecting rod, lubricate the threads of the rod bolts with a mixture of oil and moly lube. This ensures that when you torque the rod bolts, you will get a proper torque value.

I recommend having the rod bolts and nuts magnafluxed to check them for cracks. This is a worthwhile procedure since, over the years I have found a few of them with flaws. Rod bolts are another area in which to be wary of aftermarket parts suppliers. There are some aftermarket rod bolts in circulation that do not have the correct locating diameter. Beware!

There are a few other things that I have seen the inexperienced 911-engine builder inflict on the 911 engine. Pistons installed upside down, for example, so that the intake valve lines up with the exhaust-valve pocket in the piston. The result was that the intake valves hit and cracked the pistons and bent the valves. I have also seen the cylinders installed upside down, so that the longer cooling fins were up rather than down. This caused unequal cooling and resulted in the pistons seizing in the cylinders. I've even seen the air-deflector plates installed upside down so that, rather than channeling the air under the cylinders for even cooling, they deflected the air away from the cylinders, again causing the engines to overheat and ruin the pistons and cylinders.

Be sure that you lubricate the pilot bearing before installing the engine to the transmission. They will fail if not properly lubricated. Use a moly grease; a good one is SWEPCO 101. When a pilot bearing fails, the symptom is that the clutch will not release. What is actually happening is that the remains of the pilot bearing are grinding away on the end of the transmission mainshaft, trying to friction-weld the mainshaft to the crankshaft.

The following are recommended torque settings.

Component	lb-ft
crankcase, 8 mm	18
connecting-rod bolts	37–40.5
nuts for through bolts and studs, 10 mm	25
oil-screen-cover nuts	7
cylinder-head nuts, steel	25
cylinder-head nuts, Dilavar	29
rocker-shaft hold-down bolts	13
nut for fan and pulley	29
flywheel retaining bolts, six	110
flywheel retaining bolts, nine	66
1980-and-later pilot bearing	7
nut for camshaft drive sprocket	110
bolt for camshaft drive sprocket	88
covers for camshaft housing	6
crankshaft pulley	59
crankshaft pulley, double-belt AC	125
pressure-relief and by-pass piston plugs	44
oil-drain plugs	31
air injectors in cylinder heads	11
exhaust-to-cylinder head	15–17
spark plugs	18–21

Recommended tools

open-end wrench, 6 mm, 8 mm, 9 mm, 10 mm, 11 mm, 12 mm, 13 mm, 14 mm, 15 mm, 17 mm, 19 mm, 22 mm
socket wrench, 8 mm, 10 mm, 13 mm, 14 mm, 15 mm
needle-nose pliers, 90 deg, piston circlips
screwdrivers
allen wrench, 5 mm, rocker shafts
allen wrench, 6 mm, rocker shafts
allen wrench, long, 8 mm, exhaust allen nuts
allen wrench, long, 10 mm, allen head nuts
allen wrench, short, 12 mm, 12-point star wrench, flywheel
plastic hammer
steel hammer
depth gauge, minimum length 150 mm (3 in.)
vernier calipers
straightedge, minimum length 50 cm (20 in.)
⅜ drive ratchet
⅜ drive extension
⅛ drive universal socket, 12 mm
⅛ drive universal socket, 13 mm
⅛ drive universal socket, 14 mm
dowel-pin remover for cam sprocket (spark plug)
engine stand
P202 camshaft-holding wrench
P203 camshaft-nut wrench
P207 dial-gauge holder
P221 connecting-rod props
P222 timing-chain props
engine TDC indicator
dial gauge and 40 mm extension
V-belt pulley holder
torque wrench
feeler gauge 0.004 in., valve clearance
chain-tensioner holder, holds tensioner collapsed
solid tensioner, holds chain tight while adjusting right camshaft (cyl 4-6)
C-clamp, holds chain tight while adjusting left camshaft (cyl 1-3)
exhaust-manifold wrench
pliers, piston ring expanding
piston-ring compressor
valve-spring tester
valve-spring gauge, for measuring installed length
piston-pin drift, for installing piston pins
liquid graduate glass, measuring cubic centimeters; combustion chamber and piston dome
flywheel-bolt wrench
clutch-centering tool

Engine builder's checklist

1. Disassemble and check the following.
   - condition of clutch assembly and flywheel; recondition or replace as necessary
   - condition of induction system
   - condition of valve covers; early bottom covers probably should be updated
   - condition of cam chain housing, idler arms and gears; update idler arms to 1980 style
   - condition of rocker arms, rocker-arm shafts and adjusters
   - condition of camshaft for wear
   - condition of camshaft-housing cam bores and rocker-shaft bores for wear, burrs and scoring
   - condition of cylinder heads for breakage or damage
   - condition of pistons and cylinders
   - condition of crankshaft
   - condition of connecting rods
   - condition of oil pump
   - condition of intermediate shaft

- intermediate-shaft backlash in crankcase
- condition of crankcase
- condition of crankcase oil by-pass and pressure-relief pistons and crankcase bores
- each piston-cooling spray valve with compressed air and solvent

2. Clean all engine parts.
3. Magnaflux or Zyglo the following.
   - crankshaft
   - connecting rods
   - new connecting-rod bolts and nuts
   - pistons
   - piston pins
   - camshafts
   - rocker arms
4. Measure crankcase line bore.
   - 2.0-2.7 liter: 62.000-62.019 mm (2.4409-2.4416 in.)
   - 3.0-3.3 liter: 65.000-65.019 mm (2.5590-2.5598 in.)
   - bearing # 8_____ 7_____ 6_____ 5_____ 4_____ 3_____ 2_____ 1_____
5. Measure crankshaft main–bearing journals.
   - 2.0-2.7 liter: 56.971-56.990 mm (2.2429-2.2437 in.). Wear limit 56.960 mm (2.2425 in.)
   - 3.0-3.3 liter: 59.971-59.990 mm (2.3610-2.3618 in.). Wear limit 59.960 mm (2.3606 in.)
   - journal # 8_____ 7_____ 6_____ 5_____ 4_____ 3_____ 2_____ 1_____
6. Measure crankshaft rod-bearing journals.
   - 2.0-2.2 liter: 56.971-56.990 mm (2.2429-2.2437 in.). Wear limit 56.960 mm (2.2425 in.)
   - 2.4-2.7 liter: 51.971-51.990 mm (2.0461-2.0468 in.). Wear limit 51.960 mm (2.0456 in.)
   - 3.0 liter: 52.971-52.990 mm (2.0854-2.0862 in.). Wear limit 52.960 mm (2.08504 in.)
   - 3.2-3.3 liter: 54.971-54.990 mm (2.1642-2.1649 in.). Wear limit 54.960 mm (2.1637 in.)
   - journal # 6_____ 5_____ 4_____ 3_____ 2_____ 1_____
7. Measure connecting-rod big-end diameters.
   - 2.0-2.2 liter: 61.000-61.019 mm (2.4015-2.4023 in.)
   - 2.4-3.0 liter: 56.000-56.019 mm (2.2047-2.2054 in.)
   - 3.2-3.3 liter: 58.000-58.019 mm (2.2834-2.842 in.)
   - rod # 6_____ 5_____ 4_____ 3_____ 2_____ 1_____
8. measure connecting-rod small-end diameters.
   - 2.0-3.0 liter: 22.020-22.033 mm (.8669-.8974 in.). Wear limit 0.055 mm (0.002 in.)
   - 3.2-3.3 liter: 23.020-23.033 mm (.9063-.9068 in.). Wear limit 0.055 mm (0.002 in.)
   - rod # 6_____ 5_____ 4_____ 3_____ 2_____ 1_____
9. Measure intermediate-shaft backlash with dial indicator.
   - intermediate-shaft backlash: 0.016-0.049 mm (0.0006-0.0019 in.)
10. Measure valve guide.
    - intake and exhaust guide inside diameter: 9.000-9.015 mm (.3543-.3549 in.). Check by using pilot as go, no-go gauge
    - #1I_____ E_____ 2I_____ E_____ 3I_____ E_____ 4I_____ E_____ 5I_____ E_____ 6I_____ E_____
11. Measure valve-stem diameters.
    - intake-valve stem: 8.97-0.012 mm (0.3531-0.0005 in.)
    - exhaust-valve stem: 8.95-0.012 mm (0.3523-0.0005 in.)
    - valve-stem taper and out of roundness: 0.01 mm (0.00039 in.)
    - #1I_____ E_____ 2I_____ E_____ 3I_____ E_____ 4I_____ E_____ 5I_____ E_____ 6I_____ E_____
12. Measure valve springs.
    - spring pressure at 30.5-31.0 mm = 80 kp (1.201-1.220 in. = 176.4 lb)
    - spring pressure at 42.0-42.5 mm = 20 kp (1.6535-1.6731 in. = 44.09 lb)
    - #1I_____ E_____ 2I_____ E_____ 3I_____ E_____ 4I_____ E_____ 5I_____ E_____ 6I_____ E_____
13. Compression ratio calculation.
    - swept volume, 1 cyl = V1
    - deck-height volume = V2
    - cylinder-head volume = V3
    - piston-dome volume = V4
    - V1+V2+V3–V4÷V2+V3–V4 = compression ratio
14. Remove and reinstall injection tube (spray bar) from cam housing.
    - Remove plug, loosen centering screws and slide injection tube out.
    - Install injection tube; make sure bores are located correctly. Separate bores must face upward toward intake-valve covers, double bores face cam-lobe's surface.
    - Install new plug with epoxy about 0.3 mm (0.012 in.) deeper than sealing surface.
15. Measure pistons and cylinders.
    - Measure vertical clearance of rings in ring grooves with a feeler gauge. Experience indicates that the top ring-groove clearance is the most critical and that excessive clearance will cause the compression rings to prematurely break.
      Compression rings, numbers I and II: wear limit 0.115 mm (0.0045 in.)
    - Oil-control ring, number III: wear limit 0.1 mm (0.0039 in.)
    - Top compression-ring groove cyl #1_____ 2_____ 4_____ 5_____ 6_____
    - Second compression-ring groove cyl #1_____ 2_____ 4_____ 5_____ 6_____
    - Bottom oil-ring groove cyl #1_____ 2_____ 4_____ 5_____ 6_____
    - If ring grooves are not excessively worn, make other piston and cylinder measurements as specified for each different type of engine (see spec book).
    - Piston diameter piston # 1_____ 2_____ 4_____ 5_____ 6_____
    - Cylinder diameter cyl # 1_____ 2_____ 4_____ 5_____ 6_____
    - Clearance between piston and cylinder set # 1_____ 2_____ 4_____ 5_____ 6_____
16. Piston-ring end gap.
    - Compression ring I: 0.1-0.2 mm (0.0039-0.0078 in.). Wear limit 0.8 mm (0.0314 in.)
    - Compression ring II: 0.1-0.2 mm (0.0039-0.0078 in.). Wear limit 0.8 mm (0.0314 in.)
    - Oil-control ring III: 0.15-0.3 mm (0.0059-0.0118 in.). Wear limit 1.0 mm (0.0393 in.)
17. Assemble crankshaft.
    - Install gears on crankshaft.
    - Install connecting rods on crankshaft.
18. Assemble crankcase.
    - Mount right side (cyl 4-6) of crankcase on engine stand.
    - Place oil-seal-ring groove in oil-suction passage in right side of crankcase.
    - Install oil pump and intermediate shaft in right side of crankcase; fasten oil pump and bend lock tabs into place.
    - Install crankshaft in crankcase.
    - Install connecting-rod and chain props.
    - Install seal rings between oil pump and left crankcase half, and seal ring connecting the oil passage between the left and right crankcase halves.
    - Coat outer perimeter of crankcase with sealing compound.
    - Place flywheel seal into right side of crankcase flush with outer end.

- Install left side of crankcase onto the right.
- Pre-assemble through bolts. First, place the double-chamfer washer onto the bolt, and then slide the O-ring in place. Install the through bolts and slide O-rings and chamfer washers onto the nut end of the through bolts and hand tighten the cap nuts. These O-rings are very important, since many of the through-bolt holes are used as oil passages.
- In addition to the eleven through bolts, there are three additional 10 mm studs that serve the same function. The two under the oil cooler receive the same treatment as the O-ring and cap nut. The third is inside the chain housing on the left-hand side of the crankcase.
- Torque the through bolts to 25 lb-ft, preceding evenly in a crosswise order.
- Place 8 mm magnesium crush washers onto all of the crankcase retaining studs and bolts. Install nuts and torque to 18 lb-ft.
19. Install pistons and cylinders.
20. Install air deflectors. (If air deflectors are early-style, update.)
21. Install cylinder heads.
22. Coat camshaft housing with sealing compound.
23. Install oil-return tubes.
24. Install camshaft housings.
25. Torque camshaft-housing nuts progressively in a crosswise order to 18 lb-ft.
26. Install camshafts in camshaft housings.
27. Torque cylinder heads to 24 lb-ft. Keep checking the camshafts for binding during the tightening procedure.
28. Install chains, sprockets and idlers.
29. Measure parallel of the chain drive sprockets with straightedge.
    - Intermediate-shaft measurement (drive sprocket for chain to cyl 4-6): Using a straightedge and a depth gauge, measure the distance from straightedge to front intermediate-shaft sprocket face (equals A). Measure A and record.
    - Measure the distance from straightedge to camshaft sprocket for cylinders 4-6. Measure and record. This distance should also be equal to A. Note: Maximum permissible deviation = $\pm$ 0.25 mm (0.0098 in.).
    - Measure the distance from straightedge to camshaft sprocket for cylinders 1-4. Measure and record. Note: There is a fixed offset from the front intermediate-shaft gear (cyl 4-6) to the rear intermediate-shaft gear (cyl 1-3) of 54.8 mm (2.1575 in.). The resulting measurement should equal A + 54.8 mm (2.1575 in.). Note: Maximum permissible deviation = $\pm$ 0.25 mm (0.0098 in.).
30. Install distributor, point rotor at 45 deg angle toward air inlet to blower housing with cylinder 1 at TDC (Top Dead Center).
31. Install rocker arm for #1 intake valve.
32. Adjust camshaft timing for cylinders 1-3. (See spec books for timing data.)
    - #1 intake at overlap TDC.
33. Install rocker arm for #4 intake valve.
34. Adjust camshaft timing for cylinders 4-6.
    - #4 intake at Overlap TDC.
35. Install remainder of rocker arms and adjust valves.
36. Install chain housing and valve covers.
37. Install alternator, blower and engine sheet metal.
38. Install induction system, induction system type.
39. Install exhaust system, exhaust system type.
40. Run-in engine.

Engine performance modifications

4

Modifying Porsches in general and 911s in particular is quite a bit different than modifying other makes of automobiles. You probably bought your Porsche because you thought it was the best car you could buy for your money. Porsche has selected the best quality components for most applications, which makes it very difficult to improve on what the company has done.

As an example, you will often see the term "blue-printing" used to describe the process of modifying a stock engine for stock use in racing, such as showroom stock racing. The term blue-printing was coined for engines that did not resemble the original engineer's design for the engine. So when Porsche said it was blue-printing an engine, it meant that it was remaking the engine like the designer had originally drawn it in the blue-prints and not as it was built in manufacturing.

We have been cheated out of this fun by Porsche. The tolerances and quality control are such that only minimal improvements may be made using any of these so-called blue-printing techniques.

You will have to be very careful when you modify or change any of the components that Porsche has used in one of its engines. Make sure that before you change anything, you are certain that you will get the results you want when you are finished. Don't forget that almost all of the alternative components are of lesser quality than the original Porsche components. If you are not very careful with your modifications, you can actually be doing your Porsche more harm than good.

The best way to improve the performance of most of the various 911 engines is by increasing their displacement: The 2.0 liter engines can be increased to 2.2 liters, the 2.4 liter engines to 2.7 liters, the 3.0 liter engines to 3.2 liters and the 3.2 liter engines to 3.4 or 3.5 liters. If you are careful and use the correct components, you can increase the performance of most 911 engines without sacrificing the reliability. And with some of the engines, you can actually take advantage of the fact that they are apart to improve their reliability.

2.0 liter 911 modifications

Any of the 2.0 liter 911 engines can quite easily be converted to 2.2 liter 911 engines during a routine overhaul. It doesn't really matter if you have one of the early sand-cast aluminum crankcase engines or one of the later 2.0 liters with a magnesium crankcase.

When you need the engine rebuilt, it can be very easily increased in size to 2.2 liters by changing the pistons and cylinders to the 94 mm size used on the 2.2 engines of 1970 and 1971. The heads will require machining to accept the larger bore and the different style head gasket used on the 2.2 liter cylinders. You can use the pistons from the 2.2 liter 911 T, E or S. You will not have a problem with too much compression with these conversions because the combustion chamber was slightly larger for the two-liter engines so the effective compression ratio will actually be reduced by about four-tenths of a point compression.

If you have a 1969 911 E or S that you are converting to a 2.2 liter, you will have a little more of a problem with the conversion because of the mechanical-injection pump. The pump will have to be converted to the 2.2 liter specifications, but even then you will not have a perfect match because of the difference in combustion-chamber sizes and resulting difference in compression ratios and slightly

The Porsche Sports Department has offered complete cars and high-performance components to help its customers compete in the various classes of racing around the world for as long as the 911 has been in production. The components shown were the parts offered in 1970 to modify the 2.0 914/6 engine to 210 hp and the 2.2 911S to 230 hp. [The parts included in these conversion kits were replacement pistons and cylinders, twin-plug cylinder heads and twin-ignition distributor. There was also a complete replacement exhaust system with megaphones and a rally muffler to work with the megaphones. The conversion kits also offered high-lift long-duration racing camshafts. Notice that the racing camshafts are centrally lubricated. Also part of these conversions were tall manifolds and Weber 46 IDA-3C carburetors.] Werkfoto, Porsche AG

different combustion characteristics.

When you rebuild one of the 2.0 liter engines with a magnesium crankcase, whether you plan to increase the performance or not, you should plan to install threaded inserts to repair and strengthen the crankcase where the head studs screw in. The Dilavar head studs are not necessary if you limit your displacement increase to 2.2 liters because the cylinders in this size are either cast iron or Biral and do not cause the thermal expansion problem that the all-aluminum cylinders do. If you have one of the 1968 or 1969 magnesium crankcases where the inner-bearing surface of the layshaft ran directly in the magnesium, you will need to modify the crankcase to accept a layshaft-bearing insert.

If you need to replace the oil pump, I recommend that you update the engine's pump to one of the 1976-and-later-style pumps with a larger pressure pump. If you do replace the pump, be sure that you remember to modify the oil by-pass circuit and change to the newer-style oil by-pass pistons. The oil by-pass circuit modification is a good idea even if you don't change the pump, because reducing the effort required by the scavenge pump keeps the oil level lower in the crankcase and reduces wasted horsepower.

2.2 liter 911 modifications (also applicable for 2.0 liter engines)

The 2.2 liter engine is one of the combinations that is difficult to do much with inexpensively. You can put 2.2 911S pistons on a 2.2 911T engine, raising the compression and resulting performance. But to do much else becomes difficult and necessitates replacing the crankshaft and rods to increase the displacement.

There is one conversion that looks attractive on the surface, and that is using a set of the European Carrera 90 mm (2.7 Carrera RS) pistons and cylinders on one of these 2.2 liter or for that matter a 2.0 liter engine. The European Carrera pistons have been imported in fairly large quantities, which has kept the price relatively low, making this conversion even more attractive. I have built several of these conversions myself. The 90 mm bore and 66 mm stroke give a displacement of 2519 cc.

The one problem with this conversion is that the pistons provided only 8.5:1 compression when installed on their 70.4 mm stroke crankshaft in the 2.7 liter application. When you reduce the

stroke to 66 mm, you reduce the compression to something slightly less than 7.0:1. You can sneak the compression back up to about 7.5:1 by machining about 0.040 in. (1 mm maximum) off the cylinder heads' cylinder sealing surface. You will have to machine your heads in any case to work with the 2.7 cylinders with their CE-ring head gasket, and the heads will have to be angle cut to accommodate the larger pistons.

If you do machine your heads, be sure to take the same amount off of the chain

1968 and 1969 magnesium crankcases did not have provisions for bearing inserts for the inboard layshaft bearing. Because of wear problems with the layshaft running in the magnesium, these crankcases should

housings where they seal to the crankcase. This is important because otherwise you will have problems with the cam being off center in the housing and the O-ring for the cam-to-housing seal will fail to seal.

The effect of moving the heads closer to the centerline of the crankshaft is to make the chain a little too long, but a little too long you can live with. When you reassemble the engine, be sure to use new cam chains to minimize this problem. This is the reason this modification

be modified to accept a bearing insert during an overhaul. These can be modified to accept the inboard bearing insert, using reamers and a fixture for driving the reamers in a vertical mill.

Early magnesium crankcase that was modified to accept bearing insert.

is limited to 0.040 in. (1 mm)—to try to minimize the potential of this chain-tensioning problem. Even though you limit the modification to 0.040 in. you may run into a problem on the left side of the engine (cylinders one through three) when the engine has high mileage (80,000 to 100,000 miles) and the chains stretch, or wear at the links and get longer. The problem will be that the idler arm will ride too high in its travel and will actually start to hit the chain housing.

Because of the low compression of this configuration, I recommend that you use the 911T camshaft grind. I have done this conversion with both the 911T and 911E cams. The 911E cams do produce more peak horsepower, as you would expect. The 911T cams, however, provide a much broader torque curve. The subjective seat-of-the-pants results definitely favor the 911T cams. As a result, I would also recommend using the smaller 32 mm ports from the 911T engine as well.

My recommendations for the Weber carburetors in this application are to set them up as follows:

- 32 mm venturi
- tall preatomizers (secondary venturi) from the 46 IDA Webers
- main jet: 120-125
- air-correction jet: 180
- idle jet: 60-65
- emulsion tube: F3
- injection quantity: stock 0.5 cc per stroke

The idle circuit in the Webers in this application leaves quite a bit to be desired, so you will have to run fairly rich at idle to avoid low-speed surging. For idle jets you may have to run 60-65 to get rid of the low-speed, part-throttle surge problems caused by the idle-circuit problems with these carburetors.

To test for this condition, drive around on part throttle between 2000 and 3000 rpm until you have eliminated the problem. Keep trying larger idle jets until there is no longer a surge problem in that rpm range. You will want to run the idle circuit just rich enough to eliminate the lean surge, but as lean as you possibly can for the best fuel economy you can get.

We actually find that with a street car, you spend most of your driving time on the idle circuit in the Weber carburetors. A street car spends about eighty-five percent of its life near one-third load, which has the engine still running on the idle circuit. Because of the low compression and the problem with the idle circuit in the carburetors, this conversion does not provide very good fuel economy.

There is another conversion approach that allows us to take advantage of the reduction of compression caused by using pistons made for the 70.4 mm stroke on a 66 mm stroke engine. If we use the 92 mm pistons and cylinders from the 2.8 RSR engine on a 2.0 or 2.2 liter engine, the compression ratio will be reduced by about one point for a 2.2 engine and about 1½ points for a 2.0 liter engine, which will reduce the compression to a point where they are useable with the available gasoline.

The 901.101.102.7R magnesium crankcase was the best crankcase to use to build any of the engine displacements up to 2.7, and 2.8. They were stronger than all but the first sandcast aluminum crankcases, and they enjoyed all of the updates that came from evolution. There were two versions of this crankcase, one with 92 mm cylinder spigots used for 2.0, 2.2 and 2.4 liter engines, and one with 97 mm cylinder spigots for the 2.7 engines. I prefer to use one of these two versions to build any engine up to 2.7 liters.

The 901.101.102.7R magnesium crankcase with the 92 mm cylinder spigots was introduced for use with the 2.4 liter engines in midproduction. I recommend them for use with any of the smaller-engine 2.0, 2.2 or 2.4 liters because of their additional strength. Notice how thick the cylinder-spigot bases are so that they could be increased to 97 mm for use with the larger-bore 2.7 engines.

The 92 mm pistons used on a 66 mm stroke will result in a displacement of 2634.15 cc. If you use any of these larger-bore pistons and cylinders it will be necessary to increase the cylinder-spigot bore from 92 mm to 97 mm to accommodate the larger cylinders and modify the base of the crankcase main-bearing webs to provide clearance for the wider skirts of the pistons.

If the 2.0 liter or the 1970 2.2 liter engines are converted to accept either the 90 mm 2.7 liter Carrera RS pistons and cylinders or the 92 mm 2.8 liter RSR pistons and cylinders, the crankcase should have a set of the case squirters installed. In 1971, Porsche added these case squirters to provide additional piston cooling by installing six oil jets fed from the main oil gallery, which sprayed oil onto the bottom of the pistons. These jets reduced the operating temperatures at the crown of the piston by 50 deg C (122 deg F). The jets can be installed in any of the other earlier crankcases where high-performance application is anticipated. If the Nicasil (or Alusil) cylinders are going to be used on one of these earlier engines, this modification is a *must* because the piston-to-cylinder operating clearance is based on the use of these case squirters.

Also, since the engine is going to be modified to accept the 2.7 or 2.8 liter cylinders, the crankcase should be treated like a 2.7 liter engine crankcase and Time Serts (threaded inserts) should be installed for the cylinder-head studs, and the steel cylinder-head studs should be replaced with Dilavar cylinder-head studs. The Dilavar head studs are used to compensate for the thermal expansion of the all-aluminum cylinders.

There was a 2.5 liter racing version of this shorter-stroke version of the engine, which is a very nice combination if there is a class where you need an under 2500 cc racing engine. It used the 66 mm stroke and a set of Mahle 89 mm pistons and cylinders for 2463.57 cc displacement. These engines were very popular in the IMSA GTU class when the class limit was 2.5 liters. These 2.5 liter engines were very driveable engines, with good throttle response and a nice broad power curve.

You can also increase the displacement of either a 2.0 or 2.2 liter engine up to 2.7 liters by replacing the crankshaft and connecting rods with the 70.4 mm

The 901.101.102.7R magnesium crankcase with the 97 mm cylinder spigots for the 1973 2.7 911 Carrera RS. The combination of the larger-spigot base and bore in the crankcase and the Nicasil cylinders permit-ted Porsche to expand what had originally been a 2.0 liter engine to 2.7 liters. Notice the cylinder-head studs have been removed and Time Serts installed.

When you modify any of the crankcases that used the 92 mm cylinder-spigot bore to the larger 97 mm diameter, so that you can use any of the larger cylinders that fit into the 97 mm spigot bores, make sure you check the clearance for the skirt of the pistons into the crankcase. Notice the step-bore at the base of the cylinder-spigot bores. The outside diameter provides clearance for the cylinder while the inner-diameter step-bore provides clearance for the piston skirt.

You can determine how far the piston skirt will stick out the bottom of the cylinder, and then make sure there is adequate clearance for the piston's skirt when the piston is at bottom dead center. For checking the clearance, you can push the piston down into the cylinder the depth of the stroke plus two millimeters to make sure you have adequate clearance. Trial-fit the cylinder with the piston extended out the bottom into each cylinder-spigot hole to make sure the clearance is adequate.

crankshaft and a set of the matching connecting rods from a 2.4 or 2.7 liter engine. Nevertheless, with the expense involved you should consider replacing your engine with a 2.4 or a 2.7 to start out with.

2.4 liter 911 engine modifications

Because the 2.4 liter 911 engines use the 70.4 mm stroke crankshaft and rods, it is a fairly easy matter to make one of these 2.4 liter engines into a 2.7 liter. The

crankcase spigots have to be bored out from 92 to 97 mm to accept the larger 2.7 liter cylinders. The cylinder heads must be angle cut to accommodate the larger-diameter pistons. In addition to the angle cut, the conversion to larger pistons and cylinder sets often requires that additional clearance be provided in the crankcase for the piston's wider skirt at the bottom of its travel.

We have been spoiled by 911 engines in general; there are so many combinations of the 911 engine that will just bolt together and work—and work *well* at that—that we seldom run into combinations that will not work. It is always good practice to do a trial assembly before the final assembly, however, to check clearances on any combinations of engine components you are not familiar with or are sure will work. The consequences of failing to check the clearances can be a damaged engine.

It is common practice when building most engines to check both the piston-to-cylinder head clearance and the valve-to-piston clearance, and either make pockets in the pistons or deepen the existing pockets to provide adequate valve-to-piston clearance. The piston-to-cylinder head clearance should be a minimum of 0.89 mm (0.035 in.).

The only place I have seen where Porsche makes a reference to the required valve-to-piston clearance is in the original 911 workshop manual where it refers to one of the very early 2.0 engines, and says that the valve-head-to-piston clearance must not be less than 0.8 mm (0.0314 in.).

I don't feel that this is adequate clearance, however, and recommend a minimum clearance of 1.5 mm (0.058 in.) for safety's sake. All you need do is determine the existing clearance, and if it is inadequate, have the pockets deepened to provide adequate clearance. It is possible to get the piston top too thin; 5.12 mm (0.200 in.) should be the minimum thickness (Mahle says that the dome thickness should be a minimum of 5 mm or 0.195 in. thick).

To check the clearance, lay a strip of modeling clay, at least 3/16 in. thick, on top of one of the pistons, across the valve pockets, in the partially assembled engine. (Note that it is only necessary to check one cylinder.) Install the head assembly, torque the head, set the cam timing, install intake and exhaust rocker arm and adjust the valve lash to zero. Then rotate the crankshaft through two complete revolutions. This will allow both intake

In racing applications where greater than 250 hp is anticipated, dowel-pinning (or shuffle-pinning) the magnesium crankcases cuts down on the case shuffling around the main bearings. This modification will extend the life of the crankcase and the crankshaft by reducing the flexing and moving. The modification consists of installing ten dowel pins, one on each side of the main bearing, to prevent the case from shuffling around the main bearing.

Oil by-pass modification. Porsche made this change in 1976 so it could reduce the size of the scavenge pump while it increased the size of the pressure pump. This modification should be made in any car that will be used in competition, to reduce the task of the oil pump and ensure that there are no windage problems. The modification consists of plugging the original by-pass hole, where it by-passed into the sump, with a quarter-inch pipe plug and drilling a new by-pass hole into the inlet passage for the pressure pump.

and exhaust valves to open and close. After rotating the crank, carefully disassemble the head. If the valves make an impression, cut the clay in half with a sharp knife and measure its thickness at the thinnest point with a vernier caliper.

Another measuring medium preferred by many mechanics is solder in place of the modeling clay. If you use this method, use solder with an uncrushed diameter of 2.54 mm (0.100 in.). Minimum clearance for the intake and exhaust valves should be 1.5 mm (0.060 in.). If there is not adequate clearance, up to a point you can increase the depth of the valve relief in the pistons by fly-cutting for clearance, but remember you should not get the piston dome any thinner than 5.08 mm (0.200 in.).

To raise the compression in the 2.4 liter engines, people have been replacing the 2.4 liter pistons with those from the 2.2 liter engines. This modification is usually performed on the 2.4 liter 911S to take advantage of various club rules which allow cars a compression increase and still let them run in the stock class.

When Porsche went to the longer-stroke 2.4 liter engines, one of the things it did was lower the compression ratio of all of the models so that they all could run on regular gasoline. Where the 2.2 liter 911S had 9.8:1, the 2.4 liter 911S had its compression reduced to 8.5:1. Using the higher-compression pistons from the shorter-stroke 2.2 liter 911S engine on one of the 2.4 911S engines would significantly improve the engine's performance. The change in stroke will increase the compression ratio by about 0.55 points above what it would have been when used on the shorter-stroke engine, which makes a fine-running engine of the 2.4 911S.

Again, all of the clearances will need to be checked to make sure that you have no interference when the engine is assembled. Though I have never built one of these engines myself, I have heard from some people who have that they had a problem with the deck height, while others said they had a problem with the bottom of the piston skirt just hitting the main-bearing webs in the crankcase.

A race team that I worked with several years ago had a 3.2 liter 935 engine that we bought new from the factory that had a problem—just when we thought we had an unfair advantage on the competition. We didn't find the problem until qualifying, though, when one of the pis-tons broke and we were forced to use a 3.0 liter engine for the race. So much for our unfair advantage.

2.7 liter 911 modifications

The 2.7 liter 911 engines have always been a popular engine to modify. One of the most popular modifications over the years has been to use the 2.8 liter RSR 92 mm pistons and cylinders.

The only problem with the 2.8 piston-and-cylinder conversion is a misconception about the parts used for this conversion. The only quality pistons available for the conversion, the 92 mm Mahle 2.8 liter pistons and cylinders, were made for the 2.8 RSR engine which had unique cylinder heads. They were unique in that they were the only cylinder heads made with the small cylinder-head-stud spacing (80 mm for 2.0-2.8 liter engines) with the larger-diameter more-open combustion chamber required by the larger 49 mm intake and 41.5 mm exhaust valves.

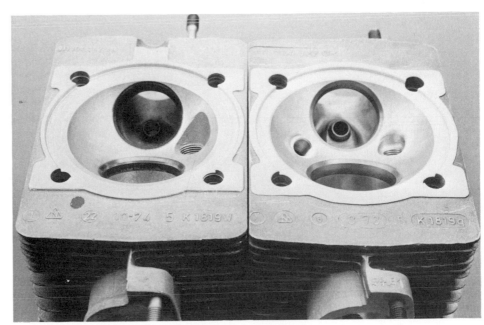

If the oil by-pass modification is performed, it is essential that you use the updated oil by-pass pistons as well. Original-style by-pass piston is on the right, and late-style, which works with the oil by-pass modification, is on the left.

Comparison of 2.7 and 2.8 cylinder-head combustion chambers. The 2.8 RSR cylinder heads were unique in that they were the only cylinder heads made with the small cylinder-head-stud spacing (80 mm for 2.0–2.8 liter engines) with the larger-diameter, more open combustion chamber. The volume of the 2.8 RSR combustion chamber was about 76 cc, whereas the 2.7 combustion chamber was a much smaller 68.1 cc.

The larger valves necessitated a reduced included valve angle of 55 deg 45 min, exhaust angle 30 deg 15 min from vertical, and the intake 25 deg 30 min from vertical. The effect of all of this was to create a combustion chamber that had quite a bit larger volume than any of the earlier (2.0 through 2.7) engines had. The 92 mm Mahle pistons were then made to work with this larger combustion chamber and still provided a compression ratio in the 10.3:1 range, which is common with most of Porsche's normally aspirated racing engines.

I measured the volume of a 2.8 RSR head and a 2.7 911 head. The RSR head had a volume of 76 cc, and the stock 2.7 911 head had a volume of 68.1 cc (I have measured other stock 2.7 heads ranging 66 to 70 cc). The effect of these volumes on the compression ratio of the engine, when used with the Mahle 92 mm pistons, is shown in the graph, *Head comparison*. The deck height in the 911 engines is usually in the 0.77 to 1 mm (0.030 to 0.040 in.) range. As you can see from the graph, that range of deck heights shown would give us a range of

compression ratios of 9.8:1 to 10.1:1 for the RSR head, and a whopping 11.3:1 to 11.75:1 for the stock 2.7 cylinder head. Notice that the compression ratios of the 2.8 RSR actually work out to be lower than the expected 10.3:1.

In my example, the dome of the piston is slightly too small to actually achieve the 10.3:1 ratio. If the dome were larger, just think what it would have done to the compression ratio of the engine using the stock 2.7 cylinder head. You might think that the alternative would be to build a 2.8 engine from your 2.7 by using the pistons, cylinders and cylinder heads from the 2.8 RSR. The problem with that choice, however, is that the 2.8 RSR cylinder heads used 43 mm ports, which are much too large for a street engine of this displacement.

I don't like to recommend altering the deck height on the 911 engines to alter the compression ratio. When you raise the compression by changing the deck height, it requires machining the heads or cylinders and the chain housings and chain-housing covers to realign the chain housing with the camshafts. Conversely, when you want to reduce the compression ratio, you need to add spacers under the cylinders and then under the chain housing to get the chain housing realigned with the camshafts. Changing the deck height can also put the chain-tensioning system out of its proper operating range, or at best compromise the tensioning system's reliability.

The most you can practically change the deck height in the 911 engine is about 1 mm (0.039 in.). As you can see on the graph, if you increase the deck height by a full millimeter, the compression will still be about 10.2:1 with the stock 2.7 cylinder head, which is probably still too high for the gasoline we have available at the gas pumps these days—unless you convert your engine to a twin-plug ignition system. For these reasons, I recommend against using the 2.8 conversion for a street car.

There was also a special cylinder made that would allow the use of the 3.0 liter RSR pistons on a 2.7 911 engine case. These 95 mm pistons and cylinders compounded the weaknesses of the 2.8 conversion with its 92 mm pistons and cylinders. The crankcase had to be bored out even more, weakening the material in the area of the spigot bases even further.

The larger crankcase-spigot bores also weakened the base material for the cylinder-head studs. The area at the top

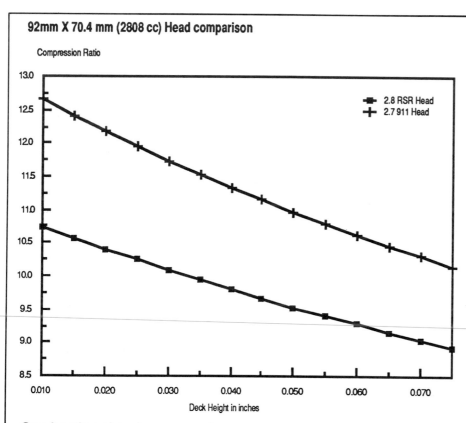

92mm X 70.4 mm (2808 cc) Head comparison

Combustion chamber comparison

The 2.7 liter versus 2.8 liter combustion chambers. The larger 2.8 RSR combustion chamber was required by the larger 49 mm intake and 41.5 mm exhaust valves. The larger valves necessitated a reduced included valve angle of 55 deg 45 min, exhaust angle 30 deg 15 min from vertical, and intake 25 deg 30 min from vertical.

The effect of all this was to create a combustion chamber that had quite a bit larger volume than any of the earlier (2.0 through 2.7) engines had. The 92 mm Mahle pistons were then made to work with this larger combustion chamber and still provide the nominal 10.3:1 compression ratio of the Porsche's normally aspirated racing engines.

For this comparison I measured the volume of a 2.8 RSR head and a 2.7 911

head. The RSR head had a volume of 76 cc, and the stock 2.7 911 head had a volume of 68.1 cc. The effect of these volumes on the compression ratio of the engine when used with the Mahle 92 mm pistons is shown in this graph. The deck height in the 911 engines is usually in the 0.030 to 0.040 in. range.

You can see from the graph, that range of deck heights shown would give a range of compression ratios of 9.8:1 to 10.1:1 for the RSR head, and a whopping 11.3:1 to 11.75:1 for the stock 2.7 cylinder head.

Notice that the compression ratio of the 2.8 RSR actually works out to be lower than the expected 10.3:1. In our example, the dome of the piston is slightly too small to actually achieve the 10.3:1 ratio.

of the cylinder was too thin to reliably support a CE-type cylinder-head gasket, even though it used one. And finally, since the combustion chamber of the 3.0 RSR was virtually identical to the 2.8 RSR, the high-compression-ratio problems were carried over to this conversion as well.

ANDIAL has made a more modern 3.0 liter conversion for the 2.7 liter engines, which addresses all of these problems and hopefully has successfully solved them all. ANDIAL has two different versions of this conversion, one for CIS-injected engines and another for carbureted or mechanical-injected engines.

The ANDIAL 3.0 liter CIS conversion has special Mahle pistons made to work with the CIS fuel-injection system. Its 3.0 conversion for the carbureted or injected engines has specially made Mahle pistons that provide adequate valve-to-piston clearance to clear 911S camshafts.

ANDIAL also has had special Dilavar cylinder-head studs made which have a longer threaded portion at the bottom so they do not require the use of a threaded insert for additional strength. The compression ratio has been lowered to 9.5:1 for the CIS conversion and 9.8:1 for the carbureted or injected-engine conversions. Like the 3.2 Carrera, the cylinders do not use any head gasket at all.

One way that people have been able to get by with these really high compression ratios of the original 2.8 and 3.0 liter conversions has been with the use of a twin-plug ignition. There was a time when you could pick up the Marelli twin-plug distributors for the 911 engines fairly inexpensively, which made this conversion very attractive.

The effect of the twin ignition on the 911 engine was to improve the flame travel in the combustion chamber and decrease the sensitivity to gasoline octane by the equivalent of about one compression point. While adding the dual ignition to a 911 engine in itself will not actually increase the power output, the effect of being able to run one compression point higher certainly does. The alternative to a twin-plug ignition for these 2.8 and 3.0 liter conversions with their very high compression ratios is to use racing gasoline.

My favorite conversion for the 2.7 liter engine for a street-driven car is to use the 90 mm European Carrera RS pistons and cylinders, 911E camshafts, a

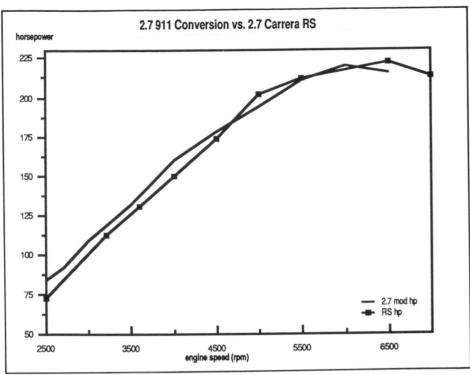

Comparison of the performance between 2.7 liter Carrera RS and 2.7 engine using 2.7 liter Carrera RS pistons and cylinders, 911E camshafts and Weber carburetors. Jerry Woods

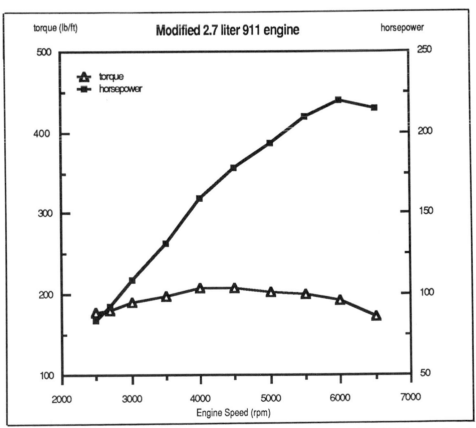

An excellent 2.7 liter engine conversion for a street-driven 911, one that uses the 90 mm European Carrera RS pistons and cylinders, 911E camshafts, a set of Weber 40 IDA carburetors and an early-style (1974 or earlier) exhaust system with a sport muffler.

If you are using a 1974 2.7 liter engine, it will already have the early-style exhaust, but you will need to replace the CIS fuel-injection system with carburetors to get the horsepower. Jerry Woods

set of Weber 40 IDA carburetors, an early-style (1974 or earlier) exhaust system and sport muffler. If you are using a 1974 2.7 liter engine, it will already have the early-style exhaust, but you will need to replace the CIS fuel-injection system with carburetors to get the horsepower.

The reason I recommend carburetors for this conversion is that the CIS system has two shortcomings. First, the CIS system is not particularly a performance-oriented system. The CIS system was utilized instead as a means of meeting the emission standards of the 1970s. The only racing car Porsche ever built that used the CIS injection system was the 934 Group 4 car, which was required to do so by the rules.

Second, the airflow metering unit used by the CIS system is intolerant of pulsations in the intake system, so relatively mild camshafts must be used in engines with CIS injection to avoid affecting the low-rpm running. So if you are going to make a hot rod of the 2.7 engine, you must replace the CIS injection system with either Weber carburetors or mechanical injection. The Webers are more readily available, and

probably a more practical solution to the problem.

If the 2.7 liter 911 being converted is a 1975-77 with either of the two later-style exhaust systems used, you will need to back-date the exhaust system to the 1974-style. The engine in my example also used a twin-pipe sport muffler.

The remainder of the conversion is a fairly simple matter. In addition to the carburetors and exhaust system, all that is needed to complete the conversion is a set of European Carrera RS pistons and cylinders and a pair of 911E camshafts. The ports will have to be increased in size to 36 mm in diameter. This is important if the engine being modified was a straight 911 with its 32 mm ports, and not one of the 911S or Carrera engines with their 35 mm ports.

The carburetion used for this modified 2.7 liter 911 engine is a set of 40 IDA-3C Webers with 34 mm venturi, F3 emulsion tubes, 135 main jets and 145 air-correction jets. Tests were done with the stock air cleaner installed. Comparison tests were also performed with larger and smaller venturi, but the 34 mm seemed to be the optimum compromise.

This is a wonderful, fun-to-drive engine, so if you are wondering what to do with your 2.7 liter 911, this might be the answer. The only downside to this conversion is a loss in fuel economy over what is available with the CIS injection system. The carbureted engine will provide fuel economy in the high teens (16 to 19 mpg), whereas the CIS injection 2.7 911 will provide fuel economy in the low twenties (22 to 25 mpg).

A really nice alternative to the carbureted 2.7 engine with 911E cams is a replica of the 2.7 RS engine—if you can round up all of the appropriate injection-system parts. The differences between the two engines would be the injection system and the use of 911S cams instead of the 911E cams to match the needs of the mechanical-injection system. The advantages to the Carrera RS engine are a little more power, improved low-speed throttle response and improved fuel economy. And where the carbureted conversion may be illegal in some states, the mechanical-injected engine in the correct car will *not* be.

3.0 liter 911SC engine modifications

There are a few fairly simple but very effective things that can be done to the 911SC engines. Many people have experimented with the camshaft timing on their 911SCs, either advancing the timing to improve the bottom-end performance or retarding the camshaft timing in an effort to improve the top-end performance.

The camshafts used in the 911SC were introduced as the camshafts for 3.0 Carrera in 1976. Porsche has advanced and retarded these cams several times over the years, and finally with the introduction of the 3.2 liter Carrera in 1984 it struck a compromise, setting the camshaft timing right in the middle of two extremes in the timing settings that were used previously.

Another very popular and very successful modification has been replacing the exhaust system with the early-style exhaust from a 1974 or earlier 911. The early-style exhaust system can be installed on any of the 911SC engines for a sizable performance gain of seventeen to twenty-two horsepower, depending on the year of the engine and the dynamometer the engine was tested on. The change requires a pair of heat exchangers, muffler, different scavenge, oil line and some pieces to adapt the heater system.

The next change is to replace the CIS fuel injection with a pair of Weber 40

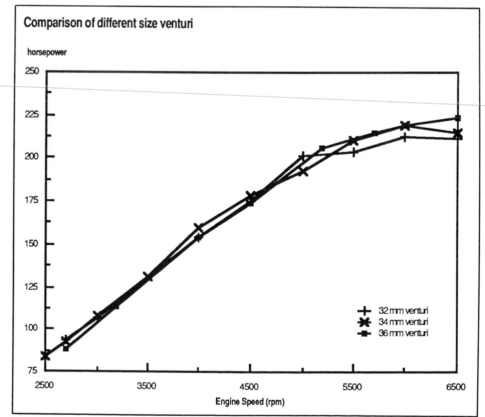

Comparison of different size venturi

horsepower

- + 32 mm venturi
- ✕ 34 mm venturi
- ■ 36 mm venturi

Engine Speed (rpm)

Venturi size selection. Tests were also performed with larger 36 mm venturi and smaller 32 mm venturi, but the 34 mm seemed to be the optimum compromise. Furthermore, the performance difference between the 32 and 36 mm was so small that it is doubtful you would be able to perceive the difference in a driving test. Jerry Woods

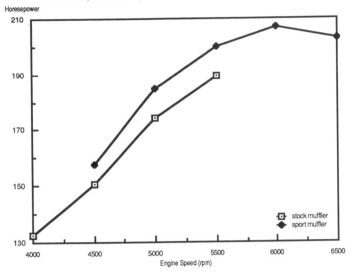

2.4 911S Mechanical Injection Muffler Test

Horsepower

Legend:
- ☐ stock muffler
- ◆ sport muffler

Engine Speed (rpm)

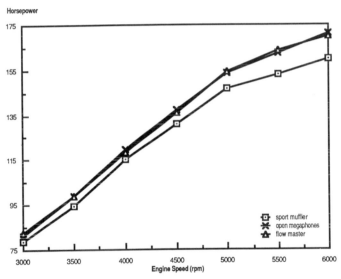

2.7 911 Muffler Comparison Test

Horsepower

Legend:
- ☐ sport muffler
- ✕ open megaphones
- △ flow master

Engine Speed (rpm)

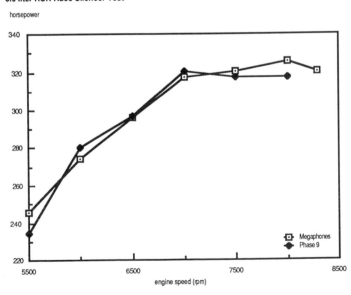

3.0 liter RSR Race Silencer Test

horsepower

Legend:
- ☐ Megaphones
- ◆ Phase 9

engine speed (rpm)

Muffler comparisons

Muffler comparison tests performed on a 2.4 liter mechanical-injected 911S engine. The test compared a stock muffler and a twin-pipe sport muffler. The sport muffler showed a significant increase in power, particularly in the upper rpm. *Paul Schenk*

2.7 muffler comparison test. This engine is used for track events where there are noise restrictions. The idea of the comparison test was to look for a muffler or silencer that would actually improve the performance while meeting the noise restriction. You can see by the results that the test was successful, and that the Flow Master racing muffler actually came very close to matching the performance of the open megaphones. Performance data by Paul Schenk. *Paul Schenk*

3.0 liter RSR race-silencer test. The consequences of this test were more severe than the muffler comparison test for the 2.7 liter engine. In the test the objective was improved performance, whereas in this test the objective was to quiet a racing car so that it was able to compete at a racetrack that had noise restrictions with a minimal loss in performance.

More and more of our racetracks are imposing noise restrictions on the cars that run on them. At a recent race in Oregon, IMSA black-flagged one of the GTO race leaders and had him put his car on the trailer because of excessive noise. If you were to just bolt a stock 911 muffler on the 3.0 liter RSR engine it would run poorly because of the camshaft timing. The choices are either to detune the engine until it will run with a stock muffler, or find a muffler that will make it quiet enough to pass the noise restrictions—without altering the engine's performance too much.

The Phase 9 race silencers were able to bring the noise of the RSR engine within the 105 dBa noise limits that most tracks require. You can see from the results of this test that it had minimal effect on this racing engine's performance. Performance data provided by Jerry Woods.

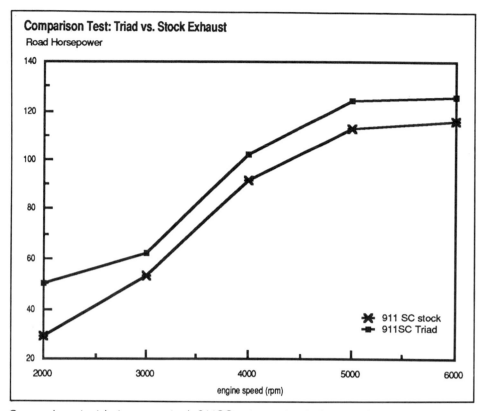

Comparison Test: Triad vs. Stock Exhaust
Road Horsepower

Comparison test between a stock 911SC exhaust system and the Triad heat exchangers and muffler system. The tests were performed on a chassis dynamometer, so the results are in road horsepower instead of the usual brake-horsepower reading. The exhaust system offered an impressive performance increase across the rpm range. Triad Industries, Inc.

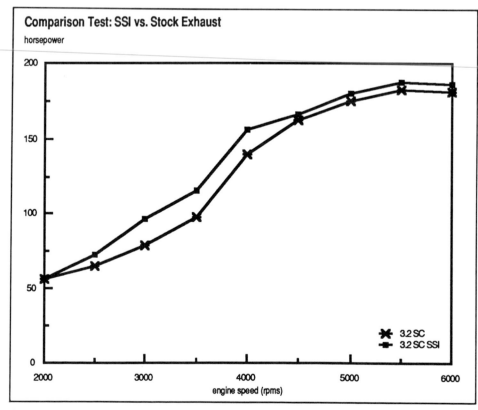

Comparison Test: SSI vs. Stock Exhaust
horsepower

Comparison test between stock 911SC exhaust system, the SSI heat exchangers and a stock early muffler system. The engine used for this comparison was a 911SC engine with a bolt-on 98 mm 3.2 liter conversion. SSI

IDA-3C carburetors. The conversion to carburetors is good for an additional ten horsepower for a total increase of around thirty horsepower when combined with the exhaust change, but because of the greatly improved throttle response you would swear the increase was more like fifty horsepower. The 34 mm venturi will be correct for this size engine. Use F3 emulsion tubes, 160 main jets, and 175 air-correction jets as a starting setup.

The engine should be tested on a dynamometer to optimize the carburetor settings. The idle jets are best selected by a driving test. You will probably need to run with 60, 65 or maybe even larger idle jets. The idle jets have to be rich enough to eliminate the part-throttle lean surge, but you will want to run as lean as possible for the best fuel economy. The distributor used with the 1978 and 1979 engines will work fine with the carburetors, but when the vacuum unit is discarded the mechanical advance curve from the 1980 and later 911SC's distributor is too short for use with the carburetors. The distributor from a 1978 or 1979 911SC will work; you can have your distributor recurved or you can use the "European" distributor.

Carburetor sizing

Since you have only two choices of carburetor sizes for your 911 you would think the choice would be a simple matter—well it's not. You are forced to choose between a little better peak power and better driveability. Even though the larger carburetors may produce more peak horsepower on a dynamometer, they may not be the best choice for day-in and day-out driveability.

If the carburetors are too small you know that you will potentially lose power. On the other hand, if they are too large you will lose torque at the lower rpm as well as driveability, so at best, carburetor selection will be a compromise. 911 street-driven engines will spend about eighty-five percent of their life near one-third load, where all carburetors are still operating in their idle-circuit range. So any carburetor you chose for street use must have an efficient idle circuit and be matched to both the engine's and your driving needs.

When choosing a carburetor for any application, you must be honest with yourself as to the application. The incorrect compromise can be quite unpleasant to drive and expensive to own. In the case of the 3.0 liter 911SC engine, the 40 IDA-3C Weber is probably the correct compromise.

The formula for selecting carburetor venturi size provided in Colin Campbell's *The Sports Car Engine*, used in conjunction with Weber's recommendations for the relationship of venturi size to throttle bore, works very well for sizing carburetors for a wide range of engine applications. Campbell's venturi size formula is as follows:

$$\text{Venturi size in mm} = 20 \sqrt{\frac{V}{1000} \times \frac{N}{1000}}$$

V = cylinder volume of one cylinder in cc
N = rpm where engine reaches peak horsepower

Weber suggests that the throttle bores of its carburetors should be between ten and twenty-five percent larger than the selected venturi. The highest-powered version of the 3.0 liter 911SC engine (Type 930/10) with stock camshafts develops its peak horsepower, 204, at 5900 rpm. The displacement for one cylinder is 499 cc, so now we can solve the equation to determine the venturi size and resulting choke size.

$$\text{Venturi size in mm} = 20 \sqrt{\frac{499}{1000} \times \frac{5900}{1000}}$$

Venturi size in mm = 34.01 (34) mm

Using Weber's throttle-bore-to-venturi size recommendations, in this example the throttle bore should be between 37.4 and 42.5 mm, showing that for the 3.0 911SC engine, the Weber 40 IDA-3C carburetors are a perfect choice for the best compromise.

Nevertheless, there is an additional problem with using the 46 IDA Webers in this application instead of their 40 IDA counterpart. Because the 46 IDAs have larger throttle bores, the idle and transition-metering signal is weaker. The available signal goes as a fourth power of the diameter, hence, changing from a 40 IDA to a 46 IDA carburetor leads to a seventy-five percent reduction in the metering signal, or simply, there will be less control and larger flat spots in the low-speed driving range.

Additionally, earlier versions of the 46 IDA carburetors had idle progression, or transition ports that were not at all optimized for use on 911 street engines. This objection has been more or less eliminated by the importers' efforts on behalf of the end user with Weber,

the manufacturer. Weber has drastically altered the idle-progression ports in the current version of the 46 IDA and greatly improved its match to street-driven 911s.

Remember when choosing your carburetors, the venturi size is responsible for the main-circuit metering signal, and that the throttle-bore size is important for the idle-metering-signal strength. If it's driveability that you want, always choose the smaller throttle bore for a street application. After all, what percentage of the time do we really drive with our foot on the floorboards?

A really nice conversion for the 3.0 911SC engine is a small increase in displacement to 3.2 liters (3186 cc) using 98 mm pistons and cylinders. I first heard of this conversion in 1979. The German customers would take delivery of their new 911SCs at the factory and then either take their cars to Werk I, the customer repair center, to have the engine modified, or they would take their cars to one of the independent German tuners for similar modifications. The only changes they would make in these conversions were to change the pistons and cylinders and reset the fuel mixture. Claimed output was 220 hp.

There were at least three different versions of this type of conversion: Porsche's version, performed for its customers at Werk I; a version the Kremers performed on their customers' cars; and the conversion Max Moritz performed for its customers.

911 model	Cam timing		Checking height at TDC overlap
1976/77 3.0 Carrera	Intake open	1° BTDC	0.9 to 1.1 mm
	Intake close	53° ABDC	(0.035 to 0.043 in.)
	Exh open	43° BBDC	
	Exh close	3° ATDC	
1978-80 R.o.W. 911SC	Intake open	7° BTDC	1.4 to 1.7 mm
	Intake close	47° ABDC	(0.055 to 0.067 in.)
	Exh open	49° BBDC	
	Exh close	3° BTDC	
1978/79 US 911SC	same as 1976-77 3.0 Carrera		same as 1976/77 3.0 Carrera
1980-83 US 911SC	same as 1978-80 R.o.W. 911SC		same as 1978-80 R.o.W. 911SC
1981-83 R.o.W. 911SC	same as 1976-77 3.0 Carrera		same as 1976/77 3.0 Carrera
1984-87 3.2 Carrera	Intake open	4° BTDC	1.1 to 1.4 mm
	Intake close	50° ABDC	(0.043 to 0.055 in.)
	Exh open	46° BBDC	
	Exh close	0° TDC	

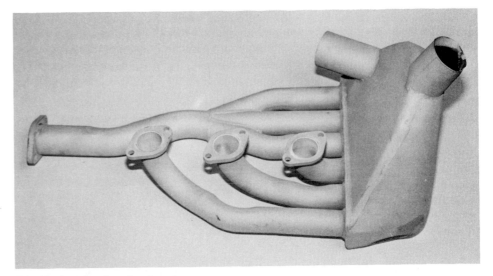

Triad Industries, Inc. heat exchanger.

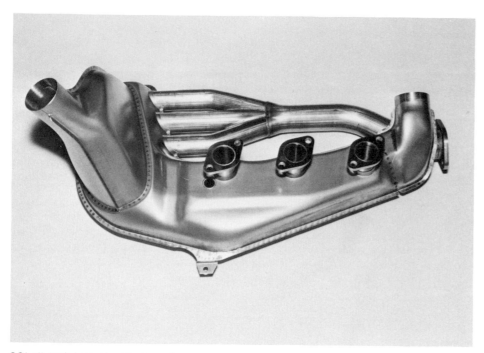

SSI all-stainless-steel heat exchanger.

Mahle made the piston sets for all of these conversions. The piston sets that Max Moritz had made by Mahle had a wedge-shaped dome which improved the efficiency of the combustion chamber. The Max Moritz pistons and cylinders have finally become a fairly popular conversion in the United States. This conversion has the advantage of offering a significant performance increase without violating the emission laws. An engine built using these pistons and cylinders can retain all of the emission control devices and comply with all of the emission tests while at the same time provide a nice performance increase.

A conversion using these 98 mm pistons and cylinders is a very nice modification to make on any 911SCs needing any major maintenance that might require the replacement of pistons and cylinders. This type of modification would have been a natural for the 2.7 911s because almost all of them required

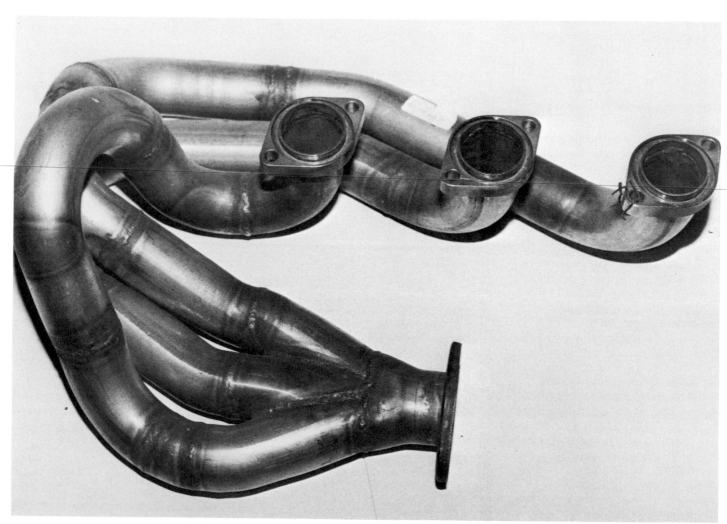

Factory equal-length three-into-one racing header for 3.0 liter 911SC engine. Left side, cylinders 1-3 (part number 911.111. 049.00) as used on 911SC RS (Type 954). Pipe diameter was 42 mm (about 1⅝ in.) inside. Werkfoto, Porsche AG

some form of major maintenance before they reached 100,000 miles. Unfortunately for the hot-rodders, the 911SCs are much too reliable and seem to want to last forever, so you may have to take a perfectly healthy 911SC engine apart just to perform one of these modifications. I have been bragging about two friends who have had over 170,000 miles on their 911SCs for some time, and I just recently talked with a shop owner who maintains a 911SC that has more than 212,000 miles on it and it still runs great. Neither of us has ever rebuilt a 911SC engine because it wore out.

These Max Moritz pistons can be combined with the carburetion change, the exhaust-system backdating and a mild cam, like a 911L cam, for a wonderful power increase. Additional valve clearance will be necessary because of the increased overlap and duration of the 911L camshafts.

I still recommend using the Weber 40 IDA-3C carburetors for this conversion. Again I used the formula for sizing the carburetors. The 3.2 Carrera engine produces its 231 hp at 5900, so 5900 rpm was again selected as the rpm and the displacement for one cylinder is 527 cc.

$$\text{Venturi size in mm} = 20 \sqrt{\frac{527}{1000} \times \frac{5900}{1000}}$$

Venturi size in mm = 35.26 (35) mm

The calculated venturi size has increased from 34 to 35 mm. Using Weber's throttle-bore-to-venturi size recommendations (throttle bore should be ten to twenty-five percent larger than the venturi size), in this example, the throttle bore should be between 38.5 and 43.75 mm, showing that even for the 3.2 conversion the Weber 40 IDA-3C carburetors are probably still the best compromise.

There are also racing pistons made for these engines, to work with the even-more-aggressive racing camshafts. There are 3.0 liter pistons available from Porsche, made by Mahle for the 954 engines that have a compression ratio of 10.3:1. There is also a 3.2 piston-and-cylinder combination available for these engines, with the traditional rounded-dome piston which provides adequate valve-to-piston clearance for racing camshafts that have a compression ratio of 10.2:1. The Max Moritz CIS pistons have a 9.8:1 compression ratio, but were not designed with adequate valve clearance for racing cams.

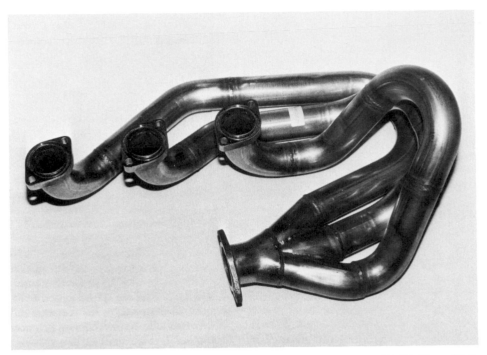

Factory equal-length three-into-one racing header for 3.0 liter 911SC engine. Right side, cylinders 4-6 (part number 911.111. 050.00) as used on 911SC RS (Type 954). Pipe diameter was 42 mm (about 1⅝ in.) inside. Werkfoto, Porsche AG

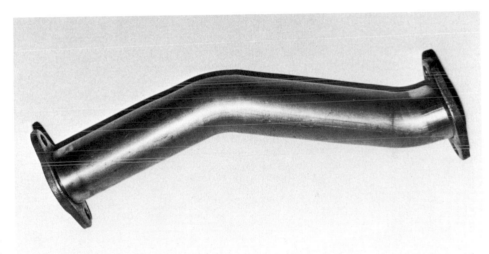

Adaptors for adapting a stock muffler or a sport muffler to a set of factory racing headers (part numbers 911.111.053.00 for the left side and 911.111.054.00 for the right side). Werkfoto, Porsche AG

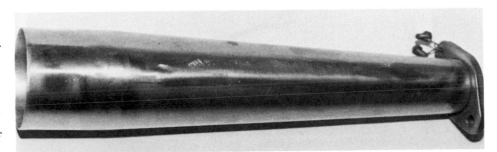

Factory racing megaphone or diffuser (part number 911.111.043.75). Werkfoto, Porsche AG

One thing you will have to watch for when you attempt to build racing engines based on the 911SC engine is that there are also RSR 3.0 and 3.2 liter pistons that can be matched to the 3.0 911SC engine's cylinders, and they just aren't the same thing. The problem is that the combustion chambers in the cylinder heads from the RSR engines were considerably smaller than those in the 911SC heads. The RSR heads had combustion chambers that were about 76 to 77 cc in volume, whereas the 911SC's combustion chamber is about 90 cc. The result is that it is very hard to get a decent compression ratio out of the RSR pistons when used in the 911SC-based engines.

3.2 Carrera engine modifications

There are several nice larger-displacement options available for the 3.2 Carrera already. We actually had a 3.5 liter normally aspirated combination available to us before the Carrera 3.2 was introduced. This was a bit of an oddball engine that used the 3.2 liter 935 (74.4 mm stroke) crankshaft and either titanium 935 connecting rods or 911SC connecting rods and 100 mm Mahle pistons and cylinders. These are the 100 mm pistons that you see listed for sale with the 22 mm wrist pins.

Fortunately, or maybe unfortunately for some of the pioneers, this original combination has stimulated a great deal of interest in these larger-displacement 3.5 liter engines, and pistons are now available with the correct-size 23 mm wrist pins and pin locations. So its fairly easy to build one of these 3.5 engines.

The pioneers who attempted to build these original 3.5 liter engines had a great deal of difficulty because of the "funny" pistons that resulted from the original combination. In addition to having the wrong-diameter wrist pin, they also had the wrist pin located incorrectly in the piston because they were made for the 0.8 mm (0.0315 in.) longer titanium/911SC connecting rods. The result was that even after you solved the wrist-pin diameter problem you still had about 0.8 mm (0.0315 in.) more deck height than you would have liked. When you build a 3.5 liter engine you will need to bore out the spigots in the crankcase, from 103 to 105 mm, to accept the larger-diameter cylinders.

Another popular size conversion for these 3.2 Carrera engines is the 3.4 liter conversion using 98 mm piston-and-cylinder sets. There is both a racing version and RUF's street version. The advantage to the 3.4 liter conversions over the 3.5 liter conversions is that no machining is required, so they are bolt-on conversions.

Again I used the formula for sizing the carburetors for a 3.4 hot-rod engine.

Let us assume it produces 250 hp at 5900 rpm and the displacement for one cylinder is 561 cc.

Venturi size in mm =

$$20 \sqrt{\frac{561}{1000} \times \frac{5900}{1000}}$$

Venturi size in mm = 36.38 (36) mm

The calculated venturi size has increased from 34 mm for the 3.0 911SC engine, to 35 mm for the 3.2 liter Carrera engine and finally 36 mm for the 3.4 liter version of the Carrera engine. Using Weber's throttle-bore-to-venturi size recommendations (throttle bore should be ten to twenty-five percent larger than the venturi size), in this example, the throttle bore should be between 39.6 and 45 mm, an indication that for the 3.4 liter conversion the Weber 46 IDA carburetors are probably the correct choice.

Turbocharged Porsches

It seems that everyone who owns a turbocharged Porsche wants it to be faster than it is in stock form. Obviously there are things that can be done quite easily with these cars to make them faster, and the easiest is simply to increase the boost. The boost comes set on all turbocharged Porsches at a pressure that, in Porsche's opinion, will give reasonable performance and reliability.

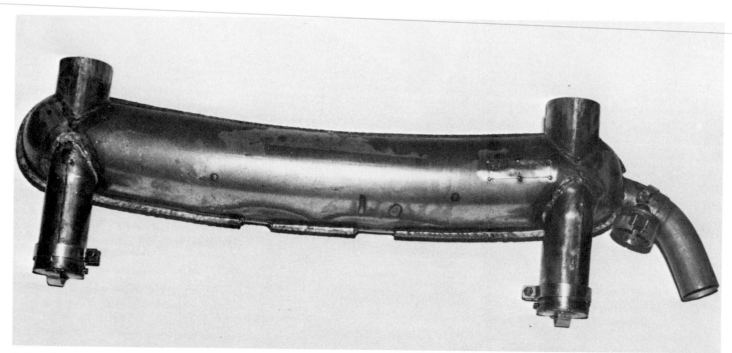

Rally silencer for use with racing megaphones (part number 911.111.010.00). These mufflers are probably not quiet enough for our track events with the megaphone outlets uncapped. They are used for European rallies where they use public roads and have special stages. For the special stages the megaphone outlets are uncapped, and for the road portions the outlets are capped so that the cars will be quiet enough to meet the noise laws of the various countries. Werkfoto, Porsche AG

On the typcial street-driven 911 Turbo (930), you can increase the boost a little for added performance without causing any damage because the cars are driven at full boost for short periods of time. I recommend that the boost never be run in excess of one bar (14.5 psi) on an otherwise stock car. Running boost above one bar puts the engine very close to its thermal limits in its stock configuration. Anything above one bar boost will exceed the fuel injection's ability to provide a proper mixture, and may cause detonation which can result in extensive engine damage.

On any turbocharged car, you should always use the highest-octane fuel you can obtain when you plan to run the car hard. Owners of pre-1978 911 Turbos (930s) should consider the installation of an efficient intercooler before increasing the boost much above the factory settings. There are several different intercooler kits available for the 911 Turbo (930): There are kits for the early cars without intercoolers, and there are larger, more efficient replacement intercooler kits available for the 1978-and-later cars that already have an intercooler. The cooler you can get the charge air, the more power your car will produce.

The correct method of modifying the preset boost is to install a pressure regulator across the diaphragm in the wastegate in a manner similar to the system used on the 935 race cars. I recommend locating the regulator back by the wastegate and using it as an adjustable preset device rather than locating it up in the cockpit where the street driver might be tempted to play race-car driver.

At the same time, you will have to modify the boost-sensitive fuel-pump cutoff switch so that it operates in the 1.35 to 1.4 bar range. This modification has to be made because when the turbo first comes up to boost it will overshoot the setting for an instant, which will cause a normally set cutoff switch to turn off the fuel pump. Some people just bypass the fuel cutoff switch. I don't feel this is a good idea either; the cutoff switch will act as a conscience for those drivers who may need a little reminding. I also do not recommend shimming up the wastegate. Before you get the desired boost you run the risk of having the spring compressed so tight that it will be in "coil bind," which will confuse both you and your car.

For 911 Turbo (930) owners who are going to modify their cars anyhow, all of this advice is offered as what I believe are the reasonable limits for these cars. Of course, for maximum safety and reliability you should not modify your cars at all. One further note on playing with the boost setting. I recommend that before you modify the boost, you have a boost gauge you are sure you can trust.

A number of Porsche 911 Turbo (930) owners who have been competing with their cars in track events also wish to increase the performance of their cars. These changes are only recommended for the 1978-and-later intercooled 911 Turbos (930s), or earlier 911 Turbos (930s) with intercoolers added. There are several things that can be done to increase performance of the 911 Turbo (930) Porsche for competition.

If the car is a US car, the first thing to do is change the exhaust system to the R.o.W. type. Note that 1986-and-late US cars already *have* this system and only need the catalyst and muffler changed.

The 1976 to 1980 US cars require a complete change of exhaust to make these other changes function properly. For instance, if the exhaust system is not changed and the camshafts are changed to the 911SC cams, the low-end performance will be greatly lacking. Increasing the compression to 7.5:1 improves the normally aspirated performance. The compression is increased by machining the cylinder heads about 0.1 mm (0.039 in.). Machine and polish the intake ports and intake duct to increase from 32 to 36 mm.

Type of camshaft	Cam timing		Checking height at TDC overlap
1975-87 911 Turbo	Intake open	3° ATDC	0.65 to 0.80 mm
	Intake close	37° ABDC	(0.026 to 0.032 in.)
	Exh open	29° BBDC	
	Exh close	3° BTDC	
1976 Carrera	Intake open	7° BTDC	1.4 to 1.7 mm
1978-83 911SC	Intake close	47° ABDC	(0.055 to 0.067 in.)
1984-87 Carrera	Exh open	49° BBDC	
	Exh close	3° BTDC	
Porsche Group B	Intake open	11° BTDC	1.8 to 1.9 mm
Turbo camshaft	Intake close	46° ABDC	(0.071 to 0.075 in.)
	Exh open	32° BBDC	
	Exh close	8° ATDC	

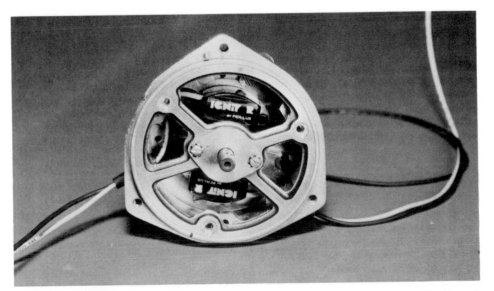

Marelli twin-plug distributor with a pair of Ignitor units installed in place of the four sets of points normally used. The Ignitor units are self-contained units with an inductive pickup, and Hall effect transistors are used as switching devices. These Ignitor units also solve a problem that the Marelli twin-plug distributors had with point bounce at high rpm.

Changing the camshafts to either 911SC camshafts or the Group B turbo camshafts makes a significant improvement in the 911 Turbo performance. If you select the 911SC grind, you may make the change either by regrinding your own turbo cams or replacing them with a new set of 911SC cams. If you use the 911SC cams, set the timing 1.4 to 1.7 mm (0.065 to 0.075 in.). And if you use the Group B turbo camshafts, set the timing 1.8 to 1.9 mm (0.071 to 0.075 in.). If you use a new set of the 911SC cams, instead of having your original 911 Turbo cams reground, you will need to add the drive piece to the left camshaft to drive air injection and turbocharger oil-scavenge pump. (The part number for this, a racing part, is 911.105.171.02.)

2.0 liter 911S piston. The 911S piston was forged and had to have a high dome to achieve the 9.8:1 compression ratio.

Note that the left camshaft also requires machining to facilitate the mounting of this drive adaptor.

The 911SC camshaft is a higher-lift camshaft than the original, whereas the Group B turbo camshaft has essentially the same lift for both the intake and exhaust as the stock turbo camshaft. If you use the 911SC camshafts, the valve springs should be reset to the same 34.5 mm for intake and exhaust that is used for the stock 911SC valve springs.

A change in the fan drive ratio is recommended to improve the engine cooling. The fan should be speeded up from 1:1.68 of the turbo to faster 1:1.8 with the larger-crankshaft pulley that was used on the 1976 and 1977 911s and the 1978/1979 911SC fans.

The twin ignition would offer the same type of advantage for the turbo engines that it offers for the normally aspirated engine by reducing the engine's sensitivity to the gasoline octane. This may be even more important for the turbocharged engines than it is for the normally aspirated engines, in that it safely allows higher boost pressure to be used. The problem is the availability of a good distributor to use for the application.

It is important to use a distributor that has an advance curve for this purpose, so the Bosch racing distributor with its fixed advance is not really advisable. With the stock distributor, the ignition timing should be set to 25 deg at 4000 rpm, with vacuum line to the distributor disconnected.

A popular conversion for the 911 Turbo has been to change the turbo-

charger to one of the K27 turbochargers. The K27 is a more modern design than the K26 that is used on the 911 Turbo. It operates more efficiently at higher levels of boost. The K27 number refers to the general type of turbocharger, or the center section of a turbocharger made by KKK. Audi diesels, Porsche 935s and the Porsche 924 Turbo have all used the K27 turbo.

There is a wide selection of different-size K27 turbochargers available for use on the 911 Turbo. For instance, there is a K27-16 that can be used to improve the high-end performance, a K27-13 to improve the midrange and a K27-11/11 to improve the low-end performance. The latter is the most popular conversion for use on the 911 Turbos.

Both the K27 turbocharger and the intercooler need to be modified so the K27 can be used in the 911 Turbo. The turbocharger should have 10 mm milled off of the mounting surface of the exhaust flange to make it fit better. The intercooler inlet tube must be modified so that it can be connected to the K27 turbocharger. The original mounting of this intercooler tube to the K26 turbocharger was sealed with an O-ring. Because there is no provision on the K27 for the O-ring, a piece of radiator-type hose and hose clamps are used instead. Intercooling or, as it is also called, charge air cooling, has proven to be very effective in the 911 Turbo. Porsche

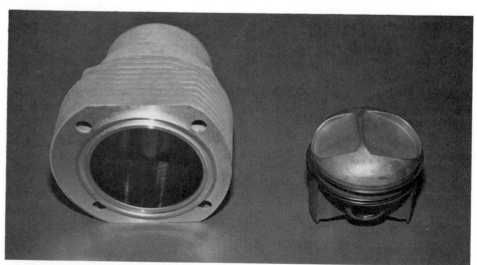

Updated piston and cylinder for a 906 or 910 racing engine. Notice the tall dome and large valve cutouts for valve-to-piston clearance. The cylinder is a Nicasil cylinder made with a CE-ring head gasket.

2.4 liter 911T CIS piston. The CIS pistons had an offset dome to alter the effective combustion chamber and ensure more complete combustion. These pistons have little practical use in a modified engine because of the lack of adequate clearance for the valves if any of the more aggressive camshafts is used.

started experimenting with intercooling on its racing cars, starting with the 917 engine. The 934, 935 and 936 all relied on intercooling to assist in reliably producing high specific outputs.

The racing cars have used both air-to-air and water-to-air intercooling. From 1978 on, the street 911 Turbo (930) has used an air-to-air intercooler, where the ambient air temperature is the cooling medium. The act of compressing the air with the turbocharger heats up the intake charge air; any increase in pressure also has a corresponding increase in temperature. This increase in temperature acts to cancel out some of the potential advantage of the increased boost because the increased temperature results in a less-dense charge reaching the engine.

This heat also raises the operating temperatures of the engine, making the engine more prone to detonation and damage caused by overheating the pistons, valves and cylinder heads. An increase of charge air temperature of ten degrees will raise the exhaust temperature by ten degrees and so on.

Intercoolers

Enter the intercooler. The intercooler is almost like perpetual motion, where you get something for nothing. Where the larger, more efficient intercoolers offer an advantage is that they allow you to safely run your 911 Turbo (930) with more boost. The limit of how much boost you can actually run is detonation, which is caused by heat. By reducing the heat of the charge air, you can run more boost. Just the act of compressing the intake air raises the temperature.

In addition to the heat caused by compressing the charge air, the combustion heat is also influenced by the compression ratio and the ignition advance. This triangle has to be played very carefully because they all increase the heat of the combustion process which can cause detonation. The idea is to get the most performance from the engine without damaging it; the engine *will* be damaged by detonation.

With more efficient intercoolers and better gasoline (higher-octane) you can run more boost, compression and ignition advance, and produce more horsepower. An example of this would be the 935 engines which ran very high boost and produced more than two and a half times as much power as the stock street 911 Turbos (930s). The cooler you can get the charge air, the more power your car will produce and the less risk of

detonation, caused by running with higher boost. The octane requirements will also be reduced for a given engine output. Nonetheless, this is usually traded off by increasing the boost again in the search for more power output.

There are several intercooler kits available for the earlier 911 Turbos (930s) that did not have intercoolers, and there are larger, more efficient replacement intercooler kits available for the 1978-and-later cars that already have an intercooler. The intercoolers must actually be judged by two criteria; we are interested in their efficiency at cooling the charge air and the restriction that they offer to the charge air passing through them. Unfortunately, the act of running the compressed air through a cooler or heat exchanger will reduce the pressure some because of the pressure drop across the cooler.

The performance from a 911 Turbo (930) engine with these modifications will be in the 350 to 400 hp range at 5500 rpm range with 0.9 bar boost. The power can be increased by approximately 10 hp by running an open exhaust system in place of the muffler. Running more than 0.9 bar boost for track use with an otherwise stock 911 Turbo (930) will greatly reduce the engine's longevity.

As an example, a 935 that ran 24-Hour races at either Le Mans or Daytona would require a complete rebuild

after just one weekend of racing. The pistons and cylinders would be worn out and often the cylinder heads would require replacement as well. This was with special engines for endurance racing and limiting the boost to 1.2 to 1.25 bar for these long races.

Similar destruction can be created in a much shorter period of time with the normal racing engines and the higher boost that was used for shorter sprint races. And the 935s had vastly superior oil cooling, intercooling and air cooling to what you will be able to accomplish with a stock street-bodied 911 Turbo (930).

With the turbocharged 911 (930) engines, like the normally aspirated 911, there is no substitute for cubic inches (unless, in the case of turbocharged engines it's more boost). RUF relies on an increase in displacement as one of the ways to increase the engine's performance. The RUF 3.4 turbo engine uses 98 mm pistons which on the 74.4 mm stroke result in 3367 cc displacement. There are also 100 mm big-bore kits available for the 911 Turbo (930) engines but they require that the crankcase be bored out to accommodate the larger-diameter cylinders.

The cylinder diameter where it fits into the cylinder head did not change when the bore was increased to 98 or 100 mm. It remained 113 mm in diameter as it had been since 1975 when the

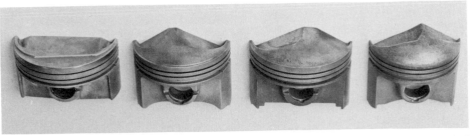

Series of pistons that are cut in half so that their construction could be observed. On the left is a 95 mm 962 racing piston; next is an 89 mm piston from a short-strokes 2.5 liter engine; next is a 92 mm 2.8 RSR piston; and last is an 80 mm 2.0 liter 906 piston.

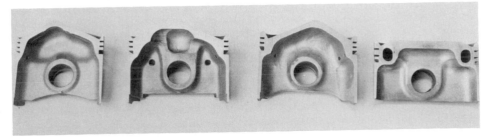

Same series of pistons from the inside, most of these pistons were cut in half so the valve-clearance pockets could be observed.

diecast aluminum crankcase was introduced for the turbo engine. At the bottom of the cylinder where it fits into the crankcase, the cylinder was increased in diameter from 103 to 105 mm and requires that the crankcase be opened up to accommodate the larger cylinders. There is also a modification for these big-bore turbocharged engines that incorporates an O-ring seal for the bottom of the cylinder, where it inserts into the cylinder spigot to prevent any oil leaking at the base of the cylinders.

Callaway Microfueler

Callaway offers its Microfueler enriching device that can be used on the 911 Turbo (930). The Microfueler is a completely separate supplemental fuel-injection system consisting of an electronic brain that senses the turbo-boost pressure and the engine's rpm and single-driver system, with one fuel injector installed in the throttle butterfly assembly. Callaway also makes double-driver systems to work with some of the larger-displacement V-8s.

The single-driver system uses one injector while the double-driver system uses two. Callaway also has twenty different-size injectors, which allows it to tailor its systems to a wide range of engine displacements and power outputs. The brain senses boost pressure and rpm, determines the amount of extra fuel needed and injects the fuel above the throttle butterfly.

Max Moritz 3.2 liter conversion for the 911SC engines. This was a really nice conversion for the 3.0 911SC engine. It provided a small increase in displacement to 3.2 liters (3186 cc). In addition, the piston had a nice wedge-shaped dome that improved the overall combustion-chamber shape.

911SC cylinder with groove for CE-ring head gasket.

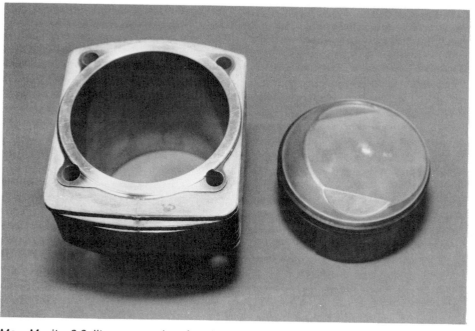

Porsche racing piston for the 911SC engine. These pistons were 95 mm, retaining the 3.0 liter displacement, and had a 10.3:1 compression ratio. They had a wedge-shaped dome similar to the one used by the Max Moritz pistons. Werkfoto, Porsche AG

935 cylinder with interlocking Ni-Resist sealing ring. Both the cylinder and the cylinder head had to be machined to accept this interlocking ring. You had to start with new cylinders that did not use the CE-ring head gasket, because the CE-ring groove was larger than the groove for the interlocking ring.

For the 911 Turbo (930), Callaway uses a single-driver system. The kit consists of the boost sensor, the brain, a wiring harness, one injector and a dash-six braided-steel fuel line that taps off of the fuel distributor for its fuel supply. The Microfueler injector system is adjustable for pressure and rpm, and starts to turn on at one and a half pounds boost pressure. Then the brain develops a curve that richens the mixture up to a boost of sixteen or seventeen pounds.

The Microfueler system permits running safely with boost increased to one bar, with an otherwise stock engine. When run with one bar boost with the Microfueler, the engine will produce an additional thirty-five horsepower.

The Microfueler systems offer even more of a performance advantage for engines that are already modified and using increased boost pressures.

Pistons and cylinders

Be careful when you consider using aftermarket pistons and cylinders; what looks like a good deal just might not be so hot. I recommend limiting your selection of pistons and cylinders to Mahle, Schmidt or Cosworth. The first two are available as both original equipment and aftermarket, whereas the Cosworth pistons are available *only* as aftermarket and must be matched with cylinders from Mahle or Schmidt.

Porsche fits the running clearance of the pistons and cylinders from a little less than 0.025 mm (0.001 in.) to about 0.064 mm (0.0025 in.). If the piston-to-cylinder running clearance is more than 0.102 mm (0.004 in.), Porsche says the bore is excessive—replace the piston-and-cylinder set.

There are some aftermarket piston-and-cylinder sets available for 911s that start out with more than 0.102 mm (0.004 in.) running clearance brand-new. If you consider buying a set of these pistons and cylinders because you think you are going to save some money, please reconsider. They may be less expensive than the Mahle pistons and cylinders, but you will not be saving any money if the running clearances are in excess of 0.102 mm (0.004 in.) because you are actually buying *worn-out* pistons and cylinders, or if you perfer, *brand-new replicas* of worn-out pistons and cylinders.

What happens if you use pistons and cylinders with excessive running clearances is that the pistons rock back and forth in their bores and the rings cannot work properly. In fact, the rings themselves can be worn-out before the engine is broken in. It really doesn't matter how cheaply you can buy something if it doesn't work, does it?

Following are some of the racing or specialized Mahle pistons and cylinders available for 911/930 type engines.

Most racing pistons for the 911 engine were made with a 10.3:1 compression ratio. However, they must be checked because they will vary depending upon their originally intended application.

Connecting-rod dimensions

The following table shows the important dimensions of the various connecting rods used in the 911 and 930 engines on production cars.

CIS fuel injection and blown air boxes

The CIS fuel-injection system was introduced on the 1973 911T in January of that year, and was utilized by all 911s from 1974 until the introduction of the 911 Carrera in 1984.

The CIS (Bosch K-Jetronic) fuel-injection system is a relatively simple mechanical fuel-injection system for gasoline engines. The air that is sucked into the engine is controlled by the throttle valve,

Bore (mm)	Stroke (mm)	Displacement (liter, cc)
80	66	2.0, 1991
81	66	2.1, 2041
85	66	2.3, 2247
86.7	70.4	2.5, 2494
87.5	66	2.4, 2381
89	66	2.5, 2464
90	70.4	2.7, 2687; Carrera RS 8.5:1 compression
90	70.4	2.7, 2687; 10.3:1 compression
91	70.4	2.75, 2747
92	70.4	2.8, 2808
92.8	70.4	2.8, 2857; 935 Turbo
93	70.4	2.85, 2869
95	70.4	3.0, 2994; 10.3:1 compression
95	70.4	3.0, 2994; 10.4:1 compression
95	70.4	3.0, 2994; CIS 8.5:1 compression
95	70.4	3.0, 2994; CIS 9.8:1 compression
95	70.4	3.0, 2994; 935 Turbo 6.5:1 compression
95	74.4	3.2, 3164, 935 Turbo 7.2:1 compression
97	70.4	3.12, 3122; 935 Turbo 6.5:1 compression
98	70.4	3.2, 3186; RSR 10.3:1 compression
98	70.4	3.2, 3186; 911SC 9.3:1 compression
98	70.4	3.2, 3186; Max Moritz wedge-shape dome originally for CIS 9.3:1 compression
98	74.4	3.4, 3367; racing pistons
98	74.4	3.4, 3367; RUF 3.4 Carrera conversion
98	74.4	3.4, 3367; Turbo
100	74.4	3.5, 3506; 22 mm wrist-pin normally-aspirated racing
100	74.4	3.5, 3506; 23 mm wrist-pin normally-aspirated racing
100	74.4	3.5, 3506; 23 mm wrist-pin Turbo

911 connecting-rod sizes

Engine size	Length measured center to center (mm)	Big-end diameter (mm)	Big-end width at crankpin (mm)	Wrist pin (mm)
2.0-2.2	130	61	21.8 (brg width 22)	22
2.4, 2.7, 3.0	127.8	56	23.8 (brg width 22)	22
3.0 SC	127.8	56	21.8 (brg width 22)	22
3.2-3.3	127.0*	58	21.8 (brg width 22)	23

0.8 mm (0.031 in.) shorter than 911SC connecting rod.

and then the volume of that air is measured by an airflow sensor which in turn controls the position of a fuel-metering piston in the fuel distributor. From the fuel distributor, the fuel goes out the various fuel lines to the injectors and is injected into the engine.

So you can see that the basis for the system is a fairly simple demand-type system controlling the engine's mixture by measuring the engine's airflow. It would be simple if that was all there was to it, however there are a number of compensating devices hung around the system to help the system run properly.

The CIS or K-Jetronic system was a reasonable solution at the time it was introduced in 1973 in that it provided reasonable performance and reasonable fuel consumption while making it easier and less expensive to meet the emission laws, which at that time where getting stricter every year.

The CIS system does have a few shortcomings, however, and some of them are easier to live with than others. Because of the method used to measure the airflow, an engine with CIS injection is limited to the use of relatively mild camshafts, thus limiting the engine's total performance potential. A bigger problem is the fact that most of the components in the system are fuel-handling components, so that the CIS system has a much greater exposure to fuel contamination.

We are still seeing fuel contamination in the CIS-injected cars. The moisture and impurities in the fuel have caused fuel starvation and poor running. It is very important to keep good-quality, clean fuel supplied to the CIS injection. Be careful of Gasohol and a lot of new premium fuels that use alcohol as an octane booster. Alcohol will put any water in the system in suspension so that it can get into the injection system to cause contamination and corrosion.

CIS-injected 911s also have a problem with the warm-up regulator being out of adjustment or nonfunctioning. Without the proper mixture in a 911 during this warm-up cycle, you may be playing Russian roulette with the air box.

Improperly operating warm-up regulators are often the cause of blown air boxes. If your 911 starts cold and runs rough for the first minute or so, it is trying to tell you something. Please listen to it. Have the warm-up regulator adjusted or replaced before you need a new air box as well. The warm-up regulator is not the *only* thing that can cause an air box to blow, however. The warm-up regulator is just one problem we can isolate.

Actually, any poor running condition should be looked into, since it is possible for any number of rough running conditions to cause a backfire that could blow the air box. Each year when it first gets cold in the winter, and again when it first gets warm in the spring, you'll actually see a few 911s that have been running fine, then backfire and blow their air boxes for what appears to be no good reason at all.

The cold-start circuit has also contributed to these random explosions in that the fuel was sprayed into the intake plenum in a fairly uncontrolled manner. The way that the process works is that if the engine is cold, when you try to start it

Modification for Weber float bowl. Weber supplied its carburetors with a little stand-off around the main-jet well in the bottom of the float-bowl chamber. This was done to prevent the main circuit from picking up dirt from the bottom of the float bowl. Unfortunately there were also some heavy-cornering conditions where this stand-off also prevented the main jet from picking up the fuel and would cause fuel starvation.

The modification to improve fuel pickup consisted of either milling away the stand-off with an end mill, or grinding it away with a rotary file in a die grinder. It had to be ground or milled down so that the fuel could be picked up off the bottom of the float bowl.

by turning the key to the start position, the voltage will be applied to both the starter and the cold-start valve.

The cold-start valve is a solenoid-operated injection valve, the "seventh injector." A thermo time switch determines if it is cold enough to operate the seventh injector, and if so, for how long. The original cold-start system relied on the high primary-circuit pressure to sufficiently atomize the fuel by the swirl of the nozzle. This spraying of raw gasoline into the intake plenum actually proved to be one of the causes of the blown air boxes, however.

In 1981 a change was made to the cold-start circuit in order to provide a more uniform distribution of the cold-start mixture to all of the engine's cylinders. Porsche added a cold-start-mixture distributor to the air-box plenum. This distributor injects the cold-start fuel into the central tube of the plenum where it is mixed with the auxiliary air from the auxiliary air regulator, and then injects it into each of the six manifold runners. This ensured that a proper mixture reached the cylinders to help with the starting process, and also prevented the raw gas from being dumped into the intake plenum just in case there was a backfire in the intake system.

A number of 911 owners have protected their air boxes by installing a Backfire Pressure Relief Valve. This valve looks very much like a little plastic valve in the bottom of the float chamber of a modern toilet.

The purpose of the BPRV is to allow any explosions or backfires in the induction system a free path of escape, the theory being that if the excess pressure from the backfire is allowed to escape through this valve, it will not seek its own path out by either blowing off the boot or exploding the air box.

Fuel

Octane is a widely used—but not well understood—term used to describe the gasoline's ability to deal with the high pressures and temperatures in the engine's combustion chamber without knocking.

The higher the octane, the higher the combustion temperature before engine knock occurs. What this means to us as end users is that high-octane gasoline can be heated more and compressed more by the pistons before the engine will knock or ping.

To finish the main-jet pickup modification, a small sheet-aluminum dam was made to fit into the float chamber and sit on top of the main-jet bores and stand-off tubes.

This dam was then glued into place with epoxy. The dam's purpose was to trap fuel around the main-jet pickup to prevent momentary fuel starvation.

Additional Weber float venting. Unfortunately, the volatility of US gasoline has greatly increased in the past few years. Prior to 1983 there was a period of about 20 years where the fuel had an average Reid Vapor Pressure (RVP) of about 9 to 9.5 psi. Since 1983 the RVP has increased to 11.5 psi (industry standard specification) and above. This increased RVP causes excessive volatility which results in vapor lock and fuel foaming, hot starting problems, poor low-speed driveability and boiling in the carburetors. The high RVP was causing the fuel in the Weber float bowls to boil and percolate the fuel out through the secondary venturi. Once this process starts it can siphon all of the fuel out of the float chamber into the throttle bore and intake port. The resulting problem from the fuel percolation is the high risk of fire when the engine is restarted. PMO offers the fixture shown in this photo for drilling additional venting holes in the carburetor top cover. The fixture aims the drill into the vent chamber for the idle air-correction jet. This vent chamber then is vented into the carburetor throat via the little square slots visible in photo. This extra venting seems to solve most of the problems caused by the excessive volatility of the fuel.

The octane ratings themselves indicate a gasoline's ability to resist detonation, and enable owners to buy the correct gas to meet their engines' needs and to prevent damage. For Porsche owners this should not be much of a problem, because the unleaded fuels that are available today will meet most of the octane needs for the various Porsche models.

It does not do any good to run a higher-octane gasoline in your Porsche engine than the engine requires, because all the higher-octane does is prevent knocking by controlling the burn rate of the gasoline. You will not get better performance by using higher-octane gasoline, you will just spend more money and in some cases actually *reduce* the engine's performance.

Remember, the United States uses a different method of rating the octane than is used in Europe. The United States uses the average method, or what is called the CLC $\left(\dfrac{RON+MON}{2}\right)$

method (US Cost of Living Council octane rating). Regular fuels in Europe have octane ratings ranging from 91 to 98 RON (Research Octane Number) which corresponds to 87 to 93 CLC (average method).

As an example, the 1977 911S/Turbo Carrera owners manual says that the 911S engine requires 91 RON octane or 87 CLC octane. So it can quite readily run on unleaded regular. The same manual says that the Turbo Carrera for racing or sustained high-speed driving requires 96 RON octane or 92 CLC octane.

RON is considered a better test of antiknock characteristics for engines operating at full throttle at low engine speeds. The MON test is considered to be a better indicator of antiknock characteristics at full-throttle high engine speed, and part-throttle low and high engine speeds. The CLC method attempts to create a more meaningful rating by averaging the two.

The CLC octane rating will usually be four to five points lower than the RON

rating. For example, the current-production European Carrera has a compression ratio of 10.3:1 and requires a fuel quality of 98/88 RON/MON leaded, or unleaded with identical octane number. Using the CLC average system, this works out to be 93 octane.

This is contrasted with the US version, which has a compression ratio of 9.5:1 and requires fuel quality of 87 CLC octane unleaded. The US version is rated at 217 hp with 195 lb-ft of peak torque, versus the Euro version at 231 hp with 209 lb-ft peak torque.

Fuel additives

What about octane? Can we get away with US pump gasolines in today's hot-rod 911s? For the most part the answer is, yes you can.

Premium unleaded fuel is adequate for any Porsche that require an unleaded fuel; most of them only require unleaded regular. Although fuel additives will not harm the catalytic converters or oxygen sensors, they are a very expensive way to go.

Most of the 911s will do fine on US pump gasoline, thank you. Nevertheless, there are a few that are marginal, and there are some combinations the owners have created themselves that overstep the bounds of reason. An example of this would be using the 2.8 RSR on the 2.7 engine, where the compression ratio ends up in the 11:1 range. In general, any of the 911s with less than 10:1 compression will do fine with the 92-and-above unleaded premium.

Our biggest need for higher-octane fuels is for the track events. The same octane ratings that you might be able to get away with in 911s for street use are just not adequate for these track events, where the cars are subjected to sustained hard running. You will have to increase the octane in these instances to protect your engine from damage from detonation.

Probably the best solution for these track events is to buy some racing gasoline, aviation gasoline or a fuel additive that contains aniline to mix in with your pump gas, and raise the octane to an acceptable level to prevent detonation.

The biggest shortcoming of octane-boosting additives is the expense. If you decide you want to use an additive, you should try to find one that uses aniline as its main ingredient. The most effective octane-boosting additive is aniline, but because it, like lead, is toxic, it is being phased out as an octane booster as well.

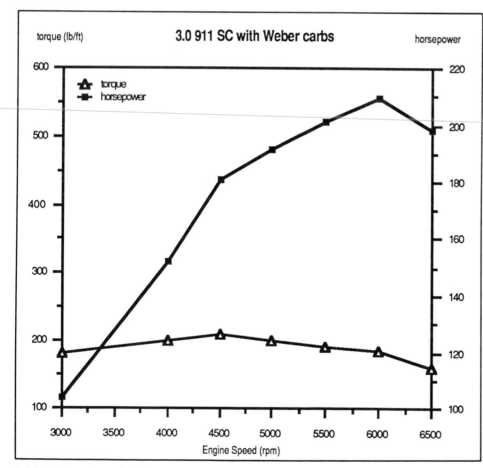

3.0 911SC engine with Weber carburetors. This 3.0 liter 911SC engine was modified by the addition of a set of 40 IDA-3C carburetors and an early-style exhaust system with a stock muffler.

Assuming that when you purchased a pint can of additive it was 100 percent aniline, it would take three cans at about $12 a can to raise the octane rating of twenty gallons of gas about three CLC octane points. The three pints work out to 1.9 percent aniline added to twenty gallons of gas. This added $36 per tank makes for an expensive fill-up.

Before the removal of lead from gasoline we were able to mix unleaded premium gasoline and leaded regular gasoline and boost the octane above that of the unleaded premium. The reason this worked was that the gasoline producers were mixing more lead than was necessary in the leaded gasoline.

Mixing unleaded and leaded gasolines doesn't do us any good anymore though, now that the lead content has been cut to 0.10 gram per gallon in the leaded fuels.

The principle of mixing leaded and unleaded gasolines together to boost the octane of the unleaded fuel can still be practiced for track events. You can use either racing or aviation gasoline, both of which still use tetraethyl lead as their octane-boosting agent.

As you can see in the chart, either of these leaded gasolines will provide a significant boost in octane to the unleaded premium used as the base stock. The aviation gasoline has a lower specific gravity, so the induction system will have to be richened up to compensate for this.

Have you ever snapped your fingers? Go ahead, try it. Sorry, that's not fast enough! The time required from when the spark plug first ignites a properly mixed air/fuel mixture in the combustion chamber until the combustion is completed is less than the time it takes to snap your fingers.

One important factor in this process is the engine's compression ratio. After the piston has moved down to suck in the air-and-gasoline mixture, it returns upward to compress the mixture before the spark plug ignites it. If the piston allows room for nine units of space in the cylinder at the bottom of its stroke, but only enough room for one unit when at the top, the engine has a compression ratio of 9:1. A higher compression ratio makes the engine more thermodynamically efficient so that it can get more work out of the fuel.

If everything goes right, in less time than it takes you to snap your fingers, you have perfect combustion and extract the maximum power from the gasoline

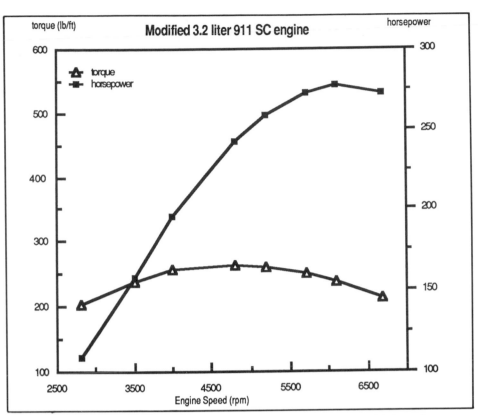

Modified 3.2 liter 911SC engine. This 3.0 liter 911SC engine has been modified by the addition of larger-bore 98 mm pistons and cylinders, special high-performance camshafts, 40 IDA-3C carburetors and an SSI exhaust system.

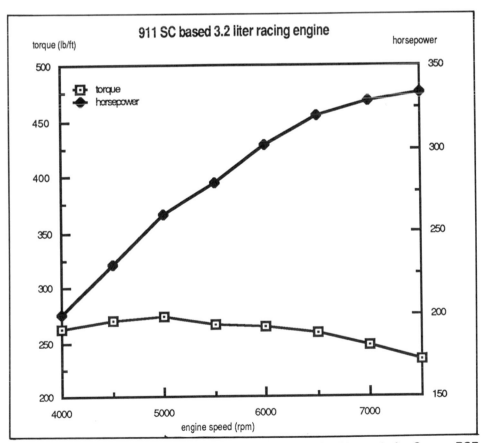

The 911SC-based 3.2 liter racing engine. This 3.0 liter 911SC engine was modified extensively with larger ports, Garretson Enterprises GE-80 camshafts, Carrera RSR racing headers and a set of 46 IDA Weber carburetors.

Gasoline's octane response to aniline

Gasoline	RON	MON	$\frac{R+M}{2}$	$\frac{R+M}{2}$ increase	$\frac{R+M}{2}$ increase for 1% aniline
92 octane unleaded	97.9	86.3	92.1	———	———
92 octane unleaded + 2% aniline	101.4	89.5	95.4	3.3	1.6
92 octane unleaded + 4% aniline	103.8	92.1	98.0	5.9	1.5
89 octane unleaded	94.9	84.2	89.6	———	———
89 octane unleaded + 2% aniline	98.9	87.9	93.4	3.8	1.9
89 octane unleaded + 4% aniline	102.0	90.3	96.2	6.6	1.6
88 octane leaded	93.0	83.5	88.2	———	———
88 octane leaded + 2% aniline	97.2	86.8	92.0	3.8	1.9
88 octane leaded + 4% aniline	100.3	89.0	94.6	6.4	1.6

Effect of mixing aviation or race gasoline with premium unleaded gasoline

Gas used as additive	Mixture	RON	MON	$\frac{R+M}{2}$	Specific gravity	Approximate lead content (g/gal)
	unleaded premium	96.8	85.8	91.3	0.7579	0
100/130	75% UP/25% Av gas	99.2	90.3	94.8	0.7416	1
aviation gas	50% UP/50% Av gas	100.9	94.4	97.6	0.7256	2
green	25% UP/75% Av gas	101.3	99.8	100.6	0.7093	3
	100% Av gas	101.5	103.7	102.6	0.6926	4
race gas	unleaded premium	96.8	85.8	91.3	0.7579	0
	75% UP/25% race gas	101.8	91.1	96.4	0.7547	1
	50% UP/50% race gas	104.9	95.1	100.0	0.7491	2
	25% UP/75% race gas	109.2	100.1	104.6	0.7440	3
	100% race gas	114.2	103.5	108.8	0.7408	4

Intercooler kit for 1975 through 1977 3.0 liter Turbo. This Garretson Enterprises intercooler kit and a later-style rear wing allowed you to adapt an intercooler to one of these pre-intercooler cars. This larger intercooler was more efficient than the factory 3.3 911 Turbo intercooler.

used. The proper air/fuel ratio for perfect combustion is a mixture of fourteen parts air to one part gasoline. In a carbureted engine, most of the fuel-air mixing is done in the carburetor itself. In a fuel-injected engine, fuel is injected into the intake airstream.

In both cases the air/fuel mixture is drawn into the cylinder and swirled around, and is further mixed on the way into the cylinder. Once the compression stroke begins, the mixing process is accelerated as the air and fuel are forced into a smaller and smaller volume. By the time ignition occurs, the fuel and air have attained a near-perfect mixing.

In some engines, a higher compression ratio can actually improve the flame propagation and combustion, and actually reduce the engine's sensitivity to knocking by reducing the size of the combustion chamber. This certainly is not always the case and the 2.0 liter 911 engine was certainly an exception.

The 2.0 911 engine has a very small, steep, hemispherical combustion chamber in a cylinder head with two large valves. The large valves displace the spark plug away from the ideal position, off to one side. When the compression is raised on these engines, the dome of the piston protrudes into the combustion chamber so that the flame front has to travel over and around the piston to get complete combustion. The higher the compression the worse the problem is, which was one of the reasons Porsche chose to use twin spark plugs for the 906 engine, which utilized this combustion-chamber shape.

In the later-model 911 engines the flame-travel problem was virtually eliminated by two different changes. For one thing, all 911 engines from 1970 on have had a more shallow, open combustion-chamber design. Also, each increase in displacement reduced the need to crowd the combustion chamber in order to maintain high compression ratios. This occurs because the compression ratio is the volume of the cylinder with the piston at the bottom of its travel, compared to the volume with the piston at the top of its travel.

Effectively, Porsche has maintained a nominal compression ratio of 10.3:1 for all of its normally aspirated racing engines. Whereas the larger-displacement engines just have a nice smooth bump on the top to maintain the same compression ratio, the 2.0 liter piston has a very steep dome. The larger pistons with their relatively smaller domes will not obstruct the combustion chamber, so the flame travel is less impaired and the engines will be much less prone to knocking or pinging.

Obviously, the choice of gasoline has a great deal of influence on detonation in your Porsche. There are gasolines available that are safe for all Porsches in almost all applications. Modern high-grade unleaded gasoline allows high compression ratios to be used with the combustion and expansion process under complete control. Special racing gas is available for purely racing purposes, to allow 10.3:1 compression ratios and turbocharged engines to also run without detonation.

With high-compression engines, it is possible to have slight detonation yet have none of the normal indications we expect with pre-ignition. For instance, the pre-ignition can happen at higher rpm when it might not be heard over the other noises the car may make.

This was a problem with some of the first 2.0 liter 911 engines and 911S engines with their tight combustion chambers. So you will want to make sure—if you own one of these early cars—that you always use the highest-octane fuel you can buy. If you still have a pinging or detonation problem, you might want to consider lowering the compression ratio of your engine by changing the pistons.

Compression ratio

Compression ratio of an engine is the ratio of the total swept volume (the volume of the cylinder when the piston is at BDC, including the volume of the cylinder head and so forth) to the unswept volume (the volume of the cylinder when the piston is at TDC).

The formula for compression is =

$$\frac{V1+V2+V3-V4}{V2+V3-V4}$$

V1 = swept volume
V2 = deck-height volume
V3 = cylinder-head volume
V4 = piston-dome-volume

To show that this formula actually works, we will go through the processes of figuring the compression ratio for a two-liter racing engine with one millimeter overbore pistons; so the bore is 81 mm and the stroke is 66 mm for a displacement of 2040.6 cc.

Calculating V1

To determine the compression ratio, you don't actually have to measure V1, the swept volume of one cylinder. In fact,

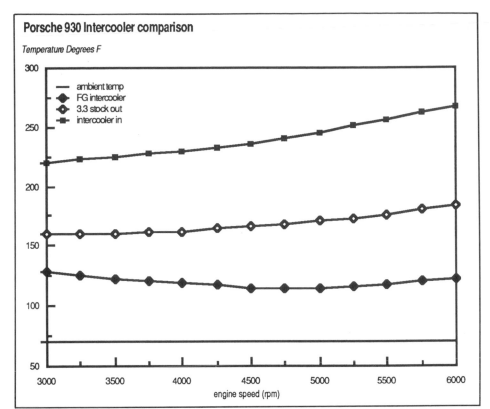

Porsche 930 intercooler comparison. This chart shows how much more effective the FG intercooler was than the stock cooler.
Fred Garretson

Larger, more efficient Garretson Enterprises intercooler conversion for 1978 through 1987 3.3 liter 911 Turbo (930).

These larger intercoolers allowed you to safely use higher boost levels and produce more horsepower.

it is easier to compute it from the bore and stroke.

$$\text{Swept volume (V1)} = \text{bore}^2 \times \text{stroke} \times 0.7854$$

The formula uses bore and stroke in centimeters, so we will have to convert the numbers from millimeters (mm) to centimeters (cm) by moving the decimal point one place to the left, and then plug the numbers into the formula.

RUF intercooler kit. The RUF intercooler was designed by Laengerer & Reich Kuehlerfabrik Gmbh. which is the same company that makes the original-equipment intercooler for Porsche. The RUF intercooler had 66 percent more surface area than the stock intercooler. A well-designed intercooler, like RUF's, provided a cool dense charge to the engine which resulted in an increase of about 30 hp. The intercoolers made an even greater difference when incorporated along with other modifications. Exclusive Motor Cars, Inc.

$$\text{Swept volume (V1)} = 8.1^2 \times 6.6 \times 0.7854$$
$$= 340.09 \text{ cc}$$

Calculating V2

First, the dome and deck heights must be measured. This involves two steps, the first of which is done with a piston-and-cylinder set that is not installed on the engine. The beginning of the dome must be determined, and then the distance measured from that beginning point to the top of the dome with a height-measuring gauge. For our example, that measurement will be 0.675 in.

Next, the height of the dome must be measured with a depth micrometer, with the piston and cylinder installed on the engine and set to TDC. Since the dome sticks out of the cylinder, the depth micrometer must be spaced up to facilitate the measurement.

In our example we have used Jo blocks to space up the depth micrometer 0.700 in. With piston at top dead center, measure down to the top of the piston. This measurement will be Depth #1, which in our example will be (0.046 in.). Knowing Depth #1, the height of the dome and the height of the Jo blocks will permit the calculation of the deck height.

$$\text{Deck height} = \text{dome height} + \text{Depth \#1} - \text{Jo block height}$$

$$0.675 + 0.046 - 0.700 = 0.021 \text{ in. deck height}$$

The deck-height volume can now be calculated using the formula used to calculate swept volume, but substituting deck height—after converting it to centimeters—for stroke in the formula.

Convert inches to centimeters by multiplying by 2.54 ($0.021 \times 2.54 = 0.053$) before plugging it into the swept-volume (deck-height volume) formula.

$$\text{Swept volume (deck-height volume V2)} = \text{bore}^2 \times \text{stroke} \times 0.7854$$

$$8.1^2 \times 0.053 \times 0.7854 = 2.73 \text{ cc V2 deck-height volume}$$

Calculating V3

Because of the irregular shape of the combustion chamber, measuring its

Kremer intercooler kit. The Kremer intercooler kit was very large and required installing a larger rear wing.

Larger rear wing to accommodate the very large Kremer intercooler.

Kremer-modified 911 Turbo engine. This Kremer 3.3 liter 911 Turbo engine was modified by using a K27 turbocharger, modified camshafts, large intercooler, modified cylinder block, modified cylinder heads and intake manifold, twin ignition and four- pipe muffler. Depending upon the boost settings, the power output for engines with these modifications is 390 to 410 hp. The Kremers recommend a front-mounted oil cooler for these high-output engines. Porsche Kremer Racing

US 911 Turbo engine's exhaust system from 1976 through 1980. Beyond increasing the boost a little and adding a larger intercooler, the exhaust system had to be replaced by the European-style exhaust before any other modifications were performed. The engine in the photo had its thermo reactors replaced with "headers." These were not really "headers," they were thermo-reactor replacements. Changing to the thermo-reactor replacements helped the engine heat, but really did nothing for engine performance.

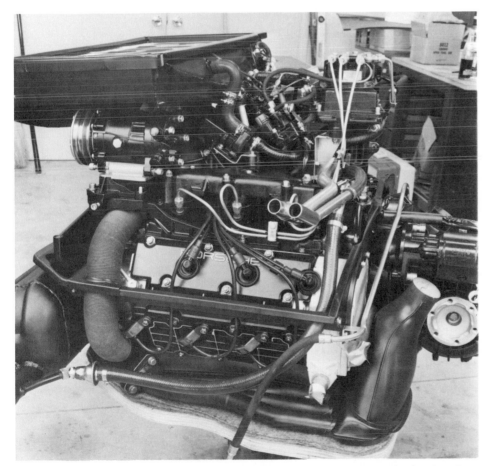

Turbo exhaust conversion. This 911 Turbo used the early-style normally aspirated type exhaust system in an effort to take advantage of the exhaust tuning of that system. Ideally you would want two equal-length primary exhaust systems with very short secondary pipes leading directly to the turbo. Unfortunately there is not enough room at the rear of one of these cars for the ideal exhaust system and all of the other things that need to be there. Tom Hanna

Euro-style 911 Turbo exhaust system. Changing to this style exhaust system will permit all of the other turbo-engine modifications. If this change is not made to one of the 1976 to 1980 US cars, the performance below 3000 rpm will be very poor after the modifications, particularly after changing the camshafts. Several different mufflers have been used with this system. All will work; some just make more power than others. The US-version 1986 and 1987 911 Turbos used this same Euro exhaust system, but with a different muffler and a catalytic converter. Both of these will also have to be changed to facilitate most of the performance modifications for the 911 Turbo.

volume involves physically filling it with liquid and then seeing how much liquid it took to do the job. The most convenient method for doing this is with a graduated chemist burette and a plexiglass disc to seal the combustion chamber.

Even if the you are not going to be calculating your compression ratio, you may want to "cc" your heads to ensure that all of the combustion chambers are within 1 cc of each other. The term cc-ing is usually used in reference to this process of comparing all of the combustion-chamber sizes. Porsche heads are generally pretty accurate, and whatever differences you find can usually be adjusted for by sinking the valves a little deeper in the heads, with the smaller combustion chambers. This, of course, requires redoing the valve job.

Before cc-ing the head, install the valves and springs and the spark plug. You can get away without installing the valve springs if you smear a light coat of grease on the valve seating surfaces. Place the head on a level surface so the combustion chamber faces upward. It is

IMSA GTO 934. This 934 had a special exhaust system with a pair of three-into-one headers leading to a large dual-inlet turbocharger. Each of the three-into-one headers was kept separate from the other and had its own wastegate. The vacuum/boost control circuits for the wastegates were connected in parallel, like they are on a twin-turbo 935. The performance for this engine was very similar to the twin-turbo 935s. In 1983 Wayne Baker won the IMSA GTO championship with this 934, winning his class championship and Sebring outright.

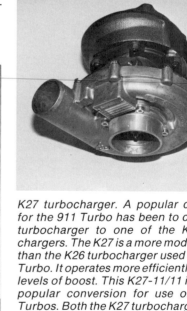

K27 turbocharger. A popular conversion for the 911 Turbo has been to change the turbocharger to one of the K27 turbochargers. The K27 is a more modern design than the K26 turbocharger used on the 911 Turbo. It operates more efficiently at higher levels of boost. This K27-11/11 is the most popular conversion for use on the 911 Turbos. Both the K27 turbocharger and the intercooler need to be modified so the K27 can be used in the 911 Turbo. The turbocharger should have 10 mm milled off of the mounting surface of the exhaust flange to make it fit better. The intercooler inlet tube must be modified so that it can be connected to the K27 turbocharger. The original mounting of this tube to the K26 turbocharger was sealed with an O-ring. Because there is no provision on the K27 for the O-ring, a piece of radiator-type hose and hose clamps are used instead.

Assembled RUF 3.4 conversion. Note "930S" wastegate, large K27 turbo and resulting clearance in tailpipes, very large

RUF intercooler and resulting modifications to the air cleaner. Exclusive Motor Cars, Inc.

very helpful to have a jig to hold the head so that it can be accurately leveled.

Cut a piece of clear plexiglass so that it will just fit into the cylinder head and seal against the cylinder-head sealing surface. The plexiglass stock must be thick enough so that it will not deflect and throw off the reading. Drill a small hole in the center of your plexiglass plate just large enough for the tip of your burette. Coat the sealing surface of the cylinder head with a thin coat of grease and press the plexiglass disc down tight against the head.

Mix some automatic transmission fluid into some clean solvent and fill the burette. The coloration of the fluid makes it easier to see what you are doing. Fill the burette to zero and the graduations on the side of the burette will be direct reading. Position the tip of the burette over the hole in the plexiglass and fill the combustion chamber until there are no bubbles.

The reading on the burette will be the cylinder head's combustion-chamber volume in cubic centimeters. In the case of the two-liter heads, the volume will be between 70 and 75 cc, partially depending on the wide range of different valve sizes. For our example V3, the combustion-chamber volume will be 71 cc.

Calculating V4

The final step before using the formula to calculate the compression ratio is measuring the volume of the piston dome. Again using a piston and cylinder not installed on the engine, insert the piston into its cylinder. Spread a light coat of grease a little below the top of the cylinder. Push the piston up in the cylinder until the top ring is sealed by the grease and the piston dome is still below the top edge of the cylinder.

Measure the distance from the top of the cylinder to the top of the piston dome with the depth micrometer. This measurement will be Depth #2. With Depth #2, the calculated theoretical volume can be calculated using the formula used to calculate swept volume, but substituting Depth #2 plus the dome height—after converting the sum to centimeters—for stroke in the formula.

Height of calculated theoretical volume
= Depth #2 + dome height

$$0.144 + 0.675 = 0.819 \text{ in.}$$

Convert to centimeters by multiplying by 2.54 ($0.819 \times 2.54 = 2.080$)

before plugging it into the swept-volume formula.

Swept volume = bore$^2 \times$ stroke $\times$ 0.7854

$8.1^2 \times 2.080 \times 0.7854 = 107.18$ cc which is the calculated theoretical cylinder volume. (This is the *calculated* volume of the cylinder, not taking into account the presence of the piston dome.)

Next is cc-ing the theoretical cylinder volume in the cylinder for the piston-dome volume calculation. Coat the edge of the plexiglass plate with grease and place it on top of the cylinder and press down so it will seal to the sealing surface of the cylinder. Fill the burette with the solvent and automatic transmission fluid to zero, and fill the theoretical cylinder volume with the fluid. When the theoretical volume is completely filled, the burette reading will be the measured theoretical cylinder volume in cubic centimeters.

In our example, the measured volume will be 70.6 cc. The volume of the piston dome can now be calculated by subtract-

RUF 3.4 liter conversion. These are all of the parts that were included in the RUF conversion to 3.4 liters. The kit included a set of Mahle 98 mm pistons and cylinders which bolt on and require no machining. The cylinders were of Porsche's conventional cooling design, and as a result needed all of the top air deflectors as well as the bottom. The conversion used Porsche Group B camshafts, RUF's own special intercooler and muffler. Notice that the intercooler required that the air cleaner be modified for clearance, and that the muffler required new valence parts to clear the extra tailpipes. The kit included a K27 turbo and the modified air duct to the intercooler. A large fan pulley (1.8:1 ratio) and fan belts were also included. Exclusive Motor Cars, Inc.

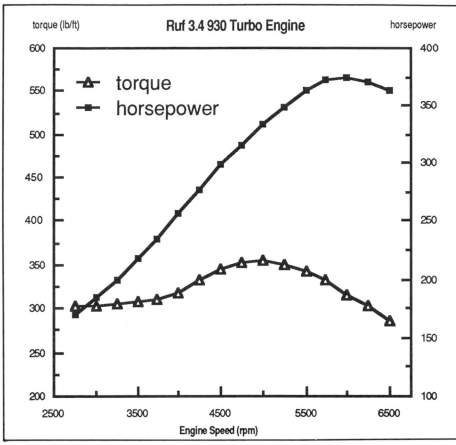

Ruf 3.4 930 Turbo Engine

torque (lb/ft) ... horsepower

- △ torque
- ■ horsepower

Engine Speed (rpm)

Power output for RUF 3.4 liter conversion.
RUF

ing the measured volume from the calculated theoretical cylinder volume.

Dome volume = calculated theoretical volume – measured volume

107.18 – 70.6 = 36.58 cc dome volume

Number of cylinders	= 6
Bore	= 81 mm
Stroke	= 66 mm
Deck height	= 0.533 mm (0.021 in.)
V1 swept volume	= 340.0 cc
V2 deck-height volume	= 2.73 cc
V3 cylinder-head volume	= 70.6 cc
V4 piston-dome volume	= 36.6 cc

Final calculation

Now that we have all of the numbers, all we need do is plug them into the compression ratio formula:

$$\frac{V1+V2+V3-V4}{V2+V3-V4} = \text{compression}$$

$$\frac{340.0+2.73+70.6-36.6}{2.73+70.6-36.6} = 10.18$$

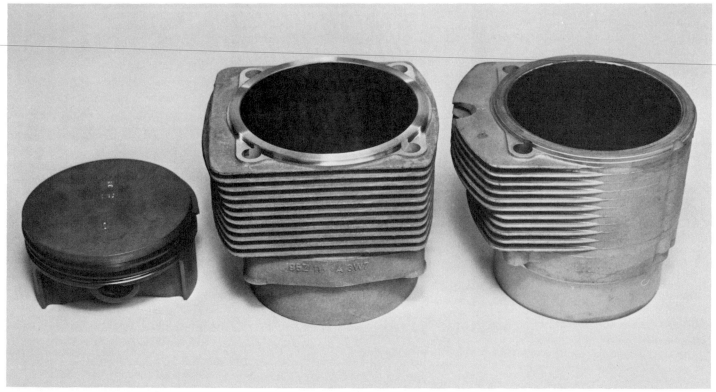

3.5 Turbo conversion. With 100 mm pistons and cylinders for 911 turbo, this conversion increased the displacement to 3506 cc. The crankcase must have the cylinder-spigot bores machined to accept these larger pistons and cylinders. 3.5 piston and cylinder on the left, and stock 3.3 cylinder on right.

Ruf "Yellow Bird" Twin Turbo 930 Engine

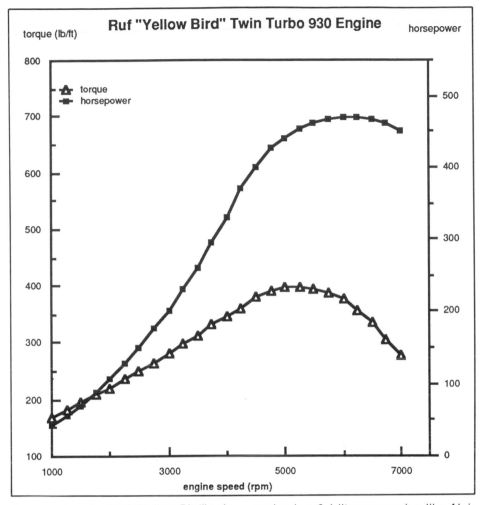

Figure: torque (lb/ft) and horsepower vs. engine speed (rpm), 1000–7000 rpm.

Our compression ratio for this engine is 10.18:1 which is just about right for a 911 racing engine. Porsche always aims for 10.3:1 as a nominal value for its racing engines.

Remember that the engine's bore, stroke, combustion-chamber size, deck height and the piston-dome size all work together to determine the compression ratio. If any of these are changed, the compression ratio will also be changed. Bigger bore and longer stroke will increase the compression ratio if the dome on the pistons is not changed to compensate. Porsche designs its engines with this fact in mind, so you will have to exercise caution when mixing pistons and cylinders for one engine-displacement size to another.

For instance if you were to use 84 mm pistons and cylinders from a 2.2 liter engine in place of the 84 mm made for the 2.4 liter engine when building a 2.4 liter engine, the compression will be increased by the effect of the longer stroke. To compensate for this change, the dome was made smaller on the pistons for the larger-displacement 2.4 liter engine

A few of the Porsche 911 engines use flat-top pistons which have no dome. It is easier to solve the equation for compression ratio for these engines—you just leave out V4 (dome volume) in the equation. The deck height is also easier to measure with a flat-topped piston. You just measure down to the top of the piston from the top of the cylinder with a depth micrometer.

Power output for RUF "Yellow Bird" twin-turbo 930 engine. Yellow Bird was the car that Road & Track used in its "World's Fastest Cars" test. Yellow Bird went 211 mph, clocked 0-60 mph in 4 sec and turned the quarter at 133.5 mph in 11.7 sec. The engine is a 3.4 liter conversion like Alois Ruf's other 911 Turbo conversions, however this one uses a special Digital Motronic Electronic fuel and ignition system in conjunction with twin turbos to achieve the extra performance. RUF

Cylinder from the same 3.3 liter 911 Turbo street engine that was run with too much boost. Notice where the melted piston also melted part of the cylinder. You can also see that the top of the cylinder had distorted and was starting to leak combustion gas. This is usually where the racing cars would fail, at the juncture between the cylinder head and the cylinder.

There is a downside to turbocharging. If you run the turbocharged cars with too much boost or not high enough octane fuel, the engines will detonate and they can seriously hurt themselves. This is a 3.3 liter 911 Turbo engine from a street car that was running very high boost with none of the other modifications necessary to allow using high boost. This engine "blew" a piston.

Checking clearance

When assembling an engine it is always a good idea to measure the deck height (whether or not you are calculating compression ratio). For the 911 engine, the minimum piston-to-cylinder-head clearance should be around 0.90 mm (0.035 in.). Because of the shapes of the piston dome and the combustion chamber, deck height and piston-to-head clearance are not the same and the minimum piston-to-head clearance must also be measured to prevent engine damage. If you are using pistons made by any manufacturer other than Mahle or Karl Schmidt, or if you have done anything to alter the compression or the valve sizes, you should plan to check both the piston-to-head and the valve-to-piston clearances.

Blown CIS air box. Almost any backfire in a CIS-injected 911 will result in a blown air box. And unfortunately the backfires can be caused by a number of things: improper fuel mixture, bad cold start, improperly set warm-up regulator or big swings in the climatic conditions.

There are always people who want more power. Until RUF's Yellow Bird engine, the practical limit for hot-rodding the 911 Turbo engines was about 400-410 hp because of limitations of the induction system. If you still wanted more power, the best way to achieve it was to detune a 935 engine. This photo shows an example of this approach.

Cold-start manifolding. In 1981 Porsche changed the cold-start circuit and provided manifolding for the fuel to the intake runners. This change alone seems to have eliminated about 90 percent of the blown air boxes. Unfortunately there are still a few engines that will backfire and blow their air boxes. These are usually caused by an injection problem or again, big swings in climatic conditions.

935 engine in street-driven 911 Turbo—detuning limited to the use of a pair of custom-built silencers.

Aftermarket pop-off valve. This little device will save the ten percent of the CIS air-intake boxes that still are going to have something go wrong and cause a backfire. This little pop-off mounts in the top of the intake plenum, and if the engine does backfire it just vents the explosion back outside the intake track, out with the air-intake filter.

Check the clearances by placing a strip of modeling clay—at least 3/16 in. thick—in the partially assembled engine, on top of the piston in the area of both the intake- and exhaust-valve pockets, and over at the edge of the piston where it will first hit the combustion chamber. Install the head, and torque it to 25 lb-ft. You can check the piston-to-head clearance without assembling the engine any further by just turning it over for two complete revolutions.

If you are interested in the valve clearance to piston clearance as well, however, it will be necessary to assemble the engine up through timing the camshaft and adjusting the valves on the cylinder under test, and then rotating the crankshaft through two complete revolutions. This will allow both intake and exhaust valves to open and close. After rotating the crank, carefully disassemble the head. If the valves make an impression, cut the clay in half with a sharp knife and measure its thickness at the thinnest point with a vernier caliper.

Another measuring medium preferred by many mechanics is solder in place of the modeling clay. If you use this method, use solder with an uncrushed diameter of 2.54 mm (0.100 in.). Minimum clearance should be 1.5 mm (0.060 in.) for the valves. If there is not adequate clearance between the piston and the cylinder head, it will be necessary to use more cylinder base gaskets to increase the clearance.

If there is adequate piston-to-head clearance but not enough valve clearance, it will be necessary to deepen the valve pockets. This all gets very tricky, and you should not deepen the pockets unless you are sure that doing so will not reduce the thickness of the piston material to less than 5 mm (0.200 in.). Doing so will weaken the dome structure and may lead to piston failure.

Studs and inserts

In 1968, Porsche changed its method of manufacturing the 911 crankcase. Prior to 1968, the crankcase had been sandcast aluminum; the change in 1969 was to high-pressure-cast magnesium. At the time, there were several advantages to this change; the pressure-cast crankcase was a more precise piece requiring less machining, magnesium machines more easily saved machining time, and the finished crankcase weighed twenty-two pounds less than its aluminum predecessor. In 1968, when Porsche had Mahle make these castings, they

were the largest magnesium pressure diecastings ever made, and Mahle won a design award from the Magnesium Association for the Porsche crankcase.

All would have probably been fine at this point if Porsche had left the 911 engine at its two-liter displacement. As a result of increasing the displacement, several weaknesses showed up in the magnesium crankcase. The crankcase itself was redesigned several times to

compensate for the displacement changes and was finally replaced with a much stronger, high-pressure cast-aluminum crankcase.

By 1978, all of the 911-derived engines were using the new, stronger pressure-cast aluminum crankcase developed for the 911 Turbo (930) and introduced with the 1975-model Turbo; all of these crankcases have a 911 Turbo (930) part number. During this evolu-

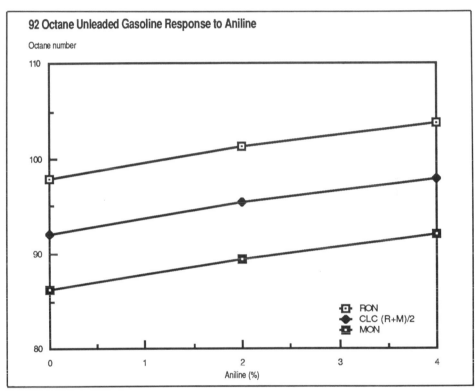

Unleaded 92 octane gasoline response to aniline.

CIS air-intake box with aftermarket pop-off valve installed. This valve was installed by drilling a hole in the intake box with a hole saw and epoxying the valve in place. I recommend a little dab of epoxy on each end of the pop-off valve's hinge pin. I have seen a couple of hinge pins work their way out, which creates an air-intake leak.

tion of the crankcase, the cylinder-head retaining studs were overlooked.

In its racing engines, Porsche had recognized the head-stud problem in the early 1970s and took steps to rectify it. Porsche had found that the difference in rate of thermal expansion for the aluminum and magnesium (which are about the same) used for the crankcase, cylinders and cylinder heads was about double that of the steel cylinder-head retaining studs.

The result was that the cold, or room temperature, stress was increased by the different thermal-expansion rates, resulting in the heads being overly torqued at operating temperatures. The overall result was that with time, many of the head studs pulled and deformed the crankcase where the head studs screwed in. Also in some instances, the head retaining studs themselves broke under this stress.

In the race cars, the solution for this problem was the use of head retaining studs made of Dilavar steel alloy, which has a thermal expansion rate about the same as aluminum and magnesium. The use of Dilavar head retaining studs greatly reduced the stress changes due to temperature changes, virtually eliminating the crankcase problems.

All 911 Turbo (930), 911SC, 911 Carrera and some of the late-1977 2.7 911 engines utilize Dilavar head studs. The 911 Turbo (930) engines use all twenty-four Dilavar head studs, while the normally aspirated 911 engines use the Dilavar studs just for the bottom row of head retaining studs.

Unfortunately, this was not the end of head retaining-stud problems. Engines built prior to the 1980 production models used a Dilavar stud that was shiny silver. Quite a number of engines built with these studs had one or more breaks, requiring their replacement. Because of a corrosion problem, the head studs have

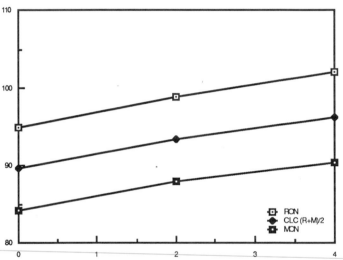

Unleaded 89 octane gasoline response to aniline.

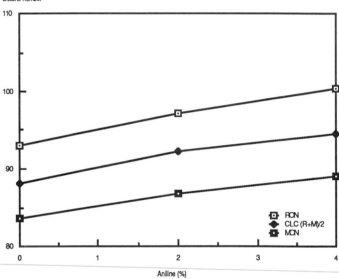

Leaded 88 octane gasoline response to aniline.

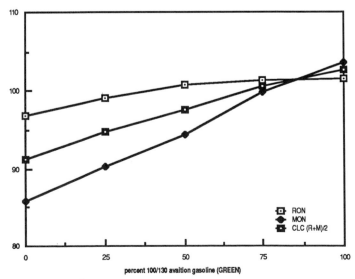

Effect of mixing aviation gasoline with unleaded premium gasoline.

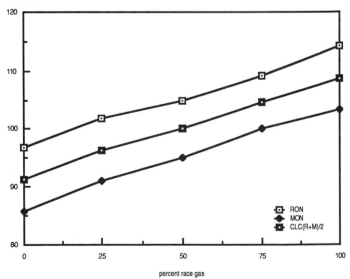

Effect of mixing racing gasoline with unleaded premium gasoline.

been changed twice since 1980. The Dilavar studs manufactured after 1980 have a gold, textured finish and the studs manufactured after 1984 have a black epoxy coating over the center portion of the stud. Both of these later-type studs have a good reliability record. Although some of the early-style studs did break—and they certainly should be checked for corrosion—their failure never approached the high failure rate of the pulled 2.7 cylinder-head studs.

A final word of caution: The Dilavar head studs are expensive enough to encourage people to make counterfeits. You don't want to go to all of this trouble and expense and end up with counterfeits. I'm not really sure what the fakes are, but they aren't Dilavar so be careful. So far, the fakes have been ferrous and thus a magnet will stick to them. The real Dilavar studs are nonferrous.

The 2.7 liter 911 is the engine that really came out on the short end of this evolution; I see a great number of these

engines with pulled head studs. An engine with a pulled head stud will sound like it has a funny exhaust leak. Further investigation will show, however, that it is not an exhaust leak, but a cylinder head leak because one or more head studs have pulled and the cylinder head is no longer properly torqued, so they don't seal to the cylinders.

The crankcases can be repaired by removing all of the head studs, installing Time Serts into the crankcase and installing the new-style Dilavar head studs. I recommend replacing all twenty-four

head studs when changing studs in any engine that will be using aluminum cylinders made of either Alusil or Nicasil. For engines using either cast-iron or Biral cylinders you should use the Time Serts when you rebuild the engine; however, you should still use the original steel-style cylinder-head studs. If Dilavar studs are used with the cast-iron or Biral cylinders it is possible that the heads will be under-torqued.

Because of the high number of 2.7 911 engines I see with head-stud problems, I recommend that this modifica-

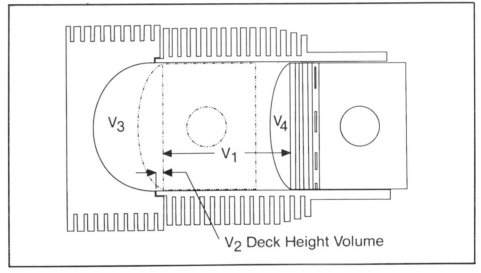

Calculation of compression. To calculate the compression for a 911 engine you measure or calculate V1, the swept volume of one cylinder, V2, the deck-height volume, V3, the cylinder-head volume, and V4, the piston-dome volume.

"CC-ing" cylinder head. For the cc-ing process, the cylinder head should be assembled and the spark plug installed. The edge of the plexiglass plate should be coated with grease so that it will seal to the cylinder head. When the burette is full, it will read zero cubic centimeters. As the solvent is drained into the combustion chamber, through the plate filling the chamber, the level in the burette will fall. When the chamber is completely full, the burette reading will be equal to the combustion-chamber volume in cubic centimeters.

Determining beginning of dome. Visualize the piston as a flat-top piston and determine that edge to be where the dome starts. Measure height of dome. The height of the dome is measured from the point determined to be the beginning of the dome to the top of the dome with a height-measuring gauge.

159

Measure dome height above cylinder, Depth #1. Install one of the pistons and cylinders on the engine and bring the piston to top dead center. Use a pair of accurate measuring spacers (Jo blocks) to space the depth micrometer up so that Depth #1 can be measured. Measure dome height above cylinder. With piston at top dead center, measure down to the top of the piston to get Depth #1. Knowing Depth #1 will permit the calculation of the deck height. For deck height, add dome height and Depth #1 and then subtract the Jo block height.

tion be done to every 2.7 911 engine when the engine is rebuilt. When installing head studs, the correct installed length is 135 mm (5 5/16 in.), measured from the end of the stud to the base at the crankcase. When you install head studs, use red Loctite on the end of the stud that goes into the crankcase. With the combination of the Time Serts and the late-style Dilavar head retaining studs, you will actually end up with a crankcase that is better than it was when new.

Removal and repair of pulled or broken studs

Broken and stripped fasteners are also problems you will have to learn to deal with. If you have a thermal-reactor car, you will find that thermal-reactor studs usually break in the middle because Porsche has tapered them to a smaller diameter in the middle. This is to allow some thermal expansion and to shift the highest concentration of stress away from the threads. You can try a pair of vise grips on these studs when they break, but I have found that the best way is to weld a nut onto the end of the broken stud, then heat the head with a torch, and then remove the broken stud as you would a bolt.

It also helps to heat any frozen nut that holds any exhaust component until

it is cherry-red before trying to remove it. This heating process does two things to help you: it loosens any corrosion or rust and expands the nut, making it easier to remove. When you assemble any exhaust-system components, it is always a good idea to assemble them with Never-Seez anti-seize lubricating compound. This will make it much easier to disassemble next time.

Conventional studs will usually break flush with the surface of the workpiece or slightly below the surface, because

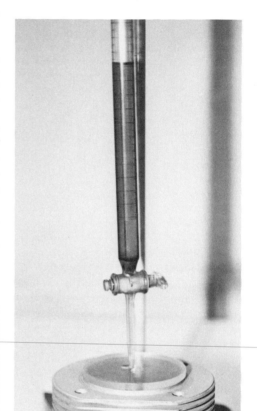

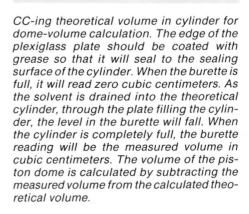

CC-ing theoretical volume in cylinder for dome-volume calculation. The edge of the plexiglass plate should be coated with grease so that it will seal to the sealing surface of the cylinder. When the burette is full, it will read zero cubic centimeters. As the solvent is drained into the theoretical cylinder, through the plate filling the cylinder, the level in the burette will fall. When the cylinder is completely full, the burette reading will be the measured volume in cubic centimeters. The volume of the piston dome is calculated by subtracting the measured volume from the calculated theoretical volume.

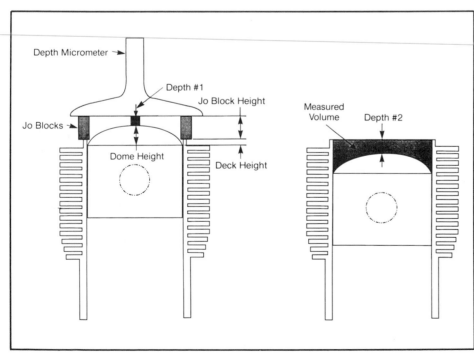

These drawings show measurement of Depth #1 and Depth #2, measuring dome volume. Install another one of the pistons into one of the cylinders. First, lightly grease the cylinder so that the rings will form a seal to the cylinder. Push the piston up toward the top of the cylinder, but stop before reaching the top. From where the piston stops, measure down to the top of the piston from the top of the cylinder. This measurement is Depth #2. With this depth, the theoretical volume can be calculated.

Improperly repaired intake-manifold stud. While this particular poor repair job is probably not causing any harm, I have seen a similar poor repair job on an intake-manifold stud for a 928 necessitate an engine overhaul.

this is where the highest stress is—at the root of the threads. A common error is to use an easy-out to attempt to remove these broken studs. An easy-out is a device intended to remove a broken-off stud by drilling a hole into the broken stud, inserting the easy-out and backing out the broken stud.

The most common error is to attempt to use one of these type devices on a broken stud that you have absolutely no hope of removing. If you have a fastener that is frozen and you broke it off trying to remove it, you will not be able to remove it with an easy-out. If you do attempt to remove this frozen stud with the easy-out, you will probably break off the easy-out in the stud. Then you really

are up the creek without a paddle.

Have you ever tried to remove a broken-off easy-out? They are made of hardened steel, and hardly anything can be done except to take the workpiece to a place that specializes in Electrical Discharge Machining (EDM) and have the offender removed, or "burned out." You can easily visualize the problem if the workpiece happens to be a cylinder head that is still attached to the engine, and the engine is still attached to the car.

It should be noted that normally an easy-out is only used on fasteners that have been broken off in shear. I recommend that under any other conditions, the broken-off stud be drilled out. Now this does not mean that you just drill out

Time Sert compared to a Helicoil. The Time Sert is a one-piece threaded insert, while the Helicoil is, as its name would imply, a wound-up coil of wire.

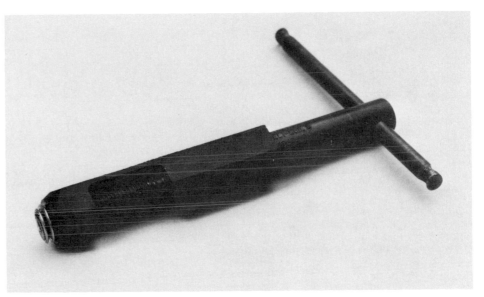

Installing tool for a Helicoil.

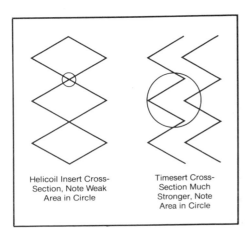

Helicoil Insert Cross-Section, Note Weak Area in Circle

Timesert Cross-Section Much Stronger, Note Area in Circle

This drawing shows the difference in concept of the Helicoil and the Time Sert. The Helicoil is just a wound-up coil of wire, while the Time Sert is a one-piece threaded insert.

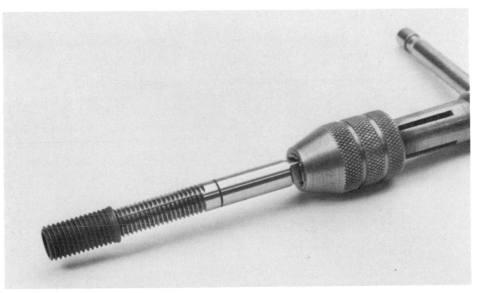

Installing tool for a Time Sert, which is a forming tap.

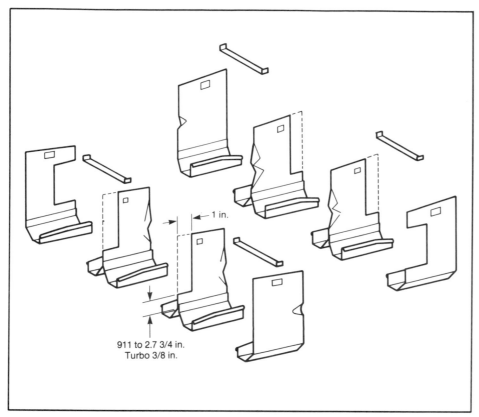

In 1977 Porsche made a modification to the middle air deflectors under the cylinders. They were made an inch narrower than on earlier engines. This change to the middle deflectors achieved lower cylinder temperatures and made the cooling-air distribution more even over the cylinders and cylinder heads. The old air deflectors can be modified with a good pair of tin snips. Drawing of cylinder air deflectors, and where the old ones should be modified. This change was made in March 1977 for all 911s and 930s, and should be made to any of the earlier 911 engines anytime they are apart. This modification has been said to drop the operating temperature by 5.6 to 8.3 deg C (10 to 15 deg F) which can't help but reduce the stud-pulling problem on the 2.7 liter engines.

the offending fastener. The proper method is to drill out the offending fastener, re-tap the hole for a Helicoil or Time Sert and install the insert. The reason is that there is hardly any chance that the drill is going to go exactly central with the existing threads, and so the drill is going to naturally damage the threads by going to one side or the other.

There is another trick you can use here if you want, and that is to use a left-handed drill when trying to drill out the offending broken stud. The beauty of this is that with the left-handed drill, every bit of force exerted is to get the stud to back out. The drilling tends to loosen—not further tighten—the broken bolt or stud.

Very often you will find that this technique will back the broken stud out as soon as you start to drill it. If it doesn't, you are no worse off than if you had planned to drill out the offending fastener and re-tap the hole for a Helicoil insert or a Time Sert. The left-handed drills are available from Snap-On tools. A set of five runs about $25: ⅛ in., 3/16 in., ¼ in., 5/16 in. and 11/32 in.

I don't know for sure, but I suspect that the Helicoil was invented about the time people started trying to make structural things out of aluminum—some 100 years ago. A Helicoil insert is a helically wound piece of wire which in its cross section is the shape of a diamond. The inside thread is the same as the thread to be repaired, and the outside is larger, but of course of the same thread pitch.

As good as they are, Helicoil inserts have certain limits. One of these is the fact that the fix is only a piece of wire, and it does not take much of a burr, cross threading and so on, to pull some of the wire out and ruin the fix. Furthermore, they depend on the spring effect of the coil to secure them in the hole. Once damaged, they can be difficult to remove.

They can also present problems on insertion because, due to the spring effect, they have to be prewound with a special tool. The problem comes when there is a lip near the hole and the inserting tool has to be held away from the workpiece. The Helicoil insert sometimes leaves the inserting tool before the threads are engaged. So much for Helicoil inserts.

Enter Time Serts. These are a more modern fix. A Time Sert is a solid piece of steel in which the threads are "timed" to one another, inside diameter to outside diameter. This device has several

Crankcase modifications. Here is what the stock crankcase looks like to a piston on its way down to bottom dead center.

162

advantages. The insert is stronger due to the increased cross section. Also, the insert is locked in place by installing with a roll tap. A roll tap is one that does no cutting, but forms the threads. This is done by pushing the material from the valleys to form the ridges of the thread—a very strong method.

On the Time Serts, the bottom few threads are incomplete (left at pitch diameter) and the roll tap forms them while swedging the bottom of the insert, locking it into place.

The Time Sert takes more time, but is a superior fix to the Helicoil inserts for most applications. The Time Sert is the only proper fix for pulled cylinder-head studs on the magnesium crankcases.

One word of advice about all of this drilling, and that concerns the importance of the work being done on a drill press, or better yet, a milling machine. If the work must be performed freehand, I highly recommend the use of a steel guide block or fixture. These inserts must be installed properly to do the job, and when done so will probably be better than the original threads.

To repair damaged male threads, there is not much that can be done. They can be chased with a rethreading die and made serviceable in an emergency. Replacement is the only proper repair, however.

Cylinder-cooling air deflectors

Porsche modified its cooling air deflectors to improve the engine cooling in March 1977. The middle two cooling deflectors on each side of the engine were made narrower by 25 mm (one inch) out by the cylinder head. The cooling fins were modified to lower the critical cylinder temperature and to even the cooling temperature on the cylinders, cylinder heads and crankcase.

When any of the older engines are rebuilt, the cooling deflectors should either be replaced with the later-style narrower cooling deflectors or modified

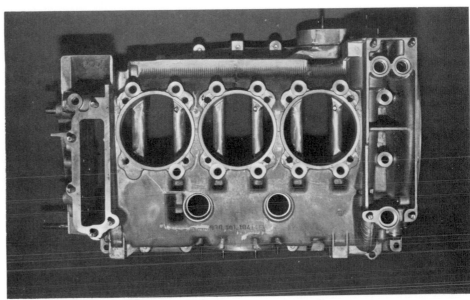

The crankcase after modifications. These modifications made it easier for the air to flow around in the crankcase, reducing wasted horsepower. There is always a piston going up when another is going down. The air being pushed by the piston going down has to find its way to the bottom of the piston that is going up. The factory recommended this modification for the crankcases for 2.0 liter racing engines, saying it would increase the output by about ten horsepower.

Turbatrol fender-mounted auxiliary oil cooler. These Turbatrol oil coolers are more efficient than any other cooler in this application. Lemke Design

The cylinders also have to be modified to let the air more freely move around in the crankcase. The cylinder on the left is stock, and the one on the right has been modified to improve this crankcase breathing.

163

with a pair of tin snips. The modification is good for a 10 to 15 deg F temperature drop. And because it provides more even cooling to the cylinders and cylinder heads, it reduces the likelihood of cylinder-head-stud pulling. This is one of the changes you can make that will help make the 2.7 engine a nice reliable engine.

Crankshafts

I strongly recommend against using damaged crankshafts in high-performance applications. I have tried to have a couple of 911 crankshafts repaired over the years, and in neither case were they suitable long-term repairs. If your crankshaft fix doesn't work, you will have to take the engine apart again to repair the engine correctly.

Send your crankshaft out to someone you are sure you can trust to be magnaflux-inspected for cracks. If the crankshaft and connecting rods pass the crack test, you should have the crankshaft micropolished. I am not fond of regrinding Porsche crankshafts. If your crankshaft is damaged and must be reground, I recommend that you either replace it or do as the workshop manual recommends and send any such crankshafts back to the Porsche factory to have them reground and Tenifer-hardened properly.

If your crankshaft did pass the magnaflux test and you had the journal surfaces micropolished, you must now thoroughly clean the crankshaft to remove any trapped dirt and grit. I don't recommend removing the plugs in the crankshaft to do this cleaning, however. I have seen more damage done by the improper replacement of these crankshaft oil-passage plugs than I have seen caused by dirty crankshafts. I have, however, seen engines ruined within the first few hundred miles because they were put back together with dirt or polishing grit still in the crankshaft. The best method of cleaning the oil passages is to use an aerosol can of carburetor cleaner with a long plastic nozzle. Thoroughly spray in each passage and then blow out with compressed air. Remember that the drillings in the crankshaft start from each end (number one and number eight main journal) and work their way toward the center, providing oil drilling for each connecting-rod throw.

For racing applications, the 66 mm stroke 2.0/2.2 liter crankshafts are almost indestructible. When Porsche stroked the crankshaft for higher-displacement engines, it had some problem with the crankshafts breaking when used at high rpm. The problem is caused by the fact that there is more of an overhang because of the increased stroke.

Porsche makes special versions of both the 70.4 and the 74.4 mm for racing. These racing crankshafts have a very large fillet which is round and makes a smooth, gentle transition from the rod journal to the counterweight of the crankshaft. Because of these special large fillets, these crankshafts require special bearings, with a relief provided for the fillet.

Porsche recommends using its special racing crankshafts for constant high-speed use above 7000 rpm. Actually with the 2.4 to 3.0 liter 70.4 mm crankshaft, I have found that if you shuffle pin the crankcase and restrict your rpm to the 7500 to 7800 rpm range, they are quite reliable.

Turbatrol spoiler-mounted oil cooler. This spoiler-mounted oil cooler was even more effective than the fender-mounted coolers. The spoiler-mounted cooler could be used instead of or in addition to the fender-mounted cooler for added cooling reserve. Lemke Design

Lemke Design spoiler, designed to complement the 911 design and the Turbatrol spoiler-mounted oil cooler. Lemke Design

Connecting rods

When you have your 911 engine apart, the connecting rods should be

164

measured and compared against the factory specifications. If they are out of specifications, they either should be replaced with new parts or reconditioned.

Reconditioning of the connecting rods consists of resizing of the big-end bores, installing new wrist-pin bushings, boring the wrist-pin bushing to reestablish the end-to-end length and honing the pin-bushing to size. All of the dimensions are critical, so this operation must be performed by a competent automotive machine shop. Specifications are given in the workshop manual and spec books.

Several years ago when the team I worked for had a 935 engine rebuilt at the factory, the factory flunked a set of titanium connecting rods and said they were out of specs. Porsche installed a new set of connecting rods in the engine, but returned the old rods with a note that said Porsche did not have the facilities to recondition titanium rods, but it knew that the rods could be reconditioned in the United States.

Indeed they can, and that set of rods *was* reconditioned and put back into service. Anytime a racing engine is taken apart, all of the components must be checked against the specifications and either reconditioned or replaced if they are out of specs.

The best connecting rods you can get for use in the 911 engine are 911 connecting rods. For most engines used for racing, there are aftermarket connecting rods that will be superior to those provided for the original application. However, this is not true for the Porsche 911 engine. The stock 911 connecting rods are suitable for racing applications for engine rpm up to about 7800 rpm. Beyond that, you should plan to use a set of Porsche's titanium connecting rods.

Balancing

Because the 911 engine is a flat-opposed six-cylinder engine with 120 deg crankshaft throws, balancing is not nearly as critical as on inline engines or V-8s. You can still have all of the reciprocating components of your engine balanced and make an improvement. The change just will not be as obvious as it would on other types of engines.

When an engine is balanced, all of the components are first balanced for static weight. The pistons, wrist pins and connecting rods are made to weigh the same by removing metal from the heavy components. The rods also have to be balanced end-to-end. Then, all of these weights are simulated with bob weights on the crankshaft, and the crankshaft is spun balanced.

It is important that if you have this work performed, that you have it performed by someone who has a reputation for quality work, because balancing is an exacting procedure.

If any of the connecting rods require replacement, be sure to replace the damaged connecting rod with one from the correct weight group. Porsche recommends no deviation greater than nine grams among the rod weights in an engine.

The 911 engine is inherently a well-balanced engine. With the 911 engine you can usually match the rods up fairly well into three pairs weightwise and install the heaviest pair on cylinders three and six across from each other at the rear of the engine, the next pair on cylinders two and five, and the final pair on cylinders one and four. If the whole set of rods was originally balanced within factory specs, this sub-balancing will give the engine a nearly perfect balance.

Shot-peening

Shot-peening is a process wherein the surface of a part is bombarded with round steel shot to produce a compressively stressed surface layer; the idea being that a crack will not propagate into a compressed layer of metal. A rough surface in compression will resist failures more than a smooth surface in tension.

Over the years, Porsche has used localized-polishing, soft-nitrating and shot-peening to prevent failure caused by crack propagation. Shot-peening has proven to offer superior durability when properly applied. Porsche is currently using shot-peening to prepare Titanium rods.

Dowell-pinning

In racing applications where greater than 250 hp is anticipated, I recommend that you have the magnesium crankcase dowel-pinned to cut down on the case shuffling. This modification will extend the life of the crankcase and the crankshaft by reducing the flexing and moving.

The modification consists of installing ten dowel pins, one on each side of the main bearing, to prevent the case from shuffling around the main bearing. If you will limit your engine rpm to 7500 to 7800 rpm, with only occasional excursions above 8000 rpm, this modification will allow you to run a stock crankshaft—and you will have a bulletproof engine.

Cylinder heads

High-performance heads are the secret to horsepower in all engines. With most production-car heads there is a great deal of room for improvement, and as a result

CMW 911 heads. These heads were machined from a solid billet of 6061 aluminum. CMW makes two versions of its newer cylinder heads, one for the 3.0 and 3.2 liter normally-aspirated engines and another for the turbocharged cars. Greg Raven

there are some people in the head-development business that have made quite a reputation for themselves. Porters and polishers are equipped to weld up and recontour ports, install seats and larger valves, reshape combustion chambers, grind valves and seats and flow-test their products when completed.

The 911 engines have a much better port design than the average production car has. So unless you are going to race your 911, you probably won't be able to justify having a set of heads ported and airflow tested.

Modifying heads is a time-consuming, expensive process. If you are modifying an engine for street use, be careful that you do not have your ports made too large and lose your broad, flexible power curve.

Over the years a few people have gained a reputation for being able to make more power than anyone else. However, today there really isn't anyone who excels in the business of making good 911 heads. Thus, if you want to have a set of heads ported and flow tested, I recommend that you contact the engine builder who is having the most success with the type size and class of engine you are planning to build, and ask them if they do their own heads—and if not, who does.

I have a Superflow bench with which I have ported and flow tested a number of heads over the years. I also have had the opportunity to test a number of "magic heads" over the years, but so far I have not seen the magic. There are no recipes for port development—just a lot of hard work. As a result there are many different approaches to port development.

The only way to tell if the port development works is by first testing on the flow bench, then the dynamometer and finally the track. Unless whoever does your heads makes the ports too large for your applicaton, however, they are not likely to do you any harm even if they aren't magic—possibly just waste your money.

I have recently heard of what may be the magic head for the 911. Bob Cousimano and his company, CMW, have just introduced Porsche cylinder heads that are made using a four-axis computerized numerical-control milling machine from a solid billet of 6061 aluminum. It makes two versions of the new cylinder heads, one for the 3.0 and 3.2 liter normally aspirated engines and another for the turbocharged cars. CMW heads are currently being thoroughly tested for both street cars and the 962 Turbo race cars.

Cousimano has worked with Indy cars and holds the patent for the D-shaped exhaust port. He feels that his Porsche heads offer more structural integrity than the cast originals, and include special design features that significantly improve engine performance and horsepower. Cousimano's unique D-shaped exhaust port provides better scavenging which, in conjunction with the development in intake port design, results in improved performance and economy.

Camshafts

Be careful when it comes to selecting the camshaft grind you will run in your engine. For a street engine, you will want to make sure you don't run a camshaft that is too wild. You will find that in day-in and day-out driving, a nice broad power curve with a lot of area under the curve makes a much more fun-to-drive car than a car that has a peaky power curve. It is equally important to select the proper camshaft for a racing engine, because you will want the engine to be producing all the power that it can.

My experiences with the street hot-rod engines with carburetors and the tuned exhaust-type heat exchangers is that either the 1966 911 cam (Solex cam) or the 911E camshafts make very nice street cams, offering a nice broad range without sacrificing power. The 911E cam has a little broader power curve than the 1966 911 cam, where the latter produces a little more peak power. These cams are great for all street cars from 2.0 to 2.7 liter.

For the larger-displacement 3.0 to 3.5 liter street engines with carburetors and the tuned exhaust, you will need a slightly more aggressive camshaft to provide performance with the same character that the smaller engines had with their 1966 911 and 911E grinds. For the 3.0 and 3.2 liter engines I recommend either the 911S camshaft or the Garretson Enterprises GE-40 cam.

For the larger 3.4 and 3.5 liter engines, I think you will enjoy the old 906 racing cam, or a GE-70 cam that Garretson Enterprises is using on an experimental basis in engines this size.

For the smaller-displacement 2.0 to 2.5 liter racing engines, I recommend either the 906 cam or the Garretson Enterprises GE-80 cams. For the larger 2.7 to 3.0 liter racing engines, I recommend the RSR Sprint cam or the Garretson Enterprises GE-80. And for the *really* big 3.2 to 3.5 liter 911 race engines, I recommend the Garretson Enterprises GE-100.

911 production engines through 1977 (2.0 through 2.7 liter) have smaller-diameter 47 mm journals. 1978-and-later 3.0 through 3.3 Turbos have the larger 49 mm journals. Racing or specially modified engines may vary.

The following table provides a comparison of the duration, lift and center-lobe spacing of a number of the camshafts available for the normally aspirated and turbocharged 911 engines.

Oil coolers

As we continue to find ways to increase the power output of the 911 engine we also need to find ways to increase its

CMW heads were machined using a four-axis computerized numerical-control milling machine. Notice the combustion chamber. Because head is machined on a computer-controlled mill, all of the dimensions can be very accurately controlled. Greg Raven

CMW 911 head with D-shaped exhaust port. Bob Cousimano holds the patent on the D-port design for racing heads. These heads are currently being thoroughly tested for both street cars and the 962 Turbo race cars. Greg Raven

Camshaft	Intake		Exhaust		Lobe center
	duration (deg)	*lift (in.)*	*duration (deg)*	*lift (in.)*	*(deg)*
Factory camshafts					
Turbo 930/53	209	.378	200	.343	108
911T	216	.387	207	.345	105
911SC	229	.455	220	.402	113
911E	229	.408	223	.393	102
911L	229	.408	223	.393	102
Group B Turbo	237	.374	220	.339	——
66 911	244	.439	234	.406	97
934	250	.408	251	.406	102.5
935	261	.446	274	.446	104
911S	267	.459	235	.396	97
3.0 RSR	278	.464	267	.450	101
906	281	.462	251	.403	95
Aftermarket camshafts					
GE 20	248	.455	230	.425	98
GE 40	256	.470	238	.440	102
GE 60	266	.490	248	.455	102
GE 80	274	.500	256	.470	100
GE 100	284	.520	266	.490	100

oil-cooling capacity. In 1969, Porsche first added its external oil cooler to the production 911S. The 911S produced 170 hp, so I guess we can use 170 hp as rule of thumb for the minimum at which we should think about adding an external oil cooler. The engine's operating oil temperature should be around 93 deg C (200 deg F). The proper operating-temperature range for the 911 engines is from 82 deg C (180 deg F) to 104 deg C (220 deg F).

You will want to be careful of some of the aftermarket oil-cooler conversion kits because their oil coolers are too restrictive. If you run a cooler that does not have large enough tubes, lines or fittings, it will restrict the oil flow. This is important because the oil cooling in the 911 engine is done in the scavenge circuit. If your oil cooler restricts the flow from the scavenge portion of the oil pump, it can cause excessive wear and possible failure of your engine's oil pump.

I have seen two engine failures that were traced to either an oil cooler that was too restrictive or the use of oil lines that were too small. What had happened was that the restriction on the oil pumps had caused the bearing surfaces in the pump to wear, allowing the pump gears to bind up and snap the interconnecting shaft between the layshaft and the oil pump. Unfortunately, both of the examples I have seen were run until the engines self-destructed. I guess the drivers did not believe the gauges and warning lights.

There are mixed opinions on whether the oil cooling in a dry-sump system should be done on the scavenge side of the oil system or the pressure side of the oil system. Porsche actually cools on both sides of the system for the 911 production-car engines.

The engine-mounted oil coolers cool the oil in the pressure side of the system, and the auxiliary front-mounted, external oil coolers cool the oil in the scavenge side of the system. In both of these cooling schemes, however, the oil is pumped through the oil cooler by one of the two oil pumps. The Porsche dry-sump systems use a tandem oil pump; one pump to scavenge the oil from the engine back to the oil tank and another to take the oil from the tank and provide the system with pressurized oil to lubricate the engine. All Porsche racing cars with 911-derived engines use the engine's oil scavenging system for engine oil cooling.

If you have a modified production 911, with more than 170 hp, you are ready to add an external oil cooler. Above these power outputs, and lacking an external oil cooler, the engine oil temperatures will increase approximately 11.2 deg C (20 deg F) for every 5.6 deg C (10 deg F) increase in ambient temperature.

I recommend that when you add a front-mounted oil cooler, you use the late-model (1974 and later) factory plumbing and thermostat, and one of the Turbatrol oil coolers from Lemke Design. These Turbatrol fender-mounted oil coolers are more effective than other types of heat exchangers because of their internal and integral helical finning. This finning agitates the oil inside the heat exchanger and produces a 250 percent improvement over heat-transfer rates of conventional heat exchangers.

Porsche engines are both air- and oil-cooled, and with their oil squirters for piston cooling and other oil-cooling techniques they are becoming more and more cooled by oil. Using engine oil for cooling has the advantage of using an internal fluid that is in intimate contact with the heat-producing surfaces in the engine, so that the engine's heat is transferred directly into the oil.

Using oil as a cooling medium also has its negative side in that oil is a very poor conductor of heat compared to conventional liquid coolants. Also, as the oil starts to cool in the oil heat exchanger, it becomes thicker and its flow is reduced. This reduction of flow at the surface has the effect of being an insulating barrier between the hotter-flowing oil and the heat exchanger.

With any of the larger-displacement high-power-output normally aspirated engines or turbocharged engines, the cooling capacity of any of the production-car oil coolers or their derivitives will be taxed beyond their limits when the cars are used for track events.

For track applications, you should consider using one of the larger radiator-type oil coolers to ensure adequate cooling. You can use the type used by Porsche for its racing cars, or any other radiator-type coolers as long as they don't restrict the oil flow. The connecting hoses and fittings used for this application should be dash-twelve or larger to prevent restricting the oil flow to and from the cooler back to the oil tank.

Suspension, wheels, tires and brakes 5

The body had to be modified to provide access to the torsion bars after the change to the new longer G-50 transmission. The rear torsion-bar tube had a bent center section to provide additional clearance for the transmission. The additional clearance was required for the new clutch disc with larger rubber-damper center section. Because the torsion-bar tube was bent in the center, the torsion bars could no longer butt up against each other in the center. Because of this change it was necessary to modify the body so that the torsion bars could be removed. Notice that they have also added lift points for repair shops to pick up the 911 with a hoist.

Suspension

For all cars the suspension design and settings are a compromise, but this is particularly true when it comes to sports or grand touring cars such as the Porsches. Porsche has established a compromise that it feels is the most reasonable for ride versus handling: If you want the car to handle really well, the car can't ride that great—it is bound to be rough over bumps.

If you *really* wanted the car to ride well, you would use high-profile tires, narrow rims, smaller-diameter rims, no sway bars, soft spring rates and light-acting shock absorbers. And this is just what Porsche did when it created the comfort group, which was standard equipment for the 911E and optional for the other 911 models back in the late-sixties and early-seventies.

We all intuitively know that this is just the opposite of what we would *want* to do to make a 911 handle better. We have grown to expect the better-handling cars to have short tires on larger-diameter wheels that are as wide as we can fit under the car, and springs and shocks that are as stiff as we can get by with—all at the expense of ride quality, of course.

And this is exactly what Porsche does when it modifies its production Porsches for racing, such as the Carrera RSR,

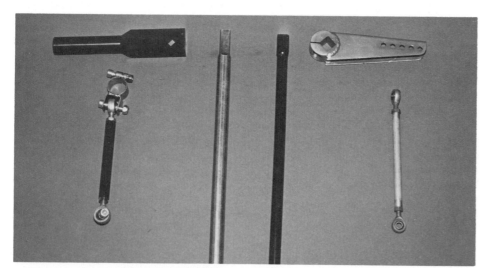

Comparison of aftermarket adjustable sway bar and drop link with Porsche factory unit for Carrera RSR. Porsche used the same sway bars and adjustable links front and rear. Aftermarket rear sway bar. The standard rear sway bar is available in 18 and 21 mm sizes, and adjustable aftermarket bars are available in 16 mm, 19 mm and 22 mm sizes.

Front sway-bar mounting torn from improperly mounted aftermarket sway bar. A larger-than-stock sway bar had been mounted in this car using a pair of U-bolts.

934, 935 and 961. For most of us, the compromise that Porsche has made with their suspension is just fine.

Shock absorber

Most other makes of cars can have their suspension performance greatly improved by just installing a better-quality shock absorber. This is because most car manufacturers use the cheapest and softest shock absorbers available. But Porsche has cheated us out of this quick fix by using quality components throughout its car. Because of this, it is important that when you think about modifying your 911, you consider the fact that if you are not careful, you will be installing parts on your 911 that are of a lesser quality than those you are taking off. Almost all of the alternative compo-

Aftermarket through-the-body style front sway bar. This type of sway bar is a must for competition purposes because it offers better control and a wider selection of bars—19 and 22 mm—and related components are available for the through-the-body style sway bar. This particular kit had a weld-in reinforcement plate to prevent tearing the sheet metal bodywork where the sway bar mounts. [The 1974 models were the first 911s with the new simplified front sway bar, which went under the front of the body and was mounted in rubber bushings to each of the front A-arms. The size was 16mm on the 911 and 911S, and 20 mm on the Carrera which also had an 18 mm rear sway bar. The 1975 and 1976 911 Turbo (930) had the original through-the-body style, but in 1977 the 911 Turbo also received the new simpler front sway bar that had been used on the 911s since 1974, with a 20 mm front bar and an 18 mm rear bar. The 911 also had its front bar increased in size from 16 to 20 mm and a rear 18 mm was added. This was the same combination the Carrera models had used since 1974. The 1986 911 Carreras had the front-sway-bar diameter increased from 20.0 to 22.0 mm and the rear sway bar was also increased in size from 18.0 to 21.0 mm.]

nents made for Porsches are of lesser quality than original-equipment components, so be careful.

Actually, shock absorber is a misnomer—they are suspension dampers that damp out the suspension oscillations. The tires and springs absorb the shock and store it as energy. The shock absorbers work in concert with the suspension's springs (or in the case of the 911, torsion bars) to damp out the suspension movement. The more damping force they provide, the sooner they will damp out the oscillations.

When you hit a bump, the suspension deflects and the spring compresses and a large amount of energy is stored in the spring. After the bump, the spring releases the energy by pushing down on the wheel, and up on the car's body. If this action is left undamped, the suspension will go into wild oscillations and the car body will oscillate up and down until it damps out in its own good time. The ride would be horrid because the car would be bouncing up and down all the time. The handling wouldn't be much better because the wheel and tire would be doing the same thing, and the weight of the car would not be on the tire's contact patch very much of the time.

935 cockpit-adjustable front sway bar. Bar was adjustable by twisting the blades on each end of it. In the photograph, the adjustable blade was in the horizontal or soft position. The blades were made of titanium and could be rotated 90 deg with a pair of Bowden cables which were controlled by a lever down behind and to the right side of the gearshift lever. When these blades were twisted vertically they were very stiff, and

The shock absorbers have to be matched to the spring rate in order to function properly, very much like a tuned circuit in electronics. Most racing cars have used double-tube hydraulic adjustable shock absorbers because of this need to be properly tuned.

The adjustable shocks can be adjusted until the circuit is properly tuned for a match to the spring rates, weights of both the car and the suspension, and the road's surface. The single-tube high-pressure-gas shock absorbers will work better over a wider range of conditions, and they do ride better over small-jounce bumps than the double-tube hydraulic shock absorbers.

The disadvantage of some high-pressure-gas shock absorbers, however, is that they are not adjustable so they cannot be matched to different spring rates. Racing teams that use these nonadjustable single-tube gas shocks are forced to carry a steamer trunk full of shock absorbers so that they will have the proper shock absorbers with the correct damping factor for each different set of spring rates that they would use.

A good rule of thumb is that the same type and brand of shock absorber should be used front and rear because their

when they were twisted horizontally they were less stiff. The range of adjustment from soft to hard was 1:8. This adjustment range was provided to allow compensation for the change in weight as the fuel was used from the 120 liter fuel cell. The change in weight from full to empty was almost 200 lb, so it would have a significant effect on the car's handling.

169

Adjustable aftermarket sway bar. The stiffness of the bar is adjusted by sliding the pickup for drop link up and down the length of the arm. Adjusting the link so that it is further out on the arm softens the effect of the sway bar, while moving the link in on the arm acts to stiffen its effect.

characteristics will be matched. There can be and are exceptions to this rule, where one manufacturer makes both types of shocks and has gone to the trouble of matching the characteristics of hydraulic and gas-pressure shocks so that they can be used as a set. There are other exceptions where the car manufacturer has matched shock absorbers from two different manufacturers, as an example. Porsche has done this with its 944 where it has used Volkswagen-made shocks on the front and Fichtel & Sachs shocks on the rear.

In the past, 911 owners have been forced to choose between ride and handling by choosing between the double-tube hydraulic shocks and the single-tube gas-pressure shocks. But now Boge has new low-pressure-gas double-tube shock absorbers for the 911. Porsche started to offer these shock absorbers as

a sport option in 1985. They worked so well that for 1986 and 1987 it made the Boge double-tube gas-pressure shock absorbers standard equipment for the 911 Carrera and 911 Carrera Turbo-look.

Koni also offers a new line of adjustable low-pressure double-tube front shock absorbers matched to work with its equally new adjustable high-pressure single-tube rear gas shock absorbers for the 911 Porsches. These new low-pressure gas shocks should prove to be the best of both worlds, particularly the Koni shocks because of their adjustability. The Bilstein high-pressure single-tube shock absorbers were still standard equipment for the 911 Turbo, and offered as an option for the other 911s for 1987.

For high-performance applications, the Koni adjustable shocks should have the edge because of their extra control and their tuneability. The 911s were available, over the years, with a number of different shock-absorber options, and some of the earlier 911s were equipped with Koni shocks.

935 rear spring plate.

935 cast-magnesium front hub carrier with ball-joint mount at the bottom. These hub carriers clamped around the shock absorber.

935 adjustable rear sway bar. Notice suspension pivots from heim joint where torsion bar mounts on production 911.

Camber adjustment on front of US-made 935.

If your 911 has Koni shocks, it is a simple matter to install new inserts. If it was originally equipped with Boge or Woodhead struts, Koni also makes inserts that will fit these (Boge and Woodhead both accept the same insert). The Woodhead shocks are a shock absorber made to the Boge license in England, so inserts for the Boge struts will work fine.

For a number of years, Koni made inserts for Bilstein front struts, but it has recently discontinued manufacturing this shock insert. These inserts (part number 282R1863) only worked in the older Bilstein front struts. If your 911 was newer than 1980 and had Bilstein shocks, these Koni inserts wouldn't work anyway

because Bilstein changed the construction of its struts in 1980.

If you want to try Koni shocks and your 911 has Bilstein shock absorbers, it looks like you will have to replace the complete front strut. There are Koni inserts available for the 1985-87 911s with Boge gas struts, however they do require an adaptor to make them work.

Springs

There are some things you need to know about springs and torsion bars. Assume you have a coil spring that is twenty inches tall and is a 100 lb per inch spring. If you cut this spring in half, you will not only have two ten-inch-tall springs, you will have two 200 lb per inch springs.

Now we know you're not likely to cut springs in half, but this might be important to you because you might cut some coils off of a spring to lower the car. If you do this, you should realize that the

resulting spring will also be stiffer. For instance, if you have a ten-coil spring and cut one coil off to lower the car, the resulting spring will be about ten percent stiffer than the original.

Another thing you need to know about springs is that whether they are torsion bars, coil springs or leaf springs, they are all springs. Porsche uses coil springs or torsion bars on its various models depending on which fits best in a given application. The MacPherson strut suspension used in front of all 911s with its torsion bars was selected because it allowed room for a much larger trunk than would have been possible with any other arrangement.

In most racing applications, Porsche will use either a combination of torsion bars and coil-over springs or just the coil-over springs to get the control that the cars need. For either coil springs or torsion bars, an increase in the diameter of the wire or torsion bar will increase

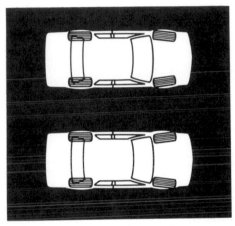

Toe diagram. Top diagram shows a car with toe in, while the bottom diagram shows toe out. Uniroyal-Goodrich Tire Company

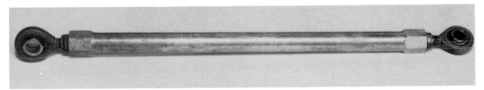

935 tie-rod. Porsche used these tie-rods because of their light weight, very positive joints and because it could set the bump steer wherever it wanted it set. Porsche set up the steering arm on the strut so that it could use spacers between the steering arm and the tie-rod to adjust the bump steer.

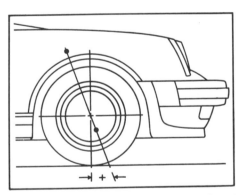

Caster diagram. Caster is the angle at which the steering angle is inclined. Positive caster helps with straight-ahead stability. Think of it as being like the front fork on a bicycle. Caster determines how much the tires lean when you steer into a turn. The 911s have positive caster, meaning that the tires lean into the turn when steered. This positive caster creates the self-centering effect that returns the steering to the straight-ahead position. B. F. Goodrich Company

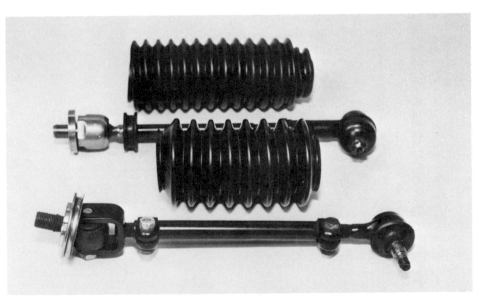

Production 911 and 911 Turbo steering tie-rods. The tie-rod closest to you was a regular 911 tie-rod and steering boot, and behind it the 911 Turbo tie-rod and steering boot. Notice that the 911 tie-rod used a rubber isolation joint at the end that mounted to the steering rack. The 911 Turbo tie-rod had a uniball joint in place of the rubber joint of the production 911 tie-rod. A very popular conversion for the performance-minded 911 owner.

the stiffness by the fourth power. What this means is that if you double the diameter of the torsion bar, you would multiply the stiffness by sixteen. So a very small change in wire or bar diameter has a significant effect in the spring rate.

The torsion bar sizes in the 911 model have changed several times over the lifetime of the 911. Originally, the front was 18 mm and the rear was 22 mm. In 1969, the rear was increased to 23 mm and in 1980, to 24.1 mm. In 1986 the rear torsion bars were increased in diameter to 25 mm to compensate for the gradually increasing weight. Because the rear of the 930/911 Turbo is so much heavier than the normally aspirated 911s, they have had a stiffer 26 mm bar all along. Porsche has used the stiffer torsion bars because of the added weight in an attempt to simulate the ride and handling of the lighter 911s, and does not make the suspension stiffer.

For high-performance applications with 911s it has become common to use 22 mm front torsion bars and 28 mm rear torsion bars in the heavier late-model 911s (1978 through 1986), and 21 mm front and 26 or 27 mm rear torsion bars in the earlier, lighter 911s (1969 through 1976). These larger torsion bars will make the 911s much more predictable and fun to drive, but at the expense of ride characteristics.

It has been the practice to use US-made aftermarket torsion bars in this application, because no larger bars were available from Porsche. Porsche now offers some larger torsion bars for its customers who wish to run their 911 Turbos (930) in the Group B class in the World Endurance Championship.

These stiffer bars are the solution for the heavier 930/911 Turbo for club events or track use. I recommend that you use these factory 22 mm torsion bars in the front and Porsche's 29 mm torsion bars in the rear. The metallurgy in these factory bars is superior to the bars made in the United States, which has the effect of increasing the stiffness-to-diameter ratio. For racing purposes, the 911s are converted to coil-over springs because still higher spring rates are required, and larger torsion bars will not fit because of the overall limitation of the spline size. The root of the spline is about 34 mm.

Porsche has used a combination of stiffer bars and coil-over springs several times in the past to achieve the spring rates it needs for different racing and rally applications. To prepare the 911SC RS (954) for rallying, Porsche has made a combination of coil-over springs and torsion bars available to permit tuning the suspension for various applications.

The components developed for the 911SC RS can of course be used for preparation of almost all 911s and 911 Turbos. For the 954, Porsche provides three different combinations of spring rates for the front, with three different matching Bilstein stock-absorber/strut units. For the rear of the 954 there are four different size torsion bars, two different rate springs and Bilstein shock absorbers of two different damping rates.

Sway bars

The function of the sway bar is to reduce body roll of the car while it is in a corner. Sway bar is probably another misnomer, because it doesn't communicate at all what the device does. We should actually be calling these bars anti-roll bars because that is what they do—resist body roll and control the weight-transfer distribution.

911 rear control arm. Standard fabricated rear control arm used from 1969 when the wheelbase was lengthened, until the arm was replaced with a cast-aluminum arm in 1974.

Drawing of 911 showing the effect of body roll on the wheels camber. If the 911 had stiffer torsion bars, was lowered and had a stiffer sway bar, the body roll and hence the camber change caused by cornering would be reduced and the car would handle better. B. F. Goodrich Company

The sway bars are used in conjunction with the springs or torsion bars to keep the stiffness relationship between the front and rear of the car reasonably constant and adjusted for neutral handling. Too much stiffness in the front will cause understeer, plow or push, and too much stiffness in the rear will cause oversteer or looseness. The difference between the two extremes—assuming you are going to ultimately lose control of your car, leave the road and hit a tree—is that if the car understeers you will hit the tree head-on, and if the car oversteers you will spin and hit the tree, rear end first.

Generally speaking, people feel that a car with a little understeer or push is easier to drive fast in very fast corners because it is less likely to spin out, but that a car with just a little oversteer or that is loose might be faster around slower corners because it will turn into the turns better. Translated, this means that you wouldn't want a car that oversteered at Indy, and you wouldn't want a car that understeered at a low-speed autocross. But anything in between is probably up for grabs.

On the late-model 911s (1974 through current) that are being modified for competition use, I recommend that the standard front sway bar be replaced with the early 911 (through-the-body) style bar with connecting drop links. This change is necessary because of the more precise control with the drop-link-style sway bar, plus the advantage of a wide selection of replacement sway bars available for this style bar as opposed to almost none for the later-style street bars.

An additional advantage of the early-style sway bar with drop links is that the rubber bushings can be replaced with plastic bushings and the drop links can be replaced with links that have metallic spherical joints for even more precise control. I do not necessarily recommend the plastic bushings or the spherical-jointed drop links for street use because of the added harshness of the ride and noise. Nonetheless, they are a *must* for racing and use with racing tires, and possibly the new super-high-performance competition versions of the radial street tires as well.

This is also true for the replacement of any of the other rubber suspension bushings with either plastic bushings or spherical bearings. Again, the replacement of all of these bushings is a must for racing cars, but undesirable, I feel, for a Porsche intended for street use because of the added harshness and excessive noise transmitted to the driver and passengers.

Bump steer

Bump steer is the change in toe setting at the wheels as the car is moved up and down on its suspension. Bump steer can happen either in the front or rear suspension. What we *really* would like is no change of the toe at all as the suspension is raised and lowered, because the resulting bump steer is the cause of many of the elusive wiggles and twitches that make the difference between an average and an excellent-handling car.

The way Porsches are designed, there isn't much you can do about the rear bump steer except to use a rear toe setting that minimizes the effect for the tires in use and the rest of the suspension settings. For the front there are steering-rack spacer kits available for the 911s, so

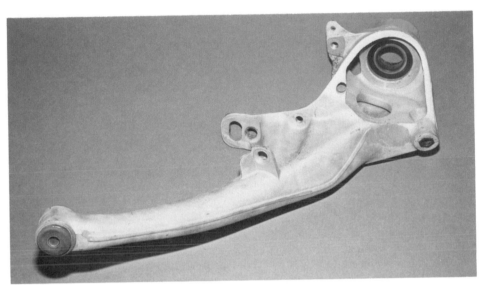

1974 cast-aluminum rear control arm for production 911s. The cast control arm replaced its fabricated predecessor while retaining the original-suspension geometry, and was stronger, lighter and less expensive than the fabricated-steel arms.

The rear-suspension pickup points for the Carrera RSR were revised to improve the handling. The change itself consisted of using a shorter rear control arm, and then moving the pickup points in toward the center by 15 mm (0.6 in.) and back to compensate for the shorter arms 47.5 mm (1.9 in.). This change actually increased the camber changes due to suspension travel, and more nearly matched the camber change to body roll.

that when the cars are lowered the steering rack can be spaced back up. Thus, the tie-rods are more nearly horizontal again, greatly reducing problems with bump steer in the front end of these Porsches.

Actually, you will still want to measure the effect of the bump changes on the toe so that you can adjust it to have zero effect in or around the static ride height. On most cars it will be necessary to heat and bend the steering arms in order to adjust the bump steer properly, once the ride height has been altered. This is an extensive procedure when done properly, but it is a *must* to get the most out of your modified Porsche.

Weight checking

The purpose of weight checking is to make sure that the weight is distributed evenly on the four tires. Assuming the 911 has a weight distribution of 40/60 front to rear, forty percent of the left-side weight should be on the left front wheel, and sixty on the left rear. This is particularly important on a Porsche that has been in a wreck. If the car does not carry its weight evenly distributed on its four tires, it is said to have weight jacked into the chassis.

People who race cars on circle tracks have made a science out of weight jacking in order to find the fastest way around a racetrack. This is not the case with Porsches, however, and sometimes after one has been wrecked and not properly repaired it can end up with the weight jacked diagonally across the car. The problem with this is that when you look at your Porsche, it may appear to set evenly on its four wheels and it may have been aligned properly. But it will have strange handling characteristics and tire wear because of this weight jacking.

Ideally the weight differences should be less than twenty to thirty pounds, but if the weights are off more than fifty pounds per wheel, the suspension must be adjusted for more even weight distribution or you will feel the effect on the handling and driveability. Porsche says the weight difference from left to right may not exceed 20 kg (44.1 lb) for the 911 or 10 kg (22.5 lb) for the 911 Turbo. It also says the difference in height from the left to the right may not exceed 8 mm (0.3 in.) on the rear axle or 5 mm (0.2 in.) on the front axle.

Special shorter RSR control arm to work with revised-suspension pickup points.

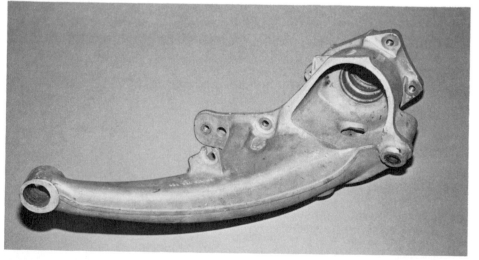

Turbo control arm. When the 911 Turbo (930) was introduced in 1975, similar suspension changes were incorporated in the rear, with the new cast-aluminum trailing arms. The Turbo trailing arms were shorter, and the pickup points were moved to relocate the suspension's fulcrum points, similar to what had been done on the RSR. In addition to being moved toward the center 15 mm (0.6 in.) and rearward 47.5 mm (1.9 in.) to compensate for the shorter arm, they were also moved upward 10 mm (0.4 in.) to give the rear suspension some anti-squat. To facilitate this change for the 930, Porsche used a new rear-torsion-bar tube (rear-axle transverse tube), with different suspension pickup points made as part of the tube.

Changing the height on one side will cause a simultaneous change in the wheel loading. When the wheel loading is changed for one wheel, it will also change the loading of the other wheels. Increasing the initial setting, or spring tension, on one side will raise the car, increasing the load on that wheel.

Decreasing the intial setting, or spring tension on one side, will lower the car, decreasing the load on that wheel. A change in load on one wheel will always effect the wheel diagonally across the car from that wheel. If the wheel load is increased or decreased on one wheel, the same will happen on the wheel diagonal from it.

Alignment

There is an excellent procedure for aligning the 911s in the factory workshop manual which goes into all aspects of setting up the 911 suspension, including setting ride height and weight checking the chassis using digital scales.

The suspension alignment is a compromise, in the case of the 911, aimed at providing a decent ride, good handling and good tire wear. In 1975 and for the rest of the late-1970s and early-1980s, the 911s were raised up on their suspensions for the US market to comply with the US 5 mph bumper laws. This change threw a new kink into the compromise, and these cars that were raised on their suspension just didn't handle as well.

When set at these ride heights, the 911s had some rather unusual alignment specifications because of suspension limitations caused by the cars being raised on their suspension. The cars were actually set 9-15 mm higher (0.35-0.6 in.) in front and 21-25 mm (0.82-0.98 in.) in the rear. These raised cars had positive camber in the front and zero in the rear.

The owners of most of these 911s that were raised for the bumper laws have had them lowered to "Euro specifications," which probably were interpreted differently at every shop that did the work. Many of these cars were set too low. If you own one of these 911 "bumper cars" that either hasn't been lowered or has been lowered too much, you should have the ride height reset and the current alignment specifications used.

The correct ride height will result in a measurement of about 25 in. when measured from the ground to the rear-fender lip. The 911 should have a very slight nose-down attitude (approximately 1 deg slope) which will result in a measurement about ½ in. higher than the rear at the front fender lip (about 25½ in.). There is a more sophisticated procedure for measuring the car's ride height given in the procedure in the workshop manual, which relates the centerline of the torsion bars front and rear to the centerline of their respective axle.

If the 911s are lowered to a height much lower than this Euro spec, they

Porsche steel wheels. When the 901 was introduced in 1963, it used steel wheels that were 15 in. in diameter and 4½ in. wide. In 1968 their width was increased to 5½ in. for the 911T, and six inches for the 911E in 1969. 1974 was the last year steel wheels were standard equipment on the 911. Having the steel wheels as standard equipment created a misleading base price for the cars, since few bought their 911 with steel wheels.

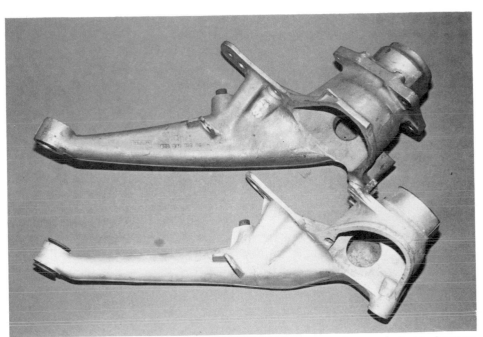

Comparison of cast-aluminum Turbo arm top and cast aluminum arm used on 911. Notice that on the Turbo arm, the brake-caliper mounting had been moved to the rear while the caliper mounted in front on the 911. You can also see that the wheel-bearing mounting had been moved farther out for the wider track of the Turbo.

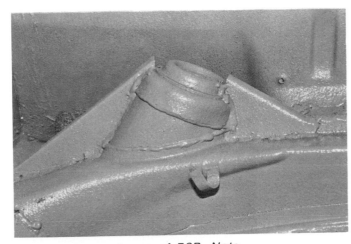

Rear shock-mount area of RSR. Note reinforcement to the shock mount and to the corner of the engine compartment.

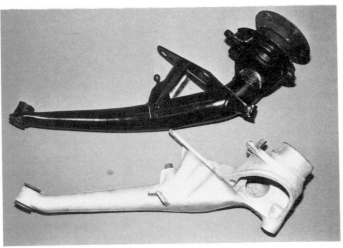

Comparison of fabricated control arm and cast-aluminum replacement arm.

will be too low and have a problem with running out of suspension travel and bottoming out. The alignment specifications were revised in 1983 for the 1983-and-later 911s when the US bumper-height laws were again revised. The current 911 alignment specifications are as follows:

Front suspension
Camber: –0 deg ± 10 min
Caster: 6 deg 5 min ± 15 min left and right
Toe-in: +15 min ± 5 min
Rear suspension
Camber: –1 deg ± 10 min
Toe-in: +10 min ± 10 min

The 911 Turbo (930) uses the same alignment specifications as the 911, with the exception of the rear-camber setting. The rear camber for the 911 Turbo is –30 min ± 10 min. The reduced camber setting is used because of the revised rear-suspension geometry. If you use larger rear wheels on the 911 Turbo than the eights or nines that the cars come with, the rear alignment becomes even more critical. With ten- or eleven-inch rear wheels I recommend that you reduce the rear camber to zero for increased stability with the wider rear tires.

What do all of these terms such as camber, caster and toe-in mean? Camber is the angle of the wheel and tire from vertical. Zero camber means that the tire's tread surface is flat on the ground. If the tires tilt outward at the top it is called positive camber. If they tilt inward at the top it is called negative camber.

Toe-in is the difference in measurement between the fronts and the rears of a pair of tires on the same axle. This can be either the front or the rear axle. Zero toe is when the tires are parallel. Toe-in is when the fronts of the tires are closer together than the rears. Toe-out is when the fronts are further apart than the rears.

Caster is the angle at which the steering angle is inclined, and it helps with straight-ahead stability. Think of it as being like the front fork on a bicycle. Caster determines how much the tires lean when you steer into a turn. The 911s have positive caster, meaning that the

The forged Fuchs aluminum-alloy wheels were introduced on the 911S in 1967. When introduced, they were 15 in. wheels that were 4½ in. wide. In 1968 the width was increased to 5½ in. In 1969 the Fuchs alloys were increased to six inches wide. The 1973 Carrera RS introduced the use of different-size wheels front and rear, with sevens in the rear and sixes in the front. Porsche used forged wheels as racing wheels for a while, and mounted nines on the front and elevens on the rear of the IROC RSRs. The 3.2 Carrera is currently delivered in the United States with 15 in. diameter Fuchs forged-alloy wheels as standard equipment, sevens in front and eights in the rear. The 911 Turbo is delivered worldwide with 16 in. Fuchs forged-alloy wheels, sevens in the front and nines in the rear.

Fuchs alloy wheels and a space-saver folding spare tire. The mixture of sizes for the front and rear wheels, along with the move to larger wheels and gas tanks necessi- tated a new solution for a spare tire and wheel. So the folding space-saver spare was a graceful solution to several problems.

Fuchs alloy wheels were made in 14 in. diameter, 5½ in. wide for the comfort group from 1969 to 1971. For 1969 the 14 in. wheels were a mandatory part of the comfort group, when it was sold with the Sportomatic transmission. For 1970 and 1971 they were sold as an option. The 14 in. wheels were offered again in 1977 as part of another comfort group.

tires lean into the turn when steered. The positive caster creates the self-centering effect that returns the steering to the straight-ahead position. The alignment specifications or measurements are given in degrees and minutes. There are 360 degrees in a circle, and sixty minutes to a degree.

If you use stiffer torsion bars you will be able to lower the 911 about an inch without problems with suspension travel, but you may have to modify the alignment slots to facilitate a proper alignment, and you will have to be very careful going in and out of driveways. The lower ride heights will reduce the roll and lower the center of gravity, which will improve the 911's cornering power and make the Porsche smoother in the corners.

A final note on lowering 911s. If your 911 was one of the cars raised up to comply with the 5 mph US bumper laws, Porsche installed a large washer on top of the shock absorber to space the shock absorber back down into its operating range. This washer is *big*—60 mm outside diameter, 18 mm inside diameter and 10 mm thick. It makes a great paperweight once removed.

When you lower your 911, you must take this spacer out; otherwise you will have the front shock absorber out of its range at the other extreme where it is very vulnerable to bottoming out.

If you are planning to run your 911 in speed events, you may wish to alter the alignment specifications by adding more negative camber. How much negative camber you use will depend upon a number of different things. If your primary application for your 911 is day-to-day use, you will not want to get too carried away with negative camber. Too much negative camber will make the 911 a little darty and will cause premature tire wear.

If, on the other hand, your primary use for your 911 is autocrosses or driver education or time-trial events at race-tracks, you will want to run more negative camber. How much camber will depend upon how low your car is, how stiff your torsion bars and sway bars are

The 1969 Mahle cast-magnesium wheel was the lightest wheel ever used on the 911, at 4.5 kg (9.9 lb). Unfortunately the Mahle magnesium wheel was only made in the 5½ in. width, so there wasn't much application for it. The forged-alloy wheels were already six inches wide for the 911E and 911S, so the only application for the 5½ in. cast-magnesium wheels was on the 911T and the 914/6.

BBS Modular Sport Wheel (RS) with its center-lock styling is the top-of-the-line road wheel by BBS and may be, as they say, the ultimate road wheel. The center section is forged aluminum, and the inner and outer rim halves are cold-rolled aluminum for stronger and lighter wheels than those that use cast centers in similar-type modular wheels. The Modular Sport Wheel (RS) has optional cooling fans (Cw) for both improved brake cooling and styling. BBS of America, Inc.

The ATS cast-aluminum "cookie cutter" wheel was introduced in 1973 as a six-inch wheel. This wheel was standard equipment for the 911E in 1973, and an option for the other models. In 1975 the ATS replaced the steel wheel as standard equipment. In 1978, they also made a seven-inch version of the ATS wheel, and the wheel continued to be standard on the 911SC.

BBS still provides two styles of pressure-cast aluminum wheels. The RA-style shown is the original-style one-piece cast wheel, while the new RZ-style wheel looks more like the new forged modular wheel and forged one-piece wheel with center-lock styling. BBS of America, Inc.

The BBS forged one-piece (RG) wheel is the newest wheel in the BBS family. These new forged wheels also have the center-lock styling of the BBS Modular Sport Wheels. BBS of America, Inc.

In 1984, with the introduction of the 3.2 Carrera, the "telephone dial" wheel replaced the cookie-cutter wheel as standard equipment.

New Etoile "shooting star" wheel, with its high-tech look and center-lock styling.

and what type of tires you are using.

On a track-type car, additional negative camber is used to help compensate for the car's body roll. Ideally, your tires would have zero camber and the car wouldn't lean, so the camber would stay at zero. A well-set-up suspension will minimize the camber change so you will not need as much negative camber to keep the tire flat on the ground. You will want to keep the outside or loaded tire flat on the ground in a corner, and too much negative camber can be almost as bad as too little camber. So you will have to be careful not to overdo a good thing.

Suspension revisions

Porsche revised the rear-suspension pickup points in 1973 on the second series of 2.7 and 1974 3.0 RS Carreras. The change was made in an effort to better match the camber changes to the body roll, so that when the suspension was properly set up, the outside, or loaded, wheel in a corner would stay more nearly vertical, or nearer to the proper suspension setting when the car leaned in a corner.

This change was only used for the RS Carreras and RSRs and was not carried over to the rest of the production 911s. The change was made on the RS Carrera so that it would be homologated and available for use by the RSR race cars. The rear-suspension change was not necessary for the production 911s and did have some negative effect on straight-line stability.

The change itself consisted of using a shorter rear trailing arm and then moving the pickup points in toward the center by 15 mm (0.6 in.) and back to com-

BBS three-piece modular center-lock racing wheel.

BBS sixteen-inch modular center-lock racing wheel with BBS wheel fan.

BBS nineteen-inch modular center-lock racing wheel with BBS wheel fan.

BBS modular wheels with BBS wheel fans on street racer 930 slope-nose. Note custom-made hubcap.

pensate for the shorter arms 47.5 mm (1.9 in.). This change actually increased the camber changes due to suspension travel.

There was also an optional raised spindle offered for the RS Carrera series so that it would be available for the RSR race cars. The spindle was raised up on the front struts by 18 mm (0.71 in.), which was 126 mm (4.96 in.) above the standard ball-joint center, instead of the standard 108 mm (4.25 in.). This change was made so that the front of the car could be lowered by the 18 mm (0.71 in.) without excessively lowering the roll center.

The modification also leaves the remainder of the suspension geometry unaltered and gives full suspension travel before bottoming out on the bump stop. The reason the spindle was not moved more than the 18 mm was that the ball joint would interfere with the rim if the spindle was moved more than the 18 mm. Of course, with larger-diameter wheels (RSRs used fifteen-inch-diameter wheels) you would be able to make a larger change in the spindle position before running into the ball-joint and wheel-interference problem.

When the 911 Turbo (930) was introduced in 1975, similar suspension changes were incorporated in the rear, with the new cast-aluminum trailing arms. The Turbo trailing arms were shorter, and the pickup points were moved to relocate the suspension's fulcrum points similar to what had been done with the RSR. In addition to being moved toward the center 15 mm (0.6 in.) and rearward 47.5 mm (1.9 in.) to compensate for the shorter arm, they were also moved upward 10 mm (0.4 in.) to give the rear suspension some anti-squat. To facilitate this change for the 930, Porsche used a new rear-torsion-bar tube (rear-axle transverse tube), with different suspension pickup points made as part of the tube.

The turbo-look cars also utilized this geometric change. So when the G-50 transmission was introduced in 1987, there had to be a special turbo-look torsion-bar tube that would both retain these revised suspension pickup points and provide room for the larger G-50 transmission.

The rear-torsion-bar tube had a bent center section to provide additional clearance for the transmission. The additional clearance was required for the new clutch disc with larger rubber-damper

RUF seventeen-inch diameter aluminum-alloy wheels. RUF has these wheels made for them by Speedline of Italy. Speedline makes several of the Formula 1 teams' wheels, and the wheels for Porsche's 962Cs and Indy cars. Exclusive Motor Cars, Inc.

There is a very nice selection of both Porsche wheels and aftermarket wheels available to the discriminating Porsche owner, so be careful that you don't buy one of the inferior makes. This example of an inferior-make wheel is one of the cast replicas of the Fuchs forged-alloy wheel. The problem with this wheel was that there was no added reinforcement to make up for the weaker casting procedure. The resulting wheel is not nearly as strong as the wheel it copied, and as you can see, the example broke. The real Fuchs forged wheels will not break; even in an accident, they will only bend. Do yourself a favor and check out any wheel that you plan to purchase very carefully.

RUF 17 in. wheels. The fronts are nine inches wide with 235/40VR-17 Denloc, and the rears are ten inches wide with 255/40VR-17 Denloc. Exclusive Motor Cars, Inc.

center section. This new center section for both the normal and turbo-look Carreras was made of cast-iron to make the part easier to make and also to provide more accurate location of the suspension pickup points and transmission mounts.

In 1974 the regular 911s also had the trailing arms changed to cast aluminum. Unlike the Turbo arms, however, the 911 arms were made as direct replace-

Tire inflation-pressure chalk test—proper inflation. B. F. Goodrich Company

Tire inflation-pressure chalk test—overinflation. B. F. Goodrich Company

Tire inflation-pressure chalk test—underinflation. B. F. Goodrich Company

ments for the fabricated steel arms and the original-suspension geometry was retained.

The front-suspension geometry on the 930 was also modified to provide some anti-dive. Modifications were made to the floor plan at the rear of the front suspension to allow raising the front cross-member by 13 mm (0.5 in.). This change raised the whole rear portion of the suspension by about a half an inch. The front mounting was also spaced down with 6 mm thick steel spacers, which had the effect of lowering the front mounting point by 6 mm (0.23 in.).

The net effect of raising the rear of the suspension by about a half an inch and lowering the front by over two tenths of an inch is a change of about three quarters of an inch. This change was made to provide anti-dive geometry in the front.

Both the front and rear suspension changes were made on the 911 Turbo (930) to provide a better basis for racing the 934, which could not have its suspension changed from the production car from which it was homologated—the 930.

Wheels

Wheels are a very important and often overlooked aspect of performance tuning. When the Porsches were slower, and for competition were just running parking-lot events, wheels were not nearly as important as they are today—now that high-speed track events and high-performance Porsches are the norm.

Porsche makes what are probably the best wheels in the world, in the form of the Fuchs spoked, forged-alloy wheels. They are probably the best all-around wheel that you can buy. When the 911 was introduced in 1963, the commonly used wheels of the day were steel wheels. The 911 had steel wheels that were 4½x15 in. when it was introduced. The forged-alloy wheels were not introduced until the 1967 model year, and they were still the 4½x15 in. wheels.

The steel wheels were still offered as standard equipment on the base 911, and in fact steel wheels are standard through 1974. Starting with 1975, first the ATS "cookie cutter" and then in 1984 the "telephone dial" wheel were standard equipment. In 1987, forged fifteen-inch alloy wheels were standard equipment in the United States, sevens in front and eights in the rear.

Aftermarket road wheels have become a big item over the past few years. The majority of these wheels are made of cast aluminum, by several different methods and many different manufacturers. There are even a few that are made by the forging process, like the factory Fuchs alloys.

A forged wheel is made by forming a piece of aluminum under high pressure, like the process for making racing pis-

Bob Strange, BF Goodrich test engineer, demonstrating use of tire pyrometer. B. F. Goodrich Company

tons. Forgings are denser and have more structural integrity than do castings, which will usually vary in density and exhibit some porosity. A quality forged wheel has both the strength and durability required of a wheel for street use, and the light weight required by a competition wheel.

For most Porsche owners, the BBS wheels are perhaps the best known of the aftermarket wheels, both because BBS has been in the business for a number of years and because Porsche has used them on several of its racing cars and offers them for sale as an option at Werk I, as part of its *Sonderwunsch-Programm* (Special Wishes Program). BBS also makes some forged wheels that are strong and yet light.

There are a number of quality one-piece cast-aluminum wheels made for the aftermarket by several reputable manufacturers. There are any number of wheels made which *look* like the original modular BBS wheels with a cast center and formed sheet-aluminum outers. The strength of some of these wheels is questionable, however, so be sure to check them out before you buy them.

Please be very careful when considering any aftermarket wheel. Some of the wheels available are just plain *not safe*. If you use any cast wheels for competition, you should plan on having them crack-checked by a nondestructive test lab at least once a year for safety, and after each time you hit something. They *can* and *will* break.

A very nice selection of wheels is available to the discriminating Porsche owner. The Fuchs forged-alloy wheels, the BBS wheels, the RUF wheels, the new Etoile wheels and many other quality wheels are approved by the West German Technischer Uberprufungs Verband (TUV).

The German TUV is like the Department of Transportation (DOT), only much stricter. Everything the West

Aluminum S-type brake caliper on 1973 Carrera RS. These brake calipers were originally introduced on the 1969 911S. The aluminum S brake calipers were used on the top-of-the-line production cars from 1969 through 1977. James D. Newton

Porsche 917-style brakes used on rear of 935/78. Note rear spring plate with heim-joint pivot and adjustable rear sway bar.

Porsche 917-style brakes as used on RSR. Note mechanical handbrake arrangement.

Porsche 917-style brakes used on the front of a 935/78. Notice clamshell air ducting for brake cooling, and cockpit-adjustable front sway bar.

German people use or consume must be approved by the TUV. Wheels are tested by the TUV's automotive division.

There is no required US equivalent to the German TUV's wheel testing. DOT doesn't require any testing and in fact, the only US test for wheels is a voluntary test by the SFI Foundation. The SFI Foundation is a nonprofit organization made up of the member wheel companies that voluntarily agree to meet the SFI's specifications for manufacturing wheels and have their wheels tested to those specifications. So do yourself a favor and check out any wheel that you plan to purchase very carefully. If one fails, the results can be tragic.

A final word on wheels. All of the modern mag wheels represent a considerable investment and deserve good care. You should schedule a maintenance program for whatever make of alloy wheel that you have.

The factory Fuchs alloy wheels require special care, however. The maintenance should start with a good wheel cleaner that is pH-balanced. Anything that gets on these Fuchs alloy wheels that is either too strongly alkaline or too acidic will stain or damage them. P21S wheel cleaner and the new Porsche light-alloy rim cleaner available from the Porsche dealers are a couple of pH-balanced cleaners that are great for cleaning these wheels, or for that matter any of the alloy wheels.

The reason Fuchs alloy wheels are so special is that instead of having a painted surface like almost all other types of wheels, they have an aluminum finish that is clear anodized. This is one of a number of anodic coatings where the surface of the metal is protected by an oxide coating or film which is produced by the process of electrolysis. This oxide coating is porous so that it is susceptible to staining.

Porsche recommends acid-free cleaning products with a maximum pH value of 10 (7 is neutral, lower values are more acidic and higher values are more alkaline). Any cleaning material that is not pH-balanced can stain or corrode the finish, ruining the wheels. The only way to restore their finish would be to send them to someone who can strip off the old anodized coating, recondition the surface and then re-anodize the surface. There are some people who can do an excellent job of reconditioning these wheels, but they will never be able to match the finish of your old wheels. So if you need to have one or more wheels refinished, send them *all*.

All of the other Porsche wheels are painted and/or have a clear protective coating over them. The finish on these wheels, as well as the Fuchs forged

Rear fiberglass cooling scoop for 935 rear brakes. Scoop mounted to the rear trailing arm with the leading edge hung down into the airstream, scooping up cooling air.

Porsche 935 big brakes used on front of 935/79. Note cockpit-adjustable front sway bar and clamshell air ducting for brake cooling.

Porsche 935 big brakes on the rear of 935/79. Notice adjustable rear sway bar and uniball pivot for spring plate.

wheels, is as fragile as the car's painted surfaces and should always be treated with great care.

The wheels should be cleaned often and with care. You should not use anything on the wheels that you would not be willing to use on the rest of the car. If you use a wheel cleaner, again be sure you use one that is pH-balanced. Porsche recommends cleaning the wheels often (every week or two) to remove road dirt, salt spray and brake dust, all of which will damage the finish and cause staining or pitting if left on too long.

Porsche also recommends that every three months, after a regular cleaning, the anodized Fuchs wheels be coated with petroleum jelly. Porsche says to rub this in well with a clean cloth. This will actually help wheels that are stained if they aren't too badly stained. Try it. Porsche further admonishes you to *never* use an abrasive or metal-polishing cleaning agent on your wheels.

Tires

Tire technology changes all the time. The hot setup street tire for competition is varying from the Yokohama A-001R to either the Goodyear VR S, Yokohama A-008R, BF Goodrich Comp T/A R or the Bridgestone Potenza RE71.

The Yokohama A-001R was the superior tire for both autocrosses and time-trial purposes for about two years. And even though we can be sure that one of the new tires will prove to be superior, we're also sure that its reign won't last two years this time—the street-car tire wars are too fierce to let that happen again. For just *good* high-performance street tires, my advice is to read all of the tire tests, pay your money and take your chances.

The stand and optional wheel and tire sizes for the 1987 911 models are shown in the chart on the next page.

I still prefer sixteen-inch tires over fourteen- or fifteen-inch for high-performance applications, but you may be

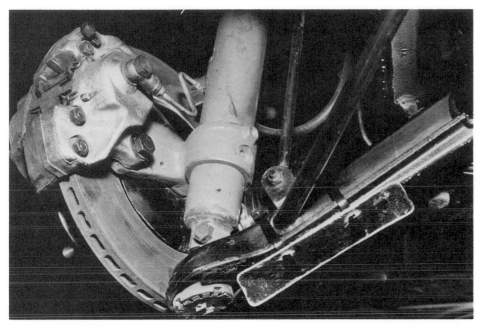

One of the first things you should try with a 911 you are using for racing or track is to duct air into the brakes. You should start with the front brakes, because the weight transfer of the car will cause the front brakes to do most of the braking. You can either fabricate your own brake scoop and ducting, or purchase one as a kit.

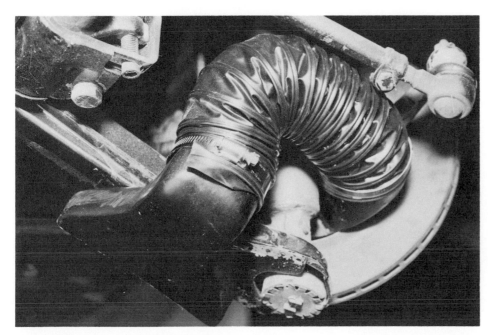

COOL-brake scoop is mounted on bottom of lower suspension arm, by the ball joint, where it is down in the airstream under the car. The air is ducted from the scoop by hose to the air funnel into the eye of the rotor.

Alternate cooling scheme used in conjunction with 935 big brakes. Instead of forcing the air into the eye of the rotor, the cool air is forced to the inside surface of the rotor.

Model	Wheel	Tire
standard front	7Jx15	185/70VR-15
standard rear	8Jx15	205/60VR-15
optional front	6Jx16	205/55VR-16
optional rear	7Jx16	225/50VR-16
Turbo standard front	7Jx16	205/55VR-16
Turbo standard rear	9Jx16	245/45VR-16

able to achieve a compromise that will better suit your needs by using either the fourteen- or fifteen-inch wheels and a higher-profile tire. Sometimes the fifteen-inch tires have a use for competition. Where allowed, you can use 50 series tires and cheat the system to get a lower center of gravity and a lower gear ratio without changing the car's suspension settings or gear ratio.

But for a 911SC or Carrera, why not sevens or eights in the sixteen-inch size? That's what most people do. The left-front-fender clearance gets a little close, but the problem is not one you can't live with if the car is properly lowered and aligned. The offset has been juggled on some brands of aftermarket wheels, and you will be able to fit 7.5x16 in the front and 8.5x16 in the rear. Check the wheel manufacturer's recommendations.

Increasing the size of wheels on the 911 Turbo (930) will transform its personality as well. The preferred sizes are 9x16 in the front and either 10x16 or 11x16 in the rear.

The wheel offset will be critical with some of the larger-wheel recommendations, so be sure to check with the wheel manufacturer for precise fitting information. You may also want to make sure the tires and wheels you do select actually fit. This is particularly true in the rear of the 1969 through 1977 cars, with their smaller rear-fender flares. Some of these cars will not tolerate the seven-inch wheels with the 205/60-15 in. tires—the wheels' offset must be correct.

I recommend that you carefully check the clearance before putting the wheels and tires on and driving away. Get two big strong friends to help you with this. Have them bounce the rear of the car up and down while you watch the tire and fender clearance. By this method of watching the arc of the tire, you will be able to determine if you will have a problem with tire clearance. You will have to judge for yourself; the penalty for a mistake is blistered paint on the rear fenders. The problem occurs about an inch and a half up from the fender lip, so that is where you will want to focus your attention while your friends are bouncing your car up and down. To be safe, you should be able to fit a finger between the tire and fender when you are all done. Don't try this while your friends are bouncing your car, though, or you may lose a finger. Just *judge* the clearance.

Also remember that during this test, as the car goes down, the camber goes more negative, pulling the top of the tire away from the fender. You can gain extra clearance by running excessive negative camber, but at the expense of excessive tire wear.

For choosing racing tires, just see a tire engineer from any of the companies that sell racing tires and ask his or her advice. This process used to be much simpler, however. You just went through the Goodyear catalog and picked out what you thought would best suit your car and driving conditions. But now everyone has gotten into the act, and recently we have seen Yokohama, BF Goodrich, Bridgestone and Hoosier tires winning races as well as the traditional Goodyears.

Tire pressures

Porsche recommends tire pressures as a compromise between handling and tire wear, and because of the wide range of potential driving conditions worldwide, this is a challenge.

When modern low-profile tires are run at high speeds underinflated, they

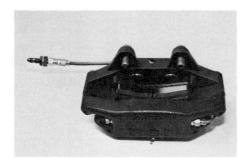

Pacific Motorsports Inc. actually makes a kit for the 911 using the Wilwood calipers. It offers the kits in a couple of stages. The Stage I Brake Solution kit replaces the A-or S-series front calipers with a Wilwood Superlite four-piston front caliper and includes mounting hardware, brake lines and Ferodo DS11 brake pads. Stage II Brake Solution uses the same four-piston front calipers and also includes a pair of the new Carrera front rotors, which have a greater heat-sink capacity. The Carrera front rotors are 0.94 in. thick versus 0.78 in. for the earlier style.

JFZ racing brakes adapted to the front of 911 club track car. Notice adjustable sway bar and cool-air ducting to the eye of the front rotor.

will probably show excessive wear in the center. This may be backward to what you may expect from experience gained with older, conventional cross-bias tires, which would wear on the outside when they were underinflated. The reason the wide low-profile tires will wear in the center is centrifugal force. Lower pressures will let the carcass flex, and the centrifugal force causes the tires to wear in the center.

The centrifugal force involved is incredible. At 65 mph the centrifugal force is approximately 250 g and at 125 mph about 1,025 g. The German driving his 911 on the autobahn at 125 mph is more inclined to having this centrifugal-force-induced wear problem than US drivers, with the 55 and 65 mph speed limits.

The following are Porsche's recommendations for tire pressures for different tire-and-wheel combinations. I suggest that you start with Porsche's recommendations, and watch your tire wear and customize the pressures for your 911 based on your observations and experiences. You might actually want to buy a tire depth gauge and check your tire wear across each tire's road surface every thousand miles or so.

If you have a newer 911 with the sixteen-inch wheels, and experience wear in the center with Porsche's recommended pressures, but you never drive over 70-75 mph, you might want to try reducing the pressure by a few pounds. At the reduced speeds in the United States, you probably will not need such high pressures to compensate for centrifugal force. In fact, some of the tire manufacturers do recommend 36 psi inflation for the 245/45VR-16 rear tires on the 911 Turbo (930), instead of the 44 psi inflation recommended by Porsche.

Competition tire pressures

Bob Strange, BF Goodrich test engineer and race driver, has a great deal of experience with radial tires on Porsches and was willing to share some information that he put together for one of BF Goodrich's ads, "BF Goodrich Update #29, Tire Inflation Pressure." The ad reads as follows:

"The question most people ask me about their tires is how much air they should put in them.

"Of all the factors that can directly affect your tires' performance, inflation pressure is one of the most important, and sadly, one of the most neglected.

"The fact about inflation pressure is that the amount of air in your tires affects the way in which the tread comes in contact with the road. By varying the pressure, you vary your car's performance.

Over and under

"Overinflation and underinflation each have their own problems. When tires are overinflated, they absorb less of the shock of driving and that puts an extra strain on suspension systems. Also, because the extra pressure lifts the shoulders off the road, traction can be substantially decreased. On the other hand, underinflation can make tires sluggish and unresponsive.

"We design our tires to have the proper balance of rolling resistance, cornering and resistance to hydroplaning when correctly inflated.

"What is the right pressure for your vehicle? For the everyday driver, the proper inflation numbers are specified

Year(s)	Standard wheels	Standard tires	Recommended wheels	Recommended tires
1965-67	4.5x15	165-15	5.5x15	185/70-15
			or 5.5x15	195/65-15
1968	5.5x15	165-15	5.5x15	185/70-15
			or 5.5x15	195/65-15
1969-74	5.5x15	165-15	7x15	205/60-15
1969-77	6.0x15	185/70-15	7x15	205/60-15
1974-75	front 6x15	185/70-15	front 7x15	205/60-15
Carrera	rear 7x15	215/60-15	rear 8x15	215/60-15
			or front 7x16	205/55-16
			or rear 8x16	225/50-16
1976-77	front 6x15	185/70-15	front 7x15	205/60-15
Carrera	rear 7x15	215/60-15	rear 8x15	215/60-15
	or front 7x15	205/50-15	or front 7x16	205/55-16
	or rear 8x15	225/50-15	or rear 8x16	225/50-16
1975-77	front 6x15	185/70-15	front 9x15	225/50-15
911 Turbo	rear 7x15	215/60-15	rear 11x15	285/40-15
(930)	or front 7x15	205/50-15	or front 9x16	205/50-16
	or rear 8x15	225/50-15	or rear 10x16	245/45-16
			or front 9x17	235/40-17
			or rear 10x17	255/40-17
1978-85	front 7x16	205/55-16	front 9x15	225/50-15
911 Turbo	rear 8x16	225/50-16	rear 11x15	285/40-15
(930)			or front 9x16	205/50-16
			or rear 10x16	245/45-16
			or front 9x17	235/40-17
			or rear 10x17	255/40-17
1986-87	front 7x16	205/55-16	front 9x15	225/50-15
911 Turbo	rear 9x16	245/45-16	rear 11x15	285/40-15
(930)			or front 9x16	205/50-16
			or rear 10x16	245/45-16
			or front 9x17	235/40-17
			or rear 10x17	255/40-17
1978-83	front 6x15	185/70-15	front 7x15	205/60-15
911SC	rear 7x15	215/60-15	rear 8x15	215/60-15
	or front 6x16	205/55-16	or front 7x16	205/55-15
	or rear 7x16	225/55-16	or rear 8x16	225/50-15
	or front 7x15	185/70-15	or front 7.5x16	205/55-16
	or rear 8x15	215/60-15	or rear 8.5x16	225/50-16
			or front 8x17	215/40 VR17
			or rear 9x17	235/40 VR17
1984-87	front 6x15	185/70-15	front 7x15	205/60-15
3.2 911	rear 7x15	215/60-15	rear 8x15	215/60-15
Carrera	or front 6x16	205/55-16	or front 7x16	205/55-15
	or rear 7x16	225/55-16	or rear 8x16	225/50-15
	or front 7x15	185/70-15	or front 7.5x16	205/55-16
	or rear 8x15	215/60-15	or rear 8.5x16	225/50-16
			or front 8x17	215/40 VR17
			or rear 9x17	235/40 VR17

Model	Wheel size	Tire size	Tire pressure front	rear
US 911,930	4.5Jx15	165HR-15	29 psi	32 psi
	5.5Jx15	165HR-15	29 psi	35 psi
	5.5Jx15	165VR-15	32 psi	35 psi
	6Jx15	185/70VR-15	32 psi	35 psi
	5.5Jx14	185HR-14	32 psi	35 psi
	7Jx15	185/70VR-15	29 psi	35 psi
	7Jx15	215/60VR-15	29 psi	35 psi
	8Jx15	215/60VR-15		35 psi
	7Jx15	205/50VR-15	29 psi	35 psi
	6Jx16	205/55VR-16	29 psi	
	7Jx16	205/55VT-16	29 psi	
	7Jx16	225/55VR-16		35 psi
	8Jx16	225/50VR-16		35 psi
	9Jx16	245/45VR-16		44 psi
Euro 930	8Jx16	225/50VR-16		44 psi

JFZ racing brakes adapted to the rear of 911 club track car. Notice the fire-slotted rotors where slots were cut into the surface of the rotors. Also notice that this club car had its own adaptation of the 935-type rear suspension pivot.

Heim-jointed rear-suspension pickup point on club track car.

on your vehicle and in your owner's manual. For all cases, the pressure should never be below the vehicle manufacturer's recommendation or above the maximum branded on the tire sidewall. For light truck tires, pressures are generally higher because they have reinforced sidewalls to carry additional loads.

The pressure of competition

"When racing, all the rules of inflation pressures change. In autocross, pressures can run much higher than for everyday driving. The higher pressure quickens steering response and can increase cornering and traction. Off-road racers run with lower pressures to provide a smoother ride, more bruise resistance and increased traction thanks to the tires' larger footprint. In competitive situations, inflation pressures are often used to compensate for oversteer or understeer. Lower front tire pressures and higher rear tire pressures generally increase understeer, while higher front tire pressures and lower rear tire pressures increase oversteer.

Check the chalk

"The most common method of finding the right inflation pressure for a competitive vehicle/tire/track combination is the chalk test. Chalk the outside shoulder sidewall area in 2 or 3 places around the circumference of the tire and after a race or practice session check how much chalk has been worn away. Ideally, the chalk should be worn away within one quarter inch of the point where shoulder rib and the sidewall meet. If the chalk remains on the tread/shoulder rib, the tire is overinflated or has too much negative camber. If the chalk is all worn away, the tire is running on the sidewalls and is underinflated or has too much positive camber. When either situation occurs, add or subtract air in 2 psi increments or modify the camber. Rechalk the tire and try again until the chalk shows your tires are properly inflated.

"The chalk method is good for rough estimates, but the method most professionals use to precisely set the right inflation pressure utilizes a pyrometer, a thermometer for your tires. After a practice session or a race, a needle-like device is inserted in the center of the tread and in each shoulder and the temperature is read. An overinflated tire runs heavier on the center of the tire than on the shoulder so the center will be hotter. An underinflated tire runs heavier on the shoulder so the shoulder will be hotter than the center.

Brakes

As the 911s and 911 derivatives have continued to go faster and faster, an improvement in brakes was needed to keep pace. The first change was in 1967 when the vented rotors were introduced on all four corners of the new 911S model. The next significant change was for the model year 1968, when all models received dual master cylinders. For model year 1969, the front calipers were increased in size and made of aluminum for the 911S model. Also in 1969, the rear calipers for all models were replaced with the larger M-caliper, which was the caliper that had been used as the front caliper on all 911s.

When used as front calipers they used larger 48 mm pistons, and when used in the rear they used 38 mm pistons. However, because the M-calipers were used front and rear, the same size pads were used front and rear for the 911T and E models. The 911Ts had solid rotors, while the 911E and S had the vented rotors. Of course, with their larger aluminum front calipers the S models used even larger front pads. In 1970 the 2.2 911Ts also received the vented rotors.

When the 1973 2.7 Carrera RS was introduced, it received the 911S brakes along with its aluminum front calipers. The 3.0 Carrera RS for 1974 had the brakes from the 917 race car, the first four-piston calipers installed on a production model 911. The 1974 3.0 Carrera RS was a very limited series, with a little over one hundred being built, and then most of those were made into the Carrera RSR race cars.

In 1975 the 911 Turbo (930) had the same combination of brakes that had been used first on the 2.0 liter 911S in 1969. In 1976 the new A-series caliper was introduced, installed on the 911s and Carreras, while the 911 Turbo continued to use the aluminum S-calipers.

The new A-caliper was an existing model that ATE made for Alfa Romeo. They were the same size as the aluminum S-caliper and used brake pads of the

JFZ racing caliper adapted for use on a street 911. Notice adjustable front sway bar in the background.

Comparison of the big brake size of the 935 pad to the pads used by the aluminum 911S. The 935 pads were probably the largest brakes ever put on a car.

Inner-suspension pickup point on club track car. This also copied the rear suspension used on the 935s. This modified rear suspension pickup allowed the camber to be adjusted at the inner end of the trailing arms.

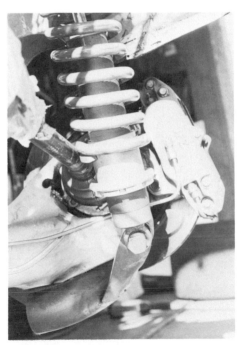

Rear-brake scoop on club track car.

187

same area. The A-caliper is a little narrower so that instead of using brake pads that are 13 mm thick, like the S-caliper, they used a thinner 10 mm brake pad.

For 1977 the 911 and the 911 Turbo (930) received power-assisted brakes. The brakes were vacuum-assisted by a seven-inch booster which acted directly on the master cylinder. The servo effect was 2.2 for the 911S and 1.8 for the 911 Turbo.

The Group 4 934s and Group 5 935s used the 917-style brakes in 1976, the 935s and the IMSA version of the 934s used them again in 1977. In 1978, with the introduction of the 3.3 Turbo, a production version of the 917-style brakes were installed on the 911 Turbo.

In 1978 the brake booster for the Turbo only was increased in size from seven to eight inches, and the internal servo factor was increased from 1.8 to a 2.25 ratio. These brakes have continued to be used on the 3.3 Turbo over the ensuing ten model years as well as the newer Turbo-look cars since 1984. The servo factor was increased again in the 1984 model year, from the 2.25 to a 3.0 ratio.

The customer 935s for 1978 continued to use the 917-style brakes. When Porsche built its Moby Dick 935/78, however, the Porsche engineers designed a new set of "big" brakes to stop this faster version of the 935. These new big brakes were made available on the customer's version of the 935 in 1979.

I can remember the first time that I saw these brakes was at Daytona in 1979, and I assumed they were only using these new larger brakes for improved brake-pad wear. To my surprise one of the drivers said that the new brakes were good for a second to a second and a half a lap at Daytona, which at that time had only one place where they did much braking.

In 1978 some of the 911SCs continued to use the aluminum S-caliper in front and the M-caliper in the rear, but by 1979 all SCs used the A-caliper, and the S-caliper was gone forever.

The brakes were revised again for the 3.2 Carrera in 1984, when the Carrera was introduced. The brake system had the following changes in 1984:

• A vacuum amplifier to increase vacuum for brake booster.
• Brake booster increased in size from seven to eight inches.
• Brake-disc thickness front and rear was increased from 20 to 24 mm (0.78 to 0.94 in.). The thicker rotors provide better heat-sink capabilities.
• Brake calipers adapted to thicker disc with spacers.
• The A and M-caliper designs were still used for the 1984 models. The brake-caliper piston diameter for the rear brakes was increased from 38 to 42 mm. The M-caliper design was still retained for the rear—Porsche just installed larger pistons. The pistons for the front calipers remained 48 mm, the same as they had been since 1969 with the aluminum S-calipers.
• Brake-pressure regulator in rear-axle brake circuit set for 33 bar.
• Brake pads-rear axle: Textar changed from Textar TP 22 to T269.

Porsche said that better rear-wheel braking effect with low brake pressure was accomplished by using the larger pistons in the rear calipers. Because the rear brakes were more effective, however, a brake-pressure regulator was needed to prevent excessive braking to the rear wheels so that the rear wheels would not lock up.

Carrera RSR pedal assembly with dual master cylinder, with a balance bar to adjust the brake balance between the front and rear brakes. This is the best setup for adjusting front-to-rear brake balance.

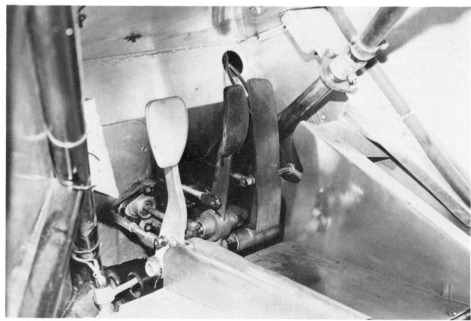

935 pedal assembly with dual master cylinder, with a balance bar for adjusting the brake balance between front and rear brakes. Notice the clutch pedal is kept separate from the brake and throttle, and that the clutch cable goes back directly under the driver's seat.

Porsche said that with the regulator, there is equal pressure in the front and rear-brake circuits up until a brake pressure of 33 bar. When brake pressure is above 33 bar, for example under full-stop braking, only forty-six percent of the additional brake pressure goes to the rear axle, compared with fifty-four percent to the front brakes.

For the Turbo-look car, the switching pressure of the brake regulator was increased from 33 to 55 bar to better match the braking characteristics to the car, with its larger brakes. Porsche made this change in the 911 Carrera's brakes in an effort to improve the overall braking effect. However, for safety reasons Porsche has to be sure the rear wheels do not lock up.

I have done some experimenting with various makes of brake pads over the years and have found pads that I feel will work better than others in some specific applications. A compromise pad is a hard thing to come up with, however, and the pads that the various Porsche models come with are probably the best all-around compromise for most applications. The real problem is that Porsche owners are unwilling to compromise their driving to make compromise solutions really work.

If you have a condition where the front wheels turn black from the brake dust and you have one of the late-model Porsches with power-boosted brakes, try Repco Deluxe pads, they seem to run cleanly and are a satisfactory compromise pad for street use. I have been very happy with the Repco Deluxe pads in 944s and 911s. They stop well and keep the wheels clean on a car that is used for street use, but they will not hold up to track use.

If you need a brake pad that will work well for track use, probably your best bet is the Ferodo DS11. All the racers have used these pads for years with great success. As well as the Ferodo DS11 pads work for track use, however, they are not a suitable brake pad for everyday street use. The Ferodo DS11 brake pads have to be warmed up before they work; it is very hard to stop a car when they are cold.

There are some other compromise brake pads available that are supposed to work well for both street and track use, but most people I know who have tried them have not been satisfied with them.

Beyond changing brake pads, there are several other things that can be done to improve the braking of your 911 for competition or track use. The first thing

you should do is work on ducting more air into the brakes, particularly the fronts. It is important for a car used on tracks to duct forced air into the brakes for cooling, because even if you have changed to Ferodo DS11 pads they will only work up to 1,050 deg F.

The first simple phase of cooling with vented rotors is to duct the forced cooling air into the eye of the rotor so that the cool air is forced out through the internal ventilating core. Start with the front brakes first; because of the weight transfer, the front brakes will do most of the braking. You can either fabricate your own brake scoop and ducting or purchase one that someone offers as a kit.

One such kit that looks like a good approach to the problem and doesn't require cutting holes in front air dams is the one offered by Holbert Racing. Holbert calls it the "COOL-brake." The fiberglass scoop mounts on the bottom of the front A-arm where there is always plenty of cool air. From the scoop, the cool air is ducted via hose and funnel to the eye of the rotor. The next step in cooling the brakes would probably be the addition of wheel fans.

Brake fluid is another very important component in the brake system as well. Porsche recommends that the brake fluid be replaced every two years. Porsche also recommends that you use only poly-glycol, DOT 3 or DOT 4 fluids and *not* DOT 5 silicone fluid. Furthermore, it says you should not add or mix DOT 5 silicone-type brake fluid with the brake fluid in your car, as severe component corrosion may result. Such corrosion could lead to brake-system failure.

Brake fluid comes in DOT 3, DOT 4 or DOT 5 ratings. The DOT standards for brake fluids were established in 1972. When the National Highway Traffic Safety Administration, Department of Transportation (NHTSA) set up the requirements for brake fluids, it determined that there was a need for two grades of fluid—until an all-weather fluid was developed with viscosity and boiling-point characteristics suitable for all braking systems.

In order to provide added protection against vapor locking and fade in severe braking service, DOT 4 fluid is recommended. But in such applications, it is important to note that the same higher viscosity that helps eliminate vapor lock-

954 pedal assembly from 911SC RS. This pedal assembly is easily adapted to a production 911 and only requires some minor modifications to the car's floorboards. Werkfoto, Porsche AG

189

ing and fade may result in poorer system performance in very cold weather.

Also, it should be noted that the high boiling points are sacrificed in the DOT 3 fluid for low viscosities for use at low temperatures. These differences between the viscosities of the DOT 3 and DOT 4 fluids are necessary to cover the specified operating-temperature ranges and as such make it necessary to maintain both DOT 3 and DOT 4 brake fluids.

Silicone fluid is DOT 5 and as such is supposed to be the replacement for both DOT 3 and DOT 4 fluids. There are some advantages to silicone brake fluid over conventional polyglycol brake fluids. It is permanent, it does not absorb moisture, it does not boil, it helps prevent corrosion rather than causing it, it will not damage paint and it helps lubricate seals and other components in the brake system.

The disadvantages, though minor, can be very annoying. Silicone brake fluid is slightly compressible, or at least it appears to be because of its affinity for air, which results in a different pedal feel from that of a system that uses a conventional noncompressible polyglycol fluid. Because of silicone brake fluid's affinity for air and its surface-tension characteristics, it tends to cling to any air bubbles which get into the system's braking, making the system very difficult to bleed properly.

When the fluid absorbs moisture, two things happen: the boiling temperature goes down and the absorbed moisture is corrosive to the brake components. Minimum wet boiling point as specified for DOT 3 is 284 deg F and for DOT 4, 311 deg F. And because these fluids are hygroscopic they commonly will approach these minimum limits. In contrast, DOT 5 silicone fluids have a wet boiling temperature of 356 deg F, and because they are not hygroscopic they will never approach the wet boiling limit.

Silicone brake fluid is inert and is the only universally compatible brake fluid. However, silicone is not miscible, it will not mix with other types of brake fluids. So, although the silicone fluids can be used with conventional polyglycol fluids, since they will not mix, the conventional fluid still in the brake system can continue to absorb any moisture in the system components.

To gain maximum benefits from the silicone brake fluids, the brake system should be completely disassembled and cleaned before adding the silicone brake fluid. Then, because of the fluid's affinity for air, it is recommended that a pressure bleeder be used for bleeding the system.

I have had personal experience with silicone brake fluid in both street and racing cars, and indeed have experienced difficulties getting the systems properly bled. Even when I was sure I had properly bled the system, the brake pedal always had a strange, soft feel to it.

I attempted to use silicone brake fluid in a Porsche 935 race car at Daytona one year for the 24-Hour race because of the problems racers have in Florida with the high humidity lowering the boiling point of the brake fluid. It probably would have achieved my objective; however, the drivers didn't like the pedal feel and requested that I change it back to conventional fluid.

In street cars, the silicone fluid has advantages that may outweigh its disadvantages, particularly for older cars that are not driven very much. Moisture absorbed by conventional polyglycol brake fluid causes serious corrosion of metal parts and deterioration of rubber seals and hoses in the brake system.

Frequent brake-fluid changes will help extend the life of the rubber components used in the brake system. One of the problems that will surface because of rubber deterioration is brake line or hose deterioration. This problem seems to take about ten years to arise, and can sometimes be deceptive and hard to diagnose because the brakes will appear to operate normally—except they will not retract when the pedal is released.

The problem is caused by the brake lines swelling up internally. The hydraulic system has enough of a mechanical-hydraulic advantage to overcome the restriction when you are braking, but the seals that retract the pistons do not have enough force to push the fluid back, so that the pistons can't retract. The swelling of the brake lines is probably caused by petroleum contamination of either the brake fluid or some other portion of the brake system.

After corrosion and rubber deterioration, the next most common problem caused by not changing the brake fluid and not bleeding the system will be the gumming up of the pistons in the calipers. When the pistons gum up, they stick in the seals when they try to retract and cause the pads to drag on the rotors, similar to the swollen-brake-line problem.

Once this problem exists, usually the only cure is to disassemble and rebuild the calipers. It is always worthwhile trying to exercise the calipers by extending and retracting each piston several times, however. Sometimes it will work. This procedure requires two people; one to pump the brake pedal to extend the pistons, and the other to force them back with a hardwood or aluminum bar. The brake fluid should be renewed and the brakes bled at the same time, since you have already lined up a helper to pump the brake pedal for the caliper-exercising procedure.

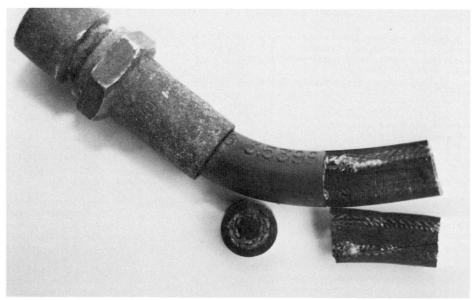

With age, the rubber brake lines can deteriorate and cause the brakes to malfunction. The malfunction is kind of sneaky in that the brakes seem to stop the car, and work fine. The problem is a dragging caliper, where the pads never fully retract, and drag on the rotor. One of the first symptoms will be one black wheel, from the brake dust.

If you ever have a master cylinder fail on your 911 and it is one of the pre-booster-brake 911s, you should plan to remove completely your pedal assembly and replace the pedal bushings. What usually happens to the pedal bushings is that the master cylinder fails and leaks brake fluid past the seal and into the pedal-box area. The stock pedal bushings are hygroscopic, so the brake fluid causes them to swell up, causing them to bind up and not return when you remove your foot from the brake pedal.

If you ever have a sticking pedal with your 911, you should check the brake-fluid level and check the floorboards around the pedals for moisture. If the fluid is low and you find fluid around the pedals, you probably have a bad master cylinder. I recommend that you use the original-style nylon-type bushings, and not the bronze-type being offered as a replacement. The new set of plastic bushings will last until the next master cylinder goes bad, which will probably be another five to ten years and nearly 100,000 miles.

If you use your 911 in speed events, you should plan to flush your brake system more often than once every two years as recommended in your owners manual. Racers will flush their brake system and bleed their brakes at each racing weekend.

If your brakes get too hot, they will boil the brake fluid. When the fluid boils, it forms air bubbles. The air bubbles are compressible so the pedal will start to go down.

The solutions for this problem are brake fluid with a higher boiling point, and the ducting of cooling air to the rotor and caliper so that the fluid cannot get hot enough to boil. Just keeping the fluid in the system fresh will reduce the boiling problem, because the fluid will not have picked up moisture.

A good racing brake fluid is AP Racing 550. This brake fluid is rated as a DOT 3 fluid, and as such has a wet boiling point of 284 deg F. AP Racing 550, however, has a dry boiling point of 550 deg F, which exceeds the DOT 4 specifications by over 100 degrees.

For competition or track use, the next step up to improve your 911's braking is to install larger brakes and/or brake calipers. Over the years, a number of people have installed the larger 917-style brakes that have been used on the 911 Turbo since 1978. With the Turbo brakes, most people who have adapted them have been installing them on older 911s and have chosen to use a twin master-cylinder assembly with a built-in balance bar for adjusting the bias between the front and rear brakes. Some people have fabricated their own and others have adapted a Neal Pedal assembly, which has built-in twin master cylinders with a balance bar.

The easiest way to solve this problem is to purchase the latest version of the pedal assembly that Porsche uses with this type of brakes. (The latest version is the 954.423.003.00, used in the 911SC RS.) The factory pedal assembly will require some slight modification to the floorboards and firewall where it mounts. As an alternative to the double master-cylinder pedal assembly, some people have installed the Turbo brakes using the vacuum-booster assembly and master cylinder from the 911 Turbo.

There are also several brands of larger US-made calipers available that may be adapted for this application. Pacific Motorsports Inc. actually makes a kit for the 911 in a couple of stages. Its Stage I Brake Solution is a kit that replaces the A or S series front calipers with a Wilwood Superlite four-piston front-caliper-mounting hardware, brake lines and Ferodo DS11 brake pads.

It also has a Stage II Brake Solution which uses the same four-piston front calipers and also includes a pair of new Carrera front rotors, which have a greater heat-sink capacity. The Carrera front rotors are 24 mm (0.94 in.) thick versus 20 mm (0.78 in.) for the earlier style.

If you are making your 911 over into a race car, or if it is primarily going to be a track car, you should probably switch the rubber brake lines to the Teflon braided-steel brake hoses. The rubber hoses are fine for a street car, in fact I prefer them. They are a low-maintenance item and the only problems I have ever seen them have are swelling from old age and contaminated brake fluid.

If you do switch to the Teflon brake lines, be sure they are dash-three size hoses. The dash-four that were so common a few years ago on the aftermarket actually cause a spongy brake pedal.

All of the successful race cars in the world use these braided-steel hoses. However, if you get an inferior product, or if they are improperly installed, you may have actually created a worse problem for yourself than the one you may think you are solving. There is probably no more frightening experience than having the brakes fail, so be very careful and check out the fit of your aftermarket brake lines carefully.

Even though it might *seem* like a good idea, I recommend against drilling your brake rotors unless you have special rotors from either Porsche or Automotive Products (AP) that were made to be drilled. The problem is with excessive cracking. The alternative is the fire-slotted rotors, where slots are cut into the surface of the rotors. The purpose of these slots is to wipe the hot brake dust from the operating surface of the disc. The slots should be cut into the surface of the rotor so that they become parallel with the leading edge of the pad as they are rotated under the pads.

Summary

Remember, you selected your Porsche because you thought it was the best car you could buy for your money. Before you get too carried away compromising the compromises Porsche has already made with your own modifications, make sure you know what you want when you are done, and that the changes you are making will indeed provide you with the results you want.

And again, don't forget that almost all of the alternative components made for Porsches are of lesser quality than the original-equipment components. This use of quality components is one of the reasons Porsches cost as much as they do. It is also the reason they work so well and get all of the rave reviews in the car magazines year after year.

You have gone to all of the trouble of selecting your Porsche because of its performance, quality and image; now don't make it a lesser-quality automobile by using lesser-quality replacement components.

Transmissions

901 transmission. Aluminum housing was used from 1965 through 1968. There was also a mainshaft available for the 904-version of the transmission that had no fixed second gear on the mainshaft as with the 911, so that all five speeds could have different ratios selected. One of the weak- nesses of the 901 transmission was the mainshaft. First gear was cantilevered out- side of the intermediate plate so that when excessive torque was applied to first gear, the tendency was to pull the gear right off the end of the shaft.

901 transmission. Magnesium housing was used from 1969 through 1971.

The original transmission used in the 911 was the five-speed 901 transmission which used Porsche's own synchronizing system. There were both four- and five-speed versions of the 901 transmission available. This was housed in a sandcast aluminum casing. The transmission housing was changed to a magnesium casting during the 1969 model year.

The 904, 906 and 909 all used their own versions of the 901 gearbox, where they used the internal components from the 901 transmission with their own unique transmission housings. This was done to take advantage of the wide selection of gears available for the 901 transmission. The 914 and 914/6 also used modified versions of the 901 transmission, with their own cases. There were three different versions of the shifting mechanism for these 914 transmissions; two with side-angled tail-shifters (one for each the four and the six) and the side-shifter for the 914/4.

The Type 916 transmission became the replacement for the racing transmissions in 1969 because of the added demands placed on the transmission by the 3.0 liter 908 engines. The 915 transmission was a development for the production cars based on this 916 racing transmission. The magnesium-cased 901 transmission was replaced by the larger, stronger 915 transmission for the 1972 model year, and the introduction of the 2.4 liter engines.

The 915 transmissions were also available in both four- and five-speed versions, continued to use the Porsche synchronizing system and used a magnesium housing until 1978, when the larger, more powerful 3.0 liter SC engines were introduced for the world market.

The 901 transmission had what was considered at the time a conventional shift pattern, with the usual H-pattern but with low and reverse placed out to the left with a spring-loaded lock-out. Reverse was to the left and forward, and low gear was to the left and back. The remaining four gears were on the regular H-pattern. When the 915 transmission was introduced, the pattern was revised and reverse and fifth were spring-loaded and placed out to the right of the H-pattern.

When the 930 was introduced as a 1975 model, it had a new Type 930 transmission as well. The 930 transmission was designed as a much larger transmission, to be able to cope with the power outputs of a generation of turbocharged race cars.

The 930 transmission was a four-speed with a conventional H-pattern, with reverse out to the left and forward. The 930 transmission continued to use the Porsche-designed synchronizing system. A large rubber-centered clutch was incorporated in 1978, so the bell housing had to be made 30 mm longer to accommodate this new clutch. For the production 911 Turbo (930), the transmission housing was made of aluminum.

There have been different versions of this transmission made for both the 934 and the 935. There are two versions for the 935: a conventional right-side-up version, and the "upside-down" gearbox which was incorporated to permit a reduction of the axle angles in the 935s.

For 1987 an all-new, much stronger five-speed transmission was introduced for the 911, which utilized a cone-type (Borg Warner) synchronizing system in all forward gears and reverse. The shift pattern was changed again; reverse was now to the left-front of the H-pattern, and fifth was to the right-front.

The pinion was a hypoid-drive design to gain the extra strength without having to increase the size over that used in the 915 transmission. The transmission had a new larger clutch which was activated by a hydraulic master-and-slave cylinder. The rear torsion-bar tube had a bent center section to provide additional clearance for the transmission.

There was also a new four-wheel-drive transmission available on a limited basis in the Type 953 Paris-Dakar car. This Type 964 transmission was based on the same design as the G-50 transmission, and will be used in the four-wheel-drive 911 called the Type 964 car for the 1989 model year.

Porsche made Sportomatic transmissions for the 911s for a number of years, starting in 1968 and phasing out in the 1980s. The Sportomatic transmissions combined a torque converter and a vacuum-operated clutch with a manual transmission to create a semi-automatic transmission. The original version was the four-speed Type 905. In 1972 a four-speed version of the 925 replaced the

901 transmission with original pivot for push-type clutch with guided throw-out bearing.

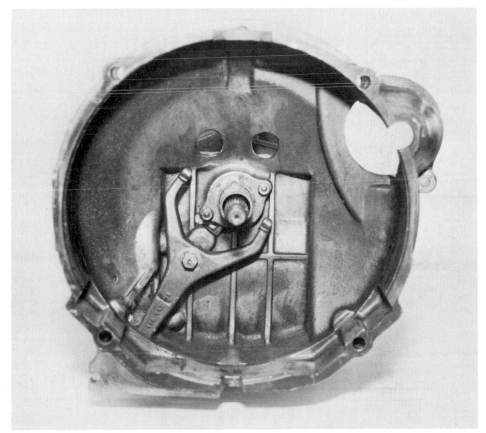

901 transmission with revised pivot point for pull-type clutch used in 1970 and 1971.

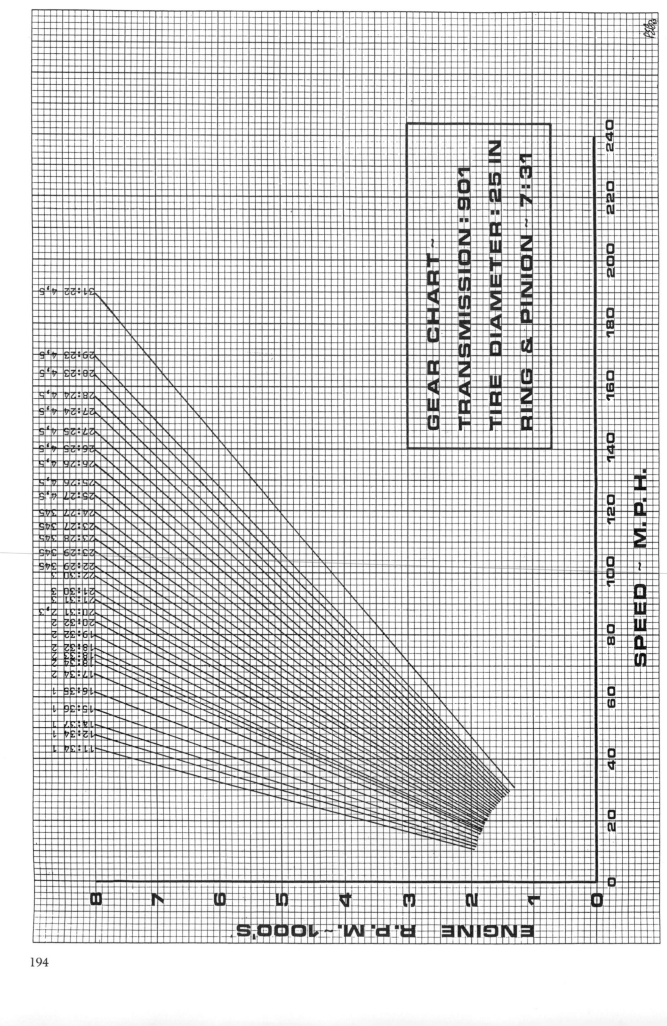

GEAR CHART ~

TRANSMISSION : 901

TIRE DIAMETER : 25 IN

RING & PINION ~ 7:31

SPEED ~ M.P.H.

ENGINE R.P.M. ~ 1000'S

31:22 4,5
29:23 4,5
20:23 4,5
28:24 4,5
27:24 4,5
27:25 4,5
26:25 4,5
26:26 4,5
25:26 4,5
25:27 4,5
24:27 345
23:27 345
23:28 345
23:29 345
22:29 345
22:30 3
21:30 3
21:31 3
20:31 2,3
20:32 2
19:32 2
18:32 2
18:33 2
17:34 2
16:35 1
15:36 1
14:37 1
12:34 1
11:34 1

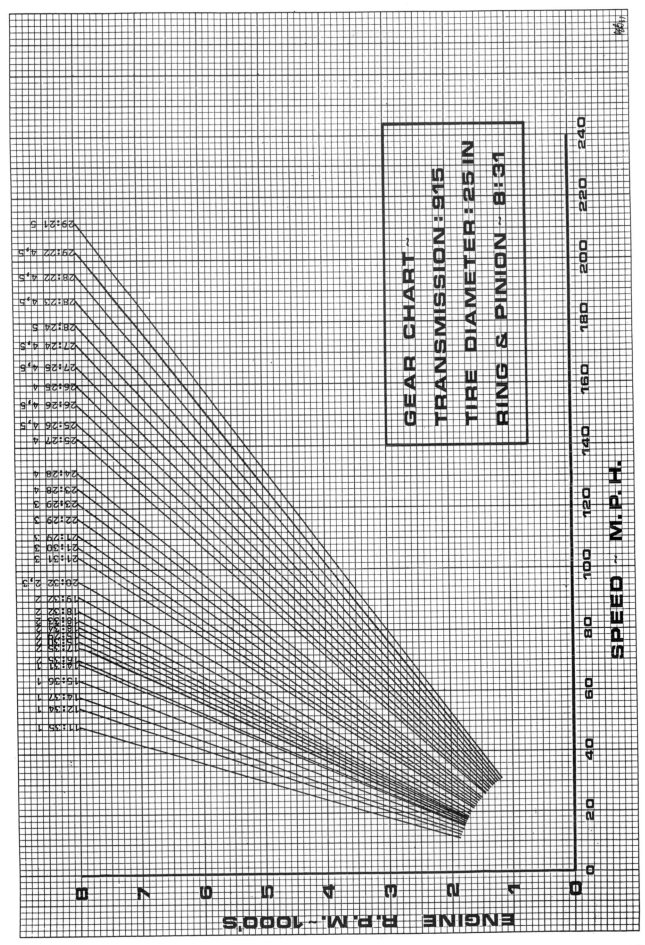

GEAR CHART~
TRANSMISSION: 915
TIRE DIAMETER: 25 IN
RING & PINION ~ 8:31

ENGINE R.P.M. ~ 1000's

SPEED ~ M.P.H.

29:21 5
29:22 4,5
28:22 4,5
28:23 4,5
28:24 5
27:24 4,5
27:25 4,5
26:25 4
26:26 4,5
25:26 4,5
25:27 4
24:28 4
23:28 4
23:29 3
22:29 3
21:29 3
21:30 3
21:31 3
20:32 2,3
19:32 2
18:32 2
18:33 2
18:34 2
16:34 2
17:35 2
16:35 2
14:35 2
15:36 1
14:37 1
12:34 1
11:35 1

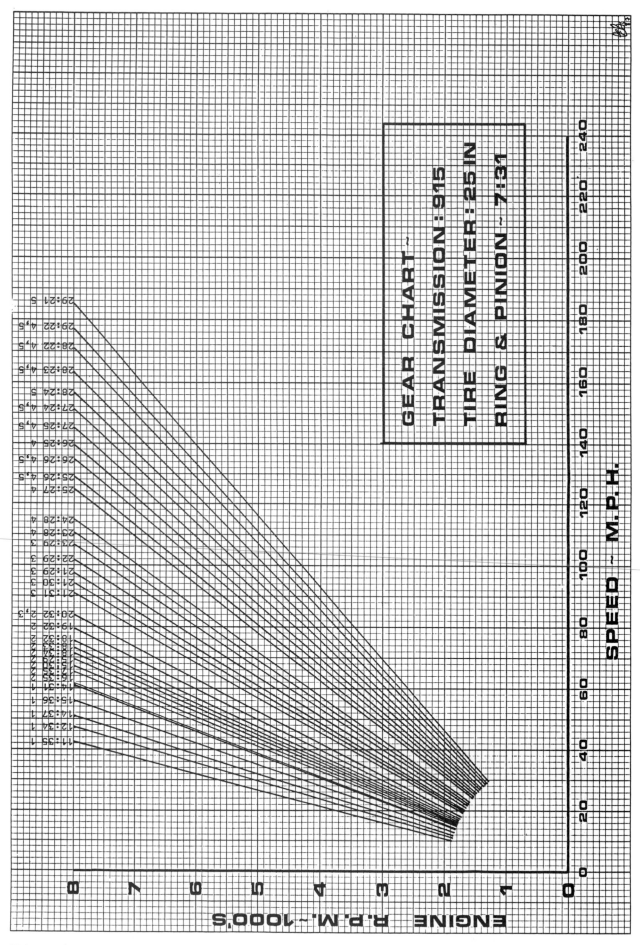

GEAR CHART ~
TRANSMISSION : 915
TIRE DIAMETER : 25 IN
RING & PINION ~ 7:31

SPEED ~ M.P.H.

ENGINE R.P.M. ~ 1000'S

29:21 5
29:22 4,5
28:22 4,5
28:23 4,5
28:24 5
27:24 4,5
27:25 4,5
26:25 4
26:26 4,5
25:26 4,5
25:27 4
24:28 4
23:28 4
23:29 3
22:29 3
21:29 3
21:30 3
21:31 3
20:32 2,3
19:32 2,3
18:32 2
15:36 1
14:37 1
12:34 1
11:35 1

196

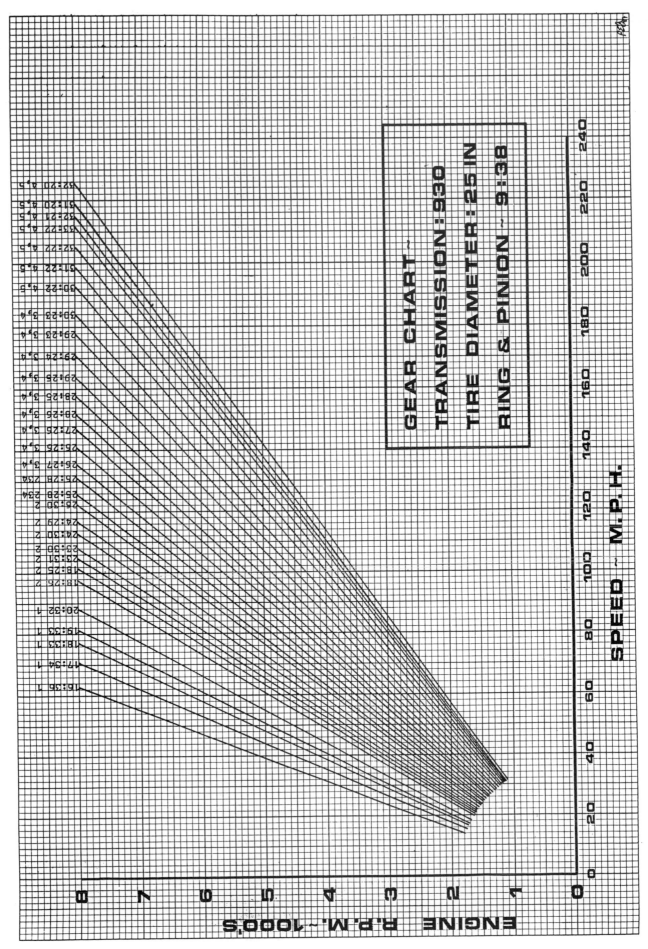

GEAR CHART ~
TRANSMISSION:930

TIRE DIAMETER:25 IN

RING & PINION ~ 9:38

SPEED ~ M.P.H.

ENGINE R.P.M.~ 1000'S

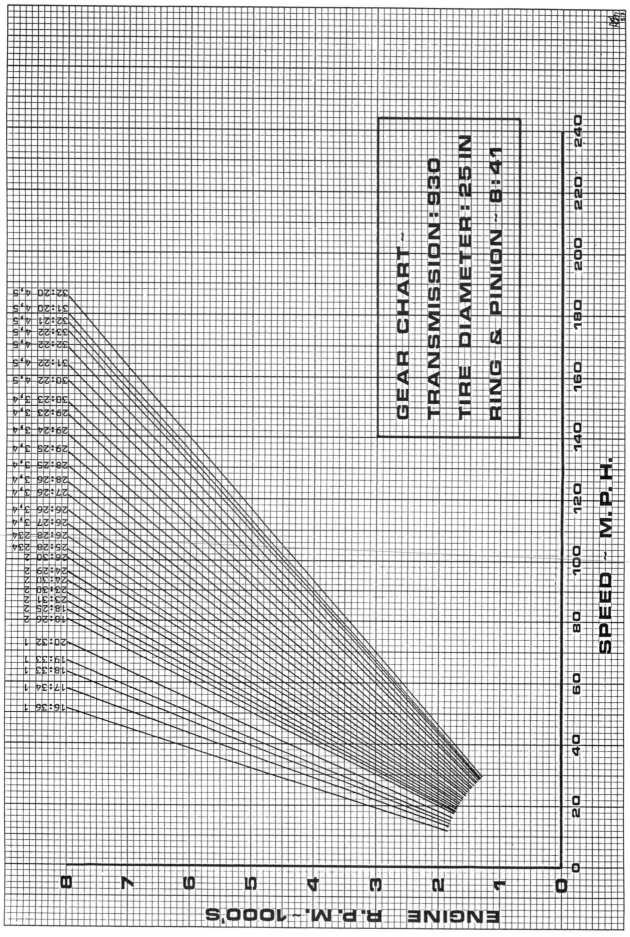

GEAR CHART ~
TRANSMISSION: 930
TIRE DIAMETER: 25 IN
RING & PINION ~ 8:41

SPEED ~ M.P.H.

ENGINE R.P.M. ~ 1000's

32:20 4,5
31:20 4,5
32:21 4,5
33:22 4,5
32:22 4,5
31:22 4,5
30:22 4,5
30:23 3,4
29:23 3,4
29:24 3,4
29:25 3,4
28:25 3,4
28:26 3,4
27:26 3,4
26:26 3,4
26:27 3,4
26:28 3,4
25:28 2,3,4
26:30 2
24:29 2
24:30 2
23:30 2
23:31 2
18:25 2
10:26 2
20:32 1
19:33 1
18:33 1
17:34 1
16:36 1

198

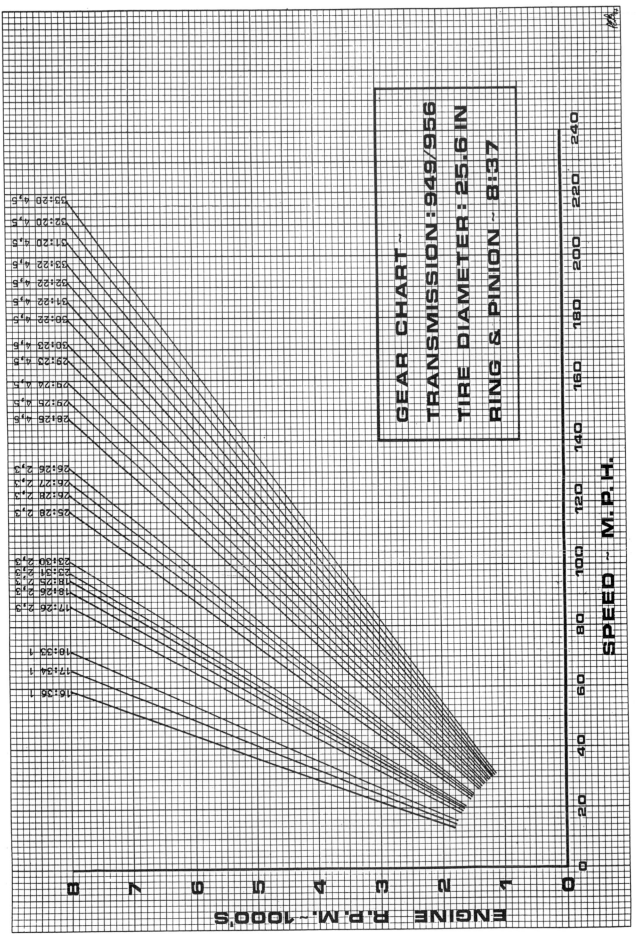

GEAR CHART ~
TRANSMISSION: 949/956
TIRE DIAMETER: 25.6 IN
RING & PINION ~ 8:37

ENGINE R.P.M. ~ 1000'S

SPEED ~ M.P.H.

33:20 4,5
32:20 4,5
31:20 4,5
33:22 4,5
32:22 4,5
31:22 4,5
30:22 4,5
30:23 4,5
29:23 4,5
29:24 4,5
29:25 4,5
28:26 4,5

26:26 2,3
26:27 2,3
26:28 2,3
25:28 2,3

23:30 2,3
23:31 2,3
18:25 2,3
18:26 2,3
17:26 2,3

18:33 1
17:34 1
16:36 1

905 transmission for most models, while the 905 was continued for the Euro 911T for 1972 and 1973.

The 925 transmission was the equivalent to the 915 transmission which had been the Sportomatic equivalent to the 901. Porsche limited the 925 Sportomatic to a three-speed in the United States for 1975 because it felt, with the broad torque curve of the 2.7 liter

engines, that the four-speed was no longer necessary. For the European market, the three-speed version was held off another year until the introduction of the 1976 3.0 liter Carrera.

The Porsche transmissions have always had an extremely wide selection of gear ratios to choose from. How do you know what gear ratios your car has? If your car is stock and no one has modified the

transmission, the type number is stamped in the transmission case. All you need do is look up the ratios in your technical specifications booklet—they're all there.

Let's assume you are choosing gears for a 911 with a 915 five-speed transmission. The first step in choosing a set of gears is to assume a differential ratio and tire diameter, and pick first gear. First gear should be a compromise between being too long (meaning too many mph/rpm) which would cause too much clutch wear from slipping to get started, and being too short (not enough mph/rpm), for example, a "stump-puller" gear.

A good first-gear ratio for a street 911 would be around 4 to 6 mph/1000 rpm. The range of a first gear for a race car could range from 4 to 10 mph/1000 rpm, depending on what first gear will be used for. In a race car, first gear might just be used as a starting gear for some tracks, and as both a starting gear and a cornering gear on other tracks.

Next is the selection of the top gear, let's call it fifth gear. This gear is determined by one of three things: First, absolute top speed of the car, second, highest speed the car will be driven (such as a long straightaway) or, third, as an economical cruising gear for the highway.

If you were gearing your 911 for top speed, you would have to either know or extrapolate from other data what the top speed of the car would be. If you were going to gear the car for the highest speed that it will reach, this will be dictated by the length of the longest sector

915 transmission with magnesium housing.

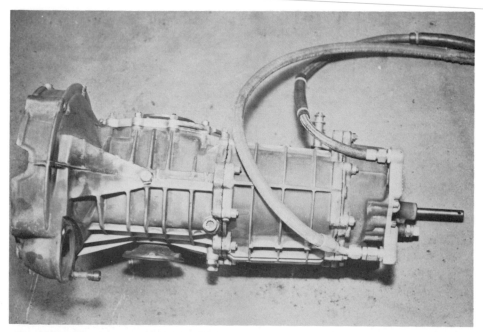

The 915 transmission with oil pump as used in the RSR competition cars. In the RSR the oil was circulated to an oil cooler and then returned to lubricate the trans-

mission, thus ensuring that the transmission was properly lubricated with cooled oil.

915 transmission with oil pump. When these oil pumps were used in the production cars, they were used just to recirculate the transmission lubricant to be sure it would provide proper lubrication to all of the gears.

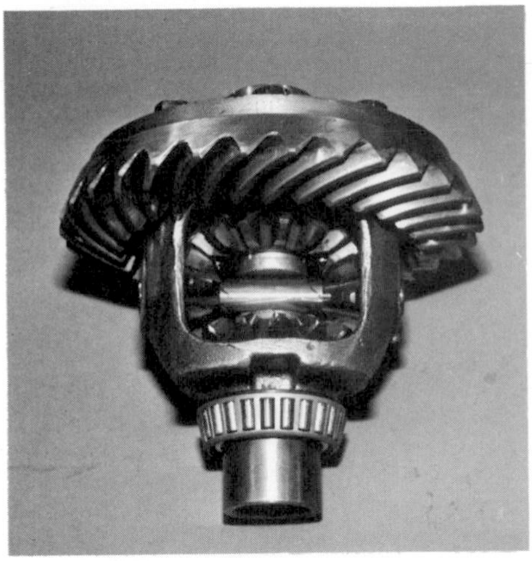

Open differential of the type used in Porsche transmissions.

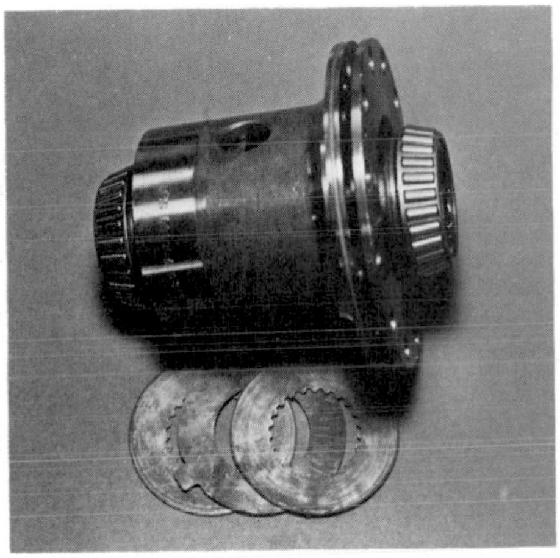

Limited-slip differential, late-style introduced in 1969. A multi-disc limited-slip differential was available from the beginning because it was used in the 904 version of the transmission. The later-style limited-slip differentials were both more reliable and more effective.

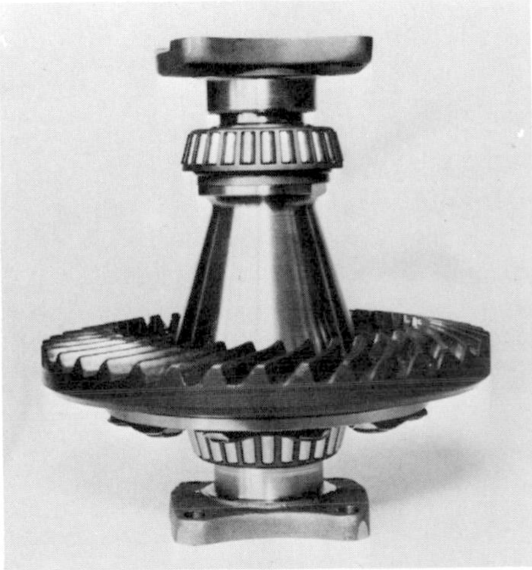

Titanium spool used in 935 instead of any differential, providing a locked rear end.

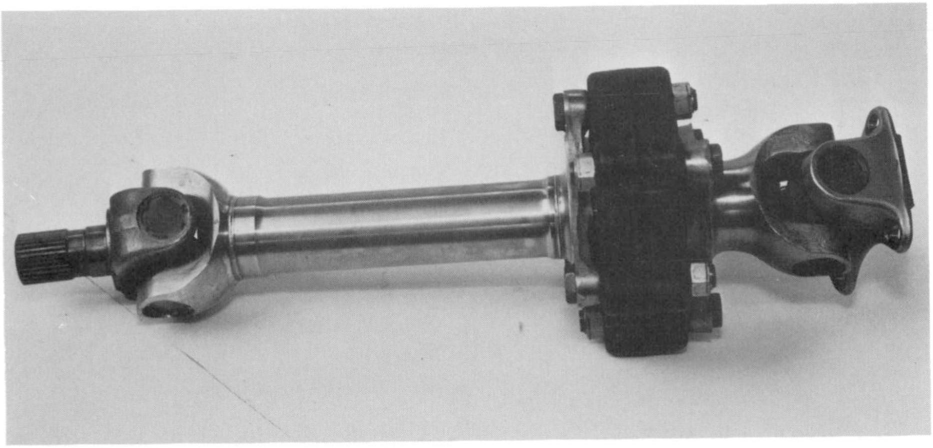

Titanium rear axle used for the 935.

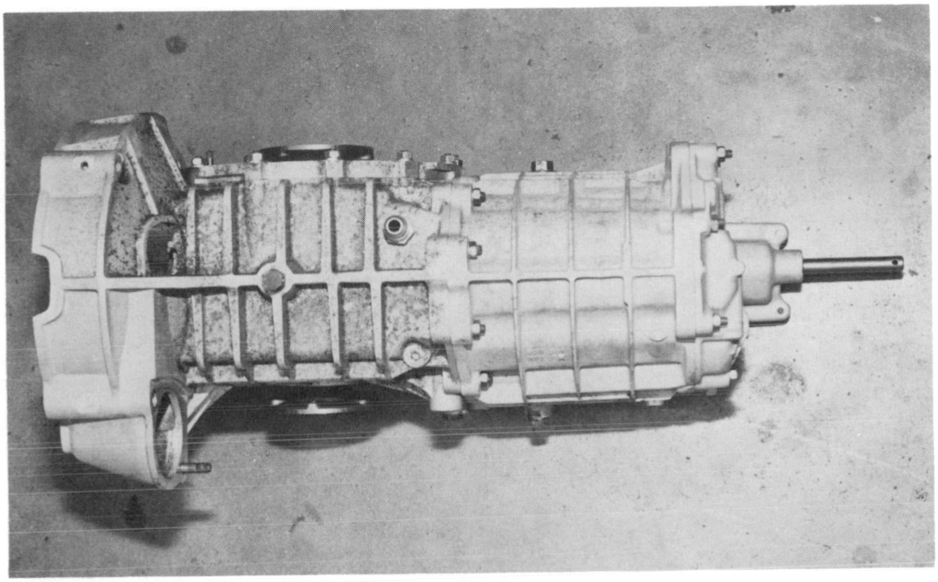

930 transmission, early-style with small bell housing.

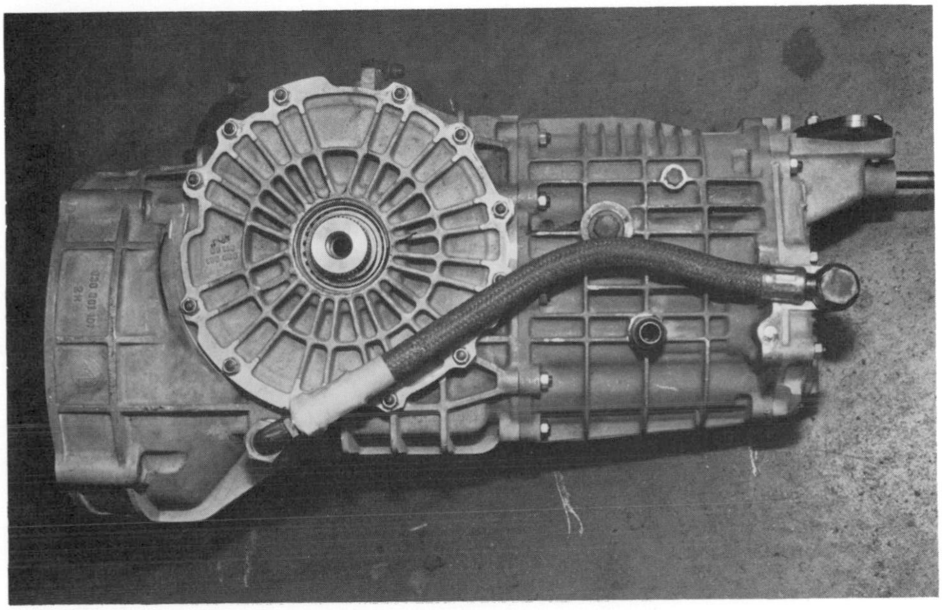

Upside-down style 935 transmission.

Upside-down style 935 transmission. Notice plumbing for auxiliary oil cooler.

on the racetrack. You would either know the maximum speed reached on a straight section of a racetrack from experience, or you could calculate it.

The maximum speed and maximum engine rpm desired at that speed are then entered into the following equation or a gear chart to calculate the fifth-gear ratio.

$$\text{T.R.} = \frac{(\text{RPM})(\text{Tire Dia})(0.002975)}{(\text{MPH})(\text{D.R.})}$$

T.R. = transmission ratio
RPM = engine speed
Tire dia = rear-tire diameter
MPH = desired speed in mph
D.R. = differential ratio

Next we will divide the range between first gear and fifth gear into even incre-

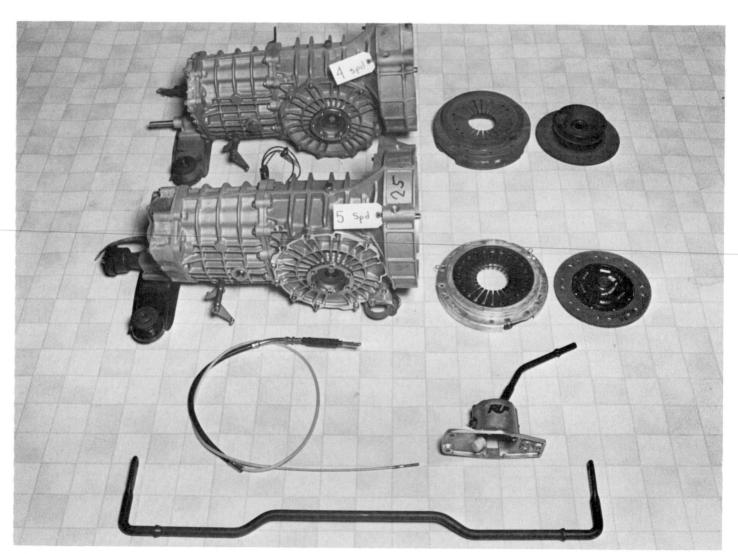

Later-style four-speed 930 transmission with large bell housing to accommodate large rubber-centered clutch and RUF five-speed transmission. The RUF five-speed had all different castings from those used by the Porsche four-speed. The differential housing was a special casting, with a shorter bell housing like the 935's. The center section was a special casting too that provided support for reverse gear. Exclusive Motor Cars, Inc.

ments. For our example, let's say that first is a ratio of 11:35, or 3.18, and fifth is 28:23, or 0.82. To divide this into even steps, a step-up ratio is calculated as follows:

$$\text{Step-up ratio} = \sqrt[1/n]{\frac{(\text{1st Ratio})}{(\text{5th Ratio})}}$$

$$\sqrt[1/4]{\frac{(3.18)}{(0.82)}}$$

Step-up ratio = 1.4 (for this example)

WHERE n = number of intervals between gears, that is, 1 less than number of gears. For instance, n = 4 for a five-speed.

This step-up ratio (1.4) is the ratio between gear ratios. If fifth gear is 0.82, then fourth-gear ratio is 0.82x1.4, or 1.15, which is approximately a 24:28 gear set. Third, then, is 1.15x1.4 which equals 1.60, approximately a 20.32 gear

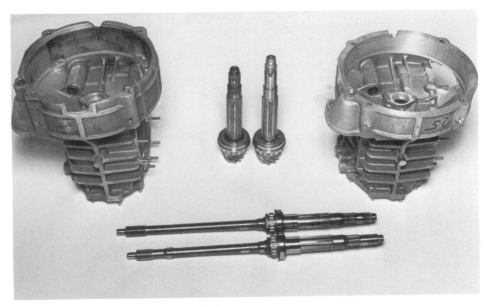

RUF five-speed compared to Porsche four-speed, some of their major differences. Exclusive Motor Cars, Inc.

RUF accommodated the fifth forward gear inside of the front cover with reverse, much like the original 901 transmission. Exclusive Motor Cars, Inc.

Porsche four-speed with only reverse out in the front cover. Exclusive Motor Cars, Inc.

203

set. Second would be 1.60x1.4 or 2.25, which is approximately a 14:31 gear set.

You can see by looking at the ratio selected on the gear chart that in each gear, the car will run for the same rpm band, from about 5700 to 8000 rpm. This may sound reasonable, but you probably won't find too many 911s geared like this. Let's analyze why.

Look at the speeds at which you would be shifting with shifts required at 8000 rpm. The first-to-second shift would be at 49 mph, the second-to-third shift at 69 mph, the third-to-fourth at 96 and fourth-to-fifth at 132 mph. As the speed increases, the range of speed in which each gear is used also would increase. The shifting is very frantic in the lower gears, but finally the car is expected to pull all the way from 132 to 180 mph. So this system that uses even geometric steps is one way to select your gear ratios, but not the *best* way.

Generally, the best way to select gears is with a method that is quite easy. Simply divide the speed range between maximum rpm in first and fifth gears by the number of intervals between gears—four in this example of a five speed—for a constant speed range in each gear.

Each gear is used for approximately a 35 mph-range, and each up-shift starts the next higher gear a successively higher rpm. Usually this is best because "long pulls," from 4700 to 8000 rpm in second gear, for example, are at low speeds where the time involved is very short. This allows the "short pulls," from 6500 to 8000 rpm in fifth, for example, to occur at high speed where the time in gear is much longer because of the aerodynamic drag.

In other words, the time lost at lower speeds is more than made up at the higher speeds. This is a fairly standard method of gear selection for street cars from 356s through 959s, including most racing applications.

The gear-selection process just discussed is great for straight-line acceleration from zero to the 911's top speed. If you are gearing your 911 for a racetrack or autocross which has corners that have to be taken at awkward speeds, your gear-selection process will require some modifications. Intermediate gear must be juggled up or down, if possible, to allow the car to exit corners at as high an rpm as possible while minimizing the number of shifts required per lap. This juggling is done based upon past experience at a particular track, or a very good course diagram that allows cornering speeds to be calculated. If you need gearing information for a track you have never been to, ask a friend for advice; most people will help. At least their recommendation will give you a place to start.

If you are an autocrosser, and the autocrosses that you participate in are all similar, you will want to try to gear your transmission to minimize the shifting—a great deal of time is wasted by shifting. Take advantage of your engine's strong characteristics. If it pulls well at low rpm, choose a gear that will take advantage of that. If it pulls well at higher rpm, choose a gear that will take advantage of that.

The most important corner on a track to consider when selecting gears is the one leading onto the longest straight. The correct gearing on this corner is vital to minimizing lap times. The gear should allow exiting the corner at a high rpm, but still allow the car to be well away from the corner before the next shift is required.

Porsche center section on left, and RUF center section on right. Exclusive Motor Cars, Inc.

Porsche end cover on right, and RUF end cover on left. Exclusive Motor Cars, Inc.

At a given speed, acceleration out of a corner is increased by running the engine nearer its maximum horsepower, as opposed to running it at its maximum torque rpm. A compromise must be made so that an up-shift is not required too close to the corner, or so that too much shifting is not required.

For a race-car mechanic, one of life's pleasures is having chosen all the gears for a new racetrack, and having the driver come back in after the first practice and say "the gears are just right!" Doesn't happen too often.

The gear charts in this chapter are all based on this equation:

$$MPH = \frac{(RPM)(Tire\ Dia)0.002975}{(T.R.)(D.R.)}$$

MPH = miles per hour
RPM = engine speed
Tire Dia = rear-tire diameter in inches
T.R. = transmission ratio
D.R. = differential ratio

The tire diameter is best determined with a tire on the car at the rated pressure. Measure the distance in inches that the car moves for a few revolutions of the tire, and then calculate the diameter from:

$$Dia,\ in. = \frac{Distance\ in.}{\pi\ Revolutions}$$

The diameter increases with speed, because of centrifugal force, until at about 180 mph the diameter has increased roughly three percent if it is a bias-ply race tire.

Differential and transmission ratios are always calculated as driven gear divided by driving gear. For example, a 7:31 ring and pinion has a ratio of 31 (number of teeth on the driven gear) divided by 7 (number of teeth on the driving gear) or 4.428. When a gear set is given on a chart, or in a parts book, the first number is always the driving gear and the second is always the driven gear. So, just divide the second gear by the first and you have the correct ratio.

In order to calculate a speed for a different differential ratio than is shown on the chart, use the following:

MPH for new ratio =

$$MPH\ for\ old\ ratio \left(\frac{Old\ Ratio}{New\ Ratio} \right)$$

To calculate speed for a different tire diameter, use the following formula.

MPH for new tire diameter =
MPH for old tire diameter

$$\left(\frac{Old\ Tire\ Diameter}{New\ Tire\ Diameter} \right)$$

915 transmission adapted for use in 911 Turbo. Extra oiling added in an effort to extend the life of the 915 transmission. Oil was sprayed at each gear set where they mesh. Tom Hanna

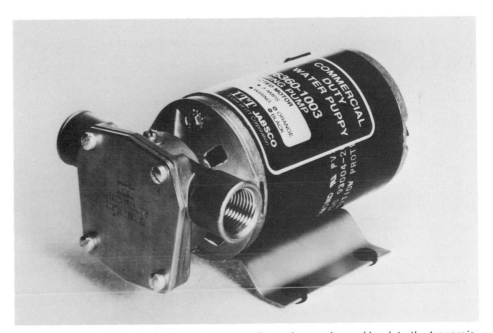

ITT Jabsco 16360-0003 flexible impeller bilge pump. These pumps worked very well for recirculating transmission lubricant through a cooler and back to the transmission. ITT Jabsco

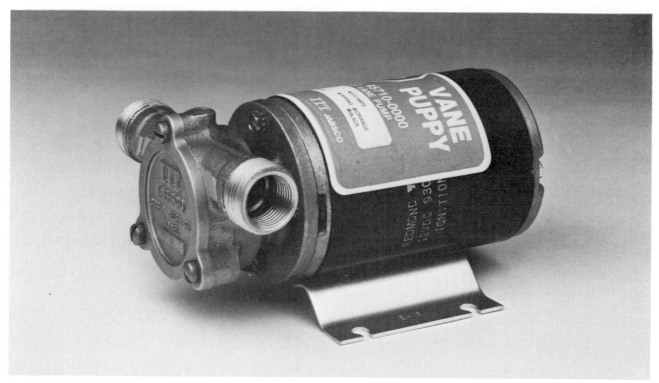

ITT Jabsco 47510-0000 rotary sliding-vane type pump. These pumps worked very well for recirculating transmission lubricant through a cooler and back to the transmission. ITT Jabsco

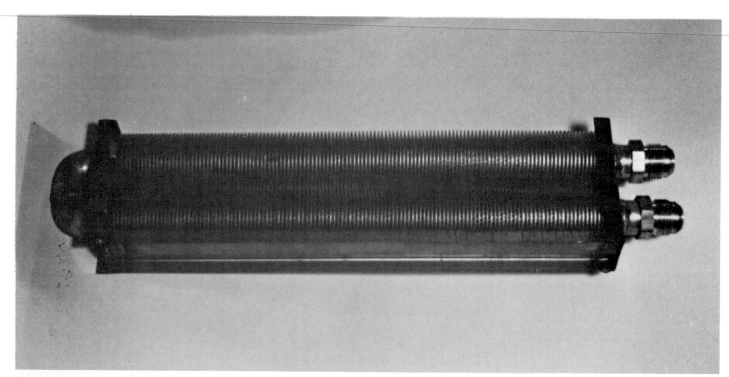

Terbatrol cooler. This type of cooler is ideal for cooling the transmission. Lemke Design

915 transmission adapted for use in 911 Turbo. A special reinforced side cover was made for the transmission. One of the later-model 915 oil pumps was incorporated in the reinforced side cover to recirculate the transmission lubricant. Tom Hanna

Bilge pump mounted in special track car for recirculating transmission lubricant to oil cooler and back to transmission. Be sure that large lines are used so that the lines do not restrict the flow.

G-50 transmission. All-new transmission used in the 1987 911 Carrera. This new transmission extended so far forward that it necessitated a new torsion-bar carrier and motor mount.

Porsche short-shifter. This short-shifter was part of the 911SC RS Type 954 (part number 954.424.010.00). Werkfoto, Porsche AG

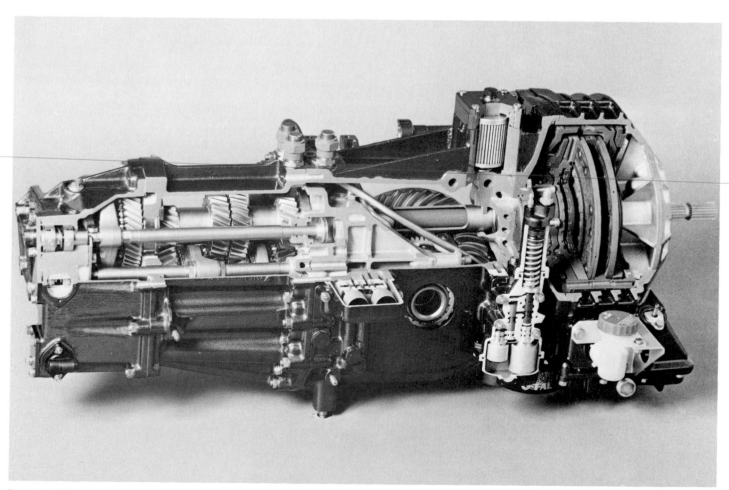

Porsche PDK transmission. The PDK transmission used two separate clutches. The driver did not have to use the clutch to shift. Two gears were engaged at one time, and the engine output was transferred from one gear to the other with the two clutches. The shift itself resembled a motorcycle shift. Pushing the gear lever forward shifted down, while pulling the lever backward shifted up. Werkfoto, Porsche AG

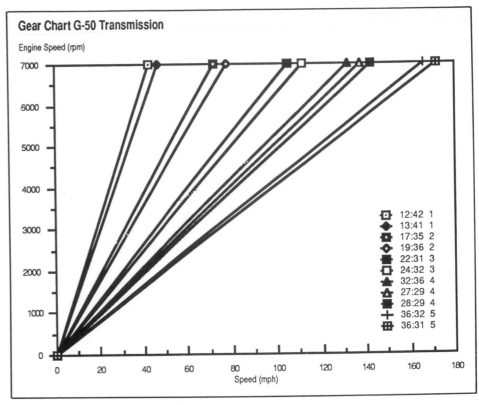

Gear chart for G-50 five-speed transmission with 9:31 ring and pinion.

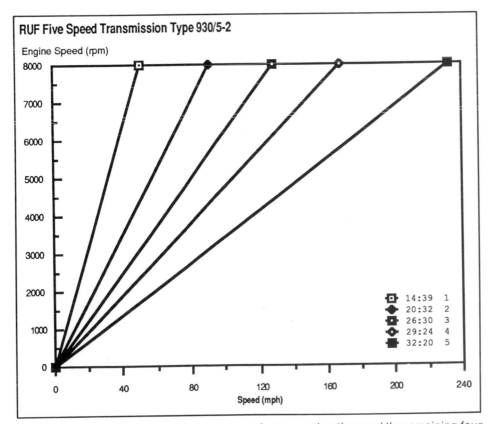

Gear chart for RUF five-speed transmission with 9:36 ring and pinion. The advantage of the RUF five-speed over the Porsche four-speed was that low gear was lower for faster acceleration, and the remaining four gears had closer ratios, allowing the engine to remain on the boost. 930 gears were interchangeable for gears two through five.

1967 Porsche Speedster. Stan Townes built this Porsche Speedster shown at the 1971 Oakland Roadster Show. He built it in the late 1960s from a wrecked 911 coupe. The fenders were flared to fit the larger American mags and tires. The Nugget

Porsche President Peter Schutz took advantage of the flexibility and skills of Porsche's Werk I to try out some of his pet ideas for the 911. Working with Rolf Sprenger at Werk I, they converted one of the 911 Turbo-look cabriolets into a coupe, with the aid of a hardtop from the Special Wishes program and then with a little magic, into a Speedster. The project was a great success. The transformation was started June 1985 with a US-legal Cabriolet chassis, including DOT, EPA and June 1985 ID plate in driver's door. The conversion took 650 hours and was finished June 30, 1986. Schutz drove his Speedster to work in the fall of 1986, putting 4,226 miles on it. The Speedster was later purchased by Bob Snodgrass of Brumos Porsche and imported to Jacksonville, Florida, in December 1986. The car's import papers stated the car's mileage was 4,962 when it was imported. It was then sold to Richard and Lori Riley, who live in Michigan. Lori Schutz-Riley is Peter Schutz's daughter. She and her husband, Rick, wanted the Speedster as a keepsake of one of her father's contributions at Porsche. Werkfoto, Porsche AG

The 911 has always been a car that people have liked to modify. When the 911R was introduced in 1967 it had fender flares in the rear to fit what were then very large seven-inch rear wheels, compared with the 4½ inch 911S wheels. It was not long after that people were flaring the rear fenders to fit larger and larger wheels and tires under the body. This was a pretty small styling statement, but it *was* a statement and the beginning of a custom craze that is still going on twenty years later.

The pace quickened when in 1970 Porsche offered both the mechanicals to convert your Grand Touring 911 into a street racer. Usually, the styling changes followed Porsche's changes to the 911s to make them competitive on the race-track—but not always. In the late 1960s a fellow named Stan Townes cut the top off of a 911 coupe and made a Speedster. Others have followed suit, including Peter Schutz, president of Porsche, who had a Speedster made at Werks I in 1985. It was the possible prototype of the production 911 Speedster.

For the most part, the custom 911s have emulated one form or another of Porsche's racing cars. The Kremers and Design Plastic were the first to capitalize on what has become the slope-nose fad, back in 1979 when they first offered their 935 street turbo. In 1981 Porsche introduced a slope-nose (or slant-nose) version of its own as part of its *"Sonderwunsche Programm"* (Special Wishes Program). Now, every population center in the world has someone doing slope-nose conversion work, and both the Kremers and Design Plastic still offer conversions of their own.

A new styling fad for Porsches is tinted windows—I mean the dark tinting like we see on the television shows such as *Miami Vice* and *Stingray*, and in many of the car ads on television and in magazines where the windows are dark—not just the stock tinting.

I recall the first time I noticed tinted windows in a Porsche, which was about five years ago on a 911. This 911 was also up from Texas, so I guess maybe *they* were trendsetters in this art. This 911 from Texas had the side and rear windows tinted a shade of gray that was almost black, with a material that was painted on the windows. The car caught my eye so I looked it over. Unfortunately, the workmanship wasn't very good; each window had a small clear border, so I wasn't impressed.

Because of that first bad impression, it took me several years before I really looked at another car with these dark-tinted windows. This car, another 911, looked great. In fact the workmanship was so good, it actually looked like it was a factory job. I was impressed.

I found out that it was done by applying a urethane film to the inside of the glass. The urethane film is precut to fit all of the windows and then applied. The rear curved windows are the most difficult to remove, particularly in the case of the 911 Targa, and also the most difficult to fit the film to.

The curved windows have to have seams cut in order to fit the material to the curved window. Most cars have rear-window heater elements; thus to hide the

It's a coupe, it's a Cabriolet and best of all, it's a Speedster. Richard and Lori Riley

The windshield removed very much like the one on the original Porsche Speedster. Richard and Lori Riley

The Speedster as a coupe. Only the black seam of the gasket showed between the top and the red paint. The Porsche hardtop was right from the Sonderwunsche-Programm catalog (Special Wishes Program) from Werk I. Richard and Lori Riley

The sideview mirrors and their fairings were built onto the wind-wing assembly so that when the assembly was removed, the mirrors went with them. Richard and Lori Riley

In 1979 the Kremers, in collaboration with Design Plastics (DP), introduced the slope-nose look for street cars. Their slope-nose was a copy of the simplest of the slope-nosed 935s. Porsche Kremer Racing

seams, the installer cuts the film along the elements so that the splices will not show when the job is done and the window is reinstalled. With the window glass removed the windows can be properly cleaned, and when the job is done the film edges do not show.

With the windows removed, all of the work can be performed in a class-two clean room. In the clean room, the intake air is electrostatically cleaned, thus the room has a positive pressure maintained at all times to prevent dirt from migrating into the clean area. In this clean room, the installer uses special tables with air-filled suction cups to hold the glass firmly in place while applying the Mylar film.

Mylar film is applied to a wetted surface, wetted with big pump-type sprayers which are also used to mist the room before laying the Mylar, to make sure no dirt gets under the film. The film is burnished to the glass with a special tool that emphasizes the body pressure. The installer uses this burnishing tool to get the material to lay well, and to get nearly all of the moisture out from under the Mylar. Edges are frosted over the edges. To refrost the edges they press Mylar over the edge of the glass and roll it so that it is pressed all the way to the top of the window. In the end, when you look at the window, it looks like it was factory done.

Probably the ultimate form of customizing, however, is building a production-based race car. Whether they are built at the factory, or by some well-known race-car builder, or by someone at home in their garage, these production-based race cars are always pushing the technology as far as the rules will allow.

Most of us will agree that a high-performance 911 or 911 Turbo deserves a high-performance sound system. Good music is one of the personal options that can enhance the enjoyment of our refined cars. I checked with several people to see what they felt was the ultimate sound system for the 911. Most agreed that the Nakamichi Tuner/Tape Deck combination and the Nakamichi crossover and amplifiers were to be included in the dream sound system. However, we had a little more trouble agreeing on what speakers you should use. Some people like the Boston Acoustics speakers, others preferred the ADS speakers, or maybe Becker, or perhaps Nakamichi, or how about the JBL speakers.

The system that most people agreed on was a three-way system with an electronic crossover with two sets of wide-range speakers and a set of subwoofers. The difference of opinion on the speakers seemed to be motivated by two things; personal perference for the sound of one brand of speaker over another, and difficulty in mounting the speakers.

Kremers' slope-nose conversions were done in fiberglass, with fiberglass components made by Design Plastics. The quality of the fiberglass work was impeccable. Jerry Woods

Porsche introduced its own slope-nose in the fall of 1981 as part of its new Special Wishes program. Porsche's slope-nose was done in metal, with only the air dam being made of fiberglass. Most of the conversions in the seventies, to the big-fender look, had all been done in fiberglass. There were conversion kits for any wide-fendered version of a Porsche imaginable, available from AIR, Hoesman and Mitcom. But now that the slope-nose look was in, the trend was toward having the conversions done all in metal. Only the originators in Europe still did their conversions in fiberglass. Porsche's original slope-nose cars were pretty simple, with their cutoff fenders, running boards and air dam/bumper. The air dam/bumpers had the headlights mounted in them, and there was nothing in the fenders. Werkfoto, Porsche AG

The Special Wishes program at Werk I was expanded and more options were available. The options included rear vents for the brakes, running board and special spoilers, but without the slope-nose. Werk-foto, Porsche AG

John Paul Racing also made a slope-nose conversion for sale, using fiberglass bodywork styled like the Kremers' K3 bodywork. Leonard Turner, Porsche Panorama

The Special Wishes program at Werk I offered the slope-nose with built-in headlights. This car also had the running boards and rear-brake vents. Werkfoto, Porsche AG

This was a very special car built for Mansour Ojjeh with a special air-dam running boards, 935 rear fenders and 935 rear wing. It also had a roll bar and a special high-output engine. Werkfoto, Porsche AG

Special Wishes didn't end with what can be done just at Werk I. There were tuners and custom-body builders both in Europe and in the United States that would convert your 911 or 911 Turbo into almost anything you could imagine. This was the Kremer line-up. The car in the center was a very special wish. It was a Kremer K3 935 that had been converted for the street. Porsche Kremer Racing

DP Motorsport 935 II Cabriolet, US version. Ekkehard Zimmermann had built all of the bodywork for the Kremers' racing cars. In 1979 they collaborated to make a road-going 935 based on the 911 Turbo. Origi- nally the cars were sold only as Kremer Street 935s with DP bodywork. They now both offered their own versions of the slope-nose 911 Turbo. DP Werkfoto

The Special Wishes program at Werk I offered the slope-nose treatment but with louvers. Werkfoto, Porsche AG

Walter Wolf's Porsche Kremer K3 street car, the ultimate weapon. Porsche Kremer Racing

Kremer slope-nose Cabriolet. Porsche Kremer Racing

Kremer slope-nose coupe with full roll cage. Porsche Kremer Racing

Strosek Design Program 911 Turbo coupe.
Strosek Auto Design GmbH offered the
body conversions for both Turbo and Carrera. Strosek Auto Design

Strosek Design Program Cabriolet. Strosek
Auto Design

Slope-nose Cabriolet by Sport Performance. Bill F. Martin

RUF 911 Turbo slope-nose, running boards,
rear-brake vents, 17 in. wheels. Exclusive
Motor Cars, Inc.

Koenig KS specials. Porsche 911 Turbo
from Koenig Specials complete body conversion included front and rear fenders,
side skirts and rear spoiler. Engine was
twin-turbo twin-intercooler 480/550 hp.
Koenig Specials GmbH

Popular headlight mechanism based on motor and light from Mazda.

Two interesting cars by Sport Performance in California. In the foreground is the owner's 935-bodied 911 Turbo, and in the background is a slope-nose 911SC without turbo-look. C. Van Tune, Sport Performance

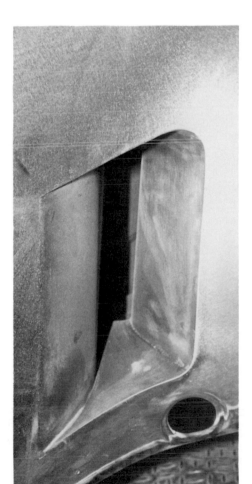

Rear-brake vent made of metal.

Slope-nose fender being made. The top was cut out of the stock fender and the flat portion was welded in, that was all there was to it.

Custom dashboard in Sport Performance 911 Turbo Cabriolet. Notice center console, LED enunciated boost gauge.

In addition to being able to purchase special gauges, you can have your gauges modified, refinished and restored by any number of people in the Porsche custom business. These gauges were done by North Hollywood Speedometer. North Hollywood Speedometer

934/935 boost gauge. This style boost gauge was the most accurate. When the LED boost gauges were standard equipment in the 935s, all of the teams that raced them added one of these.

The 935 dashboard on 1976 factory team car. Werkfoto, Porsche AG

The Davtron Digital charge air-temperature gauge. These digital gauges can be hooked up with a switch and two senders, and you can monitor the charge air temperature before and after the intercooler to see how effective your intercooler is.

Making of a 935. Note aluminum roll cage, fire extinguisher spray-bar tie-wrapped along roll cage, oil lines at bottom center of photo passing from up under the hood back to where they went through the right doorsill. Werkfoto, Porsche AG

Performance Air makes this air-conditioning vent that doubles the size of the under-dash vent and more than doubles the cooling capacity. This modification is a must for anyone with a late-model air-conditioned 911 in a warm climate.

Bob Akin's The Last 935 dashboard.

LED boost gauge.

To ensure that the film conforms to the complex shape of the Targa rear window, the film was cut into eight narrow strips. The rear window was marked with masking tape to guide the cutting of these strips.

The window was wetted and the narrow strips were laid on and burnished to the glass, one at a time.

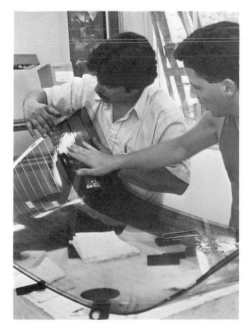

After a few strips of film were laid down and burnished, the overlap was removed by cutting along the edge of one of the rear-window heater wires with a surgeon's scalpel. The cuts were made along the edge of the heater wires so that the seams would not be visible.

One of the latest fads is tinted windows, not just stock-tinted windows, but Miami Vice-tinted windows. This was a brand-new 1987 911 Turbo Targa in the process of having its windows tinted. Removing the rear window from a Targa is a major chore, but it must be done in order to ensure a quality job of applying the tint film and ensure good adhesion and no dirt under the film. With its complex curves, the Targa window is one of the more difficult windows to have tinted.

After the film was cut along the heater wires, the overlapping strips were removed and the film was reburnished.

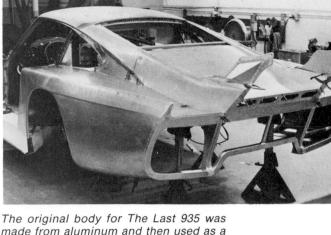

The original body for The Last 935 was made from aluminum and then used as a mold for the Kevlar carbon fiber body. Dave Klym, FABCAR Engineering

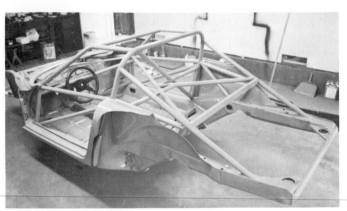

The local club rules require that cars be built from original monocoque chassis. What you see is a monocoque chassis with a steel roll cage attached. John Hammill

The Last 935 is now a club time-trial car. Moto Foto

In 1986 Porsche built the 961 which was to have been a Group B car based on the 959. The 961 utilized the complete monocoque because the rules required that it do so. Werkfoto, Porsche AG

Bob Akin had Dave Klym build what they called The Last 935 for the IMSA GTX rules. The rules required that they use steel tubing instead of aluminum tubing, but they did allow them to completely discard the monocoque chassis and make a tube-frame car. Dave Klym, FABCAR Engineering

Everyone agreed that the Nakamichi Tuner/Tape Deck combination and the Nakamichi crossover and amplifier were to be included in the dream sound system. The three Nakamichi amplifiers will fit under the seats in a 911 Turbo. Tom Hanna

The resulting car is a TopTime of Day club car. Moto Foto

One set of speakers was mounted in the front door in a custom-built enclosure. Tom Hanna

One set of speakers was mounted in a special enclosure in the back with the sub-woofers. Tom Hanna

Classic Research and Engineering Z-box enclosure mounts in the rear of the 911 provided both the enclosure for the sub-woofers and a pair of rear satellite speakers. Rick Parker, Audiovision

Classic Research and Engineering Z-box enclosure subwoofer mounts in rear side area of the 911 coupe. Rick Parker, Audiovision

ADS low-frequency driver mounted in door pocket, high-frequency driver mounted up above window crank behind perforations. Rick Parker, Audiovision

Part of ADS speakers mounted in Clover enclosure. Rick Parker, Audiovision

How to buy a used 911

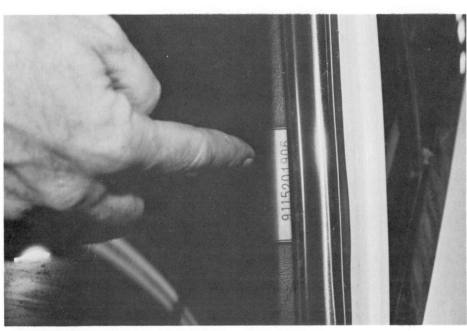

From 1969 on, the VIN number was on the 911 windshield post. Check the VIN number to see if they all agree.

A 911 ID sticker on doorjamb. VIN number should match numbers on windshield post. This sticker also tells you where the car was made, when it was made and the laws it complied with when made.

Buying a previously owned Porsche 911 can be the beginning of a long, pleasurable relationship if you do your homework and select a good sound car, *or* it can become a real nightmare if you aren't careful enough and select a dog. How do you prepare yourself to look for a used Porsche?

Well, a lot of that will depend upon what model and vintage Porsche you are looking for. If you are trying to buy a fairly new used Carrera Cabriolet, for instance, you can and should be far more critical than if you were looking for a 1974 3.0 Carrera RS. There should be a very wide selection of the 1985 Carrera Cabriolets available for you to select from, whereas there may only be two or three 1974 3.0 Carrera RS models in the country and probably not more than twenty to twenty-five left in the world.

With any of the very rare Porsche models, you will have to decide what you will accept in the way of flaws. You may have to accept some flaws in the car's condition just because the model you are interested in is so rare. If you are not willing to accept a flawed car, you might just have to decide to get something else instead.

If the 1985 Carrera is the car you want, however, you shouldn't plan to accept anything but a premium-condition 911. A 1985 Carrera is not at all rare, and since it is only two years old there is no acceptable reason for it not to be a near-perfect car.

You should start your selection process by trying to narrow down the range of cars you look at to just a few models and years. Then you should start your search by learning as much as you can about the cars you have chosen. This is fairly easy to do if you select one of the production models, but can be a real challenge if you select one of the rarer Porsche models such as a 2.7 RS. Depending upon how rare the car is that you select, you may actually have to conduct a serious research project to find out anything about the Porsche of your choice.

A good place to start your research for any of the production-model Porsches will be in the technical spec books. These are great little pocket-size books that have all of the information you will ever need to know. They are issued by model in a somewhat random manner, with seven books covering the 911 from 1965 through 1981.

If you are interested in a 911 that is newer than 1981, which will be newer than the most current 911 spec books, or if you feel you need additional information on some of the earlier 911s, a reliable source is the service information booklets that Porsche publishes each year as the new models are introduced. Although these books are not pocket-size, they are a good reliable source of the type of information you will need to buy a used car.

For instance, in 1984 when Porsche introduced the Carrera, the 1984 booklet described all of the differences between the 1983 911SC and the new Carrera, and provided a complete detailed list of the 1984 model's specifications.

Porsche Cars North America, Inc., has also started to publish a booklet that is helpful for all of the new Porsche models, called the *Porsche Fact Book*. It started last year with the *1986 Porsche Fact Book*, with was ninety-two pages. The 1987 version has been expanded to 104 pages. These books will be very handy to have ten years from now, when you are trying to figure out what equipment a ten-year-old Porsche should have. But in the meantime, study your spec books, your service information booklets and let's go look at used Porsches!

One more step before you do, however. You should try to get a good feel for what the price range is for the type of Porsche you are trying to find. How you go about this will depend upon how old the car is and how rare it is. If the car of your choice is a fairly new car, the bank is a good place to check the price range since it has books such as a *Blue Book* that list wholesale and retail prices on used cars. Banks use these books to decide how much to loan their customers for the purchase of a used car.

Another method would be to purchase the newspapers from any large city in your area and compute your own low, high and average prices. There are also people who do this on a national basis and publish newsletters listing the price ranges. One such publication is *Porsche*

Trends Gallery. If you are planning to purchase a rare car, you will probably have to establish the price range yourself by calling owners and knowledgeable people in the field to get an idea of what you should expect to pay.

Now that you have gotten this far along in the process, it's time to look at some cars. You should start this phase by prescreening the 911 yourself. When you find one you like, you should have it checked out mechanically by the repair shop that will be doing your mainte-

nance work for you. You should also have the bodywork checked out by a quality bodyshop that specializes in Porsche repair and reconstruction. This is particularly true if the 911 of your choice has had recent body and paint work or any obvious body repair work—fresh paint can conceal a multitude of sins.

When you look at your first used 911, don't be intimidated by the seller. Remember, the customer is always right and you're the customer. Take control of

ID plate under hood toward front on the early cars gives serial number, type, weight and so on. This location was used from 1965 through 1973, up until the bumper change in 1974.

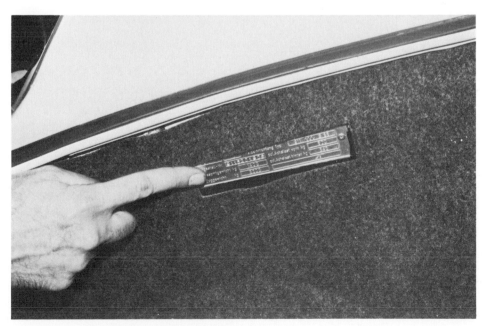

Location used for ID plate on the later cars after the bumper change in 1974. ID plate was under hood on passenger side and gives serial number, type weight and so on.

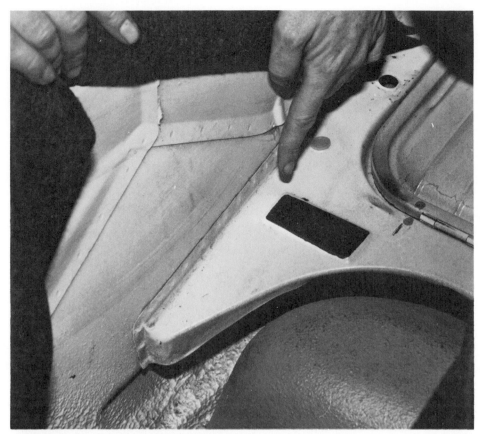

911 VIN number stamped under carpet up above gas tank. All numbers should match.

the situation and make the seller show you everything necessary to prove to you that this is the car you are looking for. Don't be afraid to say, "That's not the car I want," and walk away from it.

You should develop a system for looking at used Porsches. Even if you are lucky enough to only have to look at one car before finding the car of your dreams, having a system will help you. Start by making sure all of the serial numbers are what they should be. Check the VIN (Vehicle Identification Number) or chassis identification numbers on the driver's windshield post, in the driver's doorjamb and under the hood on post-1969 cars built for the US market.

For 911s made before 1969, the chassis numbers are *only* under the hood. The numbers should all match and be the ones called out for the model you have selected in your spec booklet or other reference book. Next, check the engine number and see if it matches the range of engines that should be in the car.

There are several good reasons for checking all of the numbers. First, you will want to make sure that the Porsche you are looking at is as it is represented. This will not be an easy task because the 911 has used six different chassis num-

911 engine type number. This number is almost as important as the engine's serial number. The internal type number was hidden on the horizontal surface behind the serial number.

911 engine serial number was on the vertical surface of fan housing support.

bering schemes up until now. You will need your spec books or service information booklets for the cars you are looking for to make any sense of the VIN or serial numbers.

The first chassis numbering system was used from the beginning of the 911 production, in September 1964, for the 1965 model 911s.

The numbering system for these original 911s utilized a sequential six-digit serial number, starting with 300,001 for the Porsche coupes built during the 1965 model year. When Karmann started producing coupe bodies for the 911 during the 1965 model year, Porsche differentiated them from the Porsche-built bodies by giving them a chassis number series that began with 450,001. The Targa was added as a new body style during the 1967 model year, and Porsche differentiated these from the coupes by giving them a chassis number series that started with 500,001. The first digit (3, 4 or 5) in this numbering scheme was actually the only designator with the remaining five digits used as a sequential serial number. When Porsche added the 911S model, it distinguished the new model just by adding an S to the end of the serial number.

In 1968, Porsche introduced a VIN or chassis numbering system that was increased to eight digits (11860001), where the first four digits had an encoded

special meaning and the remaining four digits were a sequential chassis number. With this system the first two digits (11) indicated that the car was a 911, and the third digit (8) indicated model year by giving the last digit of the model year. The fourth digit was supposed to tell everything else there was to know about the car.

The remaining four digits were used as a sequential serial number. The first

digit of this serial number was also used for further subcoding to differentiate between Karmann and Porsche bodies: 0 through 4 are Porsche, and 5 through 9 are Karmann.

In 1969 in the United States, the VIN number had to be visible on the driver's side of the car from outside the car. In 1969, Porsche also increased its VIN or chassis numbers again, this time to nine digits (119210317) where the first five

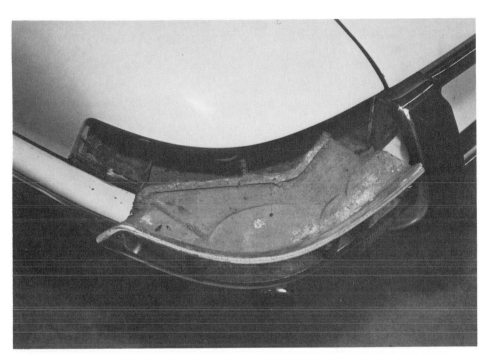

911 taillight assembly removed to expose possible damage underneath.

911 headlights can be hiding rust damage. It's a good idea to remove them when you are checking out a 911.

Broken firewall around clutch tube. We are just starting to see this problem with the

911s. This has been a problem on 914s for some time.

Type	Model year	Body version	Sequential serial number
11 = 911	8 = 1968	0 = coupe, S-version	Beginning at 0001
12 = 912	9 = 1969	1 = coupe, L-version	
		2 = coupe, T-version	
		3 = coupe, US-version	
		5 = Targa, S-version	
		6 = Targa, L-version	
		7 = Targa, T-version	
		8 = Targa, US-version	

Type	Model year	Engine type	Body version	Sequential serial number
11 = 911	9 = 1969	1 = 911T	0 = Porsche-body coupe	0317
911 = 911	0 = 1970	2 = 911E	1 = Targa	
	1 = 1971	3 = 911S	2 = Karmann-body coupe	

Type	Model year	Engine type	Body version	Sequential serial number
911 = 911	2 = 1972	1 = T-E	0 = coupe	0317
	3 = 1973	2 = E-E	1 = Targa	
		3 = S-E		
		5 = TV-E		
		6 = SC-F		

Type	Model year	Engine type	Body version	Sequential serial number
911 = 911	4 = 1974	1 = 911	0 = coupe	0125
		3 = 911S	1 = Targa	
		4 = 911 Carrera		

Crack under door by jack receiver. Car is just old and tired.

digits had an encoded special meaning.

With this system, the first two digits (11) still indicated that the car was a 911, and the third digit (9) indicated the model year by giving the last digit of the model year. The fourth digit (2) indicated the official engine type. The fifth digit (1) was used to indicate the body version. And again, with this numbering scheme the final four digits were used as sequential serial numbers.

There was a minor revision to this scheme in 1970 with the addition of a sixth digit to the encoded portion of the serial number so there were ten digits in all. The added digit was a 9 before the 11 in the type number, so that it was shown 911 instead of 11 as before (9119210001).

There was a minor revision in the system again in 1972 where, although the numbering scheme remained the same, the engine types and body versions were changed. Porsche added some engine types, and the body versions were changed to just two types: 0 = coupe, and 1 = Targa.

These engine types probably require a little more explanation, as follows:

1 = 911T-E (The E indicated fuel injection, United States only)
2 = 911E-E (The E indicated fuel injection)
3 = 911S-E (The E indicated fuel injection
5 = 911TV-E (the TV indicated that these engines were carbureted)
6 = 911SC-F (this was the 2.7 RS Carrera engine with mechanical injection)

There was a change in engine types again in 1974, with only three; otherwise the numbering system remained the same (9114410125).

The year 1975 marked the introduction of the 911 Turbo, which necessitated another change in the chassis numbering scheme. The first three digits still indicated the vehicle type, the fourth digit still indicated the model year and the fifth digit the official engine types. The body version and sequential serial number remain the same (9115610047).

For the model years 1976 and 1977, the only change was the official engine type numbers (9116300001).

For the model years 1978 and 1979, the only change was again the official engine type numbers (9118300001).

Another change was necessary in 1980 to prevent the possibility of repeating the chassis numbers from ten years earlier. Porsche continued to use a ten-digit chassis number (91A0130001), but the encoding was changed. The first two digits (91) indicated the model; type 91 = 911 and 93 = 930. The third digit (A) was actually an alpha character indicating model year; the A = 1980. The fourth digit (0) indicated the manufacturing plant. The fifth digit (1) was used as a supplemental type number; 1 = 911 and 0 = 930. The sixth digit (3) indicated the engine type or version, and the remaining four digits continued to represent the sequential serial number (91A0130001).

In 1981 a major change took place with the VIN numbering system. The new numbering system is international and uses seventeen digits (1 2 3 - 4 5 6 - 7 8 - 9 - 10 - 11 - 12 - 13 - 14 15 16 17). The first three digits (1 2 3) are the world manufacturing code, and Porsche's code is WPO. Digits 4, 5 and 6 are the VDS code for the United States and Canada.

The VDS code consists of two letters and one number. The first letter (digit 4 in example) indicates which series car it is. The character A indicates the 911 coupe series, E indicates Targa or Cabriolet, and J indicates Turbo coupe.

The second letter (digit 5) indicates that the engine is for either Canada (A) or the United States (B). The number in this sequence (digit 6) indicates the type of restraint system; 0 stands for active and 1 stands for passive. These three digits are indicated as zzz for the Rest of the World cars, and are considered as fill-in digits or specific vehicle code for the United States and Canada.

Digits 7 and 8 are the first two digits of the Porsche model type; 91 indicates 911, 93 indicates 930 and 95 indicates 959. Digit 9 is used as a test digit. Digit 10 is a letter indicating the model year; 1981 is the letter B and 1987 the letter H.

Digit 11 is a letter indicating the manufacturing location; S is Stuttgart. Digit 12 is the third digit of the Porsche model type; 1 indicates 911, 0 indicates 930 and 9 indicates 959. Digit 13 is the code for the body and engine. The remaining four digits (14 15 16 17) are the sequential serial numbers (WPOAAO910BS120001).

The various spec books also provide information on both the engine and transmission code numbers. For the engine numbers I prefer the internal Porsche type numbers, which I have summarized in the engine chapter.

If you're looking at some of the rare versions of the 911, you may not be able to completely decode the chassis number with the information given in these reference sources. You may have to write to Porsche for help.

A good example of a VIN for a rare car would be 9114600110. The first three digits 911 indicate that the car is a 911, and the next digit 4 indicates that it is a 1974 model; but our information sources do not decode the next digit 6 which is the engine type. The engine number code itself is 6840030, which does not help us much either.

The first digit 6 is the engine design and stands for six-cylinder engine. The second digit 8 indicates the official engine type, and 8 is not listed so we cannot decode the engine type. The third

Type	Model year	Engine type	Body version	Sequential serial number
911 = 911 930 = Turbo	5 = 1975	1 = 911 2 = 911S(US) 3 = 911S 4 = Carrera(US) 6 = Carrera 7 = Turbo	0 = coupe 1 = Targa	0047

Type	Model year	Engine type	Body version	Sequential serial number
911 = 911 930 = Turbo	6 = 1976 7 = 1977	2 = 911S (US 2.7 liter) 3 = 911/911S (Japan 2.7 liter) 6 = Carrera 3.0 liter 7 = Turbo/Turbo (Japan 3.0 liter) 8 = Turbo (US 3.0 liter)	0 = coupe 1 = Targa	0047

Type	Model year	Engine type	Body version	Sequential serial number
911 = 911 930 = Turbo	8 = 1978 9 = 1979	2 = 911SC (US 3.0 liter) 3 = 911SC (R.o.W. & Japan) 7 = 930 Turbo (R.o.W. & Japan 3.3 liter) 8 = 930 Turbo (US 3.3 liter)	0 = coupe 1 = Targa	0047

Type	Model year	Manuf plant	Type supplement	Engine type	Sequential serial number
91 = 911 93 = Turbo	A = 1980	0	1 = 911 0 = 930	3 = 911SC (R.o.W. 3.0 liter) 4 = 911SC (US 3.0 liter) 7 = 930 Turbo (R.o.W.)	0001

digit 4 is again the model year, which agrees with the chassis number that the car is a 1974 model.

The engine's internal type number (Type 911/74) is not any help either because it is not decoded in any of our references. So without additional information, you can not tell any more about this car. The car happens to be one of the very rare 1974 3.0 RS or RSRs, but without knowing what the engine number means, you cannot tell that.

Another equally good reason to check the VIN or chassis number is that one method of salvaging wrecked cars is to weld the pieces of two wrecked cars together to make one "good" car from the pieces. I have seen 911s that have been saved from the scrap heap this way. Not that this is necessarily all bad; if the work is done properly it is probably fine, but again you shouldn't be able to tell that it was done at all. If you *can* tell that the car in question was made from two cars, the workmanship is just not good enough. If you run into numbers that don't match or look like they have been altered, this could be what happened.

Another possibility, if the numbers have been altered, is that the car of your dreams is a stolen car. If you find a car that has funny numbers or anything else

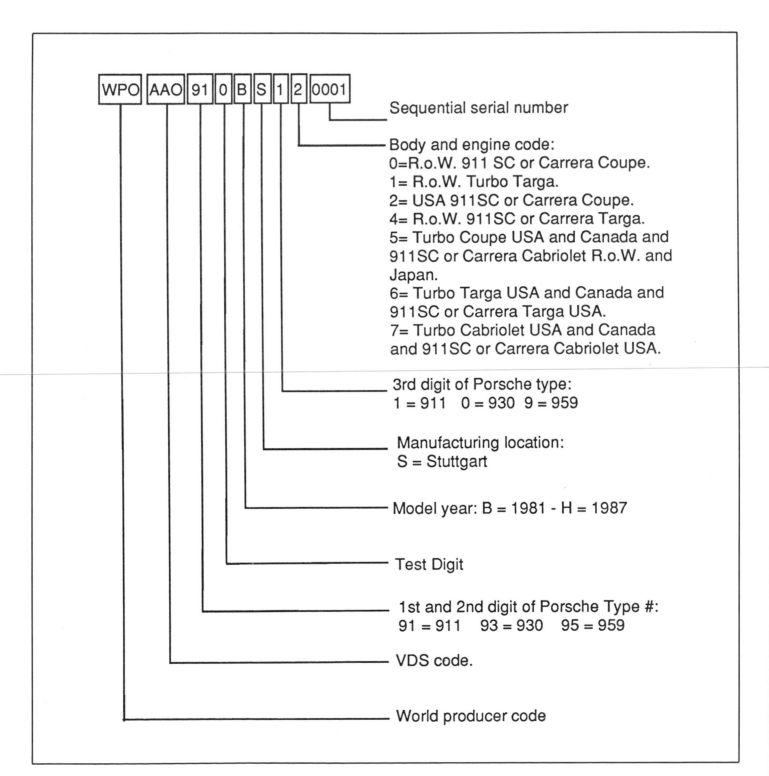

suspicious, yet you feel the car is still interesting and you want to pursue it, check the VIN or chassis number with your local police department or Department of Motor Vehicles. Possession of stolen property is against the law, and the least the system will do if you're caught with stolen property is take it away from you. If the car is not stolen and has a car title and you are still interested, you should have a quality body-shop check it out and evaluate the car's condition and explain to you what has *probably* happened to the car.

Now that the number check is done, we are ready to get down to some serious used-Porsche looking. Actually, while you were checking the numbers, you were pretty much all over the car and you should have been giving the car a quick once-over. You may decide at this stage, from what you have already seen, that this is not the car for you. If so, don't waste any more of your time or the seller's time. Say good-bye and move on to the next car. Sometimes you will reject a car after just walking around it. In this case, thank the owner and say good-bye. Do not waste your time with a car you don't like. There will be another one, and even if there isn't you may be better off than with a car you are not going to be happy with.

Now let's look at the rest of your prospective purchase. Make believe you're a concours judge and that everything must be perfect or else you will be taking off points. The big difference between this and a real concours is that the points you take off will be the money you are willing to spend for the Porsche. Go over the interior with a fine-tooth comb, looking for wear or stains on the carpeting or upholstery. Your job is to find everything that is wrong with the car, and then decide what it's worth to you and whether or not you can live with it.

Check the paint and bodywork for condition and quality of workmanship, for any repairs or repaint work that has been done. If any body repair or paint work is done properly, you will not be able to detect the work, and it is probably OK. Keep an eye out for signs of rust damage, poor-fitting panels or bad paint work, however. There are some quick checks that you can make that will give you an idea of the overall condition of the Porsche you are checking out.

With the 911, you should start with the front because most crash damage will be in the front of the car. Check for poorly repaired crash damage by lifting up the carpets in the trunk and looking for wrinkles or gaps that haven't been repaired properly. If you suspect improper repair, have that quality body-shop check it out for you.

One of the biggest enemies of any unit-body car is rust. All Porsches are unit-body construction, so keep an eye out for signs of rust. A good barometer for rust on the late-model 911s (1974 and later) is the flat rubber strip between the body and the front bumper. This rubber piece should lay flat and smooth over the rear edge of the bumper. If instead it has a bubbly or wavy look, the car may have a rust or corrosion problem.

This rubber strip is bonded to a metal mounting strip which is not galvanized so it can rust. If it has rusted, it causes the bubbly or wavy look where the rubber is separating from the metal strip. The fact

Always be on the watch for rust. Rust peeking out from underside deco under door.

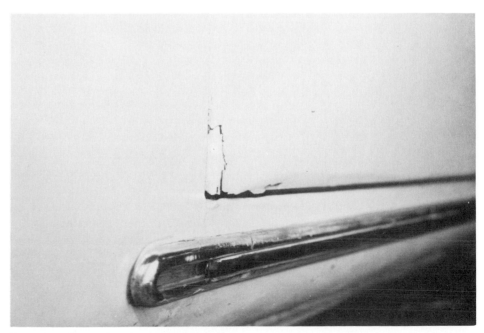

Poor door fit; car has been damaged and poorly repaired.

that the rubber strip itself has deteriorated is not that important, because it's quite easily replaced and is not too expensive. However, it is a warning that there may be other rust or corrosion, so be careful.

Check the front suspension pickups for rust because this was a very common weakness on the early cars without galvanized bodies. Check around the headlights and taillights for signs of rust. You may have to take them out to see the rust—they are good at hiding the damage. While the headlights are out, check the headlight bucket for squareness. The front surface should be flat and square. If there is a problem with the squareness of the headlight, it indicates improper crash or rust repair.

Another simple test that you can do on any Porsche built since 1969 is run your finger along the fender lip. Porsche puts a textured finish on these fender lips to protect them from rock chips. If a fender or quarter panel has been replaced, the new part will come without this texturing, and only a quality bodyshop will extend the extra effort to texture this area. If you find a fender lip without this texturing, look further because it is surely an indication of collision repair work. The bodyshop that did the work may not have been too careful about other work done on the car as well.

Another good check for rust in these cars is to remove the floor mats and wooden floorboards and inspect the pedal assembly area. If this area is not kept clean during the car's lifetime, dirt and moisture will collect and start rust and corrosion.

All of these places are fairly easy to check. If you find any rust in any of them or have reason to believe there has been recent rust repair or other body repair done, or if you have any questions at all about the condition of the body, it would be a good idea to have a quality bodyshop that specializes in Porsches look over the car of your dreams. It never hurts to get a second opinion.

In addition to having the Porsche checked out by a quality bodyshop, you should consider getting professional help to have it checked out mechanically as well, if you have not done so already. You will probably save yourself some money and a great deal of grief in the long run. Some sellers will not want you to have their used Porsche checked out. You should be very suspicious of these people—they are probably trying to hide something from you.

Take the car to your choice of quality Porsche repair shop and have it check out the car. If the car you are buying is in your home area, you should plan to take the car to the shop that will be doing your maintenance work. If the car you are buying is from some other part of the country, you might want to check with the shop that will be doing your work and see if it can recommend a shop in that area.

Some of the things you should have the shop check for are oil leaks; the condition of the suspension components (ball joints, tie-rod ends, shocks, rubber bushings); brakes, wheels and tires; and condition of drivetrain and engine. If the shop finds anything that needs repair or replacement, get a cost estimate for the repair and factor this into the price you are willing to pay for the car.

Most Porsche specialty shops will charge you extra for a compression test and/or a leak-down test on the air-cooled Porsches, because some of the spark plugs are a real challenge to reach and they all should be removed to perform either test. You should still have these tests done, however. It would be unwise not to spend the additional money to have the car completely checked out.

The compression test is a very good indication of the general health of an engine, and will pinpoint any weak cylinders. The compression readings on a healthy engine should be between 130 to 170 psi, and within fifteen percent of each other.

The leak-down test can be used to indicate how bad the problem is if any weak cylinders show up in the compression test, and give you a good indication of the source of the problem. Most people will tell you that five to fifteen percent leakage is OK, but most good-running well-maintained Porsche engines will be less than three to five percent.

The leak-down test is a method of measuring each cylinder's ability to hold pressure. The way that it works is one cylinder at a time is turned to top dead center and then pressurized. It is very easy to find TDC for each of the six cylinders on the 911 engine because there are markings for every 120 deg of crankshaft rotation on the crankshaft pulley.

Most leak-down testers have two gauges. One shows the fixed pressure being applied to the cylinder. This pressure is adjustable and should be set to 100 psi. The other will give a direct reading of the pressure retained by the cylinder under test.

As an example, the gauge may read 97 psi, indicating the retained pressure, subtracting this number from the 100 psi, will be 3 psi and 3 percent leakage. The reason we used 100 psi in our example as the original pressure is that when we subtract our leakage number from the 100 psi, we will get our leakage directly in percentage without any additional conversions.

The way this tool is used as an aid to isolating the source of the problem is by

Poor rust repair work on the bottom of this 911's door.

making a hissing noise as the three to fifteen percent leakage leaks out. All you have to do is listen for the source of the hiss. For instance, if you put your ear to the tail pipe and you can hear the hissing there, your problem is probably an exhaust valve. You should also listen at the oil filler and the intake air cleaner. If the hiss is at the oil filler, the engine's problem is probably with its rings, and it is just wearing out from old age. If your problem is at the air cleaner, the problem is probably with the intake valve.

With small percentages, this leakage sound is difficult to discern and it is therefore hard to pinpoint the source of the leakage. However, with larger leakages, fifteen percent and more, it is quite easy to hear the hissing and pinpoint the source.

Another thing to have your Porsche repair shop check for on your prospective purchase is worn valve guides. This check is very important for all of the 911s made before 1977 and particularly on the 2.7 liter 911s with their higher operating temperatures.

A good indication of worn valve guides on these cars is noisy valves; the valves should be quiet on a 911 after they have been adjusted. If you think that the 911 you are interested in has noisy valves, have the mechanic check the guide wear by pushing the exhaust valves from side to side with a screwdriver, with the valve at full lift. You can actually judge how worn the guides are with this method.

All of the Porsches up until 1977 used a copper material for valve guides. As the engines got larger in displacement and ran hotter, these valve guides started to fail earlier and earlier. Most 2.7 911s needed a top-end overhaul by the time they had 30,000 to 60,000 miles on the odometer; 30,000 for the thermal-reactor cars and as much as 60,000 for the 1977s with improved guides and for the cars that didn't have thermal reactors.

During the 1977 model year, Porsche changed to guides made of a silicon-bronze material. The new guides are a brassy color, whereas the originals were copper in color. The new valve material provides much better wear than the old copper material did. I have seen some of the newer 911SCs with over 170,000 miles that still have quiet valves—a sure indication that the valves and valve guides are still in good shape.

The 2.7 liter 911s also have a problem with pulling cylinder-head studs. Unfortunately this is a hard problem for a prospective buyer to assess when look-

ing at used cars. If the 2.7 911 has more than 60,000 miles, it probably has had some major engine work performed to repair the worn valve guides. This may be a blessing in disguise, because most Porsche repair shops have learned how to deal with the problems of the 2.7 engines, since they were built over ten years ago.

When experienced 911 mechanics have the 2.7 engines apart for a top-end overhaul, they will usually repair the head studs and any other engine weaknesses while they are apart. Check the

repair orders of the previous owners to see if anything has been done to repair the pulling head-stud problems. Some type of case saver or a Time Sert should have been installed in the crankcase, and the steel head studs should have been replaced with Dilivar studs. There are twenty-four of these studs, so you should see on the work order that all twenty-four have been repaired or replaced.

The 1978 3.0 liter 911SC and newer engines have been remarkably reliable when contrasted to the 1974 through 1977 2.7 liter engines. Very few people

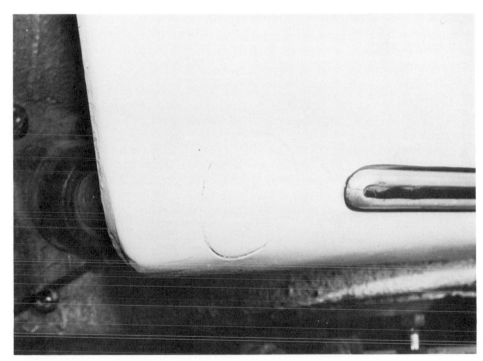

Another example of poor repair work on fender lip.

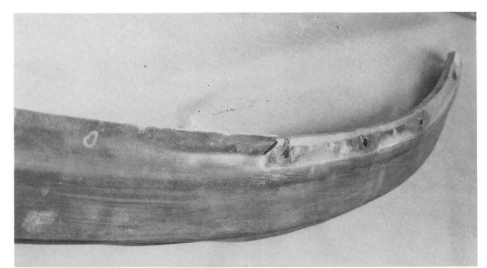

Front bumper filler strip. Note ripples in finish. These ripples were caused by rusting inner steel structure used for mounting.

have had to overhaul a 911SC engine because it has worn out. I have a friend in Seattle who drives a 911SC around the country that has almost 170,000 miles on it and it still runs great. I have talked to a couple of other friends with the early 911SCs with 170,000 to 180,000 miles on them, and they are starting to worry about whether they should continue to drive them or have them overhauled.

This is the sort of reliability and mileage that the early 2.0 liter 911s and 911Ss *used* to get. The 911SCs were troubled with two problems which were really solved during their lifetime. One is what I call the exploding-clutch syndrome, and the other was the dreaded chain-tensioner failures.

The rubber-centered (exploding) clutch was used from 1978 to 1983 when it was replaced with a spring-centered clutch. Check the repair orders for the car to see if the clutch has ever been replaced and if the replacement was a spring-centered clutch. If the clutch hasn't been replaced it will need to be, so budget for it.

The chain tensioners have been a problem throughout the life of the 911s, they are not unique to the 911SC. The failure of one of these tensioners can be expensive because of the additional damage they can do to the engine. In 1980 Porsche changed the major cause of the tensioner failures, the chain's idler arms, and in the 1984 Carrera, Porsche introduced what appears to be a bullet-proof fix for all the 911s—the Carrera pressure-fed tensioners.

If you buy any used 911 up to the Carrera, you should check the work orders or check with the seller to see if the tensioners in the car you are looking at have been updated to the latest style. If not you should budget for their updating when you purchase the car. Once the clutch and tensioners have been attended to, a good 911SC will run fine and last a long time.

The 911SC was the best of the 911s until the Carrera came out, which is a better car. Still, 911SC is still a wonderful used 911 to buy. It's just that the 911s keep getting better every year.

Be careful when you buy an older Porsche to be sure that either it is in very good condition or that you know what you are getting yourself into, or both. The parts and labor for repair has gotten very expensive over the past forty years since they started building Porsches in Gmünd, Austria. Although it is not a 911, I will use one of my own cars as an example, a 1970 914/6 that I have owned since it was new.

I am now in the process of refurbishing the car. I have already had the paint and bodywork done, and that cost me $4,000. Now all I have to do is everything else: engine, transmission, upholstery, trim items and all the little miscellaneous bits that go on forever. I'm sure

to spend more than an additional $6,000 before I'm done (probably more like $10,000) and the 914/6s are only worth $6,000 to $10,000. I know, I know, there are always people advertising them for $15,000, but I don't think many if any of them ever get that much money for one.

My point is that you have to be careful with any of the older cars, even Porsches, because you can easily invest more money in them than they are worth. This is all right if you plan to keep the car in question forever; however, if it was an investment, you may have a problem.

What this means to you is that if you find an old Porsche that needs a lot of work, you had better proceed with care. You may not be able to justify the expense to have it fixed. Now I won't say that under *no* circumstances should you buy one of these cars with horrible problems. If you make a deal with the seller so that you pay what the car is worth and the restoration is going to be a hobby, you might actually come up with a good investment for your purposes. And besides, what consenting adults do behind closed doors is their own business.

Just a word about the gray-market cars. If you find one that you think you may want to buy, please have it checked out. You should take it to whoever will be doing your Porsche service work and tell them, "I'm thinking of buying this gray-market 911, please check it over carefully and tell me if you think I should buy it. I will be bringing the car to you for service, so please check over the service items, and the components or systems effected by the conversion, and let me know if you want me and this 911 gray-market car as one of your customers."

The problem with the gray-market cars is not so much with the conversion itself, but the workmanship and corner-cutting when it comes to the selection of components used for the conversions. I'm sure that a a gray-market Porsche can be made to comply with both DOT and the EPA without destroying the car, but in truth not very many are. I have looked at a number of gray-market cars over the years and feel that their biggest problem is the lack of quality workmanship and incorrect selection of conversion components.

There has been an additional problem for the gray-market 930/911 Turbo—making them run properly and still meet the US emission laws. It has been an either-or choice with most of these cars,

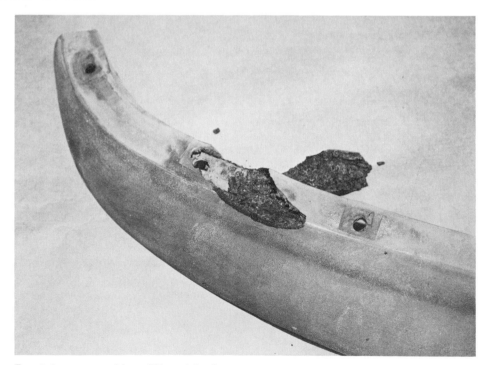

Front bumper rubber filler strip from mounting side. Note rust.

either running or complying. Now there is a US-legal 911 Turbo again, so this should be an easier problem to solve.

The people doing the conversion should use the same components that Porsche has used to make the 1986s and 1987s comply. If you are looking at used gray-market cars that have been used in Europe, be forewarned that for the most part the Europeans wear their cars out in very short order, and that whatever they use on their roads to melt the snow *and* cars does a great job. A two-year-old Euro car can be corroded so badly that it will be totally unacceptable by American standards.

I have a friend with a Euro car that has been converted and certified three times now. The first two companies were falsifying the conversions, and they have been caught and put out of business. The owner is responsible for making the car comply, so each time he has had to find someone else and have the conversion done over again.

In conclusion, I recommend that unless you are looking for a special-interest Porsche such as a 356 or a Carrera RS, what you really should be looking for is the best Porsche you can buy for your money. Because of this, you should probably plan to buy the newest 911 that you can afford. For the past ten years, each new model has been an improvement over the preceding year's model.

All auto manufacturers had trouble with their cars in the early to mid-1970s because of their inability to come up with graceful solutions for the emission laws, and Porsche was no exception. Once Porsche solved the emission problems, however, it became a leader in the technology and its cars have been just marvelous, with excellent driveability, performance and reliability.

911 options

The following is a table of the optional equipment numbers used by the 911. Since 1982, Porsche has included these option numbers on the vehicle identification labels. Some M numbers are considered standard in the country they are built for so they are not shown as optional equipment in the vehicle records or identification labels. Some numbers have been used to represent more than one option depending on model and year; in some instances several options are grouped together.

options #	Description	World	USA	not USA
M 9	3 speed sportomatic transmission	√		
M 18	Sport steering wheel with elevated hub	√		
M 20	Speedometer with 2 scales KPH/MPH	√		
M 24	Version for Greece			√
M 26	Activated charcoal canister		√	
M 27	Version for California		√	
M 34	Version for Italy			√
M 58	Bumpers with impact absorbers		√	
M 61	Version for Great Briton			√
M 62	Version for Sweden			√
M 70	Tonneau cover - Cabriolet	√		
M 113	Version for Canada			√
M 119	Version for Spain			√
M 124	Version for France			√
M 126	Stickers for French			√
M 139	Seat self heating - left	√		
M 152	Engine noise reduction			√
M 154	Control unit for improved emissions		√	
M 157	Oxygen sensor and catalyst		√	
M 158	Radio "Monterey" - 86, "Reno" 87		√	
M 160	Radio "Charleston"		√	
M 176	Oil cooler with fan		√	
M 185	Automatic 2 point rear seat belts		√	
M 186	Manual 2 point rear seat belts			√
M 187	Asymmetric head lamps			√
M 190	Increased side door strength		√	
M 193	Version for Japan			√
M 197	Higher amperage battery	√		
M 215	Version for Saudi Arabia			√
M 218	License brackets, front and rear		√	
M 220	Locking differential	√		
M 225	Version for Belgium			√
M 240	Version for countries with inferior fuel			√
M 241	Shorter shifting travel	√		
M 261	Passenger side mirror - electric - plain	√		
M 277	Version for Switzerland			√
M 286	High intensity windshield washer	√		

options #	Description	World	USA	not USA
M 288	Headlight washer	√		
M 298	Prepared for unleaded fuel, manual transmission			√
M 325	Version for South Africa			√
M 335	Automatic 3 point rear seat belts	√		
M 340	Seat heating - right	√		
M 341	Central locking system	√		
M 383	Sport seat - left	√		
M 387	Sport seat - right	√		
M 395	Light metal wheels - forged	√		
M 399	A/C without front condenser	√		
M 401	Light metal wheels	√		
M 409	Sport seats left and right leather	√		
M 410	Seats left and right leatherette/cloth	√		
M 411	License bracket, front			√
M 419	Rear luggage compartment instead of rear seats			√
M 424	Automatic heating control			
M 425	Rear Wiper	√		
M 437	Comfort seat left	√		
M 438	Comfort seat right	√		
M 439	Electric Cabriolet top	√		
M 439	Special Model "Weissach" 1980		√	
M 441	Radio speakers and antenna amplifier	√		
M 443	Tinted front and side glass, heated windshield			√
M 444	Cabriolet	√		
M 454	Automatic Speed Control	√		
M 455	Wheel locks	√		
M 462	Sekuriflex windshield	√		
M 463	Clear Windshield	√		
M 467	Drivers side mirror, convex			√
M 468	Graduated tint windshield, green side glass	√		
M 469	Black headliner	√		
M 470	Without spoilers in conjunction with Turbo look	√		
M 473	With spoilers	√		
M 474	Sport shock absorbers	√		
M 479	Version for Australia			√
M 482	Engine compartment light	√		
M 483	Right hand drive			√
M 484	Symbols for controls		√	
M 485	forged wheel rims "white gold metalic"	√		
M 488	Stickers in German			√
M 489	Symbols and insignias in German			√
M 491	Turbo look	√		
M 492	H4 headlights for left hand traffic			√
M 494	2 speakers on back shelf	√		
M 496	Black trim - painted headlight rims	√		
M 498	Without rear model designation	√		
M 499	Version for West Germany			√
M 505	Slant Nose	√		
M 513	Lumbar support - right seat	√		
M 525	Alarm with continuous sound	√		
M 526	Cloth door panels	√		
M 528	Passenger side mirror, convex			√

options #	Description	World	USA	not USA
M 533	Alarm system	√		
M 553	Version for USA		√	
M 559	Air conditioner	√		
M 566	Rectangular front fog lights	√		
M 567	Windshield green graduated tint	√		
M 568	Tinted windshield and side glass	√		
M 573	Air conditioner	√		
M 586	Lumbar support - left seat	√		
M 592	Brake fluid warning system			√
M 605	Vertical headlight adjustment			√
M 637	Sport Group	√		
M 650	Sun roof	√		
M 686	Radio "Ludwigsburg" SQM with arimat			√
M 900	Tourist delivery		√	
M 975	Velour carpet in luggage compartment	√		
M 981	All leather lining	√		
M 986	Partial leather lining	√		

Miscellaneous maintenance

Unfortunately, it is not uncommon to have a piece of carbon get between the exhaust valve and the valve seat when the plugs are removed. This condition will usually show up during a compression test, which is one of the reasons you should always perform a compression test when you are doing service on a 911 engine.

Carbon under the valves is also a common cause of bogus compression readings. Because of this, a number of people are panicked into thinking that they need engine work. If, during the course of a compression test, you find one cylinder with a low reading, don't panic. Put the spark plugs back in and run the engine for a while and then start the compression test over again. Nine times out of ten, carbon under the valve will have been the problem.

This problem should also show up when you attempt to adjust the exhaust valve in question, because the valve will appear to have excessive valve clearance. The valve adjustment is very stable in 911 engines, so if the adjustment is off by very much, it is a sure sign that there is a problem that should be looked into. If you just adjust this valve without solving this carbon problem, when the carbon falls out or blows out, you will end up with no valve clearance and probably burn the valve, and your engine will need a top-end overhaul that shouldn't have been necessary. Sometimes we even have problems with carbon fouling the valve clearances in running engines, where they will idle poorly now and then but otherwise run fine. This problem was becoming common a year or two ago, but seems to be going away with all of the gas companies' improved additive packages.

The problem was usually caused by a buildup on the intake valves. This buildup would cause the poor running condition and a loss of compression in some cylinders. Sometimes we also saw a carbon-type buildup on the exhaust valves. The symptoms would indicate that the engine needed a valve job or a top-end overhaul, when actually all that was probably necessary was a one-shot type of treatment.

My experience with this problem and resulting treatment was with a product called SWEPCO 503. It was recommended for the fuel-injector problem, and I have had good success with it as a dirty-injector cleaning agent. You can use the SWEPCO as a one-shot cleaner by pouring the additive in the intake and letting it flood the engine, causing it to die.

This has to be timed just right, so that you run out at almost exactly the same time the engine dies. Then let the car sit overnight and start it up in the morning, and drive the car around fairly aggressively for fifteen minutes or so. Be forewarned though, the car will smoke pretty badly at first—like James Bond's—so be careful.

This treatment will usually clean the carbon off the intake valves and the car should run well again. If the carbon was on the exhaust valves, the one-shot treatment may not clean them off and you might still have to have a valve job performed. Although first you should try one of these one-shot treatments; you may save yourself an unnecessary top-end overhaul.

These treatments obviously aren't magic, cure-all procedures and will not repair old, tired engines, but they may help with a premature carbon-fouling problem.

These carbon buildup problems were apparently caused by the oil companies using less and less detergent in the gasolines. In fact, some oil companies were actually using *none*. This created several fuel-related problems for motorists in general because, in addition to these problems, it allowed a buildup of fuel deposits on all of the fuel-handling components in the carburetor or fuel-injection systems.

This was particularly a problem in the fuel-injected cars because of the tiny components in the fuel-injection nozzle. There is a little pintle and seat in the tip of each injector. This pintle and seat control the flow and spray-cone pattern. Deposits on the pintle can seriously effect the pattern and the flow, seriously effecting the performance of the engine. This type of problem also usually shows up at idle or at lower rpm, where the shape of the spray pattern will have more effect on the running.

Porsche owners have had to live with this type of problem with the 911 since the CIS injection was introduced in 1973. Now that the big guys also have "multiport" fuel-injection systems with their electronic injectors, there is a great deal of concern for the cleanliness and detergent properties of gasolines.

This problem of fouled fuel systems really started to get some high-powered attention in the spring of 1986, when GM asked the gasoline manufacturers for help because a large number of its customers had started to complain about the poor running of their cars, caused by the fouling of the injectors. The oil companies met with the automobile manufacturers at the spring meeting of the Society of Automotive Engineers (SAE) and agreed to work on the problem. Soon after, the gasoline manufacturers started to advertise detergent-additive packages in their gasoline, in ads on television that would lead you to believe that they had each invented these packages.

The problem became so acute before it was solved that Porsche came out with a bulletin recommending Chevron's gasoline containing a detergent additive that Chevron called Techron. The bulletin went on to recommend the purchase of the additive separately for specific idle and low-speed running problems caused by partially restricted electric injectors used in the 3.2 Carrera.

Porsche recommended a dose of twenty ounces of Techron be added to the gas tank with a fill-up. Then it said that the car should be driven until the tank is half-empty and then refilled. Porsche recommended repeating the procedure two or three additional times.

Tune-up checklist

To ensure that your 911 is always in good operating condition, it is essential that it be well maintained. My experience with the 911s indicates that the 2.0, 2.2 and 2.4 liter 911s should have routine maintenance performed every 6,000 miles, and all of the newer 911s every 10,000 miles. In addition to this routine preventative maintenance, it is always a good idea to keep an eye out for anything that may show up in between the scheduled maintenance. Check the belts often, and keep an eye out for fuel and oil leaks.

Recommended maintenance checklist

Engine oil and filter	Change
V-belts	Adjust or replace as necessary
Valve clearance	Check and adjust
Rocker-shaft tightness	Check and correct
Spark plugs	Replace and run compression test
Dwell and timing	Adjust with electronic equipment
Fuel filter	Replace
Engine idle speed and CO%	Check with machine and adjust
Brake pads	Visual check and percent reading
Handbrake	Adjust if past five clicks
Exhaust system	Check for leaks or damage
Door hinges	Lubricate
Door latch	Lubstick
Accelerator linkage	Lubricate
Transmission oil	Check level every 10,000 mile Change every 30,000 miles
Ball joints and tie-rod ends	Check
Front-wheel-bearing play	Check
Operation of lights, horn	Check
Operation of lightswipers	Check
Headlight adjustment	Check
Battery level	Check and correct
Tire wear and condition	Check, correct pressure and note wear
Windshield-washer operation	Check and correct
Filter element for air pump	Replace
Air pump, control valves	Check
Air-injection hoses	Check
EGR, OXY counter	Reset
Evaporative control system	Check visually
Crankcase ventilation filter	Clean
Crankcase hoses	Check visually
Clutch free play	Check and adjust

Road test

Check braking, clutch, steering, heating, ventilation, cruise control and air-conditioning system (A/C should be recharged and serviced every two years).

Check all instruments, controls and warning lights.

911 tune-up specifications

Model Year / Type	1968	1969 911T	1969 911E	1969 911S
Fuel System	Weber 40IDTP3C	Weber 40IDTP3C	Bosch Mech Inj	Bosch Mech Inj
Secondary air pump	yes	no	no	no
Throttle compensator	yes	yes	no	no
Ign distributor vacuum	yes	yes	no	no
Diverter valve	yes	no	no	no
Spark Plugs	W250P21/W4DP	W225T30/W5D	W265P21/W3DP2	W265P21/W3DP2
Spark Plug Gap	0.35mm	0.6mm	.055mm	0.55mm
Ignition Distributor	Bosch	Marelli	Bosch	Bosch
part number	0.231.159.001	S112AX	0.231.159.006	0.231.159.007
Dwell Angle	38° ±3°	40° ±3°	38° ±3°	38° ±3°
Ignition Timing	30° BTDC/6000	35° BTDC/6000	30° BTDC/6000	30° BTDC/6000
Idle RPM	900±50	900±50	900±50	900±50
CO%	4.5 sec pmp disc	3.5% +0.5 at idle	3.5% +0.5 at idle	3.5% +0.5 at idle
Exhaust system	regular 3 into 1	regular 3 into 1	regular 3 into 1	regular 3 into 1
Engine Code No.	901/14 901/17	901/17 901/198	901/09 901/11	901/10

Model Year / Type	1970/71 911T	1970/71 911E	1970/71 911S	1972 911T
Fuel System	Bosch Mech inj	Zenith 40 TIN	Bosch Mech Inj	Bosch Mech Inj
Secondary air pump	NO	NO	NO	NO
Throttle compensator	NO	NO	NO	NO
Ign distributor vacuum	NO	NO	NO	Yes
Diverter valve	NO	NO	NO	NO
Spark Plugs	W225T30/W5D	W265P21/W4DP	W265P21/W4DP	W265P21/W4DP
Spark Plug Gap	0.6mm	0.55mm	0.55mm	0.6mm
Ignition Distributor	Bosch	Bosch	Bosch	Bosch
Part number	0.231.159.008	0.231.159.006	0.231.159.007	0.231.169.003
Dwell Angle	40° ±3°	38° ±3°	38° ±3°	38° ±3°
Ignition Timing	35° BTDC/6000	30° BTDC/6000	30° BTDC/6000	5° ATDC idle
Idle RPM	900±50	900±50	900±50	900±50
CO%	3.5±.05 at idle	3.0±0.5 at idle	3.0±0.5 at idle	1.5-2.0 at idle
Exhaust system	regular 3 into 1	regular 3 into 1	regular 3 into 1	regular 3 into 1
Engine Code No.	911/07 911/08	911/01 911/04	911/02	911/51 911/61

Table 1

Model Year / Type	1972 911E	1972 911S	1973 911T	1973 911E
Fuel System	Bosch Mech inj	Bosch Mech inj	BOSCH MECH & CIS in	Bosch Mech inj
Secondary air pump	NO	NO	NO	NO
Throttle compensator	NO	NO	Decel valve for CIS	NO
Ign distributor vacuum	Yes	Yes	Yes	Yes
Diverter valve	NO	NO	NO	NO
Spark Plugs	W265P21/W3DP2	W265P21/W3DP2	W235P21/W5DP	W265P21/W3DP2
Spark Plug Gap	0.55mm	1.55mm	0.6mm	0.55mm
Ignition Distributor	Bosch	Bosch	Bosch	Bosch
Part number	0.231.169.004	0.231.169.005	911.602.021.03	911.602.027.01
Dwell Angle	38°±3°	38°±3°	38°±3°	38°±3°
Ignition Timing	5° ATDC	5° ATDC	5° ATDC	5° ATDC
Idle RPM	900±50	900±50	900±50	900±50
CO%	2.0-2.5 at idle	2.0-2.5 at idle	1.5-2.0 at idle	2.0-2.5 at idle
Exhaust system	regular 3 into 1	regular 3 into 1	regular 3 into 1	regular 3 into 1
Engine Code No.	911/52 911/62	911/53	911/51/91/92	911/52/62

Table 2

Model Year / Type	1973 911S	1974 911	1974 911S	1975 911
Fuel System	Bosch Mech inj	Bosch CIS	Bosch CIS	Bosch CIS
Secondary air pump	NO	Yes	Yes	Yes
Throttle compensator	NO	Decel Valve	Decel Valve	Decel Valve
Ign distributor vacuum	Yes	Yes	Yes	Yes
Diverter valve	NO	NO	NO	NO
Spark Plugs	W265P21/W3DP2	W215P21/W6DP	W235P21/W5DP	W235P21/W5DP
Spark Plug Gap	0.55mm	0.55mm	0.55mm	0.55mm
Ignition Distributor	Bosch	Bosch	Bosch	Bosch
Part number	911.602.031.01	911.602.021.03	911.602.021.03	911.602.021.03
Dwell Angle	38°±3°	38°±3°	38°±3°	38°±3°
Ignition Timing	5° ATDC	5° ATDC	5° ATDC	5° ATDC
Idle RPM	900±50	900±50	900±50	900±50
CO%	2.5±0.5	1.5±0.5	1.5±0.5	1.5-2.0 sec air dis
Exhaust system	regular 3 into 1	regular 3 into 1	regular 3 into 1	49 state reg/Cal therm reactors EGR
Engine Code No.	911/53	911/92/97	911/93/97	49 State 911/43/48 / Cal 911/44/49

Model Year / Type	1976 911	1977 911	1978/79 911SC	1980 911SC
Fuel System	CIC Fuel Injection	CIC Fuel Injection	CIC Fuel Injection	CIC Fuel Injection
Secondary air pump	Yes	Yes	Yes	NO
Throttle compensator	Decel Valve	Decel Valve	Decel Valve	NO
Ign distributor vacuum	Yes	Yes	Yes	Yes
Diverter valve	NO	NO	NO	NO
Spark Plugs	W235P21/W5DP	W235P21/W5DP	W145T30/W8D	W225T30/W5D
Spark Plug Gap	0.55mm	0.55mm	0.8mm	0.8mm
Ignition Distributor	Bosch	Bosch	Bosch	Bosch
Part number	911.602.021.03	911.602.021.03	0.237.306.001	0.237.304.016
Dwell Angle	38°±3°	38°±3°	Pointless	Pointless
Ignition Timing	5° ATDC	49 State OT±2° Calif 15°±2° ATDC	5°±2°BTDC	5°±2°BTDC
Idle RPM	900±50	49 State 950±50 Calif 1000±50	900±50	900±50
CO%	2.0-3.5	1.5-3.0	2.5±1.0	0.4-0.8
Exhaust system	sec air disc 49 state reg/Cal therm reactors EGR	sec air disc EGR therm reactors	sec air disc CAT EGR	oxygen sensor dis 3 Way Cat Oxy Sens
Engine Code No.	49 State 911/82/89	911/85/90	930/04 Cal 930/06	930/07

Model Year / Type	1981/82/83 911SC	1984/85 Carrera	1986/87 Carrea
Fuel System	CIS Fuel Inj	L-Jetronic DME	L-Jetronic DME
Secondary air pump	No	No	No
Throttle compensator	No	Idle Stabilizer	Idle Stabilizer
Ign distributor vacuum	Yes	NO	NO
Diverter valve	NO	NO	NO
Spark Plugs	225T30/W5D	W7DC,WR7DC, WR7DP	WR7DC,WR7DP
Spark Plug Gap	0.8mm	0.7±0.1mm	0.7±0.1mm
Ignition Distributor	Bosch	Bosch	Bosch
Part number	0.237.304.016	0.237.505.001	0.237.505.001
Dwell Angle	Pointless	DME/Pointless	DME/Pointless
Ignition Timing	5°±2° BTDC	3°±3° ATDC *	3°±3° ATDC *
Idle RPM	900±50	800±20	800±20
CO%	0.4-0.8 oxy disc	0.8±0.2 oxy disc	0.8±0.2 oxy disc
Exhaust system	3 way Cat oxy sens	3 way Cat oxy sens	3 way Cat oxy sens
Engine Code No.	930/16	930/21	1986 930/21 1987 930/25

*This specification for checking DME operation is not adjustable.

Model Year / Type	1976 911 Turbo	1977 911 Turbo	1978/79 911 Turbo
Fuel System	CIS Fuel inj.	CIS Fuel inj.	CIS Fuel inj.
Secondary air pump	Yes	Yes	Yes
Throttle compensator	decel. valve	decel. valve	decel. valve
Ign distributor vacuum	Yes	Yes	Yes
Diverter valve	Yes	Yes	Yes
Spark Plugs	W3DP	W3DP	W3DP
Spark Plug Gap	0.6 mm	0.6 mm	0.6 mm
Ignition Distributor	Bosch	Bosch	Bosch 0.237.302.009
Dwell Angle	Pointless	Pointless	Pointless
Ignition Timing	5° ±2° ATDC	7° ±2° ATDC	10° ±2° ATDC / 5° ±2° ATDC, Calif
Idle RPM	950±50	1000±50	1000±50
CO%	1.0-3.0 sec air disc.	2.0-4.0 sec air disc.	2.5±0.5 sec air disc.
Exhaust system	Thermo reactors	Thermo reactors, EGR	Thermo reactors, EGR
Engine Code No.	930/51	930/53	930/61/63

Model Year / Type	1981/82 911 Turbo	1983/84/85 Turbo	1986/87 911 Turbo
Fuel System	CIS Fuel inj.	CIS Fuel inj.	CIS Fuel inj.
Secondary air pump	Yes	Yes	Yes
Throttle compensator	decel. valve	decel. valve	decel. valve
Ign desributor vacuum	Yes	Yes	Yes
Diverter valve	Yes	Yes	Yes
Spark Plugs	W3DP0	W3DP0	W3DP0
Spark Plug Gap	0.7 mm	0.7 mm	0.7 mm
Part number	0.237.301.004	0.237.302.034	0.237.302.034
Ignition Distributor	Bosch	Bosch	Bosch
Dwell Angle	Pointless	Pointless	Pointless
Ignition Timing	29° BTDC/4000	29° BTDC/4000	26°±1°BTDC at 4000 RPM vac. hosed disc.
Idle RPM	1000±50	900±50	900±50
CO%	2.5±0.5 sec air disc.	2.0±0.5 sec air disc.	0.4-0.8 measured before CAT, oxy, sen discon.
Exhaust system	Regular	Regular	3 way CAT
Engine Code No.	930/60	930/66	930/68

Sources

The following recommendations are offered as an aid to finding parts and services for your 911 or 911 Turbo. The recommendations are for the most part either based on my own personal experience or the experience of friends. When I make recommendations I realize that someone else may offer a similar service, but the ones that I am recommending are the ones that I am familiar with, and you may get just as good or better service from someone else.

Bodywork

AIR (American International Racing)
149E Santa Anita Ave
Burbank, CA 91502
    Fiberglass custom body parts, slope-nose kits in steel or Carbonfiber

Blackburn-Daly LTD.
33 N Dearborn, Suite 730
Chicago, IL 60602
    Slope-nose conversions

Bodystyle
502 W Santa Clara St
San Jose, CA 95110
    A quality Porsche bodyshop

Bruce Canepa Motorsports
1191 Water St
Santa Cruz, CA 95062
    Custom slope-nose conversions and specialty components

Hoesman Fiberglas
3072 Rubidoux Blvd, Suite J
Riverside, CA 92509
    Custom fiberglass body parts

Mitcom
12621 Sherman Way
North Hollywood, CA 91605
    Fiberglass body parts

Sport Performance
2221 Stevens Creek Blvd
San Jose, CA 95128
    Custom and slope-nose conversions and specialty components

Instruments

Davtron
427 Hillcrest
Redwood City, CA 94062
    Digital charge air temperature gauge for turbocharged cars

Palo Alto Speedometer
718 Emerson St
Palo Alto, CA 94301
    VDO repair, conversion and restoration

VDO Instruments
980 Brooke Rd
Winchester, VA 22601

North Hollywood Speedometer
6111 Lankershim Blvd
No. Hollywood, CA 91606
    VDO repair, conversion, restoration and a wide selection of custom instrument services

Brake components

Holbert Racing Inc.
1425 Easton Rd
Warrington, PA 18976
    Home of the COOL-brake

JFZ Engineering
Variel Ave
Chatsworth, CA 91311
    Source for racing brake components

Neal Products
7170 Ronson Rd
San Diego, CA 92111
    Single and dual master-cylinder pedal assemblies

Pacific Motorsports, Inc.
1503-130th Ave NE
Bellevue, WA 98005
    Brake conversion

Tilton Engineering, Inc.
McMurry Road & Easy St
Buellton, CA 93427
    Clutch, brake and suspension components

White Post Restorations
White Post, Virginia 22663
    Recondition corroded calipers, using brass sleeves

Wilwood Engineering
4580 Calle Alto
Camarillo, CA 93010
    Source for racing brake components

Pistons and cylinders

Cosworth Engine Components
23205 Early Ave
Torrance, CA 90505
    Custom racing pistons

Cosworth Engineering
St. James Mill Rd
Northampton, England
    Custom racing pistons

Race Force
4561 Horton St
Emeryville, CA 94608
    Mahle pistons and cylinders

Parts

Alan Johnson Racing, Inc.
5220 Gaines St
San Diego, CA 92110
    Good source for Porsche goodies

ANDIAL
3207-P S. Shannon St
Santa Ana, CA 92704
    Mahle pistons, cylinders and other Porsche parts for road and racing

Competition Engineering
2095 N. Lake Ave
Altadena, CA 91001
    Machining and engine parts

Electrodyne
2316 Jefferson Davis Hwy
P.O. Box 358
Alexandria, VA 22313
    Porsche aftermarket parts source

Garretson Enterprises
1932 Old Middlefield Way
Mountain View, CA 94087
    Parts, machining and service featuring GE camshafts

K&N Hi-Performance Air Filters
P.O. Box 1329
Riverside, CA 92502
    Quality high-performance air filters

Performance Products
16129 Leadwell St, Box #B-4
Van Nuys, CA 91406-3488
    Mail order parts business

Stoddard Imported Cars, Inc.
38845 Mentor Ave
Willoughby, OH 44094-0908
    The dealer that belongs to Porsche; still a good parts and service source

Troutman LTD, Inc.
3198-L Airport Loop Dr
Costa Mesa, CA 92626
    Source of all sorts of things for Porsches

Vasek Polack
199 Pacific Coast Hwy
Hermosa Beach, CA 90254
Porsche parts: "More parts than anybody, period"

Tools
Baum Tools Unlimited
7231 Owensmouth
Canoga Park, CA 91303
Source for special metric tools

Go-Power Systems
37050 Industrial Rd
Livonia, MI 48150
Dynos

Graduated Burrets
622 West Colorado St
Glendale, CA 91204
Tri-Ess Science

Mac Tools, Inc.
Washington Court House, OH 43160
Quality tools usually sold by dealers from their trucks; write or phone for the nearest dealer

Snap-On Tools Corporation
Kenosha, WI
Quality tools usually sold by dealers from their trucks; see your phone book or write or phone for the nearest dealer

Superflow
3512-D N. Tejon
Colorado Springs, CO 80907
Dynos and flow benches

Zelenda Machine and Tools Corp.
66-02 Austin St
Forest Hills, NY 11374
Source for special metric tools

Turbo equipment
Callaway Turbo Systems
Stewarts Corner
Lyme, CT 06371

Turbo Power
3250 El Camino Real
Santa Clara, CA 95051
Can modify hot housing to tighten the "snail" bringing the boost in sooner and at lower rpm

Carburetors and fuel injections
Eurometrics
PO Box 1361
Campbell, CA 95009
Rebuilds fuel injection throttle bodies and carburetor throttle bodies

H & R Fuel Injection LTD.
1648C Locust Ave
Bohemia, NY 11716
Mechanical injection pump rebuilding

Pacific Fuel Injection
1323 Rollins Rd
Burlingame, CA 94010
Mechanical injection pump rebuilding

PMO
135 17th St
Santa Monica, CA 90402
Weber carburetors

Robert Bosch Corporation
2800 S. 25th Ave
Broadview, IL 60153
Electric and fuel systems

The Carburetor Refactory
815 Harbor Way S, #5
Richmond, CA 94804
Carburetor remanufacturing

Shock absorbers and suspension components
Bilstein Corporation of America
11760 Sorrento Valley Rd
San Diego, CA 92121
Racing and street shock absorbers

Carrera Industries, Inc.
5412 New Peachtree Rd
Altanta, GA 30341
Coil springs, shock absorbers and coil-over conversions

Fox Factory Inc.
520 McGlincey Ln
Campbell, CA 95008
Gas-pressure racing shock absorbers

Koni America
111 W. Lovers Ln
Culpepper, VA 22701
Springs and torsion bars

Sway-A-Way Company
7840 Burnet Ave
Van Nuys, CA 91405
Torsion bars, adjustable spring plates and other suspension components

Weltmeister
3535 Kifer Rd, Unit 5
Santa Clara, CA 95051
Suspension parts

Lubrications and chemicals
Dow-Corning
Midland, MI 48640
Silicone lubricants and fluorosilicone sealants

HRL Lubricants, Inc.
7340 Florence Ave
Downey, CA 90240
Moly lubes for assembly

Red Line Synthetic Oil Corporation
3450 Pacheco Blvd
Martinez, CA 94553
Full line of synthetic engine and gear oil

SWEPCO (Southwestern Petroleum Corporation)
P.O. Box 789
Fort Worth, Texas 76101
Quality engine and gear oils and fuel additives

Machine shop service
Competition Engineering
2095 N Lake Ave
Altadena, CA 91001
Machining and engine parts

Garretson Enterprises
1932 Old Middlefield Way
Mountain View, CA 94087
Machining and service and featuring GE camshafts

Ollie's Automotive Machining
510 Terminal St
Santa Ana, CA 92701

Wheels
BBS of America, Inc.
33 Murray Hill Dr
Spring Valley, NY 10977
Racing and road wheels

BBS of America, Inc., Western Region
30971 San Benitio Ct
Hayward, CA 94544
BBS racing and road wheels

Highland Plating
1001 N. Orange Dr
Los Angeles, CA 90038
Refinish, polish and sell wheels

Robert W. Wood, Inc.
1340 Club View Dr
Los Angeles, CA 90024
Refinish, polish and sell wheels

Topline
2872 Walnut Ave, Suite A
Tustin, CA 92680
Etoile wheels and accessories

Crankshafts
Flecks Crankshafts
341 10th St
San Francisco, CA 94103

Sammy Hale Crankshafts, Ltd.
20 D. Pamaron Way
Novato, CA 94949
Specialist with sports car crankshafts

Exhaust system components
European Racing Headers
27601 Forbes Rd, Suite 20
Laguna Niguel, CA 92677
Racing headers for 911s

SSI, John Daniels
24 Pamaron Way
Navato, CA 94947
Stainless steel exhaust systems

Stahl Headers
1515 Mt. Rose Ave
York, PA 17403
   Builds racing headers

Triad Industries, Inc.
5623 Lawton Dr
Sarasota, FL 33583
   Exhaust systems for the 911

Stereos
Audiovision
3951 State St
Santa Barbara, CA 93105
   Quality stereo store

Century Stereo
620 S Bascom Ave
San Jose, CA 95128
   Custom car stereo installations

Heads
CMW
Mr. Bob Cousimano
8335 Lyndora St
Downey, CA 90242
   CMW 911 cylinder heads

Air conditioning
Performance Air
1885 Santa Cruz St
Anaheim, CA 92805
   All there is to know about air
conditioning and some tricks to make them
work better

Race car plumbing
Aeroquip Corporation
300 S East Ave
Jackson, MI 49203
   Lines and fittings

Earl's Supply Co.
14611 Hawthorne Blvd
Lawndale, CA 90260
   Lines and fittings

Metric Pipe and Hydraulic
1701 E Edinger E-1
Santa Ana, CA 92705
   Metric oil lines and fittings

New and used parts
Aase Brothers Inc.
701 Cypress
Anaheim, CA 92805

EASY (European Auto Salvage Yard)
1075 Second St
Berkeley, CA 94710

European Performance Parts
729 Heinz St Bldg 15
Berkeley, CA 94710
   A good source of used and new parts

Camshafts
Crane Cams, Inc.
530 Fentress Blvd
Daytona Beach, FL 32014
   Special cams for the 911 engines

Web-Cam
12387 Doherty St
Riverside, CA 92503
   Performance camshafts

Garretson Enterprises
1932 Old Middlefield Way
Mountain View, CA 94087
   GE camshafts

Alarm systems
Techne Electronics Ltd.
916 Commercial St
Palo Alto, CA 94303
   The Ungo Box alarm system

Metal processes
Metal Improvement Company, Inc.
(subsidiary of Curtiss Wright Corporation)
3239 E 46th St
Vernon, CA 90058
   Shot peening

G&L Coatings, Inc.
Leonard Warren
888 Rancheros, Unit C
San Marcos, CA 92069
   Surface coating process to improve wear
and heat radiation performance, particularly
good for cam wear surfaces

Ignition systems
Per-Lux
1242 E Edna Pl
Covina, CA 91724
   Ignitors, inductively triggered ignition

Transmission cooler recirculation pump
Jabsco Products
(a unit of ITT Corporation)
1485 Dale Way, PO Box 2158
Costa Mesa, CA 92628-2158
   Source of electric pumps for circulating
gear lubricant to transmission cooler

Window tinting
California Auto Tinting and Polishing
1610 Dell Ave, Unit S
Campbell, CA 95008
   Quality window tinting

Threaded inserts
Time Fasteners
2428 Rosemead
South El Monte, CA 91733
   Time-Certs threaded inserts

Oil coolers
Turbatronics and Terbatrol
P.O. Box 20410
Indianapolis, IN 46220

Valve guides
Lukes and Shoreman, Inc.
1011 San Pablo Ave
Albany, CA 94706
   The source of Phosphorus Bronze valve
guides

Gaskets and seals
Wrightwood Racing
2806 W Burbank Blvd
Burbank, CA 91505
   Source for quality aftermarket gaskets
and seals for the 911 engine

Fabricator, designers and car builders
Blakely Engineering, Inc.
Glenn Blakely
23052 Alcalde, Unit C
Laguna Hills, CA 92653
   Race car designer and fabricator

FABCAR Engineering
Dave Klym
2697 Fourth St
Tucker, GA 30084
   Race car designer and builder

GAACO
Charles W. Gaa
2801 Cole Ct
Norcross, GA 30071
   Design and fabrication of race cars

German tuners, specialty car builders and their agents
DP Motorsport
Ekkehard Zimmermann GmbH and Co.
KG Zum Alten Wasserwerk
5063 Overath 6, West Germany
   Custom high-performance street
Porsches

E & M Kremer
Robert-Perthel Strasse 31
5000 Koln 60, West Germany
   Famous German Porsche tuners

Exclusive Motor Cars, Inc.
256 Park St
Upper Montclair, NJ 07043
   RUF conversions, cars and parts

Koenig Specials GmbH
Flossergasse 7
D-8000 Munchen 70, West Germany
   Body styling and tuning

Kremer USA
Harvey L. Maron
2064 Briarcliff Rd, Suite 102
Atlanta, GA 30329
   Distribute Kremer cars and components
in US

RUF Automobile
Mr. Alois Ruf
Mindelheimer Strasse 21
D-8949 Pfaffenhausen, West Germany
   Famous German super tuner

Strosek Auto Design
Eduard-thony Strasse 40
D-8919 Utting/Ammersee, West Germany
   Design program for the Porsche 911
Carrera and Turbo

Art and artist

Andreas Hentrich
Gerdastrasse 11
5600 Wuppertal 2, West Germany
  Porsche art, pewter-graphics

Howard Shoemaker
1621 South 35 St
Omaha, NE 68105
  Cartoons, custom orders

Randy Owens
RO originals
9606 Percussion Way
Vienna, VA 22180
  Superb serigraphs

Driving schools

Bob Bondurant
Sears Point Int'l Raceway
Sonoma, CA 95476

Skip Barber Racing School
Route 7
Canaan, CT 06018

Publications

Auto Motor und Sport
Wereinigte Motor-Verlage GmbH & Co.
KG
Abonnement-Abteilung
Postfach 1042
7000 Stuttgart 1, West Germany
  Wonderful German language bi-weekly
magazine that emphasizes the German cars
and their success on the road and on the
track, but does cover all car activities in the
world in some depth. In addition to the
good in-depth reporting and road tests the
publication is chuck full of rumors of
future activities of the German auto
industry. Rumors have a high accuracy
quotient, but . . . issues are usually around
three hundred pages in size.

AutoWeek
965 E Jefferson
Detroit, MI 48207
  Weekly slick magazine with lots of good
race reporting and rumors, rumors are not
always accurate. They may use the leftover
rumors from *Auto Motor und Sport*.

Christophorus
200 S Virginia St
Reno, NV 89501
  Porsche factory magazine, published
every other month, a must for any Porsche
enthusiast.

Car and Driver
2002 Hogback Rd
Ann Arbor, MI 48104
  Good general interest monthly car
magazine, usually has good current
information on Porsches, sometimes seems
as though they may use the same rumor
source as *AutoWeek*.

On Track – The Auto Racing Newsmagazine
Paul Oxman Publishing, Inc.
P.O. Box 8509
Fountain Valley, CA 92728
  Quality racing publication, published
bi-monthly. Oxman also publishes and/or
distributes quality calendars, posters and
video tapes.

Motor Trend
8490 Sunset Blvd
Los Angeles, CA 90069
  General interest monthly magazine.

Newsletter
Porsche Owners Club
P.O. Box 7293
Van Nuys, CA 91409-7293
  Monthly magazine of the Porsche
Owner's Club, a Southern California
Porsche Club.

Panorama
PCA National Executive Office
P.O. Box 10402
Alexandria, VA 22310
  Monthly magazine of the Porsche Club
of America, can only be obtained by joining
PCA.

Porsche Trends Gallery
120 Filmore Ave, #944
Endicott, NY 13760
  Porsche market newsletter.

Porsche Magazine
P.O. Box 1529
Ross, CA 94957
  Quality bi-monthly publication devoted
to Porsche.

Road & Track
1499 Monrovia
Newport Beach, CA 92663
  General interest car magazine published
monthly.

VW & Porsche
P.O. Box 3719
Escondido, CA 92025
  Monthly foreign car magazine with an
emphasis on Volkswagens and Porsches.

Porsche

Porsche – Sports Department
Postfach 1140
Porschestrasse
7251 Weissach, West Germany

Dr.-Ing. h.c. F. Porsche A6
Postfach 400640
7000 Stuttgart 40
West Germany

Porsche Cars North America
200 South Virginia St
P.O. Box 30911
Reno, NV 89520-3911
  Importer for Porsche automobiles and
parts.

Porsche Motorsport North America
1425 Easton Rd
Warrington, PA 18976
  Source for Porsche factory racing cars
and parts for the United States.

Porsche Motorsport Hot Line (215)
343-9628

Porsche Motorsport Bulletin Board
  Western Union EasyLink subscribers
interested in the latest racing news and
racing results in the United States are
encouraged to check the Porsche
Motorsport Bulletin Board each week at
the beginning of the week for the
weekend's race results and later in the week
for points standings and other information.
  The procedure is as follows:
  a. Log on using normal EasyLink
     procedure
  b. When "PTS" appears, type in "/EXIT
     FYI"
  c. When "ENTER CATEGORY
     NAME" appears, type in
     "PORSCHE"
  d. When you have read the message, type
     in "/QUIT" and log off EasyLink
with your normal procedure

Units of measure

Metric conversions

Length

Metric	US
1 millimeter	0.039 inch
1 centimeter	0.393 inch
1 centimeter	0.032 feet
1 meter	39.370 inch
1 meter	3.280 feet
1 meter	1.093 yard
1 kilometer	0.621 mile
1 kph	0.621 mph

US	Metric
1 inch	25.4 millimeter
1 foot	0.304 meter
1 mile	1.609 kilometers
1 mph	1.609 kph

Area

Metric	US
1 square centimeter	0.155 square inch
1 square meter	10.763 square feet

US	Metric
1 square inch	6.451 square centimeters
1 square foot	0.092 square meter

Volume

Metric	US
1 cubic centimeter	0.061 cubic inch
1 cubic meter	35.314 cubic feet
1 cubic meter	1.307 cubic yard
1 liter	1.056 quarts
1 liter	33.8 fluid ounces
1 liter	0.264 gallons
1 liter	61.032 cubic inches

US	Metric
1 cubic inch	16.387 cubic centimeters
1 cubic foot	0.028 cubic meter
1 quart	0.946 liter

Mass (weight)

Metric	US
1 gram	0.035 ounce
1 kilogram	2.204 pounds
1 kilogram	35.273 ounces

US	Metric
1 ounce	28.349 grams
1 pound	0.453 kilogram

Force

Metric	US
1 Newton (N)	0.224 pound-foot (lb/ft)
1 kilogram/meter (kgm)	0.224 pound-foot (lb/ft)

Torque

Metric	US
1 Newtonmeter (Nm)	0.737 pound-foot (lb/ft)
1 Newtonmeter (Nm)	8.850 inch-pound (in/lb)
1 kilogram meter	7.15 pound-foot (lb/ft)

US	Metric
1 inch-pound (in/lb)	0.1130
1 pound-foot (lb/ft)	1.356

Power

Metric	US
1 Watt (1 Nm/sec.)	0.00134 hp
1 kilowatt (kW)	1.340 hp
1 PS (European hp)	0.986 hp

US	Metric
1 horsepower	0.746 kilowatt

Pressure

1 Newton per square meter (N/m²)	1 Pascal
1 pascal	0.000 psi
1 kilopascal (kPa)	0.145 psi
1 bar	100,000 Pascals
1 bar	14.5 pounds per square in.
1 atmosphere	14.7 pounds per square in.
1 atmosphere	29.9212 inches of mercury

Temperature conversion

$$°C = \frac{1}{1.8}\,(°F{-}32)$$

$°F = 1.8\ °C{+}32$

- Mega = 1,000,000 abbreviated as M or 10^6
- Kilo = 1,000 abbreviated K or 10^3
- Centi = 100 abbreviated as C or 10^2
- Milli = .001 abbreviated as m or 10^{-3}
- Micro = .000001 abbreviated as μ or 10^{-6}

Compression ratio

$$\text{Compression} = \frac{V1{+}V2{+}V3{-}V4}{V2{+}V3{-}V4}$$

- V1 = swept volume
- V2 = deck height volume
- V3 = cylinder head volume
- V4 = piston dome volume
- Swept Volume (V1) = Bore² × Stroke × 0.7854 (simplified formula)

Engine displacement

$$\text{Displacement} = \pi \times R^2 \times S \times N$$

- π = 3.141 592 65
- R = radius of the bore in centimeters
- S = stroke of the cylinder in centimeters
- N = number of cylinders

or

$$\text{Displacement} = \frac{\pi D^2}{4} \times S \times N$$

- D = diameter of bore in centimeters
- π = 3.141 592 65
- S = stroke of the cylinder in centimeters
- N = number of cylinders

Other cases
Cubic measurements

These same formulas will work for inches as well as centimeters and the resulting answers can be converted from cubic inches to cubic centimeters by dividing cubic inches by 0.061 or from cubic centimeters to cubic inches by multiplying cubic centimeters by 0.061.

Converting fractions to decimals

Divide the numerator by the denominator. As an example, ¾ to a decimal 3.0000 ÷ 4 = 0.75000

Converting inches to millimeters

Multiply by 25.4. As an example use the results from converting the fraction ¾ to a decimal which was 0.75000. Multiply 0.75000 × 25.4 = 19.050 mm. From this example you can see that ¾ inch is almost exactly 19 mm which means that you can use your ¾ inch lug wrench on the 19 mm wheel nuts used on your Porsche 911.

Converting millimeters to inches

Multiply by 0.0393701. As an example 19 × 0.0393701 = 0.7480319. From this example you can see that your 19 mm lug wrench would be a little tight on ¾ inch lug bolts.

Converting millimeters to centimeters

Multiply by 0.1

Converting centimeters to millimeters

Multiply by 10.0

Piston speed

Piston speed in feet per minute

$$(\text{fpm}) = \frac{RPM \times S}{152.4}$$

- S = stroke in millimeters

Horsepower

Horsepower is a unit of work, an effort to relate the work of an engine to the work of a horse. One horsepower is the amount of work a horse could do in one minute and is equal to 33,000 lb/ft of torque per minute. When related to an engine the torque is measured as a rotational force on a dynamometer with some form of absorption unit. With this torque figure and the engine RPM we can calculate horsepower using the following formula:

$$\text{Horsepower (HP)} = \text{Torque (lb-ft)} \frac{RPM}{5250}$$

$$\text{Metric horsepower (PS)} = \text{HP (US)} \times 1.015$$

Speed

$$MPH = \frac{(RPM)(\text{tire dia})0.002975}{(T.R.)(D.R.)}$$

- RPM = engine speed (rpm)
- Tire diameter is in inches
- D.R. = differential ratio
- T.R. = transmission ratio

The tire diameter is best determined with a tire on the car at the rated pressure. Measure the distance in inches that the car moves for a few revolutions of the tire and then calculate the diameter from:

$$DIA,\ \text{in.} = \frac{\text{distance in.}}{\pi\ \text{revolutions}}$$

In order to calculate a speed for a different differential ratio use the following:

$$\text{MPH for new ratio} = \text{MPH for old ratio}\,\frac{\text{old ratio}}{\text{new ratio}}$$

To calculate speed for a different tire diameter; use the following:

$$\text{MPH for new tire diameter} = \text{MPH for old tire diameter}\,\frac{\text{old tire diameter}}{\text{new tire diameter}}$$

Bibliography

Adler, U, ed. *Automotive Handbook*. Bosch, Robert Bosch GmbH, Stuttgart, West Germany, 1986.

Barkhouse, Bob. *Engine Repair*. McKnight Publishing Company, Bloomington, Illinois, 1975.

Barth, Jurgen. *The Porsche Book*. Arco Publishing, Inc., New York, NY, 1978 and 1983.

Boschen, Lothar. *The Porsche Book*. Arco Publishing, Inc., New York, NY, 1978 and 1983.

Batchelor, Dean. *Illustrated Porsche Buyer's Guide*. Motorbooks International, Osceola, WI, 1982.

Csere, Csaba. *10 Best Engines of All Time. Car and Driver*, January 1985.

Fisher, Bill. *How to Hot Rod Volkswagens*. HP Books, Los Altos, CA, 1970.

Frere, Paul. *Porsche Racing Cars of the 70s*. Arco Publishing, Inc., New York, NY, 1980, 1981.

———. *Porsche 911 Story*. Arco Publishing, Inc., New York, NY, 1974, 1976 and 1983.

———. *The Racing Porsches*. Arco Publishing, Inc., New York, NY, 1971 and 1973.

Haynes, J. H. *Porsche 911 Owners Workshop Manual*. Haynes Publishing Group, London, England, 1977, 1983.

Ward, Peter. *Porsche 911 Owners Workshop Manual*. Haynes Publishing Group, London, England, 1977, 1983.

Landis, Bob. *The Racers Complete Reference Guide*. Steve Smith Autosports, Santa Ana, CA, 1976, 1984.

Ludvigsen, Karl. *Excellence Was Expected*. 1977 Princeton Publishing, Inc., Princeton, New Jersey, 1977.

MacInnes, Hugh. *Turbochargers*. HP Books, Tuscon, AZ, 1984.

Mezger, Hans. *Engineering the Performance Car*. SAE Paper No. 700678. New York—Society of Automotive Engineers.

———. *The Development of the Porsche Type 917 Car*. The Institute of Mechanical Engineers Automobile Division, Reprinted from Proceedings 1972 Volume 186.

Miller, Susann. *Porsche Year 1983-84*. M&M Publishing Co., Clifton, VA, 1984.

Puhn, Fred. *How To Make Your Car Handle*. HP Books, Tuscon, AZ, 1976, Fisher Publishing, Inc., 1981.

Porsche KG. *911 Workshop Manual, Volume I and II*. Ferdinand Porsche KG, Stuttgart-Zuffenhausen, West Germany, 1965.

———. *911 Workshop Manual, Volume III — VI*. Ferdinand Porsche KG, Stuttgart-Zuffenhausen, West Germany, 1971.

Porsche AG. *911 Workshop Manual, Volume I — V*. Porsche AG, Stuttgart-Zuffenhausen, West Germany, 1984.

———. *Technical Specification Booklet, 1965-1968*. Porsche AG, Stuttgart-Zuffenhausen, West Germany, 1976.

———. *Technical Specification Booklet, 1969-1971*. Porsche AG, Stuttgart-Zuffenhausen, West Germany, 1976.

———. *Technical Specification Booklet, 1972-1973*. Porsche AG, Stuttgart-Zuffenhausen, West Germany, 1976.

———. *Technical Specification Booklet, 1974*. Porsche AG, Stuttgart-Zuffenhausen, West Germany, 1978.

———. *Technical Specification Booklet, 1975*. Porsche AG, Stuttgart-Zuffenhausen, West Germany, 1979.

———. *Technical Specification Booklet, 1976-1977*. Porsche AG, Stuttgart-Zuffenhausen, West Germany, 1977.

———. *Technical Specification Booklet, 78, 79, 80. 81*. Porsche AG, Stuttgart-Zuffenhausen, West Germany, 1981.

———. *Turbo Service Information, 78*. Porsche AG, Stuttgart-Zuffenhausen, West Germany, 1978.

———. *911 SC Service Information, 78*. Porsche AG, Stuttgart-Zuffenhausen, West Germany, 1978.

———. *911 SC Service Information, 80*. Porsche AG, Stuttgart-Zuffenhausen, West Germany, 1980.

———. *911 SC Turbo Service Information, 81*. Porsche AG, Stuttgart-Zuffenhausen, West Germany, 1981.

———. *911 SC Turbo Service Information, 82*. Porsche AG, Stuttgart-Zuffenhausen, West Germany, 1982.

———. *911 SC Turbo Service Information, 83*. Porsche AG, Stuttgart-Zuffenhausen, West Germany, 1983.

———. *911 Carrera Turbo Service Information, 84*. Porsche AG, Stuttgart-Zuffenhausen, West Germany, 1984.

———. *911 Carrera Turbo Service Information, 85*. Porsche AG, Stuttgart-Zuffenhausen, West Germany, 1985.

———. *911 Carrera Turbo Service Information, 86*. Porsche AG, Stuttgart-Zuffenhausen, West Germany, 1986.

———. *911 Carrera Turbo Service Information, 87*. Porsche AG, Stuttgart-Zuffenhausen, West Germany, 1987.

Porsche-Audi. 911S Carrera Service Information, 75. Porsche AG, Stuttgart-Zuffenhausen, West Germany, 1975.

———. *911S Service Information, 76*. Porsche AG, Stuttgart-Zuffenhausen, West Germany, 1976.

———. *Turbo Carrera Service Information, 76*. Porsche AG, Stuttgart-Zuffenhausen, West Germany, 1976.

———. *911S Turbo Service Information, 77*. Porsche AG, Stuttgart-Zuffenhausen, West Germany, 1977.

Marketing, Training & Development PCNA. *1986 Porsche Fact Book*. Porsche Cars North America, Reno, NV, 1986.

———. *1987 Porsche Fact Book*. Porsche Cars North America, Reno, NV, 1987.

Ricardo, Sir Harry. *The High Speed Internal Combustion Engine*. Blackie & Sons, Ltd., London, England, 1967.

SAE Handbook, Volume 3, Engines. Society of Automotive Engineers, Inc., New York, NY, 1983.

Smith, Carroll. *Prepare To Win*. Arco Publishers, Inc., CA, 1975.

———. *Tune To Win*. Arco Publishers, Inc., CA, 1978.

Smith, Philip H. *The Design and Tuning of Competition Engines*. Robert Bentley, Inc., MA, 1974.

Turner, B.J., ed. *Up-Fixin der Porsche Volume VI*. Porsche

Club of America, Alexandria, VA, 1981, 1982 and 1983.

———. *Up-Fixin der Porsche Volume VII*. Porsche Club of America, Alexandria, VA, 1984, 1985 and 1986.

Van Valkenburgh, Paul. *Race Car Engineering and Mechanics*. Dodd, Mead & Company, New York, NY, 1976.

Waar, Bob. *How to Hotrod and Race Your Datsun*. Steve Smith Autosports, Santa Ana, CA, 1984.

Wauson, Sydnie A. *Porsche 911 1965-1982 Shop Manual*.

Clymer Publications, Arleta, CA, fifth edition 1983.

Wilson, Waddell. *Racing Engine Preparation*. Steve Smith Autosports, Santa Ana, CA, 1975.

Smith, Steve. *Racing Engine Preparation*. Steve Smith Autosports, Santa Ana, CA, 1975.

Zimmermann, Peter M. *The Used 911 Story*. Zimmermann Publications, Fox Island, WA, 1983.

Index